S0-AHY-449

A LAW UNTO ITSELF

A LAW UNTO ITSELF

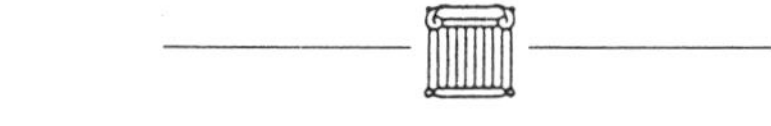

THE UNTOLD STORY OF THE LAW FIRM SULLIVAN & CROMWELL

Nancy Lisagor and Frank Lipsius

WILLIAM MORROW AND COMPANY, INC.
New York

Library of Congress Cataloging-in-Publication Data

Lisagor, Nancy.
A law unto itself : the untold story of the law firm Sullivan & Cromwell / Nancy Lisagor & Frank Lipsius.
p. cm.
ISBN 0-688-04888-9
1. Sullivan & Cromwell—History. 2. Lawyers—New York (N.Y.)—Biography. 3. Law partnership—New York (N.Y.)—History.
I. Lipsius, Frank. II. Title.
KF355.N4L57 1988
338.7′6134973—dc 19
[338.7613473] 87-35490
CIP

Printed in the United States of America

First Edition

1 2 3 4 5 6 7 8 9 10

BOOK DESIGN BY RICHARD ORIOLO

AUTHORS' PREFACE

The Supreme Court's 1977 decision to allow lawyers to advertise led to the "thirty-second soap operas," the commercials for nationwide law firms that portray death, injury, divorce, bankruptcy, and crime—the human drama and tragedy on which the legal profession thrives. Subways in New York show off the chilling frankness that makes lawyers so beloved with ads that begin in large type: "Had an accident?"

Wall Street lawyers do the same thing their own way. They avoid public contact, since their work involves corporate problems, like dealing with the Securities & Exchange Commission and the Federal Trade Commission and fighting takeovers. For this, they do not advertise on television, but the lawyers know how to get their message across.

Increasing numbers hire public relations consultants to make their names more visible and more widely associated with particular specialties. They want to be seen in legal publications and quoted in the newspapers about broad changes in the law. And they want to clobber other lawyers, as in the front-page *Wall Street Journal* story on Sullivan & Cromwell's troubles in the summer of 1987, which cited the anonymous managing partner at another big New York law firm who said, "They know the rules, but sometimes they act as if the rules just don't apply to them."

Over the course of four years of writing this book, we have seen Sullivan & Cromwell change its mind about the role of publicity in its practice.

Nancy, a sociologist of law, started the project to explore the vast terra incognita of business-law firms that serve two vital but unexplored purposes: fighting the government for their clients and making a network among clients that could seem a blatant violation of the antitrust laws.

The greatest of untouched subjects was Sullivan & Cromwell, which had not even written its own history, as many firms do. Its combination of secrecy and important clients was unmatched. It was not so surprising that the firm with the least to say publicly represented a large percentage of Wall Street's investment banks, plus many commercial banks, oil giants like Exxon, British Petroleum, and Gulf Oil, and Japanese companies like Nippon Steel, Daiwa Bank, and Sony.

Despite its old-line dignity and stuffiness, in *American Lawyer* magazine's annual Corporate Scorecard, which ranks the biggest dealmakers, Sullivan & Cromwell continues to come out on top in the company of young, aggressive firms that have specialized, where Sullivan & Cromwell never did. With a secretary of state, director of the Central Intelligence Agency, Supreme Court justice, and test-ban negotiator among its distinguished alumni, the firm ranked high among unexplored but worthy subjects in the law.

Anticipating an uncooperative response from the firm, Nancy spent two years doing library research before making an approach. Even without its cooperation, the firm was accessible through the John Foster Dulles Archive at Princeton University. This contains a treasure trove of information about Dulles's life as the senior partner of Sullivan & Cromwell for twenty years, down to his $300,000 annual income in the 1930s in the midst of the Depression (the equivalent of $12 million a year fifty years later). His brother, Allen Welsh Dulles, donated a companion library to Princeton. Though more sanitized than Foster's, it is of equal interest on the subject of Allen's twenty-year legal career at Sullivan & Cromwell before he went to the CIA. Between them, supplemented by the National Archives, the libraries expose the firm's cooperation with Hitler over almost ten years, ending only after America entered the war, an example of just what could be hidden under the capacious mantle of client-lawyer privilege.

When Nancy finally approached the firm, she started at its Los Angeles office on the analogy of Kafka's vast and poorly connected Chinese empire in which "battles that are old history are new to us." The partner in charge, Stanley Farrar, was most cordial; after checking with New York, he was the first partner to be interviewed.

With much higher hopes, but still being cautious, Nancy wrote to the retired partners in the New York office, asking to talk to them about the firm's history. When she followed up with phone calls they all said no. Most were polite, but Richard Salter Storrs—with whom she particularly wanted to speak because his great-uncle might have originally introduced Sullivan and Cromwell—blurted out, "The firm disapproves of the book." He denied that it had issued a memo instructing the lawyers not to cooperate, though in fact just such a memo had been circulated in the office.

At that point, when the project seemed to be falling into Kafka-like logic, Nancy recruited Frank, a journalist for *The Economist* and *Financial Times* of London; as her husband he had been a sidelines cheerleader through the frustrating years of isolated research. Together, we combed the National Archives, where we found, on a microfilm that was threaded backward, the Justice Department investigations that confirmed John Foster Dulles's wartime collaboration with the Germans.

We made what we thought would be a last effort to contact the firm, hoping it had changed its mind. John R. Stevenson, the chairman of the firm, had been described to us as a man with the remarkable ability to bring consensus in confrontational negotiations. When we spoke to him on the phone, we tried to explain why the input of the firm would make the book more accurate, if nothing else. He repeated to each of our arguments, "I just don't think we'll be able to cooperate."

Stevenson did at least suggest discussing the matter with Bill Willis, the lawyer who heads the firm's administration as part of the most senior management committee. Willis said he would see us. We prepared a detailed questionnaire of points that were unclear or unknown to us but central to getting a full understanding of the firm and its operation.

On a sunny summer day, we went to the firm's office at the foot of Manhattan feeling we were finally getting somewhere. Willis is a courtly gentleman with a West Virginia twang that added more informality to his short sleeves and habit of talking across his desk with his head cradled in his arm.

We pulled out our questionnaires as he mentioned the large number of former Sullivan & Cromwell lawyers who had called, asking about these people who were writing about the firm. He said he advised them that the firm was not cooperating with the book but would not want to interfere with their talking to us, if they were so inclined.

We did not get to ask a single question on our list. We spent forty-five minutes repeating the reasons why we hoped the firm would cooperate. Willis said the firm just did not cooperate with the press because it would not want to reveal client confidences or the firm's confidences. We asked how the *American Lawyer Guide to Law Firms* had gotten its list of Sullivan & Cromwell clients. Willis said the firm had been forced into cooperating because the compilers had submitted a preliminary list that was full of errors. We pointed out the same might be true of our book, with equal inadvertence. He said, "We will not be suckered into that again."

Willis said it was a firm tradition to avoid the modern practice of soliciting press coverage and that went for our book. We pointed out that Cromwell himself kept a retinue of public relations men, one of whom was called by *The New York Times* in 1905, "head of the political department of Sullivan & Cromwell."

He laughed because in many respects we knew more about Sullivan & Cromwell than he did. He agreed to take our arguments up with his partners and get back to us. Over his shoulder, the Statue of Liberty was boxed in scaffolding, which struck us as perfectly symbolic of the firm's attitude.

Nancy's greatest disappointment of the whole project, probably, was that he never called us back. Of all aspects of the firm, we had assumed the most solid was its reliability. It may not win all its cases or have the best judgment, but from the very beginning in 1879, Sullivan & Cromwell lawyers learned to follow through. It was a small thing, but it stuck in Nancy's mind. Two weeks later we called Willis, who told us his partners had decided not to cooperate with us.

The firm's willingness to talk to us grew out of its role in the *Johnson* v. *Johnson* will contest, in which both sides of the case had public relations consultants in court to deal with the press. We met our first Sullivan & Cromwell partners discussing the case. Though it was a breakthrough, as we got to see eight litigators in action who kibitzed in the halls during the trial, we were confined to asking about the Johnson case because the firm still would not talk to us about itself.

The situation altered a year later when the firm changed chairmen. The new man, John E. Merow, seemed from the outset far less interested in the firm's constricting traditions than in its present troubles and need to present its side of the case. For his promotion coincided with four embarrassing incidents in which firm lawyers, three of them important partners, had become the object of headline-making lawsuits, prosecutions, or investigations.

Merow and his partners were willing to talk with us and entirely prepared for us to draw our own conclusions, with no conditions attached to the interviews. Afterward we speculated on how the book might have turned out had we had the firm's cooperation at the beginning of the project nearly five years before. We realized the result would have been quite different, relying much more on the firm's persuasive opinion of its own accomplishments and less on the public record.

We thank the partners for their interviews and assure them that the process of writing the book has enhanced our respect for their intelligence and devotion to their clients and work. If we raise the wider issues of those loyalties, we do so in part because of the very effectiveness of their professional achievements.

CONTENTS

EPILOGUE: LEGAL ADVICE

PART I

THE LAW BENDER

1

SULLIVAN VERSUS CROMWELL

The corporation is the cuckoo egg in the commercial nest and must be cracked.—ALGERNON SYDNEY SULLIVAN

William Nelson Cromwell barely noticed the parade even though his partner, Algernon Sydney Sullivan, led the procession as it passed under their office window at Broad and Wall streets in New York. It was loud enough, with a red-uniformed band oompahing enthusiastically. The marching songs echoed through the canyon of four-story buildings in a loud celebration of capitalism, which hundreds in the parade thought would spread its beneficence to them while those actually making money labored at their desks.

The parade passed Broad and Wall, up Broadway to the corner of Exchange Place. Sullivan, as tireless a public speaker as he was a courtroom advocate, mounted the makeshift wooden platform laid over the foundation of the new Consolidated Petroleum and Stock Exchange Building, where bunting and streamers blew in the wind of a chilly September day in 1887.

A tall, erect figure with a bald pate and a dignified white moustache, Sullivan had not been able to resist the last-minute invitation to replace U.S. Senator William Evarts at the dedication of this new monument to progress and wealth. After a minister had offered a prayer and the glee club had sung "America," Sullivan harangued his distinguished audience, which included the mayors of New York and Jersey City, on the great controversy of the day: Should corporations be outlawed?

He admitted that the new building "is one more monument to the amazing increase in corporations." He had long been at odds with his own partner over the issue of corporations, and he did not hesitate to offend his listeners. He argued eloquently in favor of outlawing organizations that "live indefinitely long, without change of tenure, and without that distribution of estates which our ancestors thought was desirable as often as the death of every individual. Money and power swell in the possession of corporations as accumulating snow at the North Pole raises mountain tops to cloud land. . . . Set your face and lift up your voice against this dangerous contrivance."

Cromwell had no more time for Sullivan's views on the subject than he did for parades. Sullivan brought in business clients, went to court and public events. Cromwell stayed in the office, closed the window on the wind and Sullivan's opinions, and forced the staff to follow his demanding work schedule.

Still, the two partners got along famously. Cromwell had a head for figures, disguised by a rosy complexion, bright blue eyes, and a full mane of hair cascading dramatically over his collar. His sound advice, boundless energy, and innovative means for clients to grow, prosper, and avoid bankruptcy made their own contribution to the firm's established reputation based on Sullivan's courtroom work.

Sullivan did not interfere with Cromwell, who worked with some of the country's most notorious robber barons, keeping their assets from creditors and scheming to build their empires. The fundamental political conflict was just one more contrast between two opposites who never disagreed and who in eight years had built Sullivan & Cromwell into one of New York's most successful law firms. Sullivan was happy to let Cromwell continue his work, which brought in more clients. Cromwell, knowing that Sullivan's principles appealed to clients, was too practical to criticize him.

He also enormously respected the older lawyer, who had sent him to law school when he had been just a bookkeeper in the firm with which Sullivan was associated. The older lawyer had paid him the highest compliment in offering to start a practice with the twenty-five-year-old lawyer, who had only recently graduated from law school when Sullivan's previous firm dissolved.

Sullivan had to wrestle with his own conscience about talking against a major part of the firm's practice before the petroleum exchange crowd. But this was nothing new to a man who had spent a lifetime balancing principles and a constant need of cash.

Sullivan came from the tradition of frontier justice that brought law and order to the Wild West. Algernon's father, Jeremiah Sullivan, was a Virginia lawyer who had crossed western Pennsylvania on Indian trails to settle in Madison, Indiana. After discussing religion with all his neighbors to find some denomination they could all believe in, he picked Presbyterianism, converted to it himself, and organized the local church. Sent to the Indiana legislature in 1820, less than four years after the territory had become a state, he named the capital Indianapolis and served on the Indiana Supreme Court.

Born in 1826, Algernon Sydney Sullivan was the second son in a family of eleven children. He learned the law by clerking for his father and got enough of a classical education to quote from Sophocles in court. The Panic of 1857 bankrupted Sullivan, who had countersigned friends' and clients' loans. Just married to a descendant of George Washington, he took his bride to New York to start over again.

In the years before the Civil War, Sullivan represented southern business interests in New York. He built his practice on his wife's connections, combined with his own project to disinter the remains of former President James Monroe from a New York pauper's grave and rebury them in Virginia. Long before Presidents acquired the status of great men deserving state funerals, Sullivan arranged for Monroe's casket to be paraded down to New York Harbor drawn by eight white horses draped in black. Thousands watched the casket being delivered to the harbor and its slow, majestic departure by steamer to Virginia.

The Civil War destroyed Sullivan's practice, and almost his health. He was in no position to support the Union since, according to a Confederate who met the Sullivans soon after the war began, "his wife was a Virginia woman who influenced him. She was a genuine Confederate, very pretty and very smart. When we talked together about the South and about the Yankees her eyes just blazed and neither of us could stop talking."

If Sullivan was silent in that conversation, he moved quickly against the advice of other lawyers to defend the South in a highly emotional case. In June 1861 soon after the outbreak of the Civil War, the USS *Savannah,* one of the first Confederate warships, disguised itself as a northern vessel to capture the warship USS *Perry*. But the *Perry* overwhelmed it, and its crew was delivered to New York in chains. The men "were dragged through the streets, a show for the populace, who heaped abuse on us of every description," according to the *Savannah's* first mate, John Harleston, who survived to write about the ordeal after the war.

Because the United States had not recognized the Confederacy, the government treated the crew as pirates, whose conviction as such carried an automatic death sentence. Few lawyers would take on the case, but Sullivan did. The warnings he ignored caught up with him when Secretary of State William H. Seward had Sullivan locked up in Fort Lafayette in New York Harbor, calling his defense of the crew "treasonous." While in prison Sullivan got a severe case of dysentery that permanently affected his health.

He was released with only two days to prepare his case. Luckily his courtroom style relied more on the flamboyance of the orator than on the depths of his research. A contemporary admirer admitted, "As a lawyer he was not given to profound study of any particular case." An associate noticed that Sullivan "was not by temperament or experience a lawyer of details." But at the same time, "other things being equal, it was impossible for him to lose a case."

The trial started in New York on October 23, 1861, in front of Samuel Nelson, Chief Justice of the Supreme Court, who heard the case in the United States Circuit Court (which combined the functions later divided between the federal district and circuit courts).

The complete disruption of communication with the South prevented Sullivan's getting witnesses or documents to attest to the creation of the Confederate government to show that the *Savannah*'s crew were prisoners of war, not pirates. On the third day of the trial, a Philadelphia jury delivered a guilty verdict in a similar case, and the marshal hastily prepared death cells in the Tombs (as the federal prison in New York was already known), in anticipation of a guilty verdict.

Sullivan relied on his oratorical skills, exhorting the jurors, "Tell your Government to wage manly, open, chivalric war on the field and ocean, and thus or not at all; that dishonor is worse even than disunion," even though he represented sailors who violated the laws of the high seas. The judge called Sullivan to the bench to congratulate him on the "ability, fearlessness and fairness in the conduct of the case." The jury returned a split verdict, the case was dropped, and the sailors were returned to the South in an exchange of prisoners.

After the war, Sullivan was remembered as a southern-sympathizing copperhead, though he sponsored the first black to be admitted to the New York bar and fought the Tweed ring as a reform Democrat and assistant district attorney (working alongside Tweed's son). Because of his stance in the Civil War, he was blackballed by the committee founding the Association of the Bar of the City of New York. His once-prosperous southern clients, who were now immigrating north, begged him to take care of them.

Ultimately praised in *The New York Times* for being an honest politician, Sullivan was proposed as a mayoral candidate in New York in 1873 and was mentioned as a possible Democratic presidential nominee in 1883, but he was always more interested in causes than offices.

For a crusader, Sullivan had an extraordinarily mild and affable manner. His speech was slow, precise, and very distinct. The *New York Graphic* wrote of him, "Manful in all his ways and methods, clear headed, big brained, and widely read in all the realms of literature, he was as tender hearted as a child and as gentle as a woman."

In 1870, at the age of forty-four, Sullivan went back into private practice in the firm of Sullivan, Kobbe & Fowler, where Cromwell, who previously worked in a railroad office, had been hired as a young bookkeeper. Spotting Cromwell's talents, Sullivan offered to send him to Columbia Law School in the last class that accepted students who had no undergraduate degree. Cromwell eagerly accepted. He kept his daytime bookkeeping job and went part time to Columbia Law School, after which Sullivan offered him a place in the firm.

When Robert Ludlow Fowler became a surrogate court judge and Herman Kobbe went into practice with his brother, Sullivan asked Cromwell to start a new firm. Sullivan was fifty-three, Cromwell twenty-five and only three years out of law school.

The firm was successful from the beginning. It charged $950 for criminal defense and, if it lost the case, $250 for the appeal. Its first month it handled the incorporation of the Union Tunnel and Mining Company of Colorado, a million-dollar gold-prospecting outfit. It had to do the work twice because of mistakes in its original filing.

Sullivan worked hard to attract clients, using that period's favorite method of advertising—public speaking. His outspoken political beliefs and reputation as a reformer got him a wide variety of speaking engagements. In 1879, the first year of the firm's existence, he dedicated the memorial to General George Armstrong Custer at West Point, a delicate assignment since Mrs. Custer thought the statue of her husband, who had died at the age of thirty-nine, looked like an aging desperado—with a craggy face and two guns blazing. The same year Sullivan dedicated the Egyptian obelisk that still stands behind the Metropolitan Museum of Art in New York and presided over public dinners, like the one for Ferdinand de Lesseps, the old French engineer who was raising money to build a canal in Panama (a project that would make Sullivan & Cromwell famous two decades later).

Sullivan also served on the committee, which former President Ulysses S. Grant headed, to bring a world's fair to New York's new Central Park. He addressed the annual Christmas concert at the largest theater in New York, where a new national anthem was proposed (and rejected). He toasted Edwin Booth, the American tragedian on his way to Europe, before a Sunday farewell breakfast at Delmonico's that included P. T. Barnum and industrialist Cyrus W. Field. When Grand Duke Alexis visited from Russia, Sullivan was on hand to make one of the welcoming speeches.

Sullivan's wife, Mary, did her share to promote the firm as well. As the great-niece of George Washington, she gained entrée to the city's Four Hundred and revived the annual charity ball for the Nursery and Child's Hospital. During the forty years she was active in organizing it, the ball became the high point of the New York social season. The Sullivans conducted a weekly Sunday salon, with high tea served amid discussions of art, politics, and literature. Sullivan read the Bible in Latin and led hymns, accompanying himself on the piano.

Social contacts brought him the estate of Henrietta A. Lenox, who had one of the choicest and biggest real estate plots in the city. Lenox, a spinster who died in 1882 at the age of eighty-two, caused resentment by her choice of favorite nieces, nephews, and servants to inherit her property. Sullivan had written the will, and he defended it in court, where he drew a huge chart of how the estate, which included Fifth Avenue acreage fronting on Central Park, would be divided if the will were thrown out. The jury, asserting the injustice of any change to accommodate disgruntled relatives, voted for Sullivan's client, the major beneficiary, Rachel Lenox Kennedy, Lenox's favorite niece.

The firm was so busy in its first years that when Cromwell was sent to California on business, Sullivan recruited a stand-in, William J. Curtis. Curtis was one of his young assistants in the public administrator's office, a political appointment that paid Sullivan $5,000 a year in addition to his private practice. Curtis liked thinking of himself as "a quasi junior partner" to Sullivan, who clearly made the important decisions for the firm.

A few months later, Curtis was offered a city job, but Sullivan suggested he join Sullivan & Cromwell instead. Curtis accepted the position of a second firm lawyer who could go to court, usually alone but sometimes as Sullivan's assistant, but he also gradually took over Cromwell's chores of running the office.

By 1881, the firm was busy enough to hire a new clerk, Alfred Jaretzki, who relieved Curtis of the office work. In 1884 Cromwell agreed to hire Sullivan's son George, who soon became a partner even though he lacked the conscientiousness and sharp legal mind of the others. Since the original partnership agreement divided the profits two thirds for Sullivan and one third for Cromwell, George Sullivan could be paid from his father's share.

All the lawyers worked extremely hard, including nights and Sundays. Trials forced the small staff to stay at the office until three or four in the morning, then have to get up to start again at seven the next day. Despite the tensions of overwork and constant courtroom preparation, not even the petroleum exchange speech caused an argument to intrude on the firm's congenial prosperity.

In December 1887, three months after giving his petroleum exchange speech, Sullivan caught a chill at the office. He was carried out to his carriage and driven home. His severe cold developed "a typhoid-pneumonia complication," and on December 4 he died at the age of sixty-one. His sudden death was a shock. Cromwell, who rarely acknowledged any emotion, withdrew in seclusion.

New York City flags flew at half-staff, and the courts closed a day in Sullivan's memory, the last time they ever honored a lawyer in that way. Obituaries appeared across the country. The New Orleans *Picayune* commented, "No public occasion was considered complete unless heightened by his eloquence. His was a universal and cosmopolitan genius." The St. Louis *Republican* observed, "Perhaps no Western emigrant in New York ever succeeded in making such a pleasing impression on the natives." Even the gossipy *Town Topics* paused to note, "The announcement of the death of Algernon S. Sullivan caused many a *grande dame,* even on the threshold of a season of unusual festivities, to stop and give utterance to words of deep regret."

Pallbearers from the most distinguished Wall Street financial houses carried Sullivan's casket from his Greenwich Village town house down the street to the First Presbyterian Church on Fifth Avenue. Sullivan would have been proud of his last crowd, gathered on a bone-chilling Sunday morning. A rare mix of the city's elite and the city's poor, the mourners trudged through the snow-covered streets of Greenwich Village. They represented all the groups Sullivan had belonged to, including the Arcadian Club, the New York School of Music, the Presbyterian Club, the Literary Club, the Ohio Society of New York, and the Southern Society. Bowery bums came from the Five Points Mission, where Sullivan had preached against the gang fights that plagued the Lower East Side.

The mourners sang Sullivan's favorite hymn, "Art Thou Weary, Art Thou Languid?" The pastor was effusive in his praise of the public man, remembered for a lifetime career, who, among his other civic activities, had headed the church's Bible school. The church dedicated a memorial window in his memory and hung a portrait in the Sunday school room with the legend "As a reminder of a life worthy of emulation in every way." Cromwell might have agreed with the admiration for his partner, but he also considered Sullivan's death a chance to point the firm in another direction.

2

NOTHING BUT A PAID ATTORNEY

I could not carry you and your affairs ever in my mind for a year, without catching fire and becoming so interested in them.—WILLIAM NELSON CROMWELL (to Henry Villard)

William Nelson Cromwell sat glumly at the Astor Place Hotel restaurant, composing a letter to Sullivan's widow. "Not an unkind or harsh word to any human being, not a falsehood, not a bitter thing, not a profane or indelicate thought ever passed those lips," he wrote effusively.

When he saw his dinner companion arriving, Cromwell quickly put the eulogy in an inside jacket pocket and went back to his habitual glass of champagne. With his light blue eyes as cold as the weather, Cromwell formally greeted William J. Curtis, who had trudged across snowy Trinity Church cemetery from Sullivan & Cromwell's office at the corner of Wall and Broad streets. Curtis was at the firm only temporarily, having left its employ the year before, when he had not been made partner. But he had readily returned in the emergency of Sullivan's death, which had devastated Cromwell more than he would admit. Curtis thought Cromwell was nervous and in a state of almost physical collapse, but Cromwell insisted on hearing news of the office.

In the midst of small talk, Cromwell pulled out a piece of paper. It was not the half-composed eulogy, but a list of possible replacements for Sullivan in Cromwell's firm. Curtis, who was used to Cromwell's devotion to business, was startled by his timing and his interest in Curtis's opinion.

After looking over the list, Curtis recommended General Benjamin F. Tracy, a former court of appeals judge. An eloquent litigator, he was an old, distinguished member of the Bar who knew his way around the New York courts. Curtis thought Cromwell was lucky that Tracy was available.

Cromwell glowered at Curtis and told him he had no intention of following his advice. Curtis, a burly six-footer with a full chest-length beard, would have been imposing had he not seemed so intimidated by the slight and short Cromwell. He did not find Cromwell's grief an excuse for rudeness but, as usual, said nothing. Cromwell declared that he had already made up his mind.

He had picked Curtis to be his partner. It was typical of Cromwell to play with Curtis, just as it was typical of Curtis to swallow his pride and accept the offer with no reproach for Cromwell's rudeness. The deal was struck with a handshake, subject to Curtis's amicable parting from his own struggling firm, Larned & Curtis.

Cromwell had chosen Curtis not because he was the second litigator in the firm under Sullivan, but because he was a good subordinate. Cromwell intended to train Curtis as a business lawyer, who would in turn train others to build a new kind of practice that in the 1930s would be called "factory law"; fifty years later, it turned into the wholly respectable "institutional firm." Curtis was a good choice, having worked his way through Bowdoin College with ingenious enterprises: He had brought ministers on campus to make speeches, for which he charged admission; he had bought large quantities of discounted railway tickets and resold them at full price, a business that earned him a "substantial profit in the course of the summer."

Cromwell started Curtis's lessons with a lot of footwork. To rescue the railroad empire of Henry S. Ives, the "Napoleon of Wall Street" in the 1890s, Cromwell had to get a mandatory injunction served on Ives's creditor, Christopher Meyer. Meyer had avoided all strangers by retreating to his Fifth Avenue mansion with a reported bout of flu. Curtis hired a woman from a detective agency who, prepped with the name of an intimate friend of Meyer's, got past the butler. Armed with a layout supplied by Curtis, she forced her way into Meyer's bedroom, where she quickly handed him the papers. When the woman turned to flee, Meyer's wife refused to let her go. The intruder made her escape by claiming, "I have detectives outside waiting for my return, with instructions that if I do not come back in five minutes to break down the door."

The year after Sullivan's death, Cromwell had Curtis, a New Jersey resident, get that state's legislature to change its laws to attract corporations. Curtis operated behind the scenes with a fast-talking promoter, James B. Dill, to convince the governor that a new corporate law would strengthen the New Jersey budget.

Cromwell's package gave a lot more to companies than to the state with measures that set incorporation fees six times lower and a tax rate ten times lower than New York's. The New Jersey law gave directors the power to prevent shareholders from inspecting company books or from interfering in any way with company management. Most important, it let corporations own shares in other companies, lending credence to Reform Democrats' fears that corporations were just legal trusts. By the time the government tried to thwart Cromwell and his ilk with the Sherman Antitrust Act of 1890, he had already sidestepped the issue by finding a hospitable home for conglomerates and monopolies. At the turn of the century, New Jersey was the address for more than 700 corporations worth together $1 billion.

The first two companies to incorporate under New Jersey's new corporate law were Sullivan & Cromwell clients, the Southern Cotton Oil Company trust and the North American Company. For the cotton oil trust, Cromwell locked himself in with the client at 6:00 P.M., drew up 175 agreements, and had them signed and registered by morning. His fee was $50,000 for one night's work.

Ten years later the Clayton Antitrust Act and Supreme Court decisions restored the teeth to the Sherman Act by redefining trusts to include corporations. But Cromwell had bought a decade of freedom for corporations to bypass the country's concern that they had usurped the nation's wealth and stood above the law.

Once Cromwell pioneered a procedure, Curtis repeated it for other clients. In 1889 the Louisiana Supreme Court outlawed the American Cotton Oil Trust because it was "an illegal and invalid association . . . guilty of usurping, intruding into and unlawfully holding and exercising the franchise and privileges of a corporation without being duly incorporated. . . ."

Cromwell went down to Louisiana and hired the best local counsel to fight the decision in court. The lawyers assured Cromwell they could win the appeal; so he left them to it while he chased around the state in tugboats to get the members of the trust to sell their shares to a Rhode Island company.

The new company was exactly like the trust but registered in Rhode Island, which tolerated trusts. The day the appeal was to be heard, Cromwell walked into court and told the justices that the companies had been dissolved and that therefore no action of the attorney general was necessary. The local officials were so angry they threatened to throw Cromwell in jail. He left the city that afternoon, and nothing more was heard of the case.

Cromwell told Curtis to do the same in Texas for the local cotton oil trust. When Curtis was in Texas, he read in the state charter that the attorney general had to be informed of the dissolution of a company. Local counsel said there was no way around the law. Curtis sat in a Galveston hotel room on a hot April night, devising a plan. He arranged to have all the companies amend their charters to expire simultaneously the following month. He went to all the companies to change their certificates of incorporation and had them filed with the secretary of state a day before they took effect. The ruse worked, and the trust became a Rhode Island company on the pattern Cromwell had set.

Meanwhile, Cromwell applied his organizational and business skills to the firm itself. He ran the office like a skinflint. He expected the staff to reuse rubber bands and paper clips. He rebuked a clerk for not turning off the light in a closet; when the clerk said it turned itself off,

Cromwell did not believe him and had to be shut in the closet to see it work for himself.

He was a penny-pincher by habit, not necessity. The rewards for traditional lawyers were the intellectual gratification of making the best arguments and convincing juries; the rewards for Cromwell's work were extraordinary fees. In 1891 Cromwell made $260,000 for rescuing the prominent stockbrokerage Decker, Howell & Company from bankruptcy. Even though the client ended up with only $2,000, he was so grateful to be solvent that he gave Cromwell a silver Tiffany tea service.

The year after Sullivan died, Cromwell moved from a modest Brooklyn boardinghouse to a town house at 12 West Forty-ninth Street in the center of Manhattan, off Fifth Avenue adjacent to the Columbia University botanical gardens. After walking up an imposing staircase to a double front door, visitors found the house dark, especially because Cromwell's heavy furnishings made the place look like a museum to his newfound eminence. The front hallway had a gold organ, used for public occasions; Cromwell relaxed by playing a more modest organ on the third floor.

The house contained marble, mahogany, ivory, and bronze fashioned into urns, pedestals, statues, and carved furniture. The oil paintings and tapestries depicted ladies in powdered wigs surrounded by cupids and doves. The floors, including those in the bathrooms, had expensive red oriental rugs in rich curlicue designs, while the shelves of the china closet sagged with complete sets of the most expensive tableware. Everything imaginable bore a monogram.

The house reflected Cromwell's taste, not that of his wife, Jennie Osgood Cromwell, a widow (with a son) whom Cromwell had married in 1878. Taller and older than her husband, she shared few of his enthusiasms or intimacies. He was master of the house, as he was of the firm, though he spent more time at the latter than the former.

Mrs. Cromwell preferred to play cards with her women friends and to rear her son, in whom Cromwell took little interest. Cromwell spent his time working or playing the organ upstairs, one of the few activities to remind him of his obscure childhood. Born in 1854, he had grown up in Brooklyn. His father was a Union officer who was killed in Grant's march on Vicksburg when Cromwell was seven. As a teenager, Cromwell went to work for a railroad. He moved to

Sullivan's law firm at the recommendation of the pastor of the Church of the Pilgrims, Reverend Richard Salter Storrs, for whom Cromwell played the organ. (Storrs's great-nephew and namesake joined Sullivan & Cromwell in 1935 and was a partner until his retirement in 1980.)

Another childhood habit Cromwell never lost was his capacity for hard work. He rose at five to start the day, dressed himself after a valet had laid out his clothes, and was taken by limousine to the office at nine. He eventually shifted to working almost entirely at home, but he kept his expansive corner office at the firm while his associates were increasingly squeezed into the library and bullpens on the floors below.

In a period of violent swings in economic conditions, it paid to do bankruptcy work, which Cromwell started while Sullivan was still alive. In 1884 he had kept Henry Villard, the German aristocrat and American railroad magnate, from losing his beloved home, which stood across from St. Patrick's Cathedral in New York City, when his railroad went bankrupt. To save the property, Cromwell had Villard sign a note to his wife with Villard House as collateral. This would prevent creditors from taking the house while Cromwell worked out a sale to newspaper publisher Whitelaw Reid.

After that success, Villard involved Cromwell in rescuing his Northern Pacific Railroad, which the financier had built at the tremendous rate of ten miles of track a day. Villard's downfall came only after the railway was finished and he had taken a crowd of investors and celebrities to the western terminus to celebrate the event. When the visitors saw how deserted the vast stretch of country to Portland, Oregon, was, they rushed to sell their shares. In the precipitous fall of his stock, Villard turned all his business over to Cromwell, who spent three years threatening to give creditors less if they hesitated to settle.

Cromwell was developing an extraordinarily mature and suave manner that flattered clients while getting what he wanted. He had the calculating instincts of a master manipulator. Writing to Villard, he said, "Frankly, my thought was not so much of meeting any liabilities for the past, as it was of making a future possible to you. . . . It shall be my aim to continue to do for you precisely what I would have another do for me."

Cromwell developed the reputation of being a clever lawyer "who taught the robber barons how to rob." In the Northern Pacific bankruptcy in 1893 he showed all ten lawyers then at Sullivan & Cromwell how to handle receiverships. To stop creditors from dismembering the railroad, at a time when there was as yet no federal bankruptcy law, Cromwell had to file bankruptcy papers in every state where the Northern Pacific operated. He sent lawyers across the country to prepare papers for the local courts. When he telegraphed them simultaneously, "File," they had all performed their first bankruptcy work.

Cromwell also had to fight against a separate jurisdiction and different receivers for the western part of the railroad. Curtis argued before the Supreme Court to keep the railroad intact, and won the case, which established the principle that federal courts are units of one whole. Where a federal court already had jurisdiction, another could not claim a separate one.

He called his bankruptcy procedure the "Cromwell Plan," as though it were a patented product of Sullivan & Cromwell. The premise of the Cromwell Plan was to hold off creditors for as long as possible while awaiting an economic upturn. Cromwell handed out promises to pay creditors more than they would get in immediate, drastic liquidations. The plan relied completely on the confidence Cromwell inspired, but it was well placed because a panic was the worst time to liquidate.

During the Panic of 1893, caused by a shortage of dollars, Cromwell spread his bankruptcy work around the office. Alfred Jaretzki, a young associate who had been at the firm since 1881, proved adept at reassuring the market. The New York *Tribune* quoted him saying, in reference to Sullivan & Cromwell's client, insolvent stockbroker H. I. Nicholas & Co., which had failed because it could not sell its shares in the Evansville & Terre Haute Railroad, "I think that the collateral is splendid paper and if the creditors will not become frightened and sell it out, I am sure that they will receive 100 cents on every dollar which the firm owes them."

Success bred success: Having rescued the broker, Sullivan & Cromwell got the Evansville & Terre Haute as a client when its stock plunged in value from $125 to $75 a share.

* * *

The year after Sullivan died, Cromwell moved the firm out of its four-room office on the fourth floor of the Drexel Building at the corner of Broad and Wall streets. Having crammed a 1,000-volume law library (bought from a retired judge) into the space, along with the two partners, an associate, an embosser of wills, a bookkeeper, clerks, and office boys, Cromwell started over in spacious quarters in the United States Trust Company at 45–47 Wall Street. By 1900 Sullivan & Cromwell had grown to fourteen lawyers working four to a room in bullpens surrounding the library. The firm had a reputation for having one of the most modern offices in Wall Street. Under Sullivan, the firm had more partners than associates in the style of litigation practices, in which juniors supported the work of the partner in court. Under Cromwell, three associates worked for each partner, establishing a ratio that prevails a century later in major corporate law firms.

Paul Cravath, of Cravath, Henderson & de Gersdorff (now Cravath, Swaine & Moore), is credited with instituting the legal training system that has lasted ever since: Take top Ivy League graduates, pay them well, and work them night and day. A meritocracy supplanted social status to make partners. Cromwell went further. He gave each associate independence and client contact practically from his first day in the office. It was a perfect match of the law school graduates' wanting to feel important and the firm's wanting to get as much work out of them as possible. Sullivan & Cromwell acquired a reputation for being the best firm to work for despite the long hours and hard work; in turn, clients came to trust the firm's lawyers, even the most junior, because they were the best graduates.

Not that they worked alone. Cromwell prowled the halls of the firm night and day, supervising associates. He poked a finger into their chests and grilled them about their work. When they were not at their desks, he made sure they were in the office by checking the hatrack. He considered anyone who fooled him, who was known as a "two-hat man," the lowest form of life.

Neither did he trust the newfangled invention the telephone. He had a phone installed in 1881 but left it in the outer office until desk phones arrived in 1889. Clerks were not allowed to use the phone, and Cromwell avoided it because all the city's 140 law firms and 600 lawyers used the same exchange, LAW, on a party line. Even when the firm got its own private line, Cromwell followed up conversations with written confirmation. After airplanes started carrying mail, he sent regular letters chasing airmailed ones and filed papers by train, mail, and personal messenger to ensure delivery. Once, when a train was delayed by floods, an airplane grounded, and only the messenger got through, Cromwell remarked, ''Accidents don't happen, they are permitted to happen by fools who take no thought of misadventure.''

Cromwell's methods took their toll on the lawyers. Curtis suffered a nervous breakdown in court in 1902 but kept going to the trial—with a doctor—until he had finished the final plea. The unrelenting pressure obviously still rankled twenty-five years later when he wrote, ''I did not recover from this breakdown, and was compelled a few months afterwards to go to Europe in the hope of recovering my health.'' He got only six months off and so ''did not recover for some years.'' He concluded, ''The fact was, the previous twenty or twenty-five years of intense and unremitting labor, had resulted in a nervous attack which was more serious than I at the moment realized.'' If Cromwell was destined to be remembered as the founder of the firm, Curtis set the dubious precedent for a Sullivan & Cromwell underling, whether associate or partner, to be overworked, underrewarded, pushed to his limits and beyond.

Having organized the firm so meticulously, Cromwell could devote himself to the clients who interested him the most. They were not all, as one might have expected, the most eminent or lucrative ones. Cromwell acted for eight Pittsburgh bishops who had written asking him to bring ''daylight out of [P. J.] Kiernan's darkness.'' This case was over a fast-talking Irishman who had lent money to poor Catholic parishes in return for powers of attorney and for big life insurance policies on the nuns and priests. Cromwell negotiated with Kiernan to give back the control he had taken in return for not being prosecuted.

Cromwell instructed executives on how to attract investors, telling the president of the Cotton Oil Company that the ''annual Reports do not give a clear, nor convincing idea of the variety and value of our properties—the extent of operations—the magnitude of interests involved. In my judgment, this accounts for the lack of interest by the investing public in our securities.''

He sent the executive copies of the annual report of the National Tube Company, of which Cromwell was a director, because "you will notice . . . [it] betrayed no secret of our business, nor anything that would give a competitor advantage; but we stated significant facts upon which intelligent investors desired information, and with the consequence that in the first year of our existence our stockholders are nearly 3,000 and the securities daily growing in confidence without any fictitious methods."

J. P. Morgan called on Cromwell's business acumen to organize the United States Steel Company, the first American corporation capitalized at more than $1 billion. Cromwell may have even given Morgan the idea to consolidate the steel industry into U. S. Steel, as Morgan's public-relations man, Ivy Lee, averred. But others also claimed the original idea because instead of just admitting his desire to sell out and retire, Andrew Carnegie spread rumors that he would set up in competition to two Morgan-backed businesses, the Pennsylvania Railroad and the National Tube Company. Morgan was forced to buy out the wily Scotsman to avert these challenges. But even though Morgan paid Carnegie $500 million, he had the last laugh a few years later when Carnegie confided, "I should have asked you for a hundred million more," and Morgan replied, "Well, you would have got it if you had."

Since Cromwell had organized the National Tube Company with Morgan's backing in 1899, he was the logical choice for putting together the steel company. The tube company was more than a dry run for U. S. Steel. Its consolidation of twenty-one companies created an $80 million corporation which was the largest consolidation to that time, and controlled 90 percent of the country's pipe manufacturing.

National Tube was also one of the eight components of U. S. Steel when it was formed in 1901. The first step in creating a near monopoly in the steel industry (the one major holdout being the Rockefeller interests) was Cromwell's starting U. S. Steel Corporation with the modest capitalization of $3,000. Cromwell had his partner, William J. Curtis, put up $1,000; in return he became, for a month, the company's first president.

Cromwell exchanged most of the shares in the component steel companies on a one-for-one basis, though his original client, National Tube, got one and one-quarter shares for each share of their company's stock. The contributors first received U. S. Steel certificates of deposit and the last dividends of their old companies in the spring of 1901. Meantime, Cromwell oversaw the issuance of $550 million in stock and $550 million in bonds to capitalize the new company.

The bonds represented the asset value of the new company, and the shares its profit potential. Bonds were considered a safe investment, the shares a risk based on the company's growth. Three hundred insiders, including Cromwell, got $200 million of the new company's stock for $25 million. Within the first month the stock rose 10 percent as the price of steel rails, which over twenty years had dropped down to $16.50 a ton, rebounded over the next fifteen years to $28 a ton.

Cromwell himself got $2 million in shares, for which he paid $250,000. He and the other insiders were paid back with a special dividend of three times their original investment, and despite periodic sales of shares, U.S. Steel stock remained a major part of Cromwell's estate when he died nearly half a century later.

In 1906 Cromwell attracted as a client one of the most notorious railroad robber barons, E. H. Harriman. Described by President Theodore Roosevelt as a "malefactor of great wealth" and an "enemy of the Republic," Harriman controlled 12 percent of the railroad track in America, an empire that earned $300 million a year with assets as large as U. S. Steel's. Harriman wanted Cromwell to win two tough fights for him—proxy battles to gain control of the Illinois Central Railroad and to retain control of the Wells, Fargo Company against dissident shareholders.

The Illinois Central connected the Great Lakes with the Gulf of Mexico and would add a north-south route to Harriman's holdings, which stretched from the Union Pacific and Southern Pacific in the West to his recently acquired Baltimore & Ohio in the East. Knowing the value of his franchise, Stuyvesant Fish, the cagey president of the Illinois Central, had tried to insulate the railroad from a takeover by accepting tax exemptions from the state of Illinois in return for giving the governor a seat on the company's board of directors. Fish had also encouraged a wide shareholding among small investors, who, just as he had hoped, rallied round when Harriman accumulated 20 percent of the company stock.

Fish tried to outsmart Harriman by soliciting proxies for the next annual meeting in his own name rather than the board's. After Cromwell threatened to send out his own proxies on behalf of the board, Fish agreed in a compromise to vote the proxies with a majority of the board.

Cromwell forged an alliance with two board members, John Jacob Astor and Charles A. Peabody, who were already angry at Stuyvesant Fish for starting an investigation of the Mutual Life Insurance Company, of which Peabody was president. When Cromwell lacked one vote for a board majority, he offered to make J. T. Harahan, the railroad's general manager, president if he cooperated to oust Fish.

In a battle recounted on the front page of *The New York Times,* Cromwell stood at the annual meeting and demanded that Fish cast his proxies according to the new Cromwell majority.

Fish declared, "I will never under any circumstances vote [that way]. The issue today is whether the Illinois Central Railroad Company shall or shall not continue to be an independent corporation."

While Cromwell attacked, supporters on the floor defended Fish, and called Cromwell, "nothing but a paid attorney." Cromwell made a spectacle of the meeting, shouting and threatening from the floor before Fish cast the votes and defeated Cromwell 600,000 to 21,000. At the end of the meeting, Cromwell called a press conference to warn, "There will be a meeting of the board, probably in November. This board will elect the officers of the railroad. You can draw your own conclusions."

Cromwell and Harriman nursed their wounds for only three weeks before calling the special board meeting in New York. The date was election day, and it was chosen specifically to keep the governor of Illinois from attending. Reluctantly, the governor traveled to New York for the meeting, but he could not help Fish, who, behind closed doors and out of the glare of publicity, was replaced as president by Harahan.

The day after the Fish ouster Cromwell disingenuously told the press that the "board [is] composed of gentlemen of strong individuality, and it is ridiculous to suppose that three or four of their number would control the destinies of the Illinois Central."

He added later, "All that is wanted is a close working agreement between the two roads, through which all the advantages that might accrue from a lease could be obtained without any of the possible legal complications."

Despite Cromwell's reassurances, Harriman's takeover of the Illinois Central was universally condemned as a ruthless abuse of proxies to take control without a majority of the stock. The best *The New York Times* could say about Harriman was that "there was no hemming and hawing, no indirection, no concealment, none of those hesitations and timidities that men weaker than Mr. Harriman often exhibit upon such occasions." The Richmond *Times-Dispatch* remarked that "Mr. E. H. Harriman has again raised the black flag of piratical high finance," and the *Philadelphia Press* called it "one of those ruthless exercises of the power of sheer millions which diminish public confidence in railroad investments and make the small investor feel that he has no security, no adequate defense for his rights, and no efficient way to exercise power."

Fish shifted the fight to the courts, where he argued that a majority of the board of directors had to live in Illinois according to the company charter. Cromwell replied that a majority had not lived in Illinois for more than a decade, including Fish's tenure.

At the same time that Cromwell waged the Illinois Central fight, he masterminded a four-month effort to defend Harriman's control of Wells, Fargo. Small shareholders wanted the company to increase its dividend to reflect its fabulous profits. Led by a former Harriman business associate and friend, W. C. Stokes, the dissident group knew of Harriman's abuses; whether they could get redress was another question.

Cromwell stopped the dissidents with deceit, bribery, and trickery. It was all legal, insofar as the deceit was perpetrated through the accountants, who concealed the real value of the company. The bribery was conducted by buying out small shareholders at a premium over the stock market price. Cromwell sent a Sullivan & Cromwell associate through New England with $198,000 to buy as many shares as he could. The associate, Hjalmar H. Boyesen, a tall, good-looking athlete of Norwegian descent, went house to house sweet-talking and offering $90-a-share premiums for Wells, Fargo stock that, the dissident leader pointed out, proved the stock was worth much more than anyone realized.

Curtis got a New York court to agree that stockholders had to apply to see the company books in Colorado, where the company was incorporated. But because the charter had been drawn up while Colorado was still a territory, it could keep its books in any state in the Union. So even a favorable ruling by a Colorado judge would not gain access to the books, which were actually held in New York.

Cromwell called the Wells, Fargo annual meeting on a hot August day in a claustrophobic space at company headquarters in the Wall Street area. The room was right above the din and smell of trolleys and horses, which could be eliminated only by closing the windows. Cromwell insisted that every vote go through an elaborate counting procedure, which dragged the meeting through the whole day. He wore down the opposition, and with 4,000 shares bought door to door in New England, kept Wells, Fargo in Harriman's control.

Cromwell capped the campaign with the typical hyperbole he lavished on his clients, saying of Harriman, "It is not on the business acumen of the officers, but on his wonderful executive genius on which the shareholders must rely if the prosperity of the company is to continue. He cannot be replaced for he moves in a higher world into which we may not enter."

The age of playing Monopoly on a life-size scale came to an end with the Supreme Court's decision in the Northern Securities case in 1904. Instead of confining the Sherman Antitrust legislation to trusts, the Supreme Court applied it to the Northern Securities holding company. Reflecting the populist sentiments ushered in by the energetic young President, Theodore Roosevelt, the government's case against Northern Securities put monopolists on notice that they would no longer have a free hand to transform America in their own interests.

The new President had finally thwarted the men who seemed to be riding roughshod over the American economy and the gullible people who entrusted their investments to them. With the government starting to assert itself, Cromwell had a new client in mind—the President of the United States.

3

CROMWELL THE REVOLUTIONARY

No other great work now being carried on throughout the world is of such far-reaching and lasting importance as the Panama Canal. Never before has a work of this kind on so colossal a scale been attempted. Never has any work of the kind, of anything approaching the size, been done with such efficiency, with such serious devotion to the well-being of the innumerable workmen, and with a purpose at once so lofty and so practical.—THEODORE ROOSEVELT

The completion of the Suez Canal in 1869 represented the pinnacle of engineering achievement for Ferdinand de Lesseps and his daring and talented French builders. But when the same team went bankrupt trying to repeat its success with a Panama canal, they precipitated a French national tragedy. The failure marked a watershed in French history, an embarrassment on a monumental scale that bankrupted more than two hundred thousand French people who had staked their personal fortunes as well as their national pride on the engineering skill associated with the Eiffel Tower and the Suez Canal.

But there remained the assets which the Paris-based New Panama

Canal Company hired Cromwell to sell to the United States for *its* projected canal. Besides an excavation of 19 million cubic yards, the French Panama Canal Company had left the remnants of a civilization in the jungle. Their $260 million investment included roads, housing, and hospitals rusting along with the rotting, hastily buried corpses of 4,000 Frenchmen who had died of yellow fever.

The French failure made Americans all the more determined to dig their own canal in Nicaragua. The site had been selected as far back as the 1850s, and it had the support of the southern states. Because a Nicaragua canal was closer than Panama to the ports of Galveston, New Orleans, and Biloxi, southern senators made it an understandable obsession.

Cromwell took the entrenched opposition as a challenge. Before he went to Washington to persuade Congress to take over his client's Panama lease, "there was scarcely a person in either house who would willingly espouse the cause of Panama," William J. Curtis ruefully admitted. But Cromwell and Curtis went down there to argue that too much work had been done in Panama just to abandon it. Other investors would buy the French lease, finish the canal, and create competition for the American project, they contended. Cromwell and Curtis tried to show as many legislators as possible the statistics, maps, and cost estimates backing the French assertion that the canal was already 40 percent finished.

Thinking he could disarm the opposition, Cromwell made the first presentation to the Democratic senator from Alabama, John Tyler Morgan, the chief proponent of the Nicaragua site. He was a thirty-year Senate veteran who had fought for the South in the Civil War and saw the Nicaragua canal as the culmination of his life's work. Though he listened politely, he used the information Cromwell gave him to make "a most vigorous and vicious attack against the Panama Canal project," Curtis noted.

Having taken the measure of his competition, Cromwell set himself up in the Birdcage Bar at the elegant Willard Hotel, where he sipped champagne with a growing list of Washington contacts. Curtis sought an interview with the Speaker of the House, Republican Thomas B. Reed, who invited the lawyer to his apartment at the Shoreham Hotel. After Curtis presented the case for Panama in great detail, Reed, like

Curtis a plain-speaking man from Maine, asked, "What is it that your Company wants, Mr. Curtis, an appropriation?"

Curtis said, no, all he asked was "that you *investigate* before you act."

"That is a perfectly fair proposition," Reed agreed.

It was a crucial conversation. Senator Morgan tacked a simple rider onto the Senate version of the 1899 rivers and harbors bill, asking for $2 million to start building the Nicaragua canal. The bill easily passed the Senate, but as an addition to the original House appropriations bill, it had to be reconciled in a conference committee of the House and Senate.

Reed appointed to the conference committee three House members sympathetic to Panama. Not until the last frantic hour of the congressional session did the Senate understand that Reed would block the whole rivers and harbors bill if it had the Nicaragua provision. The House version finally passed, giving $2 million for an investigation of both routes.

With the investigating commission to be appointed by the President, Cromwell ingratiated himself with President William McKinley and his right-hand man, Republican Senator Mark Hanna of Ohio. Cromwell got an introduction to Hanna through Hanna's banker, Edward Simmons, who was an old acquaintance of Cromwell's and president of the Panama Railroad, which was owned by the New Panama Canal Company.

Meeting Hanna in Simmons's office, Cromwell explained the benefits of the Panama route and donated $60,000 of the New Panama Canal Company's money to the Republican party. The effect was immediate: The 1900 Republican platform abandoned its previous endorsement of Nicaragua and advocated a canal chosen by the experts.

Of the nine members of the commission, which was named after its chairman, Admiral John G. Walker, three were Cromwell's choices. Cromwell persuaded the group to go first not to Central America, but to Paris to meet with his client, the New Panama Canal Company.

Cromwell spent six months preparing for the commission's visit to Paris. Taking advantage of the French company's ten years' experience in Panama, he gathered far more information than any American had ever considered before. He set up a press bureau of three writers run by Roger Farnham, a former journalist. It was the beginning of a lifelong association with Farnham eventually being called the head of Sullivan & Cromwell's "political department." For Panama, Farnham prepared releases for the general press, the scientific press, and the international press. He accompanied Cromwell to meetings, arranged appointments, and found out whom Cromwell had to impress. He also produced a three-volume study of Panama. Cromwell made sure that Farnham's efforts were not ignored, writing bluntly at one point to President McKinley, "Advise the Congress of the facts in the case." He then got the Senate to pass a resolution forcing the President to transmit all the documents relevant to Panama to Congress.

Cromwell sailed ahead to France and met the commission on its arrival, presenting them with a detailed itinerary covering their business and social activities for their five-week stay. Cromwell scheduled the key company personnel to explain the work that was done, the work that remained, and the geology of the area. Each commissioner sat in front of 340 documents with Sullivan & Cromwell's name embossed on the covers; they included engineers' reports, geological studies, plans for everything from dam and lock sites to usable equipment and property, a complete set of scale maps, elevations, and detailed graphs of the whole Panama enterprise.

The second week, a highly respected American engineer, General Henry Abbot, told the commission that another country would take over the Panama route if the United States did not. He considered the canal feasible and already past phase one of what he defined as a three-phase operation.

At a final eight-course "breakfast" at the Pavilion Paillard on the Champs-Élysées, Cromwell—until then a hovering presence, solicitous, guiding, attentive—finally spoke. He summed up the evidence produced during the commission's stay. Eloquent and flowery in his private conversation, he spoke effusively in public. He used notes to recall all the facts and figures that showed just how advanced the Panama project was. He told the commissioners that a German consortium was thinking of taking over Panama. He thanked them for their visit and toasted their voyage and deliberations. Admiral Walker stood to toast his hosts and especially Cromwell, who had done so much to enlighten them about Panama.

Cromwell stayed in Paris to convince his clients to sell the canal to the Americans. He told the French company that on financial grounds the commission would pick Panama, but not unless the French were no longer involved.

Company president Maurice Hutin was not a businessman but an engineer whose pride overwhelmed his pocketbook on the subject of Panama. He let Cromwell speak, but he said nothing, determined to make America build the canal on his terms, with the French at least partners in the project.

Cromwell rushed back to America to stop another bill pushing Nicaragua even before the investigative commission had had a chance to report. Cromwell and Curtis lobbied the Senate to delay its vote and won by a narrow margin. An infuriated Senator Morgan railed publicly against Cromwell's "interference," which he found "repulsive . . . direct, constant, and offensive." Cromwell "insult[ed] . . . the intelligence of Congress," but, worst of all, won.

Senator Morgan should not have worried. The commission's preliminary report recommended Nicaragua for one reason: It was the only route the United States could "control, own and manage." Panama had its advantages, but complete control was the overriding issue. Before submitting the final report, Admiral Walker called on Cromwell. The admiral had been on a previous commission that recommended Nicaragua, so Cromwell assumed he had to work around him.

But Cromwell had underestimated the old admiral, who said that if the French company were to accept the commission's recommended $40 million price for the canal lease and all remaining property, the final report, due to be released the next month, would opt for Panama.

The commission valued the excavation at $27,474,033; the Panama Railroad stock at $6,850,000; the maps, drawings, and records, $2 million; and an added 10 percent for contingencies. Though the French had sunk $260 million into Panama, the New Panama Canal Company was capitalized at only $12 million, with an agreed division of any income of 60 percent to the original Panama Canal Company and 40 percent to it. A $40 million sale would represent a profit of $4 million for Cromwell's client.

Cromwell cabled Paris the same day, urging the company to take the $40 million as a reasonable settlement. Instead of French consent, Cromwell got back a letter firing him. When Hutin arrived in America insisting on $109 million for the canal, the final Walker report overwhelmingly supported the Nicaragua site. American newspapers called the French arrogant and obstinate, an appraisal with which Cromwell had to agree (but only privately). Curtis, who had to accompany Cromwell to Washington, regretted that the firm was involved at all. He pleaded with Cromwell to take the firing as a chance to escape this client, whose national pride was tragically and fatally blinded by its overblown expectations.

Cromwell continued to follow the issue on his own while the New Panama Canal Company fired Hutin and replaced him with a banker and major creditor of the canal company, Marius Bô of Société Génçrale. At his first shareholders' meeting as president, Bô pushed them to accept the $40 million American offer. Police had to break up the riot, which pitted the thousands of small stockholders of the original Panama Canal Company who faced major losses against the financiers who had picked up the bankrupt company and could make a killing on even a $40 million sale. When the dust settled, the angry and disappointed stockholders agreed to accept $40 million.

But the offer came after the United States had already negotiated a treaty with Nicaragua and after congressional bills to appropriate the needed funds had easily cleared the necessary committees. Congress awaited only the end of the Christmas holiday to vote in the full House and Senate. A Nicaragua canal was almost a foregone conclusion.

Philippe Bunau-Varilla, a former engineer in Panama, who had a $200,000 investment riding on the canal, cabled Bô from America; "FAILURE TO REHIRE CROMWELL WILL ALIENATE SYMPATHIES INDISPENSABLE TO SAVING THE SITUATION."

On January 4, 1902, Bô cabled Admiral Walker to inform him that the company was willing to accept the $40 million while reinstating Cromwell to negotiate the sale. He added the insulting conditions that Cromwell accept a fee set by the company, subject to arbitration, and that Cromwell not spend any more company money on political contributions.

Three days before the debate on the Nicaragua bill at the opening session of the Fifty-seventh Congress, Wisconsin Senator John C. Spooner, one of the most powerful Republicans, submitted a simple amendment substituting the word "Panama" for "Nicaragua" in the canal bill. Spooner was Cromwell's secret weapon, a leader of the most conservative Republican faction and a staunch admirer of Cromwell's. When the Northern Pacific went bankrupt in 1893, Cromwell had used Spooner's Milwaukee firm as local counsel, and at that time, Spooner wrote admiringly of Cromwell, "He is wonderful in his energy, in his quickness of comprehension, his mastery of details, his power of rapid generalization, his fertility of resources, etc. etc. and with it all he is generous, full of good impulses and altogether a lovable man. In addition to his other accomplishments, he can bulldoze like damnation when he wants to, and I have seen him when he wanted to."

The vote on Spooner's amendment was too close to call until the issue literally exploded when a volcano erupted in Nicaragua. No one was killed, but the damage went perilously close to the canal site, or so Cromwell contended. He had Farnham prepare a map of all major volcanoes in the region, active ones in red, extinct ones in black. The Nicaragua route showed almost a solid band of red dots from the Atlantic to the Pacific; Panama had none within 200 miles of the canal site.

In the final debate, Senator Hanna gave an impassioned speech for Panama with notes Cromwell had prepared for him. He spoke for hours, and when he was too exhausted to go on, he stopped, only to start again the next day. Though no orator, he brought out the salient factors, like the fact that it would take half the time to cross the Panama Canal than the canal in Nicaragua; Panama needed fewer locks and was the only site that could be built at sea level.

Under Cromwell's influence, Hanna rose to eloquence, declaiming, "It is the great, broad, liberal American policy for which we stand in the building of a world canal. I sympathize with all those who in other days, laboring for an isthmian canal, had but one star to guide them—Nicaragua—and who must now naturally feel like giving up an old friend to pass it by. But in an age of progress and development, Mr.

it, the American people are looking to Congress to answer to this question without regard to sentiment. . . .''

Considered his finest speech, it was so convincing that some started referring to the ''Hannama canal.'' The Spooner bill passed by a vote of 42 to 34 and was signed, June 28, 1902 by President Theodore Roosevelt, who had assumed the presidency the previous September after the assassination of William McKinley. A bitter, defiant, and almost violent Senator Morgan got up on the floor of the Senate to bray, ''I trace this man Cromwell back to the beginning of the whole business. He has not failed to appear anywhere in this whole affair; and . . . I have dreadful fears that Mr. Cromwell wrote pretty nigh the whole [Commission] report.''

Though a defeat for Senator Morgan, it was not yet a victory for Cromwell. By the end of the 1902 Congressional session, Colombia, which owned Panama, had to endorse the sale of the New Panama Canal Company's lease to the United States or the President would turn once again to Nicaragua.

Colombia wanted to be paid to transfer the concession to America. The United States refused, and the President threatened to take up the Nicaragua route. The next day, January 23, 1903, Tomás Herrán, the Colombian chargé d'affaires in Washington, signed the treaty at Secretary of State John Hay's home on Lafayette Square. Hay gave Cromwell, who had drafted the treaty, the pen used to sign it.

Senator Morgan submitted sixty amendments to the Hay-Herrán Treaty, hoping to prevent its ratification. He raged about the ''crowd of French jailbirds cleverly advised by a 'New York railroad wrecker' [to] . . . unload an otherwise worthless property on the United States for an exorbitant sum . . . to build a canal over a poor route, infested with disease, in conjunction with a depraved, pest-ridden people whose constitutional government was a myth.''

Once again ignoring Morgan, the Senate ratified the Hay-Herrán Treaty, but the *Colombian* Senate refused to ratify it, gambling on the lapse of the French concession to get the $40 million Cromwell's client was expecting. If they could hold out until 1910, all French rights would revert to Colombia, a delay harmful primarily to the interests represented by Cromwell. He was lucky to have in the White House an activist whose impatience matched his own. Roosevelt called the Colombian senators "foolish and homicidal corruptionists" who should not be allowed to "bar one of the future highways of civilization."

On June 13, 1903, Cromwell met twice with President Roosevelt to discuss the Colombian impasse. The next day, the New York *World* ran an unsigned "special report" predicting that if Colombia rejected the treaty, Panama would secede and get quick recognition from the United States. Roosevelt and Cromwell hoped that the story, which Farnham had delivered to the *World,* would scare Colombia into ratifying the Hay-Herrán Treaty.

But the Colombian Senate remained adamant. The only way around Colombia's obstinacy, Cromwell decided, was a revolution in Panama. He was the conduit between Washington and the revolutionaries, who were led by officials of the Panama Railroad Company, Cromwell's client. The organizers of the revolution, who later became the top officials in the Panamanian government, included the railroad's general superintendent, assistant superintendent, freight agent, land agent, and even company surgeon.

Cromwell summoned the railroad's freight agent, James Beers, to New York, promising to "go the limit" for revolution. Beers returned to Panama with a cable codebook containing special instructions from Cromwell.

The physician for the Panama Railroad Company, Dr. Manuel Amador, sailed from Panama to New York to talk with Cromwell. Amador, though seventy years old, was ready to fight, as long as the United States government supported the revolution with arms and prompt diplomatic recognition. Cromwell gave Amador full assurances of help and money.

The same ship that docked with Amador brought another conspirator, J. Gabriel Duque, the proprietor of the Panama newspaper and the local lottery. Cromwell suggested that if Duque financed the rebellion with $100,000, he could become the first president of Panama. Cromwell telephoned Secretary of State Hay and arranged for Duque to see him the next day.

The secretary of state promised Duque to stop Colombian troops from landing to protect the Panama Railroad, as permitted by the Treaty of 1846. But the plan backfired when Duque went from

Secretary of State Hay to the Colombian chargé d'affaires, warning him that if the treaty was not signed, Panama would revolt and Colombia would lose everything.

Herrán wired Cromwell that if there were a revolution in Panama, Colombia would hold him and the New Panama Canal Company responsible. Cromwell bombarded Secretary of State Hay with letters and telegrams disavowing any role in Duque's double cross.

The next day, when Amador came to Cromwell's office, Cromwell refused to see him. Amador sat for hours with the receptionist until Cromwell appeared and told him to leave at once and not return. Cromwell telegraphed the superintendent of the Panama Railroad to avoid all connection with the revolution. But Cromwell's refusal to see Panama Railroad officials did not stop Farnham from receiving a full briefing as the plot unfolded.

Cromwell escaped to Paris on the pretext of conferring with his clients. His place in the revolution was taken by Bunau-Varilla, whose $200,000 investment in the canal represented an emotional, as well as a financial, commitment. The Frenchman, who was first mesmerized by de Lesseps's Panama scheme as a schoolboy twenty years before, set up a one-man central headquarters in New York to assume the arrangements originally promised Amador by Cromwell.

Bunau-Varilla underwrote the revolution with a $100,000 loan and provided a declaration of independence, a constitution, and a flag designed by his wife. In return, he demanded to be made the diplomatic representative of Panama in Washington. Bunau-Varilla, after seeing Secretary of State Hay, wired the conspirators at the isthmus that American warships were ready, signaling the start of the revolution.

With the American warships *Nashville* and *Dixie* protecting the Panamanian harbor, the bloodless coup occurred on the night of November 3, 1903. The revolutionaries arrested the governor and bribed the Colombian officers to flee into the jungle. The Panamanians declared their independence, and seventy-two hours later the United States recognized the new republic.

A contingent from Panama, including Dr. Amador, waited in New York for Cromwell's return from Paris. They went together to Washington to negotiate an American-Panama treaty.

But Bunau-Varilla and Roosevelt had already signed a treaty on behalf of Panama and pushed it through Congress. Guided by the Hay-Herrán Treaty, which Cromwell had written for the deal with Colombia, Bunau-Varilla made changes even more beneficial to the United States, which were rescinded only under the Carter administration in 1978.

Instead of the ninety-nine year lease Cromwell had negotiated with Herrán, the treaty granted the United States a ten-mile-wide canal zone "in perpetuity as if it were the sovereign of the territory . . . to the entire exclusion of the exercise by the Republic of Panama of any such sovereign rights, power or authority." In return, the United States guaranteed Panama's independence and promised to pay an initial $10 million and $250,000 a year after completion of the canal. Bunau-Varilla sent the treaty to Panama for quick ratification and tried to get the Panama Railroad to delay one of its boats so that the signed treaty could be quickly returned to Washington.

But Cromwell instructed the company not to wait for the signed treaty because he was incensed at Bunau-Varilla's hasty swindle of Panama. He cabled Panama that Bunau-Varilla was compromising the country's interests and a Panamanian should be appointed in his place. The provisional government ratified the treaty anyway, and the United States Senate approved it on February 23, 1904.

Cromwell fed the New York *World* a news story attacking Bunau-Varilla as the head of a group of French and New York speculators who financed the Panama revolution and made $4 million on New Panama Canal Company stock. Bunau-Varilla immediately suspected Cromwell since he was excluded from the accusations. Indeed, Bunau-Varilla eventually found out that the *World* had paid one of Cromwell's press agents, Jonas Whitley, $100 for the scoop.

A month later the Hay-Bunau-Varilla treaty was ratified, and Dr. Amador became the country's first president. The new president's son hosted a New York celebration at the Waldorf-Astoria for four Panama Railroad officials and five Sullivan & Cromwell lawyers. He gave the first flag raised in the republic to Cromwell for presentation to President Roosevelt.

J. P. Morgan & Company, fiscal agents for the transaction, arranged to pay $40 million in gold bullion and currency directly into the Bank of France for the New Panama Canal Company and the liquidator of the old de Lesseps company. The liquidator of the original Panama company distributed an average $156 to 226,296 of its bondholders; stockholders got par value plus a 3 percent annual dividend on their ten-year investment in the reorganized New Panama Canal Company. It was another successful Sullivan & Cromwell liquidation, even confined to the $40 million price set by the Isthmian Canal Commission in early 1900.

Not quite satisfied, Cromwell submitted a claim on behalf of his client that the canal company get an extra $2 million to cover the four years it had spent holding on to the concession. He appealed directly to President Roosevelt, who agreed to be the sole arbiter. Roosevelt ruled against any further compensation on the ground that the original calculation had given a 10 percent margin to preserve the canal concession. Cromwell was extremely disappointed, but some people thought that the $40 million was already too much, and Senator Morgan had not given up his attacks on the choice.

Cromwell submitted to his client a bill for $800,000, amounting to 2 percent of a tough transaction. The company rejected it and brought the payment before a French arbitrator. To represent it, Sullivan & Cromwell picked Raymond Poincaré, a French senator, lawyer (*avocat*), and, a decade later, the president of the country, who received Curtis at his apartment on the Champs-Élysées. "It was the practice then, as I suppose it is now," Curtis reported, "for those who desire to consult *avocats* to go to their homes and wait in the parlor adjoining the library, each taking his or her turn in regular order. It mattered not who called or how important the business, they must each wait their turn." However Poincaré failed to get the firm more than $200,000 for its eight years' work, and Curtis complained, "We were very inadequately paid."

Cromwell at least got appointed Panamanian general counsel and fiscal agent. He invested the $10 million Panama got and arranged to repay Bunau-Varilla $100,000 through a loan from the Bowling Green Trust Company, a bank Cromwell had reorganized and on whose board of directors he sat.

With the construction of the canal about to begin, the United States wanted complete control of the Panama Railroad to avoid obstruction by minority shareholders. Secretary of War William Howard Taft, as overseer of the canal, empowered Cromwell to acquire the 2 percent of the shares the government did not already own. Cromwell paid three times the government's offer for one block of shares but told Taft he would give the government an irrevocable proxy if it decided not to pay the higher price.

When the Panama Railroad elected new directors in April 1905, among the group, *The New York Times* reported, was "Roger L. Farnham, who has long been employed by William Nelson Cromwell in connection with the political department of the law firm Sullivan & Cromwell." It was the beginning of a stellar business career for Cromwell's publicist, who became vice-president of National City Bank and president of the Haiti Railroad (the latter a Sullivan & Cromwell client).

Despite Sullivan & Cromwell's paltry fee, all the work and controversy, Cromwell was bursting with pride over his part on the world stage. In reply to the government's effusive praise, he grandiloquently claimed he worked so hard so that "my country and mankind may in our day and generation secure the inestimable blessings which will flow from the reshaping of the globe and thus bringing closer together the family of nations."

Panama had occupied Cromwell nearly full-time for four years, marking the end of his regular presence at the New York office. When a New York newspaper described him as a shyster, he laughed it off, as he did Senator Morgan's persistent criticisms, not realizing the epithet would color his reputation. The writer made him sound as intriguing as he was roguish:

> There is nothing theatrical about his methods. He can dig deeper and do big things more quietly than almost anyone downtown. His eyes are a brilliant light blue, as clear as a baby's and as innocent looking as a girl's. His complexion also would not shame a maiden. He can smile as sweetly as a society belle and at the same time deal a blow at a business foe that ties him into a hopeless tangle of financial knots. A wizard with figures . . . he is one of the readiest talkers in town. No life insurance agent could beat him. He talks fast and when he wishes to, never to the point. . . . Mr. Cromwell has an

intellect that works like a flash of lightning and it swings about with the agility of an acrobat.

Cromwell never regretted the Panama work, but Curtis recognized that "We possibly suffered somewhat in reputation, due to the scandalous and malicious libels and unfounded attacks and suggestions in the newspapers. Personally I have never ceased to regret our identification with the Panama business, which did not result in any reward commensurate with the cost, time, labor, strength, and energy involved, and which possibly affected our reputation in the minds of strangers."

Cromwell felt differently because he was in Washington at a perfect time to see the capital blossom as a lobbyists' delight, where determination and contacts could do wonders for clients. He was half a century ahead of his time, and so had the field to himself. He advised the President, negotiated both with and for the government, and interceded for the Panamanian revolutionaries.

In contrast with Curtis, Cromwell relished every moment and spent the rest of his semiretired life recounting his exploits to young Sullivan & Cromwell lawyers. People assumed that the Panama Canal made him rich; it did not. But it did make Cromwell the most famous lawyer in America, and Sullivan & Cromwell the only household name among American law firms.

As a lasting tribute to his work, in 1908, when the Panama victory was secure, the Bar Association of Alabama, home of Senator Morgan, instituted the first canon of professional ethics, a direct attack on and reform of Cromwell's use of publicists, lobbying, and unlawyerly conduct in fighting for the Panama Canal.

4

CHANGING OF THE GUARD

Darling Mother: Spend money and give away all that you wish, for there is plenty more to come as fast as you want it.—WILLIAM NELSON CROMWELL

Cromwell had stayed in Washington too long. In his absence Sullivan & Cromwell made only one partner, though the firm had grown to twenty-eight lawyers. The staff was demoralized and somewhat paralyzed without him. He was constantly drawn away, as when in 1906 Senator Morgan used his interoceanic subcommittee to conduct an investigation meant primarily to discredit Cromwell.

During the hearings, Pennsylvania Senator Philander C. Knox asked Cromwell whether "the only compensation you have received or expect to receive or have contracted to receive has been from the New Panama Canal Company."

Cromwell responded, "Absolutely, correctly, solely, completely, and truly.'' He did not mention that along the way he had bought 22 percent of the electric company in Panama.

But that revelation had no bearing on Senator Morgan's contention that if the French had just gone broke, the United States could have bought the lapsed concession from Colombia at a fraction of the cost. He had whittled his complaint down to the unprovable charge that Cromwell had made a bad deal for the country.

The weeks of Cromwell's testimony produced front-page headlines like CROMWELL DODGES, MORGAN LEARNS LITTLE and STILL AT MR. CROMWELL, MR. MORGAN BAFFLED, SAYS WITNESS HAS ''A REMARKABLE CASE OF LOCKJAW.'' Morgan asserted preposterously, ''The assets and franchises were held to be worthless; its stockholders little better than common thieves; its officers paid schemers to be trusted under no conditions.''

Morgan's vindictiveness ultimately turned against him. *The New York Times* editorialized that he behaved like a ''farm dog that has once chased a woodchuck into his hole, and cherishes thereafter the imperishable belief that it is his duty whenever he has an afternoon off to go and bark at that hole.''

Impressed by Cromwell's tranquillity throughout the examination, the *Times* credited him with ''the patience of Father Time, as persistent as the attraction of gravity, and smarter than chain lightning.'' It suggested that if as much energy were put into building the canal as into this investigation, some real progress would be made. Morgan's constant badgering only seemed to confirm that without Cromwell, America would have made an entirely different choice.

Cromwell stayed even longer in Washington to help Secretary of War William Howard Taft, who was overseeing the Panama Canal excavation, in his bid for the 1908 presidential race. President Roosevelt warned Taft that Cromwell's ''past reputation in New York has been such that, as was said to me by a businessman in whose judgment I have entire trust, I can never be sure that some day he will not be working for a big fee in connection with this very matter, while you and I are entirely ignorant of what he is doing.''

Senator Philander C. Knox said, ''We are in grave danger of public scandal of an unpleasant type if he is permitted to appear as too close to us.''

Still, Taft asked Cromwell to be his campaign treasurer. Cromwell chose instead to remain behind the scenes while recommending "a [J. P.] Morgan man," George R. Sheldon, who took the official title. Cromwell assured generous business support for Taft by giving him a $50,000 campaign contribution. Though Taft admitted, "We are greatly in need of money," he urged Cromwell to take the money back. It "will be misunderstood and the inference drawn from it will not be just or kind either to you or to me." Cromwell refused, he said, because of "the blessings to the whole land which will come from the selection of such a great, wise, and good man as President."

Ironically, Cromwell's enormous contribution allayed the suspicions of the President, who told Taft to take the money. He compared the donation to the one he got from another New York lawyer, Elihu Root. Not only had Roosevelt taken Root's money, but he had made him secretary of state, a job many thought Cromwell wanted from Taft. Roosevelt told Taft to put Cromwell on the candidate's public advisory group.

Taft kept the contribution but refused to put Cromwell on any public body of support. He explained to Cromwell that Sheldon's corporate connections and Cromwell's ties to railroad robber baron E. H. Harriman made the Republicans too vulnerable to charges of being the party of special corporate interests.

Cromwell stayed behind the scenes, arranging details and trouble-shooting organizational problems, like the fights between campaign workers. He also prepared position papers on railroads and utility regulation, two issues close to his heart that needed the look of reform without jeopardizing business interests.

During Taft's campaign, blackmailers, failing to get a payoff from Cromwell, publicly claimed that an American syndicate, including Cromwell, had made enormous illegal profits from the New Panama Canal Company. Cromwell decided to sue, surmising that the extortion claims might be part of a Democratic plot to smear Taft.

Curtis discussed the subject with the New York assistant district attorney, who agreed to collect evidence quietly until the election was over. Curtis stressed the confidentiality of the subject. The next day the New York *World* ran a front-page story asserting that "William Nelson Cromwell in connection with M. Bunau-Varilla, a French speculator, had formed a syndicate . . . that included among others Charles P. Taft, brother of William H. Taft, and Douglas Robinson, brother-in-law of President Roosevelt.'' Other prominent New York financiers were also mentioned. According to the *World,* the syndicate parlayed a $3.5 million investment into $40 million ''because of a full knowledge of the intention of the Government to acquire the French property at a price of about $40 million.''

Cromwell issued an immediate denial and defended his alleged accomplices. ''No member of the Taft family or Mr. Douglas Robinson ever had the remotest connection with Panama Canal matters either directly or indirectly. . . . The names of Caesar and Napoleon might as well have been used.''

The *World* had gotten the story inadvertently from one of Cromwell's three press representatives, Jonas Whitley, who had called the paper to make a denial after the story had been dropped for lack of information. A good newsman on the *World* got Whitley to tell the whole story in the process of denying it.

Cromwell drew attention to himself in order to keep it away from Taft. The controversy continued through election day, but Taft won a decisive victory, which elated Cromwell and vindicated their Panama policies. The district attorney dropped the suit for lack of evidence.

If Cromwell had harbored hopes to become secretary of state, the final Panama controversy scotched the idea, and Taft appointed Senator Knox. As eloquent in defeat as he was in victory, Cromwell wrote Taft that Knox's ''recognized position and preeminent qualifications fitted him for the premiership of your Cabinet as no other man in public life.''

Before leaving office, President Roosevelt asked Cromwell to send him a complete list of New Panama Canal Company stockholders and a certified copy of the final liquidation report of the de Lesseps company. The documents showed there was no American syndicate involved in the canal purchase. Roosevelt forwarded the papers to Congress and in early December 1908 Roosevelt brought criminal libel charges against the New York *World* and the Indianapolis *News.* The *World* sent investigators and lawyers to Paris, Panama, and Bogotá to collect evidence but in court successfully filed for dismissal on the ground that the suit should have been brought before a state, not a federal, court. Far from vindicating Roosevelt and Cromwell, the suit left the impression that the newspaper accusations were well founded.

Cromwell finally returned to New York after Taft had been safely elected in November 1908.To make amends for his long absence, he established the Sullivan & Cromwell Society with a $10,000 donation. It funded an annual dinner for new recruits, old associates, and partners. The first dinner was held on December 29, 1908, in a private room at the high-society restaurant Delmonico's. The twenty lawyers there had their caricatures drawn and their renown assured when Cromwell, rather than let them take the pictures home, hung them on the office wall, where they stayed for many years.

Cromwell put his mind to rebuilding the firm. He was determined to make new partners, for though the firm was thirty years old, it was dominated by its first-generation partners—Cromwell, Curtis, George Sullivan, and Alfred Jaretzki. There was only one young partner, Francis Pollak, in an office of more than two dozen lawyers.

With Cromwell away, the office was run by Jaretzki, the only partner able to take on the work. Curtis had had a nervous breakdown and gone deaf just at the point in 1902 when the issue of Nicaragua or Panama hung in the balance. Though the same age as Cromwell, at the age of forty-eight he suddenly seemed like an old man, burdened with a three-foot ear horn around his neck. The only new partner made between 1898 and 1908 was Pollak, a litigator who became partner in 1906 at the young age of thirty-one, but died unexpectedly ten years later.

The next new partner, made in 1911, was Royall Victor, a tough corporate lawyer capable of supervising the firm's dull but lucrative practice raising money for utilities. The job of writing endless indentures and contracts for a continuous process of money raising was tedious and routine, a task for associates who built the firm from eighteen lawyers in 1898 to twenty-eight in 1908. It had not yet instituted its policy of taking young lawyers just out of law school to train them in the Sullivan & Cromwell way. Instead, associates came and went haphazardly, reflecting no policy except that they could not expect to become partners.

The lawyers who joined Sullivan & Cromwell just out of law school hoping to make their careers there found instead that they remained associates for an unconscionably long time. Hjalmar Boyesen stayed an associate for twenty years before he decided to quit to fulfill a lifelong ambition to live in Paris. Emery Sykes worked at the firm for forty-seven years, nearly as many as William Corliss's fifty. But neither became a partner. In contrast with them, a succession of associates came and stayed for extremely short times, including the eventual Chief Justice of the United States, Harlan Fiske Stone, who spent less than a year at the firm in 1898 and 1899, but was always proudly claimed as one of the most illustrious Sullivan & Cromwell alumni.

Royall Victor became the managing partner in 1915, at the age of thirty-eight. Despite his comparative youth, he was a man of definite opinions and habits. Associates knew they had to work until at least four o'clock on Saturdays because that was when ''Mr. Victor'' made a regular tour of the office. Known for his severity, he liked to keep a garden and was greatly trusted by clients, like the American Agricultural Chemical Company, a major conglomerate in the chemical business, of which he was a director and vice-president. He was also a director of Detroit Edison and the Gold Dust Corporation, a popular soapmaker.

Tall, handsome, and self-assured, with jet black hair parted in the middle, Victor ushered in a new era to fill the middle ranks of the firm. He started recruiting lawyers from law schools to establish a pool from which future partners would be chosen. He also began the practice of farming out rejected associates to clients, which, like the firm, were just beginning to build up their staffs.

To overcome the entrenched position of the existing partners, Victor appointed partners in pairs. For every one who worked his way up in the firm, he made a partner of an existing partner's relative. Victor's strategy encouraged his partners to accept additions to their ranks more readily, even when promotions entailed reductions in their own share of firm profits. The two partners made after Victor were Henry Hill Pierce, Curtis's son-in-law, and Edward H. Green, Jaretzki's cousin. Two of the next five partners were also Jaretzki relatives, his son Alfred Jaretzki, Jr., and his son-in-law Eustace Seligman, both of whom played an important part in the firm over the next four decades. They constituted an unusually large Jewish contingent for a Wall Street firm of that era, though, as one former Sullivan & Cromwell lawyer pointed out, "They were all relatives."

Jaretzki, Sr., had been a poor Jewish boy who went to Harvard with George Sullivan, the son of Cromwell's original partner. Jaretzki showed that social standing was irrelevant to a practice like Cromwell's, which relied not on contacts as much as on a good head for figures. Cromwell established the liberality of the firm not from high-mindedness but because efficiency and prejudice don't mix.

The young partners were also not practicing Jews. Jaretzki, Sr., made no attempt to hide his background, generously supporting such charities as the Hebrew Immigrant Aid Society, the Baron de Hirsch Trade School, and the Jewish Agricultural and Industrial Aid Society. As president of the agricultural aid society, Jaretzki provided loans for Jewish farmers and underwrote the *Jewish Farmer,* an agricultural monthly in Yiddish. But Seligman, son of the famous Columbia University economist, E.R.A. Seligman, was a leader of the Ethical Culture Society and his cousin Edward Green took an active part in the Riverside Church. Seligman, whose relatives considered him violently anti-Semitic, divided his active social life, giving Jewish and non-Jewish cocktail parties, both of which his relatives found stuffy and stopped attending.

Under Victor, Sullivan & Cromwell made the most of Cromwell's utilities clients. In the forefront of both technological and financial advances, by the early 1900s the utilities were replacing railroads as the most powerful force in the economy. They benefited from increasing efficiency to cut costs at the same time that they raised rates because they needed massive amounts of capital to fund their expansion.

Cromwell had pioneered the utilities work in the 1890s for his old client Henry Villard, who had returned to New York after the Northern Pacific bankruptcy to represent Germany's largest bank, the Deutsche Bank, and the Siemens electric company. Cromwell got Villard to buy out Thomas Edison, who wanted to go back to working on his next batch of inventions, including "ink for the blind" and "artificial silk."

Cromwell encouraged Villard to start a new enterprise to pick up electric companies and trolley car franchises in industrial cities throughout the Midwest, like Cleveland, Milwaukee, Cincinnati, and Pittsburgh. In 1890 they created the North American Company, which survived strictly as an electric utility after the trolleys disappeared. Sullivan & Cromwell represented the giant utility under different owners until it was broken up in New Deal legislation forty years later.

Sullivan & Cromwell lawyers helped manipulative utility owners place the rising profits into holding companies that by the 1920s gave three quarters of the country's electric business to ten companies. For its client Union Electric, Sullivan & Cromwell created more than 1,000 subsidiaries. These companies in turn were dominated by a few individuals. Instead of issuing common stock, the management issued preferred shares and bonds that did not carry voting rights. To make money raising easier, Sullivan & Cromwell pioneered the open end mortgage with which companies could borrow on corporate assets; so borrowing grew automatically with assets. "Never had the architects of corporate finance built with such craft and mystification," noted historian Arthur M. Schlesinger, Jr.

The holding companies themselves were interlocked through their board members, like the two Sullivan & Cromwell lawyers William Nelson Cromwell and Henry Hill Pierce, each of whom served on the boards of nine utilities. Alfred Jaretzki was on even more electric company boards of directors—sixteen—including Detroit Edison, of which he was a vice-president.

Using techniques developed for the utilities, Edward Green helped the National Dairy Products Company become a nationwide milk and cheese company. Taking advantage of advances in refrigeration and dairy processing, National Dairy acquired a string of regional dairies and provided them with economies of scale and new products. In 1930 it acquired the Kraft-Phoenix Cheese Company, which was already a large international company, with a brand name (eventually the corporate name Kraftco) and a new product, processed cheese, that transformed a perishable, localized service into an international conglomerate.

Green specialized in the financial side of innovation. He drew up the contracts that allowed Warner Brothers to make the first talkie films under contract from Western Electric. He established the patents for Sanforizing fabric to prevent shrinkage and oversaw the merger of Merck & Company with Sharpe & Dohme. He also applied his financial skills to the firm's own practice, acting as treasurer for many years and taking care of clients' tax needs until a separate tax department was established in 1934.

John Foster Dulles, ultimately the most important lawyer of the new generation, joined Sullivan & Cromwell after being turned down by Spooner & Cotton (the predecessor of Cahill, Gordon & Reindel). Even to get into Sullivan & Cromwell, he had to rely on the influence of his grandfather, former Secretary of State John Watson Foster, who had known both founding partners. Cromwell had hired the elder Foster to work on the initial stages of representing the New Panama Canal Company in Washington. Foster had also clerked for Algernon Sydney Sullivan in Ohio in 1855.

The young Dulles was a lanky bon vivant with a pipe-smoking swagger that belied his intellect. He got an academic prize at his Princeton graduation, which provided him with a year's study at the Sorbonne in Paris. Instead of going to Harvard or Yale Law School after Paris, he wanted to stay in Washington, where he could attend George Washington University Law School and take advantage of his grandfather's political clout and social connections. He took the socializing as seriously as the law school. His diary was full of entries about White House parties, at which he sat next to the President's daughter, Helen Taft, while his law school notebooks contained only doodles even when he was required to show them to the professor. Still, he got top grades, causing one of his teachers to remark, "He is the most brilliant man I have ever taught and, moreover, he is very ambitious. Any firm he is with is likely to do very well."

Starting in 1911 at $12.50 a week, the twenty-three-year-old Dulles found the routine of a new associate boring and frustrating. Used to things coming easily to him, he needed his grandfather's reminder his first summer at the firm not to allow himself "to tire of the drudgery of the office. I was janitor and char-woman, having to open the office in the morning, sweep the room and get everything in shape for the day's work.''

Grandfather Foster passed through New York later that summer to remind Cromwell to look after the new man. Dulles soon brought himself to Cromwell's notice by writing a pamphlet on the debate over whether American ships should have free passage through the Panama Canal when other countries' vessels did not. Dulles contended that trips between American coasts through the canal should be considered domestic traffic and free of tolls.

Cromwell wrote Dulles that the American secretary of state had contradicted his argument, but Dulles's pamphlet got him invited to speak before the American Society of International Law, of which, not coincidentally, his uncle Robert Lansing was chairman. When his speech was included in the organization's proceedings, Dulles had 100 extra copies printed to pass around to his well-placed contacts in Washington and New York, and at Sullivan & Cromwell.

After a trip to Trinidad to scout out Caribbean trading possibilities for clients, Dulles practiced the art of verbal assault with the unfortunate shipping company that delivered him a crate of rotten avocadoes. ''I made a trip through the British West Indies as the representative of large American interests, who desired a study to be made of trade relations between the United States and the British West Indies . . . ,'' he arrogantly lectured. ''I can emphatically state, however, that . . . it is folly to attempt to create a market in this country for tropical fruits. . . .''

During the trip, he contracted malaria. The cure, massive doses of quinine, left one of his eyes subject to excess tearing and a tic he never lost. The malaria also forced him to take a nurse as chaperone on his honeymoon, after he had married Janet Avery in the summer of 1912. Among the 200 guests at Grandpa Foster's compound in upstate New York was long-term associate Emery Sykes, bearing a $200 Tiffany gift certificate on behalf of the firm. Six months later, Dulles was admitted to the New York bar.

In 1913 Robert Lansing wanted his nephew to join a diplomatic mission to Britain. Lansing, who owed his own blossoming State Department career to his father-in-law, John Watson Foster, assured

President Woodrow Wilson, "there was no nepotism involved" in picking Dulles. Lansing, known as "Uncle Bert," lived with his wife in the Fosters' Washington house, even when he was secretary of state during World War I.

But Sullivan & Cromwell considered the offer too unimportant for Dulles, who wrote his uncle, "It did not seem to Mr. Victor that it would be advisable for me to absent myself entirely from my work here for a year, at this time when I am just beginning to get more intimately in touch with the work of the office and with its clients."

The firm, however, was impressed with his contacts, and soon had Dulles write his uncle to ask if the State Department could recommend a lawyer in Peru. As soon as war broke out in Europe in August 1914, Dulles wrote to his uncle asking the State Department to locate people on behalf of firm clients. When one German was discovered languishing in a Japanese prison camp, Dulles had the audacity to ask the department "in some way to parole this young man so that he could return to the United States, where Mr. Merck will assume personal responsibility for him."

Dulles asked such favors with no qualms or apology. His younger brother, Allen, was more appreciative of the family's extraordinary influence and the privileges it afforded him. Allen wrote home from a round-the-world trip, "It is a great thing to have had illustrious relations. I am certainly profiting by what others have been."

Foster Dulles put even Cromwell in his debt when the United Fruit Company and a New York banker tried to get Panama to remove Cromwell as the country's fiscal agent. After secret correspondence with Panama, the State Department solicitor (none other than Robert Lansing) lobbied heavily for Panama to keep Cromwell because "he was appointed with the approval of the Department of State, he has served with ability and generosity, and a change does not appear desirable."

Not content just to save Cromwell, the State Department Solicitor's Office abandoned its customary reserve and attacked Cromwell's enemies, claiming that "the Fruit Company [is trying] to extend its dominion into Panama, which effort, if successful, might or might not have happy results. Judged by the results which have obtained from the

Fruit Company's activities in Costa Rica and Honduras, it would seem that one result of its efforts in Central American countries is to stifle competition in the fruit business.''

World War I started when Dulles was a third-year associate at Sullivan & Cromwell. To take advantage of it, he volunteered to go to Europe to get war risk insurance for the American Cotton Oil Company's European shipments. Dulles was working on such short notice that, without a birth certificate, he wrote his uncle, ''I trust you can still put through my application and secure a passport.'' Along with the passport, Lansing sent Dulles letters of introduction to the American ambassadors to Britain and France and the consul general in Rotterdam. All the letters, at Dulles's request, included assurances ''that they [the ambassadors] may rely on the truth of any representations'' Dulles might make.

Dulles traveled as a one-man commercial envoy, scouring Europe for business. His main job was to get war risk insurance for his clients to continue to do business in Europe. In Holland Dulles advised the Holland-American Line about placing its own war risk insurance, though he admitted to his wife he was not sure he was ''telling them right.'' While waiting for the results of the insurance company's deliberation on American Cotton Oil's war risk policy, Dulles visited the Rijks Museum and played golf and tennis. After getting approval from the Dutch insurers, Dulles headed for England, where the streets were full of French refugees during the day and at night searchlights eerily broke the blackout looking for Zeppelin bombers.

He wrote his wife one letter on the back of an advertisement for intimate apparel with the slogan ''Every common sense Eve wears pyjamas nowadays for if the 'Zepps' come and one had to flee from the sanctity of the house one wouldn't feel quite so—so—much of a refugee as in a nighty. The Last Word in Ladies' Lingerie.'' He expressed his shock at the ''German policy of attempting to terrorize other people by ruthless murdering and torturing (mentally and otherwise) noncombatants—women, children and neutrals.'' He realized that the constant barrage of recruitment posters meant English soldiers were dying as fast as they shipped out and felt that ''it would be hard to put one's life to a more useful service than to help wipe out the German military systems which make all this horror possible.''

He relished the role of a neutral in the midst of battle. As a student at the Sorbonne after Princeton, he had stuffed paper in his bowler to ward off gendarmes' truncheons while wandering among the student rioters. He was an adventurer but not a fighter. In Liverpool he also did some business arranging war risk insurance.

Dulles had to rush back to London to take care of Mrs. Bilicke, a firm client who had survived the *Lusitania* sinking but lost her husband. Dulles arranged for another passport for her, wrote a new will including her husband's estate, and booked her onto a crowded ship back to America.

Dulles returned home consumed with interest in the war. He spread maps out on the floor of the study in his East Side apartment and used colored pins to show the German advances and the French and Belgian retreats. He fumed at German victories.

He finally had a chance to do something about the war when his uncle Robert Lansing became secretary of state in June 1915. William Jennings Bryan had resigned after the *Lusitania* sinking because he thought President Wilson, who had vowed to stay neutral, had purposely provoked German aggression to get America into the war. Since the *Lusitania* was an armed British ship, the Germans had advised the United States not to let its citizens go on board. Wilson ignored the warning, in part, Bryan suspected, to arouse American anger at the Germans.

Lansing recruited Dulles to go to Nicaragua, Costa Rica, and Panama on the pretext of firm business but really to find out which leaders would support the United States against the Germans. Dulles was cruising to Central America, playing bridge and listening to the wireless, when on April 6, 1917, he heard America's declaration of war on Germany.

He advised Washington to support the vicious dictator Federico Tinoco in Costa Rica because he was anti-German and ran ''a Government and people with more sincere friendliness to us than any other Central American state.'' Dulles got the dictator General Emiliano Chamorro, president of Nicaragua, to issue a proclamation suspending diplomatic relations with Germany.

Chamorro was particularly cooperative because the year before, Dulles had played a major role in Chamorro's election by introducing the Central American to his uncle. During the election, Lansing assured Dulles that the State Department had found "the best means of advancing the interests of General Chamorro. Of course you realize," he added, "it is a delicate question to interfere in any way with the franchise in Nicaragua, and your policy must be very carefully considered."

In Panama, his last stop, Dulles offered on behalf of the American secretaries of state and the treasury to let Panama continue to get its annual $250,000 canal fee tax-free as long as Panama declared war on Germany and protected the canal for Allied shipping. The new 1913 income tax law would have made these payments subject to American tax, a sticky issue Washington was glad to resolve to Panama's advantage as long as the country was an American ally.

Dulles's trip was a complete success and qualified him to work closer to his uncle in Washington during the war. Dulles got a commission as a captain for a position in military intelligence, working for the War Trade Board. Arranging to keep goods out of enemy hands, he got Spain to provide mules and minerals exclusively to the Allies in return for cotton and oil. He worked out an intricate legal scheme to secure thirty-seven Dutch ships in American harbors without compromising Holland's neutrality. He dictated the confiscation order for the President to sign.

With his brother, Allen, an American envoy in Switzerland, Foster worked "very hard lately on getting grain to Switzerland. . . . We now have the grain and the ships, but as you know the safe conduct from Germany is not forthcoming," he told his brother. He did send Allen tennis balls, which he wanted "both for my own use and as propaganda among my Swiss friends." The propaganda proved so successful Allen needed "as many good tennis balls as possible"—indeed, "every week until further notice one dozen balls."

When Dulles talked about war policy with his grandfather and uncle over breakfast, they constituted a formidable foreign-policy contingent, as a former, present, and future secretary of state. Dulles mentioned the problem of important Sullivan & Cromwell clients, the major Cuban sugar plantation owners. They were worried about a rebellion by the Liberals, who had lost the recent election but maintained a stronghold in the area of the sugar fields. Dulles wrote a memorandum urging the State Department to recognize the Liberal claims that the election was stolen by the incumbent Conservatives. He cited as his authority Sullivan & Cromwell's "unusual and diversified means of obtaining information," as well as its "special representative [in] Havana who has interviewed and obtained the views of men prominent in banking, railroads, insurance, tobacco and sugar businesses." Sullivan & Cromwell concluded that the rebellion could not be suppressed and recommended "appointment of commission of three . . . [to] investigate election troubles immediately."

Dulles's overriding concern was not the Liberals but American property interests in territory controlled by the Liberals.

A Cuban Liberal representative huddled with Alfred Jaretzki, Sr., in New York and wrote a four-page letter to the State Department emphasizing "electoral fraud perpetrated by the government" and "calling on the United States to install a leader more favorable to American business."

Sullivan & Cromwell wrote its own letter asking the government to "protect American property," especially the firm's thirteen clients who owned $170 million worth of Cuban sugar fields. One of them alone, Cuban Cane Sugar (organized by Sullivan & Cromwell two years earlier in 1915), accounted for 15 percent of the country's sugar output. Lansing sided with Dulles's support for the Liberals, but President Wilson decided that the "strong moral support of this government should be given to the established Cuban government." While the President refused to help the Liberals, he did protect American interests by sending 1,600 troops for "training purposes" and "as a protection for the sugar industry." They remained in Cuba until 1922.

Sullivan & Cromwell's New York office had more prosaic problems but contributed to the war effort by reorganizing the Aetna Explosives Company in 1918. Companies and rich people had to be extricated from German involvements, like Antoinette Converse, the hapless daughter of the National Tube Company and U.S. Steel organizer

E. C. Converse. She was repeatedly unlucky in love. Though she was in the process of divorcing a German count when war broke out, the final decree had not come through and the State Department was forced to write to Sullivan & Cromwell that "the Government . . . could not properly assist her in any official capacity."

With America in the war, Mumm Champagne & Importation Company, a German-owned company, faced seizure by the Alien Property Custodian. In a letter to the State Department, Dulles deceptively called the U.S. importer for Mumm a "New York corporation [with an] extensive organization which is entirely American in its character."

The Alien Property Custodian found the instructions the Germans gave Sullivan & Cromwell to "sell" the company to its American management with Mumm's money but hold on to the stock while pretending the company was American. The firm willingly helped the company try to evade the Alien Property Custodian, but luckily the war ended only a year and a half after the United States entered it, with no casualties to Sullivan & Cromwell personnel or reputation.

5

PARTNERS FOR PEACE

> If you lived in this atmosphere and daily witnessed the magnificent universal sacrifices, sufferings, sorrow, you would feel as I do that mere personal gain is unworthy and that nothing now counts but humanity and the Allied cause.—WILLIAM NELSON CROMWELL

Living in Paris during the war, Cromwell vicariously shared the suffering of the French. Though he stayed at the Hôtel Ritz and had his meals delivered to his room, he felt the heroic spirit, if not the sacrifices, as he described to his partners in New York. "EACH DAY IS AS A YEAR AND EACH YEAR HAS THE SIGNIFICANCE OF A HUNDRED," he cabled them. "THIS IS PROBABLY THE LAST GREAT EPOCH IN WHICH WE OF MATURITY WILL EVER BE PARTICIPANTS."

Cromwell lived in an upstairs suite, while two secretaries and a bookkeeper worked out of a room below. Only his principal secretary, Jane Renard, ever went up to his apartment. For this reason, she was assumed by the New York partners to be Cromwell's mistress. The other secretary was Madeleine Regnier, a small, delicate woman who remembered Cromwell as a rotund but jolly old man with flashing blue eyes and a resemblance to British Premier David Lloyd George. "But he got so mad when anyone stopped him in the street to ask to take his photograph as Lloyd George," she recalled sixty years later.

Cromwell devoted himself to the French cause by helping the finance minister borrow money, and subscribing to 2.5 million francs ($500,000) of French war bonds, which were not a secure investment while the war hung in the balance. Cromwell explained by telegram to New York: IT IS NOT HOW MUCH I CAN GAIN BUT HOW MUCH CAN I GIVE OF SERVICE AND FORTUNE [TO WHICH] . . . I INTEND TO DEVOTE THE WAR PERIOD IN AMERICA AND EUROPE. As the war produced more casualties, he endowed a workshop for the wounded at the Grand Palais in Paris, a school for 400 war-orphaned children, and, when America joined the war, a club for American officers in Le Mans.

Cromwell's devotion to the war made him all the happier to see a young lawyer from the firm join the American negotiators of the Versailles Treaty. Dulles participated in redrawing the world's boundaries in the peace of World War I, but the work's greatest impact was in making him a Sullivan & Cromwell partner. The last time Dulles had lived in Paris, he was studying at the Sorbonne, absorbing Henri Bergson's views on intuition and the supreme role of all living creatures to adapt to reality. As a member of the American delegation to the Paris Peace Conference just ten years later, he had already proved what an apt student of reality he was.

Dulles latched on to the delegation from the War Trade Board. It went to Paris as the Reparations Committee, for which Dulles became counsel. He arrived late in Paris and was shocked at all the "confusion, jealousy, wire-pulling and lack of accomplishment. Any one new coming is regarded as an interloper and has to meet the united efforts of the 'already established' to 'absorb' him." Idealism was being reduced to petty bickering within the American delegation housed together in the Hôtel Crillon, and it had not even started dealing with the Europeans.

Dulles avoided the bickering and stuck to his own personal allies in the delegation. His uncle Robert Lansing bore no resentment when

Dulles found his own way to the Crillon after the secretary of state had turned down his request to go with him. Lansing had wanted to keep his nephew from the infighting that had already pitted the secretary of state against Wilson's personal adviser, Colonel Edward M. House. Younger brother Allen was there, too, as a State Department representative handling the redrawing of central European boundaries.

Dulles used the first month of jockeying and stock taking to host luncheons for his colleagues. He held a lunch at the Ritz for two members of the Reparations Committee, Norman Davis and Vance McCormick, and George Sheldon, the "Morgan man" whom Cromwell had chosen as Taft's campaign treasurer in 1908. Sheldon, now the War Trade Board's European representative, remained a useful link to Cromwell. Dulles found his distinguished guests "nice though not awfully exciting." He blithely noted that the lunch "will cost me a month's salary, I suppose, for the Ritz is hardly cheap these days."

Dulles asked Sheldon "to hustle around and pick up gossip and extend Uncle Bert's sphere of influence" the way, he found out, Gordon Auchincloss was doing for his father-in-law, Colonel House. Over tea in the delegates' rooms, Dulles and Sheldon discussed whom Colonel House was seeing and what the colonel said about Lansing, the President, or the Europeans.

Dulles indulged Cromwell's interest in the proceedings and patiently listened to his opinions. After one afternoon-long visit with Cromwell, Dulles concluded, "He is certainly verbose."

On the day of the organizational meeting of the Inter-Allied Reparations Commission, Dulles came down with the mumps. Since this commission would determine how much the Germans had to pay the victors, every country put its top men on it, including John Maynard Keynes, the young Treasury man from Britain, and Louis Loucheur, a member of the French cabinet. Besides being disgusted at missing the meeting, Dulles was worried that he might have given the mumps to Cromwell, who was the last person he saw before getting sick.

Forced to stay in his room, Dulles wrote up a memorandum on how the Reparations Commission should proceed. The next day Dulles discussed the memo in front of the American reparations committee. He incorporated their suggestions in his memo while, he noted gleefully, "haranguing this distinguished group in my bath robe." The third day he got dressed and presented the memo to the international commission on behalf of the U.S. members. He showed that even mumps can be a blessing to an ambitious man.

Dulles entertained the Chinese minister of foreign affairs, Tseng-tsiang Lou, at dinner at the Ritz, to which he invited Cromwell along with Lansing and William Graves Sharp, the American ambassador to France. Sharp was also the father of an eventual Sullivan & Cromwell partner, George Sharp, who met Dulles then, as his father's secretary. The dinner cost Dulles $110. "Still it was worth it, don't you think?" he wrote his wife, Janet, for it showed off contacts even Cromwell could admire.

So social had the peace conference become that Dulles had his wife join him in March. She elevated the entertaining side of the conference to an art form, spending her days shopping and sightseeing in the War Trade Board car. Once Janet Dulles had arrived, the Dulleses entertained in the secretary of state's suite with its high ceilings, red brocade drapes, and dignified portraits of French nobility. They drank with twelve guests in front of a huge fireplace. When the waiter called them to dinner, he pulled away a screen hiding the table in another corner of the room. Between social engagements, Janet Dulles went to Cromwell's reception for Queen Marie of Romania, who had arrived with an entourage that took twenty-two rooms at the Ritz.

Janet Dulles was not completely sheltered from her husband's work. She reported proudly to her mother, "Messrs McCormick, Baruch, Lamont and Norman Davis [of the Reparations Committee] seem to depend on Foster for every step they take—and I hear from them and others all sorts of wonderful things about Foster's ability and work. I think it was a most fortunate thing for him that he got over here and had this chance as counsel for the Reparations Committee. It is really very important—aren't you *proud* of him?"

Meeting with President Wilson, Dulles argued against including pensions in Germany's war debt. He was afraid that "to accept pensions would involve admitting against the enemy all war costs. . . ." Wilson replied that he "did not feel bound by considerations of logic and that . . . it was a proper subject of reparation under the agreed terms of peace." The American legation put the reparations demand at $30 billion compared to British demands for $90 billion and France's $200 billion. Colonel House concluded, "I thought the British were as crazy as the French but they seem only half as crazy which still leaves them a good margin of lunacy."

Dulles had the greatest impact on the reparations debate by proposing a permanent Reparations Commission, which the British and French prime ministers embraced to shelve the issue. Janet Dulles was able to write her mother-in-law, "Foster has a copy of the treaty and a great deal of the Reparation and Indemnity clauses in it are exactly as Foster wrote them!"

Taking time out from the deliberations, Dulles had lunch with Cromwell to discuss Brazilian railroads, which Cromwell was reorganizing after bankruptcy. While Cromwell was trying to get a shareholders' group together to prevent an immediate forced liquidation, Dulles reported that he had met with the president of Brazil, with whom he had discussed reparations and the prospects for Brazilian coffee. Although the topics did not bear directly on Sullivan & Cromwell business, the Brazilians were impressed with the importance of Dulles and his law firm. It was not surprising that Cromwell and Dulles got around to discussing the future of Sullivan & Cromwell—and Dulles's role in it.

Dulles hoped to return to New York with his wife and Mr. and Mrs. Cromwell, but the American Commission to Negotiate Peace cabled Alfred Jaretzki, Sr.: WE ARE INSISTING THAT DULLES SHALL NOT GO QUITE YET BECAUSE OF THE FACT THAT WE CONSIDER HIS PRESENCE HERE OF THE UTMOST IMPORTANCE. . . . WE FIND THAT WE CANNOT DISPENSE WITH DULLES' SERVICES. . . . HIS PRESENCE HERE IS OF SUCH IMPORTANCE TO THE PUBLIC INTEREST THAT WE HAVE UNDERTAKEN PERSONALLY TO SEE TO IT THAT HIS FORTUNES DO NOT SUFFER BY REASON OF THIS COMPARATIVELY BRIEF EXTENSION OF THE NOTABLE SERVICE THAT HE IS RENDERING TO HIS COUNTRY AND THE CAUSE OF PEACE.

Jaretzki wired back: IN RESPONSE TO YOUR KIND MESSAGE WE ARE GLAD THEY WILL HAVE DULLES MAKE EXTENSION CONTRIBUTION HIS SERVICES. OF COURSE YOU CAN ASSURE HIM HIS INTERESTS WILL NOT BE PREJUDICED BY DOING SO.

Janet Dulles left with the Cromwells. A month later, Dulles had to write her, "McCormick, Baruch, Lamont and Davis . . . all told the President that they would have complete confidence in the situation if I stayed and that he might also. At the same time it is a bitter disappointment'' to postpone his return home. The subject now was the financial and reparation clauses of the treaties with Austria, Hungary, Bulgaria, and Turkey, in which Dulles acted as principal American negotiator.

Dulles proved himself indispensable as a negotiator with no point of view of his own. Some of the other young American delegates quit because, as one of them, William C. Bullitt, wrote, ''our Government has consented to . . . new oppressions, subjections and dismemberments—a new century of war.'' Dulles, on the other hand, deferred respectfully to his elders, to whom he made himself useful.

Besides, he had the confidence of his uncle the secretary of state. President Wilson, who knew Dulles as a fellow Princeton man, wrote him, ''I hope that you will not feel that I am imposing a too onerous or too unwelcome duty upon you if I beg very earnestly that you make arrangements to remain in Europe for the present to handle the very important and difficult matters with which you have become so familiar and which you have so materially assisted in handling.''

Dulles sent a copy of the President's letter to Cromwell, ''which, as you will see,'' he noted, ''has made it impossible for me to return upon the signature of the German Treaty today.''

The French government made Dulles a member of the Legion of Honor in a ceremonial dinner on Bastille Day, July 14, 1919, which he celebrated by wandering around Montmartre with his brother, Allen, until 4:00 A.M.

Wanting to get back to New York, Dulles faced a further obstacle, the permanent Reparations Commission. He wrote to Cromwell a little nervously, ''I hope very much that you will let me know whenever any definite plans are made for any reorganization. You know the deep interest which I take in the firm.'' Dulles was lucky that the Senate Foreign Relations Committee refused to appoint an American representative to the Reparations Commission. Its argument was that since the treaty had not yet been ratified, no permanent representative was required.

Dulles stayed on in Paris for almost another month, mediating a reparations dispute over what to do with 800 tons of German dyestuffs held by the Allies. The British did not want the German goods flooding the European market and suggested the United States take them. As

Dulles pointed out to a New York *World* reporter, "Without an American member on the commission, our own dye industry may be seriously affected." He got the material distributed in Europe.

Dulles relinquished the world's burdens on August 28 when he finally set sail for England. He spent a few days there relaxing with American Ambassador John W. Davis, playing golf and taking it easy, before he returned home in early September. It had been an extraordinarily fruitful trip that had guaranteed Dulles (if not Europe) a secure future.

6

DULLES'S PRIVATE FOREIGN POLICY

> The reparation creditors had built up within Germany a machinery which was intended to enable Germany to pay reparations, but which, in fact, enabled Germany to wage the most destructive war of all time.—JOHN FOSTER DULLES

John Foster Dulles's role in the Versailles negotiations, which continued long after the senior delegates had gone home, was a sign of how little Americans cared, with the result that the peace only perpetuated hostilities and instability in Europe. But Cromwell, impressed with his thirty-year-old underling's role as an international negotiator, made Dulles a partner as soon as he arrived back in New York.

Cromwell recognized in his young protégé a kindred spirit. Both men were passionately concerned about international affairs, with access and ability to charm world leaders. For Cromwell, Dulles was the perfect link between his own interests and the otherwise lucrative but prosaic practice of the firm. For Dulles, Cromwell provided a Wall

Street legal career outside the humdrum life of most lawyers. They made a perfect pair. Cromwell could live comfortably in Paris and have news of the office through regular visits from Dulles.

Dulles got to travel and avoid the hostility from fellow lawyers for his charmed life, which they resented as they slaved eighteen hours a day and weekends on boring contracts and bond issues. For everyone else, even a partnership was no guarantee of being above the drudgery of ordinary work, but for Dulles his partnership was the confirmation that he would never have to look at routine again.

Cromwell and Dulles shared an urge to rehabilitate Europe. Cromwell followed his French war relief with imaginative programs for recovery and rebuilding the devastated country. Though he returned to New York twice a year, in 1924 he made his Paris life more permanent when he moved to a huge Gothic apartment on the fashionable avenue Bois de Boulogne. He hired a household staff of six, including a waiter, and brought over his American decorator to fix up the place with fancy seventeenth-century Belgian tapestries and an American electric organ (the first in France).

Besides his two secretaries, he wrote Dulles, "In truth I should have had, from the beginning, some one of the juniors at my side, as I am kept working from 5 A.M. (whence this is drafted by my own hand) until 9 P.M. to bed and do not go out once a month in the evening. It is the only way I can conserve my health and energy."

He donated fruit trees, chickens, and fountains to farmers and villages throughout France. He gave 100,000 francs to reestablish the lace industry of Valenciennes, a district near Belgium which was completely destroyed in the German advance on Paris. Working through an organization called Le Retour au Foyer ("Return to the Hearth"), Cromwell sent livestock and equipment by truckfuls to needy farmers. Newspapers carried photos of the trucks with GIFT OF CROMWELL written across the side to broadcast the generosity of this eccentric American.

Cromwell had books printed in Braille in several languages through the Permanent Blind War Relief Fund, Inc., of which he was president. In one month in the summer of 1924, he gave away more than 200,000 francs to a variety of causes. Cultivating important

French politicians by asking their advice on where to make donations, Cromwell gave 100,000 francs to each of ten scientists, a total gift of about $200,000 to further their research. In 1923 he endowed the town of Bailleul with a lace-making school and, following the advice of former French Prime Minister André Tardieu, gave $20,000 to the top 325 lace-makers.

When one newspaperman, using Cromwell's secretaries as interpreters, asked why he was so generous, he answered, "Because it is France. Does one know why one loves one woman above all others? Well, France is like a woman I admire and cherish. Her serenity is never indifferent, her grace is never fatuous, her pride is never haughty. I would like her to be happy after having paid so dearly for her honor."

He gave more than half a million francs to build the Museum of the Legion of Honor in Paris and deeply resented another American's willingness to match his gift. A jealous suitor to his adopted country, he tried unsuccessfully to have the Legion of Honor return the other donor's money. He also paid $125,000 to build a monument to the American fliers of the Lafayette Escadrille who were killed fighting for France before the United States entered the war.

Cromwell's Paris philanthropy did not stop his getting lucrative legal work. He made $1 million handling the litigation over robber baron Jay Gould's estate on behalf of his daughter Anna Gould. The first of the American "million-heiresses" to marry impoverished European nobility (a fashion that soon caught on), Anna Gould stopped her brother George Gould from bankrupting the $93 million estate in his attempt to outdo their father. Cromwell worked with another prominent lawyer, Samuel Seabury, to win a $40 million judgment against George Gould, though the amount was halved on final settlement.

Cromwell soon became part of the Gould household because "my mother had complete confidence in him. She trusted him and she didn't trust very many people," recalled Violette Palewski, the daughter of Anna Gould and the duc de Talleyrand. But "I don't know if my father liked it too much," she said of Cromwell's habit of slapping her father on the back with the greeting "Hi, Duke." She remembered Cromwell as a charming old man who arrived promptly for Sunday lunch and sat with her, a five-year-old girl. He uncurled her hair and handed her red leather gift boxes from Cartier. "He covered me with jewels," she said. "Even to a small girl he brought precious jewels—bracelets, necklaces, all kinds, which he picked out himself. They were very well chosen."

Dulles wanted to help Germany the way Cromwell was helping France. He had never lived there, but he felt responsible for the country's shabby treatment at the Versailles negotiations, even if publicly he claimed the treaty did the best that could be done. He had the honorable and imaginative idea of using trade to initiate postwar revival after the United States government had turned its back on Europe. He provided an American commercial presence in Europe at a time when most Americans had little interest in the economically depressed, war-ravaged continent.

But two differences separated the philanthropy of Cromwell and Dulles. Cromwell used his own money to fulfill a scheme of his own devising, while Dulles was dependent on his clients' participation. Cromwell also recognized the limits of his ambitions and accomplishments in France while Dulles was never realistic about the conditions he found in Germany or the potential of his efforts.

Part of the difference was Dulles's wishful thinking, but part was a lack of scrupulousness shown in a small matter Cromwell was involved in. Despite Prohibition, which started in 1920, Cromwell tried to get crates of champagne shipped to New York to satisfy his consumption of a daily pint of bubbly. Cromwell and Dulles corresponded on the subject for more than a year, at the end of which Cromwell had to warn Dulles, who had offered to deal with high State Department officials, "Above all, we must not do anything which would subject us to criticism or even of serious doubt as to the course of conduct." Cromwell ultimately succeeded in getting two crates legitimately because they had been in transit before Prohibition started. (The incident showed another difference: Cromwell offered to reward Dulles with one of the crates, but Dulles preferred gin, which he quietly smuggled in from Canada through his brother-in-law in upstate New York.)

Dulles returned to Europe only three months after leaving Paris. He boarded the RMS *Mauretania* in February 1920, despite Cromwell's advice not to tax himself. Convinced that individuals could succeed in securing peace where governments had failed, Dulles went to Czechoslovakia, Poland, and Germany to scout new opportunities. He did not visit Paris because he was embarrassed to see old colleagues after the Senate had rejected the League of Nations.

He had persuaded various of the firm's clients to go along with a scheme to give the Europeans raw materials on credit. They would pay once they had sold the finished goods, a no-risk deal for the Europeans.

His first business stop was Frankfurt to meet the Merton brothers, whose Metallgesellschaft needed copper. Dulles was particularly taken with Richard Merton, who had been a German delegate in Paris, where Dulles jumped to the conclusion that "he was doing in Germany about what I was doing for the U.S."

Dulles was always drawn to foreigners like Merton who spoke fluent English. After spending so much time in Europe, Dulles was assumed to speak foreign languages, especially French from his year at the Sorbonne. But when he was asked in French, "Do you think German rearmament is a good thing?" he answered, "I am sorry she isn't here."

Unfortunately, knowing English did not make a person as trustworthy as Dulles assumed. He arranged to get the Mertons a large loan through Goldman, Sachs & Company to import American copper. Dulles found the Mertons perfectly agreeable trading partners, but several years later they embroiled him in a headline-grabbing court case in which the United States attorney general Harry M. Daugherty was caught taking a bribe from them. Dulles had to testify to his relationship with them, which was innocent because Goldman, Sachs ultimately backed out of the copper deal.

From Frankfurt Dulles hired a chauffeur to drive him to Prague, where he represented four American textile companies working in a consortium called the European Textile Corporation. Dulles was sympathetic to the feisty Czechs, especially to Eduard Beneš, who had helped establish his country at the Paris Peace Conference. Within a week Dulles had arranged a $15 million deal for the export of

American textiles, while Beneš introduced him to the country's first president, Thomas Masaryk, and escorted him around the beautiful central European capital.

On Sunday, March 14, 1920, the hotel operator rang Dulles's room to tell him that a military putsch had taken over Berlin. With boy scout enthusiasm, he got an American legation officer to produce, as he put it, "a magnificent letter stating that I was the special representative of the Legation and Diplomatic courier to go to Berlin and that all persons were requested to give me assistance and protection." Beneš gave him a special Czech government pass, and by Sunday evening Dulles was on a train to Germany with an American who spoke fluent German.

When German frontier officials stopped Dulles for not having a visa, he told them he "hadn't known what Government to get one from." They didn't either, and let him go. With Dresden in the midst of a general strike, Dulles rented a car and a chauffeur for a pittance in dollars but a king's ransom in German marks. He hired a porter who made Dulles walk ahead of him so it would not look as if he were carrying Dulles's luggage. In Berlin he found milling battalions of the Kapp putsch, led by a rough group of right-wing junior officers wearing ominous-looking helmets and brandishing hand grenades. Dulles picked his way carefully past the barbed wire, cement barriers, and machine-gun-wielding troops to the American embassy.

Allen Dulles, an embassy official, had just arrived from Poland on the last train that got into Berlin. The two brothers wandered the streets, watching the revolution unfold around them. Crowds filled the streets night and day. Foster noticed the "anti-Jewish propaganda which met with considerable response." During the Kapp putsch, he detected "very bitter feeling against the Jews which [*sic*] have come into Germany in great numbers from Russia and Poland, and they are popularly blamed for the shortage in food and lodgings and with being profiteers. Many of the hand bills which were given out by, or with the approval of the Kapp people were most bitterly anti-Jewish and one of the real dangers was a 'pogrom.' " He was far more conscious of anti-Semitism in 1920 than he would be after Adolf Hitler came to power.

As for business, Dulles admitted, "Practically no one was at their [*sic*] offices, however, as there were no means of getting there, and if they got there [they had] nothing to do, without clerks, mail or telegraph.'' Allen Dulles had his brother meet Dr. Hjalmar Schacht, an economist at the beginning of a stellar career that would ultimately lead to his being tried as a war criminal at Nüremberg after World War II. Born and raised to the age of twelve in Brooklyn, New York, Schacht was one of those beguiling figures who spoke perfect English. (His full name was Hjalmar Horace Greeley Schacht.) But he also considered himself a true German patriot. In 1920 Schacht helped found the Democratic party before supporting Hitler a decade later—and, after this meeting, taking Dulles along with him.

''Of all that I met in Berlin,'' Dulles recalled in 1930, ''Dr. Schacht alone looked forward with hope to the future and felt it worthwhile to do something, to try to save something out of the wreckage which everyone else felt was permanent.'' Dulles had a lot in common with the tall, ramrod-erect economist who wore a high, stiff collar that squeezed his throat and made his crew-cut head look as if it were set on a pedestal.

Both had originally thought of becoming Protestant ministers. Dulles flattered himself that he knew something about economics, a conceit Schacht encouraged in discussing ''plans for financing the importation of essential raw materials into Germany,'' as Dulles put it, ''which would again put industry into motion.''

Dulles and Schacht talked while machine-gun fire from the Kapp putsch echoed in the street below. In Dulles, Schacht had the perfect instrument for luring America into Germany's problems. Their relationship would last more than a decade and cost Americans a billion dollars because Schacht seduced Dulles into supporting Germany for far too long.

The putsch vacated Berlin, leaving the streets to marauding troops, who put the city into a panic. People offered Dulles fabulous sums for his car, one of the few in the whole city. But he kept the car until the day after the putsch dispersed, returned it to Dresden, and took the overnight train back to Prague.

He wrote his wife that he had seen ''a remarkable testimonial to the fundamental orderliness of the German people, as during the whole period there was no strong central government, and even regular police service was wholly disorganized.'' Dulles might have wanted to keep poor Janet from worrying about her adventurous hubby, but even to American legation officials in Prague he reported, "The failure of the Socialists to seize Government shows that the great majority of them are moderate in their views and that the extreme radicals are weak."

Dulles was not concerned about conditions in Germany, but his clients were. Just as he was concluding $15 million of cotton sales in Prague, the client cabled to cancel the deal. Dulles cabled back that it was too late.

Wanting to reassure his clients, Dulles begged his brother, Allen, to send encouraging reports to Washington from the embassy in Berlin. In the effort to tether clients to his own agenda, Foster asked Allen, "Is there nothing that you can do either through the State Department or through the newspaper men to give a more truthful picture of the situation?" Allen Dulles refused.

Clients pursued Dulles to Frankfurt, where he went to finalize the copper sales to Metallgesellschaft. He wrote with exasperation to his brother, "Today we have long cables from New York stating that it will be impossible for many months to make the public sale of securities which is necessary to finance our copper transaction. We must call it off or hold it in abeyance."

Rather than admit defeat, Dulles arranged to meet his clients in Cologne to review the deals. But when their ship was delayed, he set out on an adventure that confirmed just how precarious German stability was. The Kapp putsch had inspired a left-wing takeover of the Ruhr region. This was the beginning of a progressive polarization in Germany that culminated in Hitler's rise to power as a safer alternative to Communists, though the Ruhr Reds struck Dulles as merely comic.

Claiming his right "to confer with their leaders," Dulles bribed a chauffeur with chocolate and went to Duisburg, where the revolutionary government was holed up in the city hall. Dulles pushed through the hordes of hungry people waiting for food rations to explain to a guard the importance of his mission. The guard used a rifle to poke his way through the crowd.

"The sight was really pathetic," Dulles recounted, looking at this band of what he called, "uneducated workmen chiefly jews [*sic*], I should say, looking as one pictures Trotzky [*sic*], unshaven for days, dirty and I imagine not having gotten much sleep since they started to govern!"

Dulles explained to someone who spoke English that he had come all this way for a safe-conduct to get out again. A commissar pored over a typewriter for ten minutes, tapping out twenty-five words. Handing the pass to Dulles, he explained apologetically that he could "not guarantee how good it would be," confessing, "The revolutionary region was so divided and their differences were so acute that their pass might not be generally recognized."

Dulles's chauffeur, impressed with his rider's importance, picked a fight with some soldiers who did not show the proper respect. But Dulles extricated him and fled to Cologne, where his impatient clients wasted no time telling him the deals were off.

Dulles would have preferred to get some business out of the trip, but he was content to watch the country fall apart while concluding reassuringly: "Taking into account that here was a concentrated population of a rough class, miners, steel workers, etc., who had been underfed, only partly employed and underpaid for a long time and who were not, through red guards who had the only arms, in entire and unopposed control of the situation, the order and respect for property which was [*sic*] displayed was remarkable."

As Dulles left Germany, the right-wing army brutally put down the Ruhr revolt, and two months later the democratic Weimar coalition collapsed as the moderate Social Democrats lost their power. The Weimar Republic started to crumble as the country's judges prosecuted the left wing while justifying right-wing retaliation as peacekeeping. But Dulles had had his adventure and was off to new hotels, clients, and deals with no thought for the implications of what he left behind.

Having completed no work for the firm, Dulles managed to make himself $10,000 on the way home. Bernard Baruch, with whom Dulles had served on the War Trade Board and who had attended the Versailles negotiations, approached him through Cromwell to ghostwrite a book on the Versailles Treaty, which, Baruch assured him, would take only about two weeks.

Baruch was a speculator who used his fortune to buy influence and reputation. Having made a stock market killing on a tip that America had destroyed the Spanish fleet to win the Spanish-American War, he hovered around the powerful with the look of a do-gooder while hiding the manipulative skill he learned in smoked-filled back rooms. Dorothy Parker once said that two things confused her: "the theory of the zipper and the exact function of Bernard Baruch."

As a member of the Reparations Committee at the Versailles negotiations, Baruch felt compelled to counter the devastating criticism of John Maynard Keynes, the brilliant British economist who had quit Versailles because of its punitive provisions against Germany. On his way to Europe, Dulles had read Keynes's new best seller *The Economic Consequences of the Peace,* which disturbed him as much as it did Baruch. While still in London before going to the Continent, Dulles had written a letter to *The Times* of London which published it in nearly two full columns of the paper.

In answer to Keynes's complaint that Wilson had betrayed the principles on which he promised Germany peace, Dulles replied that Wilson should not have been faced with a choice. The French were unreasonable. It was all *their* fault. In *The Times* letter Dulles argued that the Reparations Commission could make amends. "The whole operation is akin to that of a settlement in which the creditors recognize that their own interest lies in preserving and enhancing the economic vitality of their debtor." But he ignored Keynes's point that unlike relations between a creditor and debtor, France wanted to destroy Germany in revenge for World War I and the humiliating loss in the Franco-Prussian War of 1870–71.

Dulles anonymously wrote *The Making of the Reparation and Economic Sections of the Treaty* in Baruch's name as an elaboration of the letter. By merely justifying America's actions, Dulles ignored Keynes's major concern about the instability caused by the Treaty of Versailles. The Baruch book looks an impressive 353 pages, a prodigious achievement on Dulles's cruise back to New York; but it is really only 124 pages of new material, followed by a lightly annotated text of the reparation and economic sections of the treaty and appendices of speeches of delegates in Paris, including Dulles's.

Having rationalized the peace with Baruch in 1922, it was to him that Dulles confessed in 1945, "The reparation creditors had built up within Germany a machinery which was intended to enable Germany to pay reparations, but which, in fact, enabled Germany to wage the most destructive war of all time.''

Witnessing two revolts in Germany in two weeks in no way changed Dulles's opinion that ''the Reparation Commission in the process of enforcement might become a flexible instrument of wisdom and justice.'' He had no second thoughts about the adventures he had just been through—the hunger, the anti-Semitism, the violent swings of right- and left-wing politics.

Dulles's partners could not have been too happy to see him return to the office with nothing to show for two months of adventure. But Cromwell approved, writing to Dulles, ''This kind of work is the most effective and far reaching in the future (as well as the present) of S & C. It is only a matter of time when you will be called to take a more active part in these great questions.''

Cromwell's confidence was well-founded. Though Dulles had gotten nowhere in Europe, in New York he immediately attracted clients with European problems. The New York Life Insurance Company, which had $525 million in policies outstanding abroad, asked Dulles to sort out the immensely complicated results of the war on its business. New York Life had increased its coverage in Europe while other American companies had withdrawn, so that by 1913 it did more than half of all the United States' European insurance business. Its policies varied from standard life insurance to endowment policies, which Russians took out at a daughter's birth to guarantee her a dowry.

In 1885 the clever Russian court adviser Count S. Y. Witte had forced American insurance companies to invest their Russian premiums in Russia. New York Life had 20,000 policies worth $40 million in Russian insurance and a comparable investment in Russian bonds and property. In 1918 the Soviets annulled the bonds and confiscated New York Life's property, while claiming payment on the policies on behalf of the 20,000 policy holders.

The Soviets won a landmark case on the policies in New York state court, getting a judgment amounting to millions of dollars. Dulles made New York Life settle with the Russians, but the Equitable Life Assurance Society appealed and won a reversal. Those cases took six years, nothing compared to New York Life's counterclaim for its property confiscated in 1918. In 1931 the Litvinov Accord set aside $9 million of Russian property in the United States for all claimants like New York Life to divide proportionately. The actual distribution occurred twenty-five years later, in 1956.

"It was a wonderful legal exercise but economically a total disaster," according to Frederick Seibold, who rummaged around in New York Life Insurance Company's attic looking for prerevolutionary Russian documents; it was fascinating as his first assignment at the firm. "But the firm lost a lot of money on it." New York Life's claims in central Europe and Russia were a nagging reminder of the Old World which Dulles had helped to bury without necessarily creating a satisfactory replacement.

When in 1920 the American Bankers Association set up a foreign trade organization with $100 million to bankroll exports to Europe, Dulles claimed a special expertise "as [an] American Member of the Reparations Commission and an American Member of the Supreme Economic Council." He added, in a letter to the president of the ABA, "I had, perhaps, exceptional opportunities to study the financial problems involved in Europe securing its necessary commodities."

He did not mention his failures when he also wrote about his "recent private trip to Europe, including Central Europe, studying particularly the problem involved in the nations' financing imports from the United States." The bankers were impressed and invited Dulles to a meeting in Chicago.

Reviving Europe through private industry was an idea whose time had not yet come. Cautious businessmen would not lend to Europeans while German inflation reached, at its height in 1923, a rate of 4.2 *billion* marks to the dollar, compared with eight marks to the dollar in 1919. In 1923 France invaded the Ruhr Valley on the pretext of Germany's refusal to deliver coal under the Versailles Treaty while Germany embarked on a general strike. Dulles could do little work for the bankers then, but their taking notice of him would yield the firm dividends later.

In the summer of 1923 some of the biggest industrialists in Germany invited Dulles to defend them after their arrest for refusing to send coal to France. Besides having a good reputation as a lawyer (though he had never tried a case in court), Dulles was useful to the Germans by being able to publicize their predicament abroad. He met his potential clients in the elegant executive quarters adjacent to the Krupp steelworks, known locally as the "Krupp Private Hotel" near Essen.

After an elegant and hearty lunch that surprised Dulles for its refinement in the midst of crisis, he asked to see some of the proceedings of the French military tribunal before deciding whether to defend the executives. A mine manager who had transported coal without a French permit had received a fine and a one-year sentence. A professor accused of propaganda against the army of occupation because of a newspaper clipping found in a room next to his had gotten a heavy fine and a five-year sentence. A French soldier who had carelessly killed another French soldier but blamed a German had gotten a one-year sentence. Dulles concluded that the trials were "summary affairs. . . . It is part of the general policy to sentence a certain number every day."

Under the circumstances he declined the work, even though, he told the German chancellor, "there were admittedly many individual cases of grave injustice which, under other circumstances, I should have liked to help remedy." For a lawyer with no experience he had a high opinion of his own worth, adding to the chancellor, "The situation did not permit of work of a really professional character and I doubted that I could accomplish any real good."

The chancellor, Wilhelm Cuno, who was head of the Hamburg-America shipping line (which Sullivan & Cromwell later represented), pleaded with Dulles to find "a solution to the whole matter." He assured Dulles of the reasonable attitude of his government.

Dulles conducted a private round of negotiations among the Germans, French, and Belgians to try to resolve the impasse over the Ruhr occupation. Dulles found French Cabinet Minister Louis Loucheur, whom he knew from the Reparations Commission, "very bitter as regards the Germans." He told Dulles that the Germans had played "into the hands of extremists like Poincaré and had in fact proved that these extremists were right when they had said that the moderates were indulging in false illusions." The Belgian prime minister had railed that "only a more socialistic government can make the necessary sacrifices and take the necessary action against the great industrialists.''

Besides passing messages among the European leaders, Dulles warned them all of ''disintegration'' in Germany and ''political problems which would disturb all Europe for years.'' He devised the strongly pro-German solution of paying reparations with a tax on beer, wine, and tobacco instead of delivering valuable coal to the French. He wanted the Germans to reindustrialize while German consumers paid the country's reparations. His ideas satisfied German demands but did nothing to placate the concerns of the other Europeans.

Dulles also suggested that the money collected for reparations be applied in Germany ''for internal use . . . [as long as] the Reparations Commission shall be satisfied that Germany is loyally seeking to carry out her fiscal reforms and make deliveries in kind.'' In return Germany would try to get back to normal, as long as the occupation troops were reduced in number.

Dulles made a constructive effort to break the impasse, but he had no official standing, and so he sailed home a week later, concluding to his wife that the trip was ''an interesting but not financially profitable time.'' The profits were to follow.

Dulles's proposals of the year before were revived in April 1924, with Germany faltering on its Reparations payments and French troops still occupying the Ruhr. The Inter-Allied Reparations Commission sent Charles Dawes and Owen Young to an international committee to stabilize the mark and balance the German budget. With Dulles as his special counsel, Dawes, chairman of the committee, arranged for the United States to rehabilitate Germany by using Dulles's suggestion of a ''trustee'' (calling it a ''transfer agent'') to apply reparations payments within the country. The levy was pared from $55 billion to $33 billion and made payable in marks, not foreign currency. As a further boost to German stabilization, the J. P. Morgan bank spearheaded a $200 million international private loan.

Keynes had recommended that the United States participate in rebuilding Germany, but the Dawes Plan relied far too much on private loans rather than on Keynes's idea of government aid. From 1924 to 1931 Dulles arranged more than $1 billion in loans, which he liked to say were issued under the Dawes Plan. When the State Department forced him to be more accurate, he revised his statement: "I do not mean under the control of the organization set up by the Dawes Plan, but that it was in accordance with the general recommendation contained in the Dawes Plan that capital should be supplied to German manufacturing interests." Unless pressed, he always preferred his original formulation, which made the bond-buying public believe its money was being lent under some official sanction when it never was.

The Dawes Plan initiated an era of German prosperity based on American lending, a disastrous formula which Sullivan & Cromwell vigorously promoted. The firm organized the very first American bond for a German company, the Krupp steel company, "one of the best known and most important steel works in the world," as the prospectus put it. The bottom of the Krupp prospectus, as prepared for the bond issuer, J. & W. Seligman & Company, read "This offering is made in all respects when, as and if issued and accepted by us and subject to the approval of Messrs. Sullivan & Cromwell, of New York."

For the Krupp loan, Dulles called Leland Harrison, the assistant secretary of state on a Saturday in December 1924, asking casually, "If you felt you could, in your talks with the newspaper men, do anything to soft-pedal this talk" of renewed dissension between France and Germany. He added that the issue was coming out the day after next. Harrison was incensed because the department had issued a circular asking to see foreign loan applications before they were approved to monitor the export of American funds. But as Dulles knew, the department had no authority to stop the transactions.

Dulles claimed he thought the circular applied only to governmental loans. Harrison reminded him, "Several members of the syndicate were well aware of the Department's desire to be consulted in such matters."

Dulles offered to go to Washington on the midnight train but was told he could not get a reply on Sunday. On Sunday Dulles changed tack and tried to get around Harrison by calling the department's economic adviser. After being very apologetic, he admitted the bankers wanted State Department approval because "they felt that the disagreement between the Allies and Germany as to evacuation of occupied territory would injure the sale of the notes.'' But they still planned to go ahead on Monday.

The Krupp bond was successfully issued on the Monday without State Department approval. Ten days later the department sent Sullivan & Cromwell a copy of the year-old circular with the tart comment ''Inasmuch as the financing in question was not brought to the attention of the Department . . . this Department does not feel in a position to express any views on the matter at this time.''

Dulles wanted to avoid State Department scrutiny of whether the German factories were producing military hardware in violation of the Versailles Treaty. Sullivan & Cromwell had accepted Krupp's own pallid assurances that ''all special equipment for the manufacture of war materiél has been destroyed, except for certain pieces of machinery.''

A year later Dulles wrote in *Foreign Affairs* magazine, ''Few bankers would wish, and fewer still would dare, to ignore the expressed desire of the State Department that it be consulted.'' However, by avoiding the State Department he had already ushered in the era of private loans to rebuild Germany.

It was a telling start to an incredible era when Sullivan & Cromwell dominated a major segment of American investment. Banks competed with each other to get the firm to find them German loans. Within the first year, Americans lent $150 million to Germany, a sum that worried even the German government. It warned against ''indiscriminate placing of German loans in the American market, particularly when the borrowers are German nationalities and the purposes are not productive.''

The concern was well founded. The prospectus for a Prussian state loan approved by Sullivan & Cromwell noted that ''the entire proceeds . . . are to be applied by the State for revenue producing purposes,'' though a third of the money was being used to improve harbors, which are hardly a revenue producer for paying back loans.

When the State Department issued more warnings, Dulles called it ''a pretty poor effort'' that ''ties up several matters upon which I have been working.'' He wasted no time neutralizing the department by ingratiating himself with its loan supervisors, starting with Robert E. Olds, the undersecretary. Using the Council on Foreign Relations, a prestigious New York club of businessmen and academics interested in foreign policy, Dulles invited Olds to a dinner in New York. Within three years, Olds had joined Sullivan & Cromwell as a partner to head the Paris office in what *The New York Times* called "a significant increase in the ranks of 'American Ministers of Foreign Finance.' "

While the State Department privately alerted bankers and lawyers of its concern over the growing levels of German indebtedness, Dulles publicly promoted the loans. His speeches were covered in the newspapers, especially when he praised himself and his colleagues for the Dawes Plan and the "financial and economic revival which is, perhaps, the most notable achievement of its kind that the world has ever known . . . a wise and constructive and firm employment of the financial power of this nation."

After one of his *Foreign Affairs* articles had appeared, Dulles admitted to a Sullivan & Cromwell partner, "In some quarters there is a tendency to criticize my article as representing too much the 'Wall Street' attitude of wanting to get rid of any sort of restriction with reference to financial matters."

Sullivan & Cromwell supervised endless series of German bonds. They came so fast that errors the firm would theoretically have never tolerated proliferated. Some prospectuses had just not been proofread carefully, which was probably not surprising, considering how frantic the efforts to acquire new loans became. Others were purposely deceptive. A 1926 Bavarian bond prospectus began, "Bavaria has an excellent financial history," discussing the period prior to 1914 when, the year before, in 1925, the state had defaulted on its debts.

Candler Cobb, a garrulous American with a veneer of cosmopolitan manners covering a base of sheer persistence, worked at Sullivan & Cromwell's Paris office, looking for loans to pass along to bankers. Not himself a lawyer, he roamed Eastern Europe from Frankfurt to Budapest, scouting prospects in an increasingly competitive market, where, for instance, "36 houses, most of them American, competed for a city of Budapest loan and 14 for a loan to the city of Belgrade. A Bavarian hamlet, discovered by American agents to be in need of about $125,000, was urged and finally persuaded to borrow 3 million dollars in the American market."

Even Dulles chased customers. The director of the Dresdner Bank in

Hamburg wrote him in 1925, "You encouraged me to remind you of the possibilities for placing American capital here, secured by first mortgages at from 5–10 years. It is the only object of this letter to bring this matter once more before your eyes, and I shall be very much interested to hear from you in due time whether you have been able to promote interest at proper quarters."

Cromwell got into the act once, with his typical showmanship and mixed motives. He hosted a visit to America for the queen of Romania, one of the most beautiful women in the world, who came to launch a successful Romanian debt issue in October 1926. As president of the Society of the Friends of Romania, an organization he had founded after falling under the queen's spell in Paris, Cromwell sponsored a dinner for 1,000 at the Waldorf, with a glittering guest list that he had had published in its entirety in the *Herald Tribune*. Handsome Sullivan & Cromwell associates were put into blue satin uniforms trimmed in gold and taught to whisper to entering guests, "There shall be no curtsy to the Queen—just a slight handclasp." After the ball, which was fully covered in the society columns, Cromwell escorted the queen, with whom he had a purported romance, on a cross-country tour in a seven-car private train donated by the railroads.

Cromwell never revealed his attitude toward the firm's active solicitation of bonds, but his support of the Romanian effort implied no more enthusiasm for the whole practice than his defense of Mrs. Frank Leslie's will had implied personal support for the women's suffrage movement. Yet he *was* instrumental in the success of the movement when he made sure that the estate of Mrs. Leslie, who had inherited a magazine empire from her husband and had greatly enhanced it, went to "my friend, Mrs. Carrie Chapman Catt of the City of New York. It is my expectation and wish that she turn all of my said residuary estate into cash . . . to the furtherance of the cause of women's suffrage, to which she has so worthily devoted so many years of her life."

Cromwell had written the clause in the will that "should any . . . beneficiary or next of kin of mine contest this will, . . . I hereby direct that he or she shall thereupon be deprived of all interest in my estate." But Mr. Frank Leslie's son sued both the estate and Cromwell as an executor to throw out the will. The son tried to make the case that Mrs. Leslie was both illegitimate *and* the daughter of slaves. He failed and the suffrage movement got the money that helped get women the vote in 1919.

It was not that Cromwell sold Romania to the Americans so much as that he sold himself to the queen. Normally, Sullivan & Cromwell found borrowers to pass on to the bankers, who then used the firm to supervise the loans. It willingly put its prestige on the line with clauses in the loans like the one for the Saxon State Mortgage Institution, which claimed, "It is believed that the adoption of the Dawes Plan has rendered extremely remote any attempt to enforce such charge against either the revenues or assets of the States."

Such reassurances helped build a huge structure on an increasingly shaky foundation. From 1924 to 1931, Sullivan & Cromwell handled $1.15 billion in loans to Germany and Europe as well as $250 million to Latin America and $139 million to Japan, a total of more than $1.5 billion.

To handle its accelerating volume of European work, the firm started a law firm in Berlin—Albert & Westrick. Heinrich Albert had been a German spy in the United States before it entered the war, buying up industrial ceramics to cripple the United States' chemical industry. His attaché case, which he accidentally left on a New York subway, revealed subversive activities, like smuggling rubber to Germany in coffee sacks and raising money from émigré Germans "to create an army of hyphenated voters to wage political warfare against the Government." Albert was deported amid loud objections to what *The New York Times* called "impudent activities." After the war he was German secretary of state and a key means of access to major German borrowers. As a high German government official, Albert left the legal work to his young associate, Gerhard Westrick.

To the bankers and to Sullivan & Cromwell, the loans produced no risk once the banks had sold the loans to unsuspecting buyers among the general public. In the defense of his client bankers, Dulles claimed, "It is the function of the bankers to pass upon matters of lending money and [they] should be held primarily and exclusively responsible." It was a heavy responsibility, but as Dulles knew, it was moral, not financial. And since he himself had bought no bonds, he had nothing to worry about.

PART II

THE LAWBREAKER

7

THE RISE AND RISE OF JOHN FOSTER DULLES

The real culprits [are] some of the leading law firms who make such a fat killing out of the abuses which brought the Securities Act into existence. They really want to do business at the old stand. [They] have come out of their storm cellars of fear—not to improve but to chloroform the Act.—FELIX FRANKFURTER

Sullivan & Cromwell managing partner Royall Victor was within sight of the Oyster Bay Yacht Club on the second day of the season's first regatta. It was a beautiful, sunny day with a light breeze in May 1926 when he gasped and fell to the deck of his yacht, the *Snookabuss*. Another racer, noticing the boat buffeted in the wind, came alongside. With Victor lying on the deck, a launch towed the boat to shore. Victor's inert body was carried into the clubhouse, where a doctor pronounced him dead. The third day of the regatta was canceled, and in a front-page obituary in *The New York Times*, the forty-eight-year-old lawyer was called "one of the ablest lawyers engaged in corporate practice in the city."

His death caused a succession crisis at Sullivan & Cromwell because it quickly followed the loss of three other major partners. Columbia Law School Dean Harlan Fiske Stone, who had sent his best students to the firm, rejoined the firm in September 1923 to head the litigation group. At a time when the firm was making $1.2 million, Stone was promised $100,000 a year. But he quit within a year to accept the appointment of U.S. attorney general from his Amherst classmate Calvin Coolidge in the new Republican administration. Though Stone had expected to return to the firm, he was appointed to the Supreme Court fifteen months later. Dulles wrote his congratulations "with a heavy heart," admitting that "it is a matter of great personal disappointment that this seems to postpone indefinitely the prospect of your return here with us."

In March 1925, Alfred Jaretzki, Sr., died at the age of sixty-three after a two-month battle with stomach cancer. Henry Hill Pierce, who was a leader in utilities work and training associates, contracted an unspecified illness called sleeping sickness at the time, which grew worse as the decade drew on. He shuffled slowly, spoke with an increasing stutter, and finally resigned in 1928.

To tide the firm over, Cromwell decided to appoint a four-man directorate composed of John Foster Dulles, Wilbur L. Cummings (a corporate law expert), and the two cousins Edward Green and Eustace Seligman. Dulles had worked his way into the heart of the firm and now fully involved himself in its domestic work by taking over from Cromwell such important clients as International Nickel, American Bank Note, Cuban Cane Sugar, and the Gold Dust Corp. He continued to conduct his European work through a number of associates who became important partners. They included Arthur H. Dean, Norris Darrell, and George Sharp.

Handling recruitment and pay in the new regime, Dulles immediately offered a job to his brother, Allen. Allen, who worried about "keeping my head above water financially," had attended Foster's alma mater, George Washington University Law School, while continuing at the State Department. He found Foster's overture "more flattering than a neophyte in the law has a right to expect" but hesitated. To placate him, Foster discussed his brother's belated legal career (at the age of thirty-three) with John W. Davis of Davis, Polk,

Wardwell, Gardiner & Reed, but gradually won him over to Sullivan & Cromwell. Allen Dulles started at the firm in October 1926, five months after Foster Dulles had taken over recruiting.

Not everyone, not even a future Supreme Court justice, could expect the same treatment. William O. Douglas remembered being interviewed for a job at Sullivan & Cromwell in 1926, at which time he found Foster "pontifical. He made it appear that the greatest favor he could do a young lawyer was to hire him. He seemed to me like a high churchman out to exploit someone. In fact, I was so struck by Dulles's pomposity that when he helped me on with my coat, as I was leaving his office, I turned and gave him a quarter tip."

In 1927 Dulles became sole managing partner and, despite continuing deference to Cromwell, remolded the firm in his own image and habits. His style reflected the aloofness of his personal relations and lax disregard of details. This made Dulles easy to work for, according to lawyers close to him, like George Sharp, the son of the American ambassador to France when Dulles was at the Versailles Treaty negotiations. Sharp said that Dulles "never would say, 'You must do this,' or 'You mustn't do that,' but he would put up certain guideposts that he knew would be of help to me, and I always felt that I had his entire confidence in going ahead and using my own judgment on the spot." Not surprisingly, Sharp considered this "a great pleasure" and "a welcome relief from the attitude of several other of my partners, who always felt that they had to, you know, dot the i's and cross the t's by cablegram."

Dulles leaned back in the chair in his spacious corner office as lawyers paraded in to keep him abreast of clients' affairs. He bought his suits at the annual Brooks Brothers sale after Christmas, preferring those of a sickly green color that were always in stock during the clearance sales. From his bout with malaria in the Central American jungle he retained a tic in his eye two decades later, and he constantly patted down his hair. He sucked on a pipe as he listened, incessantly tamping it, making his lawyers nervous as he seemed to drift off into his own thoughts. The pipe routine was altered after dinner, when he smoked a cheap White Owl cigar for its laxative effect.

To go with his new position, he cultivated a dignified, reserved, old-man air. If he was asked for an opinion, he stood up, paced the floor silently for about five minutes, and recited all the facts given to him until he had formulated his thoughts and had droned his opinion in a slow monotone. He showed that he had been listening by getting to the central points but he did not drill subordinates the way Cromwell did. Dulles was relaxed, trusting, not a worrier. ''Once he had considered a matter, made up his mind, I don't think he ever gave it another thought,'' George Sharp believed. ''He certainly didn't carry it home and toss about it in bed at night. I think that he felt that he'd done everything he could do, and that was that.''

Despite his forbidding air and professional reserve, Dulles attracted great loyalty from those close to him. He had a small coterie of colleagues who saw an entirely different side of the man. To them, he was playful and engaging. The wife of banker George Murnane chided him every time he visited them: ''For God's sake, Foster, get yourself a larger hat. You look like Humpty Dumpty.'' And Dulles laughed uproariously.

He was considered more able to appreciate than initiate a joke, but he wrote an elaborate spoof letter to Polly Dean, the jolly wife of Dulles's young partner Art Dean. Having convinced Polly to make book (be the banker) at Henry L. Stimson's annual Columbus Day races at his Huntington, Long Island farm, Dulles sent her a letter with the typewritten return address, ''Office of Collector of Illegal Revenue, Bridge of Sighs, New York.'' The joke involved not only her untaxed racetrack earnings, but also the legalese used in their professional writing.

> ''Dear Madam:'' it began, purporting to be from a tax inspector, ''Information has come to me from unimpeachable sources that you currently are, and for some years past have been, in receipt of large sums as a result of bookmaking activities. A careful audit of your Federal Income Tax Returns shows that you have wholly failed to disclose this important source of revenue or to pay any tax thereon. The fact that this income is illegal does not alter its taxable status as held in the closely analogous case of *U.S. v. Al Capone,* of which you have perhaps heard. In view of your sex, the Government is disposed to adopt a lenient attitude. The least that it can ask is immediate payment of the tax with interest and penalties. If,

> however, this is done, the Government will urge upon the court that prison sentence be suspended, conditioned upon you[r] future good behavior. Do not think you can minimize the amount of your gains, as the Government field agents, who customarily attend all important racing events, have full information which will be used to check the adequacy of the belated restitution which you are called upon to make. With high regard for your ability, I am, Very truly yours, Collector.''
>
> A postscript noted, ''Do not delude yourself with the vain hope that because your husband is a partner in a famous Wall Street law firm, the services of this firm can be obtained by you to extricate you from your present predicament. Doubtless they have given aid and comfort to many other malefactors of great wealth. But in the instant case, we learn that even this great firm, with all its reputation for sagacity, has become one of your victims and will act accordingly.''

Thinking it was from the Internal Revenue Service, Polly Dean was in tears meeting her husband at the train station after getting the letter. When he laughed at Foster's obvious joke (starting with ''Illegal'' for ''Internal''), she almost threw him out of the car. He convinced her that it was a joke, and when she confronted Foster, he turned it into a homily, warning her, ''Well, you were so brash. You wanted to make book. You were so determined and you were having so much fun. Now just let that be a lesson to you.'' Dean called Dulles ''a master theologian.''

The informal Dulles at home, drinking gin during Prohibition and stirring it with his finger, would have been unrecognizable to most firm lawyers who saw the managing partner as a stern moralist with no humor. He rarely mixed business and home life, but when he took his children sailing, they stopped in at ports where clients had offices for factory tours he had arranged for them. He also let his son Avery use the firm office on Saturday to type up schoolwork, which Dulles had printed by the firm's securities printer. To the public and to most Sullivan & Cromwell associates, the only humor associated with John Foster Dulles occurred in 1957 when Carol Burnett launched her career with the song, ''I Made a Fool of Myself Over John Foster Dulles,'' which her subject got a copy of because he enjoyed it so much.

* * *

As managing partner, Dulles cast his influence over all firm business, domestic and foreign. A high priority, it seemed, was to make sure he did not miss the final surge of the stock market boom. Though he had not participated before, he jumped at the chance when former associate Waddill Catchings, who had gone to Goldman, Sachs, offered "to include you [Dulles] in the selling group which will give you the selling commission." It proved to be one of the most overblown financial concoctions of the whole crazy 1920s, the Goldman Sachs Trading Company. The frenzy hit Dulles when he replied to Catchings in two letters on the same day in November 1928, the first asking for $50,000 in shares and the second to "raise my participation in the G. S. Company to $75,000."

Dulles even reserved shares for his mother, who wrote him gratefully, "I certainly thank you very much for getting me such a good investment and for letting me have the benefit of your price." As astute bankers, Goldman, Sachs had avoided the manic Wall Street craze of the 1920s until the very end. Then, throwing caution to the winds, it not only put together an investment trust at the very last gasp of the boom but also named it the Goldman Sachs Trading Company, which tied the reputation of the bank to the fortunes of its new business.

The public was so eager to buy shares that Goldman, Sachs decided to double its initial capitalization and raised $100 million instead of $50 million. It had a hard time deciding even where to invest so much money until John Foster Dulles put the bankers together with his utilities client Harrison Williams to make a speculative alliance of fiendish magnitude.

Williams was the father of the New Jersey senator jailed in the Abscam scandals of the 1980s and a schemer of the first order. With Goldman, Sachs, he created two trusts, the Shenandoah Corporation and the Blue Ridge Corporation. Williams paid $5 million for 40 percent of Shenandoah while the public paid $17 million for 20 percent. He then paid himself back out of the public subscription, making an overall profit (including his shares) of $40 million just on the initial public offering. The Goldman Sachs Trading Company shares jumped up in eight months from an offering price of $100 a share to $280. Shenandoah and Blue Ridge, with assets of $200 million, offered to buy twenty-one of America's leading companies, including American Telephone & Telegraph, U.S. Steel, General Electric, and Eastman Kodak. Williams was a paper billionaire; his wife, regularly voted America's best-dressed woman, expected a Sullivan & Cromwell lawyer to take care of her seventy-four trunks when her private ship docked in New York.

Despite his personal stake, Dulles's first reaction to the stock market crash on October 24, 1929, was relief. He wrote a London banker, "On the whole I think it is a healthy development. . . ." But as a member of the board of directors of Shenandoah and Blue Ridge, Dulles faced numerous shareholders' lawsuits as the stocks plummeted in value from $280 to $1.25 a share. One of the suits, *Austrian et al.* v. *Williams,* Sullivan & Cromwell won in the Supreme Court because the statute of limitations had run out; another, *Marco* v. *Dulles,* Arthur Dean finally won after a determined fight he waged "because of the slurs on Foster's reputation and the money involved." The court of appeals decision came in 1968, forty years from those heady days of carefree investing in 1929 and ten years after Dulles had died. His wife never got any of his legacy because the case was not finally settled until after her death in 1969. But she lived comfortably, since Dulles had taken the precaution of putting most of the family money in her name so that his estate was only $1 million compared with her $7 million (which greatly surprised their children).

The market crash *was* healthy for the firm, but not to clear the air for further investment in Europe, as Dulles had assumed. This was no mere "correction" but a financial bloodbath. As usual it gave Sullivan & Cromwell more work. There was, to start with, a huge volume of stock trading, certificates of which lawyers in those days transferred for stockbroking clients. Lauson Stone, one of more than sixty lawyers in the firm, handled $20 million of securities in one day as market volume exploded in the wake of the crash.

Goldman, Sachs & Company, which dearly regretted putting its own name on its investment trust, faced "suits on every conceivable basis," according to the bank's partner Walter Sachs. "I mean, on the basis of the fact that people had lost money. That's the basis—they charged us with neglect and with fraud and this and that, you see.

That's a long, long history. [To find the answers] you'd have to delve into the files of Sullivan & Cromwell.'' Goldman, Sachs lost altogether $13 million and settled with the biggest plaintiffs, while Sullivan & Cromwell made money from the suits of Dulles's labor.

At Sullivan & Cromwell 1929 was best remembered for the increasing evidence of John Foster Dulles's lavishness. Dulles's ambition made him want Sullivan & Cromwell to have extensive international connections, prestige, and domestic importance to reflect well on its managing partner. He quickly expanded the firm around the world.

He opened offices in Berlin and Buenos Aires. In Paris the firm hired half a dozen lawyers and moved out of Cromwell's one room in the Ritz into a whole floor of an office building behind the hotel. In New York the firm moved to opulent new quarters at 48 Wall Street. At a time when the existing standard of law office decor was rolltop desks and cracked leather sofas, Dulles preferred the elegance of wall-to-wall carpets and a winding staircase connecting the floors. One of the partners of Davis, Polk, Wardwell, Gardiner & Reed came over and commented, implicitly comparing the decor to a call house, ''It's very nice; I might stay for a drink but I don't think I'll go upstairs.''

From the time Dulles took over and for two succeeding decades, Sullivan & Cromwell was the largest law firm in the world. ''White shoe'' firms like Sullivan & Cromwell included Davis, Polk, Wardwell, Gardiner & Reed; Shearman & Sterling; Milbank, Tweed, Hope & Webb; Cravath, de Gersdorff, Swaine & Wood; White & Case; and Cotton, Franklin, Wright & Gordon.

Dulles's taking over as senior partner raised the firm's social standing; after all, he had had his first White House appointment at the age of four to attend the birthday party of President Benjamin Harrison's grandson while Dulles's grandfather was secretary of state. But other firms had great social distinction. Every partner of Davis, Polk, for instance, was in the social register. According to novelist Louis Auchincloss, whose father was a Davis, Polk partner, ''The firm would have been shocked that its senior partner would ever be Jewish,'' as occurred in the 1980s. Where Davis, Polk epitomized aristocratic law, which included most of the white shoe firms, Sullivan

& Cromwell, with its hard-working Jewish partners, epitomized and anticipated the meritocracy that would ultimately overtake all Wall Street practices. As the largest firm, Sullivan & Cromwell seemed more than the others to have the archetypal big-business practice.

The term "legal factory" applied to Sullivan & Cromwell even before it became familiar in the 1930s. In 1929 the firm doubled its entering class by hiring thirteen lawyers to increase its size to sixty-three. The next year Dulles took on the firm's first women associates, four intrepid souls, to prove the progressiveness of the senior partner while filling the ranks with lawyers who did not expect to become partners. One resigned within a year, but another, Lois Rodgers, spent more than twenty-five years at Sullivan & Cromwell.

Half the new recruits stayed fewer than three years, forcing the firm to continue its active recruitment policy; that meant six new associates in 1931, four each in 1932 and 1933, and eight in 1934. Dulles was a master at building up the firm but he was not an administrator, a drawback that the world got to know when he became secretary of state in 1953.

At Sullivan & Cromwell this failing was hidden behind the backup authority of William Nelson Cromwell, who spent a considerable amount of time hounding the young lawyers in the office. Now well into his seventies, Cromwell roamed the halls of the office, acting as though he were boss. He had a right to approve prospective partners, but his questioning of them became desultory and sometimes vague. Yet he still terrorized the lawyers in the office. Associate Joseph Prendergast was shocked at the different environments at Sullivan & Cromwell in New York and Berlin, where the eighteen-hour day, a New York routine, was unknown. Though Dulles made Prendergast something of a protégé because he had played football at their alma mater, Princeton, Prendergast soon soured on Sullivan & Cromwell. When he got back to New York after a year in Berlin, he noticed the "Sullivan & Cromwell tic" on partners that seemed to go along with the Park Avenue apartments and houses on Long Island. Even Dulles had his habitual hair patting and squint. "They all had something, if only an ulcer," Prendergast noticed. "It did not seem worth it to me," he decided.

Cromwell remained sharp in business—and controversial. A congressional investigation revealed that he was one of seventeen rich Americans who had donated more than $10,000 each to the Republican party and arranged significant tax refunds for clients from Secretary of the Treasury Andrew Mellon. Over eight years as treasury secretary, Mellon dispensed $3.5 billion in refunds. Cromwell collected $222,652 for clients American Water Works & Electric Company and Manati Sugar Company, on whose boards of directors he sat.

Cromwell gained further notoriety when he refused to abandon his house to make way for Rockefeller Center, even though the house was owned by Columbia University, which was participating in the new project. Cromwell wanted John D. Rockefeller, Jr., himself to ask him to leave; when he didn't, Cromwell declared, "My wife died here. I will die here. You can talk to my executors," thus preventing the building of 1 Rockefeller Center for nearly two decades.

Sullivan & Cromwell had a strict hierarchy imposed by the dominating share of income Cromwell controlled and the large number of associates compared with partners. At the time in 1934 when the firm employed sixty-eight lawyers, there were only sixteen partners, a ratio of more than four to one. That year, besides constantly hiring new associates, the firm had eight senior associates who had been there more than fifteen years and never expected to make partner. This holdover senior associate status from Cromwell's day enhanced the firm's profitability, especially in adding weight to the litigation and the trusts and estates groups, each of which had three senior associates with only one partner in trusts and estates and two partners in litigation.

Despite the rigid hierarchy within, the firm expected the lowliest associate to be treated by the outside world with the same respect as the senior partner. The firm did not put lawyers' names on its letterhead. The main reason was convenience, since changes occurred so often it would be hard to keep the stationery current. Dulles did not share Cromwell's penurious habits, but it would have been cumbersome if not expensive. The lack of individual names also blurred the lawyers' status in the organization, and the practice of giving responsibility to young recruits allowed the firm to maintain the fiction that every lawyer was an equal because of his Sullivan & Cromwell label.

Within the firm, it was considerably more complicated. Senior associates did not fit the standard pattern of making partner or leaving the firm. They did the work of partners but did not have to be paid as much. For this reason, litigation and trusts and estates could get away with fewer partners because they had more senior associates, while the general practice, with thirty-six lawyers, had only two senior associates. One was Walter G. Wiechmann, the nephew of conductor Walter Damrosch, and appropriately an expert in copyright law (the firm represented ASCAP, the songwriters' and publishers' association); the other, Paul W. McQuillen, a public utilities lawyer, eventually became a partner in 1944, after twenty-six years as an associate.

Even when it affected partners' income, Dulles did not hesitate to expand the firm. He was prepared to spread the wealth, which became an issue only when, in the mid-1930s, Sullivan & Cromwell considered merging with Cotton & Franklin (previously known as Spooner & Cotton), the firm that had rejected Dulles when he first tried to find a job in 1911. But the other firm's partners made more money than Sullivan & Cromwell's, scotching the deal.

Most partners approved of Dulles's policy. As Eustace Seligman described it, "Under Mr. Dulles, Sullivan & Cromwell, I think, went almost further than any other firm, in bringing in additional younger men as partners. . . . Under his leadership we always tried to recognize the younger man and bring them in and give them greater financial rewards than they might get."

Dulles headed a senior committee convened to recommend a new financial structure for the firm based on the division of a share of profits that Cromwell was willing to relinquish as his contribution to modernization. Dulles turned the deliberations into a two-pronged effort to give junior partners more of a share and to provide the firm with its own capital base. He accomplished both by letting the juniors buy into the firm to provide the capital. Until then, working capital came from undistributed partners' shares "in an amount (over $1,000,000) which, if the demands were exercised, would leave the Firm wholly bereft of working capital," Dulles explained.

In 1934 he designed a new partnership agreement to give the firm a pool of $750,000 provided by the junior partners who "are in a better position to do so than the seniors because their income tax rates are much lower.'' This was true, of course, only because their incomes were so much lower.

Included in the new package of firm finances was a provision to withhold the shares of partners who quit and went to work for a competing firm within five years. Dulles cabled the proposals to Paris, where Cromwell mulled them over and ratified them for institution on January 1, 1935.

Dulles took the lead in limiting his own shares, which inspired others like Seligman, who said, ''The only quarrels we ever had with Mr. Dulles on percentages were that we never could get him to take enough. He was remarkably unselfish and unwilling to agree to what we thought he should agree to.'' Still, in 1936 Dulles's share of firm income, despite the reduced percentage to accommodate juniors, was $377,000. (It was no aberration. Dulles earned $345,000 in 1937, $249,000 in 1938, $199,000 in 1939, and $203,000 in 1940.) At the time associates in the firm earned $2,100 a year. Robert T. Kimberlin, who joined Sullivan & Cromwell in 1934, felt ''in the middle of the Depression, that $2,100 was damned good.''

In 1934 William Nelson Cromwell bought Janet Dulles an ermine coat and cabled her, SHORT STYLES ARE IN THIS YEAR, NOT LONG AND IF YOU WISH [YOU] COULD CUT COAT SO AS TO FURNISH ONE [FOR DAUGHTER] LILIAS ALSO! In 1935, when nearly half the American lawyers were earning less than $2,000 a year, Janet Dulles got monthly allowances for household expenses that ranged from $2,000 to $5,000. Her Christmas present from her husband, who took about the same amount as his wife for expenses, was $25,000.

Until the mid-1930s, the Dulleses had a chauffeur-driven Lincoln. Avery Dulles would sit in the front seat with the chauffeur, Thomas Sweeney, while his mother sat in the back, ringing a bell to get the chauffeur to get back in his lane. ''Sweeney would get so mad,'' Avery Dulles recalled. Later, Herbert Green, the gardener, doubled as the chauffeur when Dulles wanted to look less ostentatious during the worst of the Depression years.

It is hard to conceive just how stupendous Dulles's income was in the 1930s, but as one example, if associates at Sullivan & Cromwell in 1987 were making $71,000, the senior partner would have had to take home $12 million a year to make as much as Dulles did in 1936. Dulles's $377,000 in 1936 contrasts with the experience of fifteen hundred lawyers in New York City who in that same year were prepared to take a pauper's oath to get work relief. And Seligman thought that Dulles should have taken even more, indicating just how much they were all making throughout the Depression.

The firm was earning so much money that Dulles suggested Cromwell invest in some of their hard-up clients. Dulles arranged for Cromwell to put $50,000 into the First Boston Corporation, which Sullivan & Cromwell helped put together as the investment-bank spin-off of the First National Bank of Boston and Chase National Bank's investment arm, Harris Forbes. After six months' negotiations, the new company ultimately decided to raise $9 million as a public corporation. The relationship between First Boston and Sullivan & Cromwell has endured to this day, after an auspicious start when Sullivan & Cromwell recommended former associate Robert Goldsby to work there.

In 1934 Dulles asked Cromwell to invest in a partnership Dulles himself concocted between two bankers he trusted, Jean Monnet and George Murnane. Dulles wrote Cromwell that Monnet, whom he had met at the Versailles negotiations, was "one of the most brilliant men that I know" and "an intimate friend [who] has the full confidence of many of the most important financial people." Later to be the architect of the Iron and Steel Community and the founder of the European Economic Community, Monnet worked as an investment banker in France. Dulles teamed him up with Murnane, who had been a partner in Lee, Higginson & Company, a Boston investment bank that had failed because of one major mistake—backing Ivar Kreuger, the Swedish match king, whose suicide in 1932 was one of the stunning events of the Depression.

Dulles introduced the two men, set up Monnet, Murnane & Company as a private investment bank, put up $25,000 of his own money, and got Cromwell to put up another $25,000 to underwrite its activities.

Dulles convinced Cromwell to support the two bankers because they "should produce a large amount of legal business for us," to which

Cromwell replied in a long telegram, USE YOUR DISCRETION AS TO PRECISE TERMS . . . [BUT] MUST BE STRICTLY ON LOAN BASIS ENFORCEABLE AS SUCH AND SO DECLARED IN DOCUMENTS [BECAUSE I] AM NOT SO CONCERNED ABOUT A LOAN AS THAT I FORESEE THIS DANGER OF LAWSUITS BY CREDITORS IN ALL NEW RESURRECTIONS OR VENTURES.

With Monnet conducting business in France and China, Dulles channeled Murnane toward the businesses he wanted to promote. The two men were close friends, both having weekend houses in Cold Spring Harbor, Long Island. In his role as senior partner at Sullivan & Cromwell, Dulles had to entertain lavishly to large numbers of firm clients as well as hosting an annual firm New Year's cocktail party. But in the intimate setting of his New Year's Eve party for his family and less than a dozen friends, Murnane and his wife were invariably included. The Dulleses and their guests performed an annual ritual of guessing where the Dow Jones stock average would end the following year and what would be the major events and personalities of the next year. Dulles kept the previous year's answers in his office safe and pulled them out on the last working day of the year to present at the party.

Dulles and Murnane thought alike, having together helped the conservative Heinrich Brüning escape from Germany just ahead of his planned murder by Hitler's orders. They arranged for him to hide in a Long Island monastery in Cold Spring Harbor, a testimonial to their enduring financial and emotional support of Germany regardless of the regime in power.

Both also shared the embarrassment of seeing investments they supported in Europe go bad. Murnane's answers to inquiries indicated Lee Higginson's carelessness in the collapse of Kreuger's empire. The bankruptcy investigations after Kreuger's suicide revealed that the International Telephone and Telegraph Company had warned Murnane about fraud in Kreuger accounts, but Murnane admitted, "It never occurred to Lee, Higginson & Co. [of which he was a partner], even on hearing IT&T accuse Kreuger of falsifying a balance sheet, to suspect the balance sheets that he had given them." Murnane felt that "the situation seemed serious only because it might result in a public challenge to Kreuger's honesty, which might injure his prestige and his companies." Such contempt for the public, another characteristic he shared with Dulles, actually reflected a carelessness that Cromwell recognized in cautioning Dulles over the Monnet, Murnane investment.

From the incorporation of Monnet, Murnane in 1935 to its dissolution in 1939, it steadily repaid its backers while engineering deals like the Nash automobile company's merger with Kelvinator refrigerators to make Kelvinator-Nash, a precursor of American Motors, which remained a Sullivan & Cromwell client into the 1980s. Dulles introduced Murnane to Solvay & Cie, the Belgian chemical company, whose interests the banker represented in America, and Murnane became a member of the board of Allied Chemical after Sullivan & Cromwell had fought its management in 1933.

The Depression had its biggest impact on Sullivan & Cromwell when the Democratic administration of Franklin D. Roosevelt demanded new legislation to curb the excesses of the investment community. Dulles and Cromwell inveighed bitterly against the Democratic hostility to capitalism and the financial markets. Dulles had endorsed President Herbert Hoover's optimistic belief that "if someone could get off a good joke every ten days, I believe our troubles would be over."

Sullivan & Cromwell partners reacted angrily to the securities regulation proposed at the beginning of the Roosevelt administration during the famous Hundred Days, when fifteen statutes fundamentally changed American society. The first draft of the Securities Act, written by Huston Thompson, a former member of the Federal Trade Commission, went beyond the President's demand for "full publicity and information. . . ." A young Sullivan & Cromwell partner, Arthur Dean, called the Thompson bill a "hopeless confusion of ill-assorted provisions." Eustace Seligman objected that holding corporate directors responsible for the truth of registration statements was "revolutionary . . . and without precedent in Anglo-Saxon law."

The chorus of objections prompted a revision supervised by Felix Frankfurter, later a long-serving justice of the Supreme Court but at the time a professor at the Harvard Law School and a member of Roosevelt's Brain Trust. The new draft was made in a single day. It limited its demands to "full and fair disclosure" and a waiting period between registration and the sale of a security. Sam Rayburn, the wily Texas legislator who headed the House Committee on Interstate and Foreign Commerce, channeled the bill to a subcommittee to prepare a final draft.

Before the subcommittee sent the final draft to the full committee, Raymond Moley, the head of Roosevelt's Brain Trust, let Dulles and Dean raise their objections. Rayburn was against the idea, but went along if Dulles and Dean would meet with the bill's drafters, James Landis, later head of the Securities and Exchange Commission (SEC), and Benjamin V. Cohen, who knew Frankfurter from Harvard.

Dulles agreed, but thoroughly alienated Rayburn's Saturday morning subcommittee meeting with unsubstantiated and indiscriminate accusations. Rayburn, the deft, slow-drawling, political manipulator, demanded that the "system live up to its pretensions." But Dulles was so violently opposed to the whole New Deal, he took out his rage on Rayburn, claiming that he "was sponsoring legislation that would undermine our financial system."

While Dulles abandoned the reserved and dignified manner that underlay his talent for smoothing ruffled feathers, Dean concentrated on details. He showed a much firmer grasp of the legislation and its effect on business, staying in Washington to work on the bill while Dulles defiantly returned to New York.

Though most Sullivan & Cromwell lawyers were heavily involved in securities work required by the newly formulated acts (as discussed in Chapter 11), Dulles continued his vendetta against the New Deal. He recruited clients to defy the 1935 legislation designed to break up the public utility holding companies. The act had several unique features giving the SEC wide powers, which Dulles decided to fight in the courts. Its "death sentence provision" in Section 11 gave the utilities three years to cut back into single integrated systems with natural geographic bases. The SEC was to supervise all service and construction contracts and the institution of a uniform accounting system. Never before had a peacetime American government taken such powers to restructure and control an industry.

The head of the new SEC, William O. Douglas, suggested that business people help draft the legislation. "[I] pointed out to them the great financial rewards available to those who took over the job of redesigning and reorganizing these systems and floating the new securities.'' When Dulles urged noncooperation, Douglas commented wryly, ''For once principle transcended greed.''

Dulles gathered together the holding company heads in a conference room at 48 Wall Street and fumed, ''The men who drafted and promoted this law obviously do not know the law or the Constitution. I can assure you that it violates basic constitutional guarantees and that the Supreme Court will strike it down. My strong advice to you gentlemen is to do nothing. Do not comply; resist the law with all your might, and soon everything will be all right.''

It was at this time that Dulles decided to start a litigation group. Previously the firm had preferred the British system of considering itself ''solicitors'' and hiring well-known ''barristers'' like Charles Evans Hughes, Jr., George Medalie, and Judge Joseph Proskauer to appear for it in court. To start its litigation group, Dulles tried to lure Harlan Fiske Stone away from the Supreme Court to return to Sullivan & Cromwell. Though polite and regretful to Dulles, Stone was concerned that ''steadily the best skill and capacity of the profession have been drawn into the exacting and highly specialized service of business and finance. At its best the changed system has brought to the command of the business world loyalty and a superb proficiency and technical skill. At its worst it has made the learned profession of an earlier day the obsequious servant of business, and tainted it with the morals and manners of the market place in its most anti-social manifestations.''

When that attempt failed, Dulles hired a reputable West Coast litigator, John Higgins, who arrived at the firm to fight the new securities legislation. Higgins tried harassing the Justice Department by postponing the substantive issues with a procedural case he took up to the Supreme Court. He wanted to force the attorney general to prosecute all the utility companies at once, rather than let there be a test case to be decided first, which would save time and money.

Higgins established Sullivan & Cromwell's tradition of inundating the other side in paper as part of the tactics that gave the firm a reputation for bullying with limitless resources and tireless work. Higgins was extraordinarily hardworking. He had no regard for his own time or anybody else's. Day and night, weekends and holidays, he was at the office and expected the same of others. Higgins won the procedural case, so the Justice Department was swamped with work, simultaneously filing all the utilities cases, each entrenched in its own intricacies and convolutions.

The firm's extensive litigation against the New Deal created an awkward dilemma for Harlan Fiske Stone, who kept facing Sullivan & Cromwell in Dulles's campaign against the New Deal. Stone was the only Supreme Court justice to occupy every seat based on seniority, before Franklin D. Roosevelt appointed him chief justice in 1941 to cap a twenty-one-year career on the Court.

Stone had a policy of not sitting on Sullivan & Cromwell cases if the client or lawyer arguing the case had been at the firm when he was. But because two other justices also disqualified themselves for their role in New Deal legislation, Stone had to sit on the case brought to break up Harrison Williams's North American Company under the Public Utilities Holding Company Act of 1935, even though he admitted, "As a youngster in the office, I ran errands for [the North American Company]. It was one of the important clients after I became a partner in the firm."

But he helped provide the majority that upheld the law, costing the utility companies millions of dollars and resulting in their breakup. Cyrus Eaton, later famous for entertaining Nikita Khrushchev at his farm in Ohio, who headed Otis & Company, an important Cleveland investment house, concluded, "I came to distrust John Foster Dulles's judgment completely. . . . He was so wrong [about the constitutionality of the Public Utility Holding Co. Act]. . . ."

Sullivan & Cromwell made money when Dulles's constitutional opinion was proved wrong and even more money later by helping break up the public utilities it had put together only the decade before. Now the firm was carving up the empires and creating some of the country's major regional utilities. West Penn Power Company, Allegheny Power Company, and Monongahela Power Company all came out of one client, the American Water Works and Electric Company.

The firm had represented the Union Electric Company of Missouri, a subsidiary of the North American Company, which had bribed practically the whole Missouri legislature. Sullivan & Cromwell then hired a former associate, Walter Lundgren, as independent counsel, and he tried to prevent an SEC grand jury investigation. The firm also hired another independent counsel, Homer Cummings, soon after he resigned as U.S. attorney general in 1939.

Cummings invited Chester Travis Lane, general counsel to the SEC, to lunch at the swank Metropolitan Club in Washington. According to the SEC lawyer, Cummings "pulled the heavy father on me" to deter the grand jury investigation.

Lane refused to cooperate. Sullivan & Cromwell backed away from a confrontation and the SEC investigators uncovered the utility's "slush fund" for paying off legislators. More than half a million dollars had been collected through five sources, including an insurance company, which kicked back premiums, and local lawyers, who kicked back fees.

The company allowed a vice-president, Albert Laun, to make a detailed confession showing the registered letters that went to the Jefferson City legislators with small sums: $50 here, $100, $500 there. "It was that kind of thing," recalled Chester Lane of the SEC. "I don't suppose that any law enforcement official in Missouri would have cared to prosecute the entire state legislature," he concluded.

Laun and Frank Boehm, the first vice-president, went to prison for perjury over their initial testimony. The SEC found "fairly substantial indications" that similar bribery systems were operating in Williams's companies in Iowa and Illinois.

Lane set up a grand jury in Springfield, Illinois, to find out whether the top officials of the North American Company itself and its attorneys, "including Mr. John Foster Dulles," had participated in the scheme. "It is only fair to say," Lane concluded, "that a great deal of pressure was brought on me not to press for the indictment of Dulles. . . . There were visits from lawyers in New York, partners of his whom I knew much better than I knew him, to tell me their own personal views of his integrity and of the impossibility of his having taken part in any such scheme as was involved here."

Lane claimed, "It seemed to me that a man of Mr. Dulles's well-known intelligence and ability could hardly be supposed not to have known what was going on and approve it tacitly." But the grand jury did not return an indictment, which failure Lane somewhat cynically attributed to "Mr. Dulles's charm and the charm of other of his associates" who convinced the prosecutor "that it was impossible that such a nice man could have been involved."

Remarkably, the firm was able to find prospering clients to work with in the 1930s. But it also had its share of bankruptcies, including the celebrated case in 1939 of McKesson & Robbins, a pharmaceutical distributor. The company had been falsifying its books for years by showing fictitious Canadian inventories, which the auditors had never checked. The president, F. Donald Coster, needed the stolen money to pay blackmailers who had known him under his real name, Philip Musica, when he was a "bootlegger, stool-pigeon and jail-bird," as the press put it.

Sullivan & Cromwell associate Malcolm MacIntyre was working late one night when Arthur Dean came in with three of McKesson & Robbins' bonds, which Sidney Weinberg, the senior partner of Goldman, Sachs, had given him. Dean distributed the bonds to three associates, telling them to "petition for involuntary bankruptcy." By midnight they had prepared the papers and found a judge to put the company into bankruptcy.

As the scandal unfolded, Coster shot himself, having earned a place as one of the most notorious swindlers of the century. Sullivan & Cromwell showed complete sangfroid. "The accountants were very embarrassed. Sullivan & Cromwell was very embarrassed too—for twenty-four hours. But then the firm very skillfully switched sides to show that it was representing the directors and that it was as angry with the crooked president as anyone else," recalled Judge Macklin Fleming, at the time a young associate in the firm. "It hadn't hurt them at all."

For Sullivan & Cromwell, the Great Depression was just a healthy bout of deflation, which sent prices lower for young lawyers but gave great investment opportunities to those still flush with cash and a constant stream of business.

8

NAZI CLIENTS

The statement that I have been legal representative of Nazi financial interests is literally without foundation.—JOHN FOSTER DULLES

The Sullivan & Cromwell headquarters in Berlin, a suite at the Esplanade Hotel, was decorated in gold with carved bronze bedsteads and a huge bathroom tiled in marble. Established in 1929, the office was meant to produce prospectuses for bonds. But after the stock market crash, three Sullivan & Cromwell associates spent their time watching the rise of Hitler and waiting for the semiannual visits from John Foster Dulles.

Their surfeit of free time allowed associate Joseph Prendergast to attend street demonstrations, where once, caught between Nazis and Communists, he was beaten up. Norris Darrell, the head of the Berlin office, warned him, "We don't want headlines, 'Sullivan & Cromwell lawyer killed in street brawl.' "

But Dulles continued to disregard the dire conditions in Germany. In 1931, along with George Murnane, he arranged a final effort to prop up the conservative Brüning government with a $285 million loan. To Dulles partisans, it was the "most constructive loan ever made. The aim was to keep Europe afloat."

But even some Germans were reluctant to go along. When Dulles's old friend Schacht heard about the Brüning loan he "was horrified. Once again the German government was endeavoring to conceal the true economic situation by piling up fresh debts abroad." He was especially disturbed by America's high tariffs, which kept Germany indigent.

In January 1930 Schacht quit his position as president of the Reichsbank in protest at the Young Plan, which lowered reparations to a manageable level but extended the payment period to 1988. He retired to his Brandenburg farm to raise pigs and prepare lectures for a speaking tour of the United States. After writing twelve speeches, precise man that he was, he asked his New York agency to arrange a dozen engagements. When the agency was inundated with offers, Schacht made four dozen speeches in fifty days, sometimes as many as three a day.

In October 1930 Schacht appeared with John Foster Dulles at a dinner meeting of the Foreign Policy Association at the Astor Hotel in New York. Speaking from carefully prepared notes, Dulles gave a rosy picture of Germany's economy, contending that reparations represented only 3 percent of the national budget because of economic expansion in the 1920s. Germany's exports finally exceeded Great Britain's and gave the country a net balance of trade favoring exports over imports. Dulles minimized the elections held the month before, when the Nazis had become the second largest party in the Reichstag, and declared that the "difficulties are of a character which are largely psychological and consequently subject to ready reversal."

This theme of the superficiality of Germany's problems echoed Dulles's assessment of the Depression. Dulles told his listeners that "the underlying conditions are far more satisfactory and favorable than they have been during any preceding period of like crisis." Considering the tenor of his remarks, the word "crisis" surprised the crowd of 600, who had come to see Dulles as an international figure with a firsthand knowledge of Europe. They did not know of his own interests in fostering a sanguine view after having just raised $285 million to lend to Germany to prop up the Brüning government.

"My friend Dulles will forgive me if I follow him only in part of his statement," Hjalmar Schacht began as a prelude to shattering Dulles's cozy picture of Germany's recovery. He countered Dulles's numbers with his own to prove that the country was desperately poor and unable to make reparation payments. Germany's export surplus, he contended, was no sign of prosperity; on the contrary, "We are, under home market depression, forced to export and we obtain a surplus only by decreasing our imports." In an appraisal that became more familiar as the decade wore on, Schacht declared, "The middle classes have entirely disappeared. They have become extremely poor, and it is from that part of the country that Hitlerism received its main backing."

Though much of his talk had the impersonality of economic calculations, he dealt emotionally with the question of why Germany accepted the Young Plan, even though he contended it could not afford to pay further reparations. Despite his bullet-headed stiffness, Schacht could recite poetry with great feeling. He asked his audience almost plaintively, "Don't you think it was worthwhile to sign the Young Plan in order to get rid of the occupation? Can you think of a people which still has some self-respect—occupied by foreign troops fifteen years after the war?"

From the speakers' table Dulles stared intently at Schacht and listened to his reproaches with no emotion. He contentedly puffed his cigar, while Schacht won over the audience. Schacht moved from defending Germany to attacking its creditors, declaring ominously, "You must not say that the responsibility is entirely with Germany."

Schacht projected the rigid authority of his military bearing as Dulles slouched in his seat and nervously patted his hair. Dulles acted as though Schacht were merely debating, rather than voicing the threat that Germany was prepared to repudiate its international debts. Schacht impressed the audience by overwhelming Dulles's optimism with a sobering appraisal that they enthusiastically applauded.

The next day *The New York Times* carried the front-page headline

SCHACHT PREDICTS GERMANY WILL STOP PAYING REPARATIONS, reflecting the alarm that Dulles had ignored. If he knew more, he did not appear to let it bother him. In public Schacht said, "All the credits given to Germany by private people certainly Germany . . . will pay," but privately during the same visit, Schacht slyly told George Murnane, "You'll certainly get your money back, Murnane; whether it will be precisely on the dates agreed upon may be open to doubt."

The whole of Schacht's trip was a great success, for though he soon tired of nearly four dozen chicken-and-ice-cream dinners, he got across his point that Germany would not long live up to its international obligations. Americans seemed grateful more than resentful about the warning, which Schacht was glad to provide as a forecast of his future role in Germany.

Usually it is the creditor who puts a stop to a deteriorating financial relationship. This time the debtor sounded the alarm, a role reversal particularly awkward for the far too optimistic Dulles. He made Schacht look disarmingly honest, while Dulles was obviously putting the interests of Americans second to those of the Germans. He had done it since 1924, when he issued the Krupp loan without State Department approval.

Schacht realized that Dulles had more of a position to defend than he, a German who had been—and would be again—responsible for his country's economy. Schacht spoke frankly in a forum meant to teach Americans more about international affairs. Dulles merely made excuses for the superficial, self-serving foreign policy he had devised for his clients and himself.

The relationship between Schacht and Dulles grew in the 1930s to a close collaboration. Schacht recognized the value of an American with his own reasons to promote German interests, and he used Dulles and Sullivan & Cromwell from the time the Nazis took power to the Second World War.

Within months of Schacht's speaking tour in the United States, the European economy collapsed just as he had predicted. On May 11, 1931, Credit Anstalt, an Austrian bank for which Sullivan & Cromwell prepared a share issue in America in 1927, declared bankruptcy, precipitating bankruptcies throughout central Europe. In December

1931 Germany arbitrarily reduced interest on some bonds to 6 percent, which, as a letter from Sullivan & Cromwell to the State Department complained, "is not a mere moratorium postponing the payment of interest or principal but actually reduces the interest rates." Hungary did the same later in the month.

More than $1 billion in bonds that Sullivan & Cromwell had arranged in Europe were merely paper by the time Hitler took power in January 1933. In truth, a series of repayment postponements, moratoriums, and suspensions had rendered them virtually worthless even before Hitler. But it was Hjalmar Schacht, reappointed Reichsbank president in March 1933, who delivered the coup de grâce. At the end of May, he summoned a debtors' conference to meet in Berlin within the week. The American banks that had issued the bonds had to ask for an extra day to make sure their representative, John Foster Dulles, would get there on time. He sailed from New York on the *Bremen* on May 20 and arrived in Berlin on May 29. The firm's three associates in Berlin set Dulles up in a suite at the Esplanade while he hurried off to the classically formal Reichsbank for the opening of the debtors' conference.

Schacht started the meeting with the threat "Consider the problem on the hypothesis that Germany would declare a virtually complete transfer moratorium." Schacht let the delegates, representing most other European countries and the United States, look at books prepared at the Reichsbank to "prove" that Germany could not repay its debts. Throughout the proceedings, Schacht pulled delegates aside for one-on-one pleas.

Three years before, talking to the Foreign Policy Association in New York City, Schacht had complained that Germany had had to cut consumption to boost exports and gain a trade surplus. That surplus prevented Schacht from defaulting on loans to countries that owed Germany money since they could seize German assets in their countries. As a result, all of Europe was saved from a German refusal to service its debts, while the American creditors suffered from Dulles's failure to assure that there was collateral for the loans he had arranged.

Dulles was humiliated by Schacht's deal for all the creditors except Dulles's clients, the long-term dollar bondholders. Dulles reacted angrily to Schacht's "precipitate and drastic action" suspending bond repayments, which, he noted in his only reference to the matter, "came on top of intolerant treatment of the Jews."

Privately Dulles and Schacht met over dinner at the Esplanade Hotel to discuss other business. The results were soon evident when the only debt Dulles represented that continued to be paid was the Brüning loan arranged by George Murnane and Dulles. Murnane boasted later that "by and large we did very well, about ninety percent" on the 1931 loan that had "horrified" Schacht when he first heard about it.

Three days after Dulles and Schacht's dinner meeting, Sullivan & Cromwell mounted a campaign to unseat the management of the Allied Chemical and Dye Corporation, which had defied the German-led chemical cartel and secretly built a nitrogen factory in Hopewell, Virginia. It more than quintupled American nitrate exports from 28,630 tons in 1930 to 185,000 tons in 1933 and infuriated Allied's major stockholder, Solvay & Cie., the Belgian company that also owned part of the cartel leader, the notorious German I. G. Farbenindustrie. (I. G. Farben later ran part of the Auschwitz concentration camp as a private chemical factory.)

Sullivan & Cromwell had the perfect pretext for mounting a proxy fight against Allied because the New York Stock Exchange was in the middle of an effort to force more information out of the company. The company president, Orlando F. Weber, justified his secrecy as a means of keeping information from "those foreign-subsidized cartels which are now engaged in a bitter struggle with your Company in the markets of the world."

Sullivan & Cromwell associate Rogers Lamont, who had worked in the firm's Berlin office, was assigned to be "secretary" of the "Committee for Allied Chemical and Dye Corporation." In a letter to Allied shareholders he claimed to represent the "right of stockholders to receive adequate company reports." But one shareholder, James W. Gerard, voiced the concern of many when he contended, "Much as I deplore the attitude of the company in withholding information from its stockholders, I would deplore even more a successful campaign of a committee which might result in the election to the board of directors of interests representing a large foreign competitor."

On behalf of Solvay's 20 percent holding in Allied, Sullivan &

Cromwell got a resolution to convene a special shareholders' meeting to elect four new board members. When Weber and Allied's management agreed to provide more information, Lamont dropped the demand for the special meeting and an uneasy truce prevailed for the three years until the irascible Weber retired.

His successor, H. F. Atherton, proved more pliant. In 1936 George Murnane was elected to Allied's board of directors; the company joined a chemical cartel with I. G. Farben, Imperial Chemical Industries, and Solvay. Sullivan & Cromwell became the company counsel.

Sullivan & Cromwell thrived on its cartels and collusion with the new Nazi regime. On August 2, 1933, the day that President Paul von Hindenburg died and Hitler seized the presidency of Germany, Schacht became economics minister as well as president of the Reichsbank. Though Hitler did not like the outspoken Schacht, he recognized his economic genius and made him responsible for rearming the country. Hitler also knew that Schacht's apparent independence made him invaluable as a representative to the outside world. He seemed to be an anti-Nazi Nazi, capable of reassuring foreigners who either were gullible or wanted an excuse for justifying their relations with the Hitler regime.

Schacht could make the worst extremes of the Nazi government palatable. He never denied the persecution of the Jews but claimed that his ministry should be a "tower of justice."

Dulles celebrated Schacht's appointment as economics minister by promoting a crucial cartel arrangement with Inco, the International Nickel Company. Without Dulles, Germany would have lacked any negotiating strength with Inco, which controlled the world's supply of nickel, a crucial ingredient in stainless steel and armor plate. Dulles played up I. G. Farben's patent for an efficient method of extracting nickel from ore. The cartel's control of the ore meant that efficient extraction was irrelevant, but Dulles convinced Inco that I. G. Farben could get nickel from previously unusable ore.

He spent many hours in the 1930s negotiating with I. G. Farben officials in his New York office. The original agreement in 1934 cut the Nazis in on Inco's ore. In return for an exclusive right to share I. G.

Farben's patent, Inco guaranteed to supply unrefined nickel to the German company, and I. G. Farben promised to sell refined nickel "through distributing organizations utilized by Inco, Ltd . . . at prices fixed by Inco Ltd."

In 1937 Inco expanded its agreement with I. G. Farben because the Germans "proposed to erect an additional refinery." Dulles helped inflate the Germans' empty threat. A supplemental agreement increased I. G. Farben's quota of unrefined ore for domestic use so that it clearly had no purpose other than to let Hitler stockpile weapons. Under the agreement, moreover, Inco officials were "to cooperate with the German authorities in developing the use of nickel in Germany," according to a United States government complaint against Inco.

Dulles's influence over Inco went far beyond the normal lawyer-client relationship. He was a director and member of the executive committee. Since William Nelson Cromwell had organized the company in 1902, a steady stream of Sullivan & Cromwell lawyers had become company executives. Among the most prominent was Henry S. Wingate, who, not coincidentally, joined Inco in 1935 in the midst of the machinations with I. G. Farben. Wingate rose from assistant to the president to chief executive officer and chairman of the board. He, in turn, hired a phalanx of Sullivan & Cromwell lawyers as corporate vice-presidents and secretaries, making Inco one of the firm's very closest clients.

Dulles worked with the company throughout the interwar period, resisting Canadian and British government efforts to curtail the shipment of nickel for military use. In a *Foreign Affairs* article, Dulles had argued that the United States always supported free movement in arms and led the assault on Canada's effort to restrict the export of nickel as a strategic war material. The Canadian government, yielding to the nickel company's influence, accepted the contention that "it would be impossible to control the ultimate destination of the material." The company argued that Germany, Italy, and Japan were buying only a little more than a $1 million worth, while ignoring how much nickel was going to them through intermediaries. Legislation prohibiting Canadian export of nickel was never enacted, and Dulles assured the Germans of a steady supply of nickel.

Disdaining the perceived national interest, Dulles justified his cartel-making to Lord McGowan, chairman of Imperial Chemical Industries and a fellow cartel participant. ''The word 'cartel' has here assumed the stigma of a bogeyman which the politicians are constantly attacking. The fact of the matter is that most of these politicians are highly insular and nationalistic and because the political organization of the world has under such influence been so backward, business people who have had to cope realistically with international problems have had to find ways for getting through and around stupid political barriers.''

As international monopolies, cartels, in Dulles's mind, were one step better than the domestic monopolies that Sullivan & Cromwell had always promoted. The only drawback, but a major one, was that the Germans insisted on controlling the cartels; still, Dulles helped them achieve their goal.

Even more insidious than the major cartel arrangements were the small everyday interactions that were unnoticed yet infiltrated and compromised a variety of American interests. In 1933, for example, Dulles helped Berlin attorney Heinrich F. Albert reschedule $17 million of bonds for the North German Lloyd shipping company, even though Sullivan & Cromwell had represented the bondholders in the initial offering in 1927.

While European bonds were being repaid on schedule, Dulles secured an agreement to lower the interest on the dollar-denominated North German Lloyd bonds by 50 percent, from 6 to 4 percent, a reduction applied retroactively by six months. Future repayments depended on earnings, but as Dulles noted privately to Schacht, ''there is, of course, always considerable latitude in the Company in calculating the existence of earnings.'' Dulles mentioned to Schacht that the negotiation was ''most difficult'' because ''the leading bankers, Kuhn, Loeb & Co., are somewhat prejudiced in their attitude toward Germany.''

Dulles was proud to commend this ''plan for radically reducing fixed bond interest'' to Schacht because ''there will, I think, be far more ready acceptance of the bondholders as a whole of the general regime established by the Reichsbank.''

Dulles also tried to mislead the State Department about the nationality of the Possehl Works in Poland, in which his client the Overseas Securities Company held a 20 percent stake. Dulles told the State Department, "we are advised . . . that Possehl was established in 1920 as a Russian company for the manufacture of scythes." The State Department, however, learned through confidential sources in Warsaw that "the consortium now owning the shares is merely a blind under which the German Government has attempted to conceal its real interest in the factory; and that the Montan A.G., a Swiss company which dealt in the shares of the factory after the war and eventually distributed them to the present holders, was the usual agency of the German Government in such transactions." When Dulles pressed the State Department to protect Possehl from Polish government confiscation for being German, the department wanted more explicit information, but, "over the space of several years, Dulles proved reluctant to provide the State Department with this information."

The Germans were far more successful in using Dulles than he was in using them. In the 1930s one of the wealthiest Czech families, the Petschecks, wanted to sell its Silesian coal mines before they were seized by the Nazis. Dulles had known the Petscheks since his trading efforts in the early 1920s and he had visited them in their elegant Prague home, which after World War II became the Soviet embassy (another of their houses became the American embassy).

Dulles arranged for George Murnane to "buy" the mines to hide the Petscheks' ownership and then offer them to Schacht. But the Nazi economics minister asked Murnane, "Why should I buy them now when I can confiscate them later?" When Murnane explained that *he* owned the mines, Schacht bought them, and Murnane made a commission of about $100,000. But the American government charged him a huge tax based on the sale price (as though he really did own them) and Murnane had to liquidate assets to pay it.

Despite Dulles's expensive miscalculation, Murnane blamed the United States secretary of the treasury, Henry Morgenthau, for the loss. Fifty years later, his son, George Murnane, Jr., became furious at the mention of Morgenthau, whom he compared with Hitler in being a dictator and a hindrance to the effort to help Europeans like the Petscheks.

After arranging the mine sale for the Petscheks, Dulles became a director of the Consolidated Silesian Steel Company. Its sole asset was a one-third interest in Poland's largest industrial concern, the Upper Silesian Coal and Steel Company. After the removal of the Petscheks, two thirds of the company was owned by one of Hitler's main business supporters, Friedrich Flick, who was ultimately tried as a war criminal at Nüremberg. Through the coal interests, Dulles established ties to Flick, an example of the Sullivan & Cromwell practice of retaining clients through changes in ownership, whoever the buyers and sellers were.

Dulles was not alone in pursuing his European activities. Though most members of the firm had stopped commuting to Europe, and the Paris office no longer had a partner in charge after 1932 (when Robert Olds died unexpectedly at the age of fifty-seven), the firm maintained its European offices, to which Dulles's brother, Allen, increasingly became the emissary from New York.

After joining the firm in 1926 Allen was made a partner in the remarkably short time of four years. He became in many respects his brother's eyes and ears around the world, a role that earned him the nickname "the little minister." He was envied but not resented because he came to Sullivan & Cromwell with such a rich and useful background. He had German contacts going back to his State Department posting in Berlin in the 1920s, when he introduced Foster to Hjalmar Schacht. It was a source of permanent envy to his older brother that Allen had met Hitler but Foster never did.

While Foster Dulles met foreigners in conference table settings that bordered on state visits, Allen was a practical problem-solver with a canny knowledge of the world. Even in the State Department he was known as a fixer, which was a lucrative reputation for a lawyer to take to Sullivan & Cromwell.

His talents had many applications. The Mellon family hired him, for example, to convince the Colombian government not to confiscate its $1.5 million investment in the rich oil and mineral fields of the Barco concession. He succeeded by helping to rig the 1932 Colombian presidential election of a candidate who flew to New York to pick up a $1 million personal loan and who recognized the Mellons' Barco claims as soon as he was elected. Allen Dulles did not know how much to charge his client until he was in a plane that suddenly plunged 2,400 feet. When the plane stabilized, Allen ordered a scotch and decided on $2,400 as the fee.

Allen regularly went to Paris where he flattered and indulged Cromwell in place of Foster, who was far too busy to spend time with the old man. He arranged to take Cromwell and two women to lunch at the Trianon Palace in Versailles, where they "gave the girls a good time" and stopped for races at Longchamps on the way home. He reported back to Foster that Cromwell "hasn't touched a drop for weeks . . . and was not only in fine mental shape but seemed delighted with the way the Paris office was going."

A committed womanizer, Allen Dulles had become a lawyer to assuage his guilt over his affairs by buying jewels for his wife, or so the Sullivan & Cromwell scuttlebutt had it. She found out about them from her husband himself, who wrote her during one European visit, "I dined with the Shoops and played bridge. The fourth was an attractive (but not beautiful) Irish-French female whom I took to Scheherazade where we stayed until the early hours as usual—somewhat to the annoyance of her husband, I learned, as he was not in on the party. Her name is 'Gregoire.' "

Amidst the socializing, there was plenty of work. W. Averell Harriman, then a banker, hired Sullivan & Cromwell for his pet project: financing the electrification of Poland. Harriman had agents in Poland, but Norris Darrell, the head of the Sullivan & Cromwell office in Berlin, traveled there twice a month to negotiate the terms and help pass the necessary legislation. Though Harriman had nothing but contempt for Dulles personally, Sullivan & Cromwell was the perfect choice for this work because Dulles had negotiated the loan that stabilized the Polish currency in 1927. As part of that work Dulles created a Polish federal reserve system for the first public bond issue ever made in the country. For relaxation he played golf in Poland on a course that was a cow pasture in which the farmer held the flag over holes in the ground. But Darrell's visits to Poland ceased when he returned to New York in the summer of 1930 and General Jozef Pilsudski, the Polish premier, refused to let

Harriman control such an important domestic industry, making a deal with the French instead.

Sullivan & Cromwell also represented American holders of $50 million in Kreuger & Toll bonds that defaulted with Swedish match king Ivar Kreuger's suicide in 1932. Negotiations to obtain the collateral backing the bonds followed a tortuous path. Creditors of Kreuger's operating company, the Swedish Match Company, did not want to share their assets with the bondholders, and the Swedish government objected to Swedish assets' being dispersed abroad. Sullivan & Cromwell associates trekked up to Stockholm from Berlin to attend negotiations, until Dulles paid former American peace negotiator Norman Davis $75,000 to represent the American bondholders (while Sullivan & Cromwell earned $540,000).

The negotiations ended in New York in April 1935 when the bondholders got only $2.5 million in settlement of more than $100 million in bonds from poor central European governments like Latvia and Serbia to which Kreuger lent money in exchange for getting the local match monopoly. He then used those bonds to back his own. Candler Cobb, the persuasive and suave American who had placed millions of dollars of bonds for Sullivan & Cromwell in the 1920s, spent the 1930s trying to collect on them. He continued to work out of the Paris office, where the debtors met to discuss their obligations. He relied on the advice of Cromwell, who coached him, "You cannot get money out of an unwilling debtor, and the way to make the debtor willing is to come down in your demands to what you are convinced is his capacity to pay."

With Cromwell peering over his shoulder, Cobb made "the fatal mistake of asking [the Romanians] for some figures on their tobacco monopoly, having in mind the old idea of capacity to pay and they'd say, 'Oh, we haven't got those figures but if you want them . . . we'll go back to Bucharest and get them.' So we'd all adjourn for a couple of months while they went back to Bucharest to get those figures," Cobb related.

After getting an agreement on the debts in Romania, Cobb went to Yugoslavia to ask the head of the national bank "to consider if Yugoslavia couldn't do the same." The banker answered, "The day you get a payment from Romania, let me know."

The rest of the Kreuger & Toll business switched to America in April 1936, when Dulles started Kreutoll Realization, an American company that bought the bonds to hold until repayment. The wait lasted to the 1980s, when Sullivan & Cromwell partners continued to have Hungarian land reform bonds. In 1985 George Murnane, Jr., whose father had originally issued the Kreuger & Toll bonds was still holding on to his certificates.

Once the Nazis came to power in 1933 cables from Sullivan & Cromwell's Berlin office bore the salutation "Heil Hitler." It was demanded by German regulations, but it still shocked lawyers like Lauson Stone who received the correspondence in New York. Dulles's ties to the Nazis were making his partners uneasy. There were the frequent appointments with representatives of I. G. Farben and Solvay et Cie. They were perfectly civilized businessmen, Dulles would say. Others were not sure, even though the visitors were polite and deferential to the secretary, who came down to escort them up the steps to Dulles's office at the head of the staircase. To any outsider, they were just another name in a lawyer's appointment book, but their growing familiarity with the office routine was a reminder of Dulles's cooperation with the Nazi-run cartels in Europe.

By 1934 Dulles was publicly supporting Hitler with a philosophy that rationalized Nazi brutality as being the spontaneous outbursts of an energetic people. He wrote a long article, "The Road to Peace," for the *Atlantic Monthly* of October 1935 that began with the ridiculous fatalistic claim that "the changes which we recognize to be inevitable over a hundred years must begin sometime." He excused Germany's secret rearmament because "Germany, by unilateral action, has now taken back her freedom of action."

Knowing what he did about Nazi agreements with Inco and German weapons stockpiling, Dulles was purposely misleading when he maintained, "If other countries like Germany, Japan, and Italy adhere only reluctantly if at all to such projects [for perpetual peace], it is not because these nations are inherently warlike or bloodthirsty. They too want peace, but they undoubtedly feel within themselves potentialities which are repressed and they desire to keep open the avenues of change,"as though Hitler were a misunderstood progressive.

To most people, Dulles's article was just another part of his abject appeasement of the Axis powers in a campaign that culminated in his 1939 book *War, Peace, and Change*. His law partners, however, were shocked that he could so easily disregard law and international treaties to justify Nazi repression he saw more intimately than most. Cromwell chided Dulles: "You will be the first to recognize the inevitable application of this principle by nations for revision of territorial expansion and treaty provisions—as in the cases of Germany, Japan, Italy, Hungary, Austria, etc. Doubtless your article will be quoted in support of such national claims."

Even if Dulles acted as though German companies were like other clients, the Sullivan & Cromwell Berlin office remained a glaring admission of the firm's support for Hitler. It had little use, but Dulles did not want to give it up. He would not be cowed by his partners' qualms.

In June 1935 Allen took a whirlwind tour of Europe, visiting London and Budapest as well as Berlin in a pioneering *Clipper* commercial flight. He was met at the Berlin airport by Joseph Grazier of the Sullivan & Cromwell office and then spent a day seeing some foreign ministry and embassy people and "our lawyer friends Albert, Westrick, etc."

When he returned home Allen told his brother to get rid of the Berlin office. It was an awkward time, Foster said, because Heinrich Albert's son, Christian, was clerking at Sullivan & Cromwell in New York.

It was hard for Allen to fight his brother. After all, Allen would not even have been at Sullivan & Cromwell except for Foster's encouragement and sponsorship. And their family ties went deep. Their father, on his deathbed, had made all the children take an oath accepting Foster as the head of the family. In the late 1940s Allen turned down an offer from the Democratic Truman administration to be the American ambassador to France to avoid embarrassing Foster, who would have become secretary of state in a Republican Dewey administration.

But this was not just a dispute between brothers. It entailed the future of the firm. Louis Auchincloss, who knew both brothers, considered Allen cold and calculating, despite his apparent warmth, while Foster was much more capable of kindness despite his formidable reserve. The difference, according to Auchincloss, was that Allen could anticipate others' reactions and Foster could not, a difference apparent in the conflict over Sullivan & Cromwell's Berlin office.

When Allen got nowhere privately with Foster, he brought the subject before a partners' meeting. Foster was stunned by the affront of his partners' objection. He resisted, using the loss of potential profits to defend his position. Allen argued that the firm "would suffer more if they *didn't* abandon" the Berlin office. "You couldn't practice law there," he recounted. "People came to you asking how to evade the law, not how to respect the law. When that happens, you can't be much of a lawyer."

Arthur Dean added, "In view of the fact that Edward Green, Eustace Seligman and Art Jaretzki, Jr., were Jews, it would seem better to me if we didn't represent in any way any German clients."

"Finally," one version has it, Foster Dulles "capitulated, 'in tears.' "

No partners' meeting has ever been so acrimonious and divisive—or so subject to revision after the fact. Arthur Dean insisted later, "There was no argument, no confrontation, no threat to take action if Foster didn't agree." Foster Dulles soon obfuscated the date of the office's actual closing—conveniently moving it back to 1934.

The rebuff over the Berlin office did not change Foster Dulles's attitudes or *modus operandi*. The firm's European business continued. Candler Cobb was still chasing after debts in central Europe. "I got the story from someone in the Hungarian Foreign Office," Cobb proudly wrote Foster Dulles in 1936, "that I collected more money from Hungary than any other creditor. The strange part of it was that the Hungarians rather liked it."

Succumbing to a revolt led by his brother did not harm Foster's leadership. In fact, the two brothers recognized the value of Allen's insurrection in limiting the repercussions so that the office returned to normal and the defeat was passed over as almost a display of democracy.

Foster soon came to see his brother's value as a safety valve. At the next dinner for partners and associates of the firm, Allen had the unpleasant task of discussing the firm's decade of disastrous foreign loans, a policy pursued with full enthusiasm by Foster. But Allen could speak about it impersonally since he had become a partner in 1930, after it was virtually over.

In the cozy clubhouse atmosphere of the Down Town Association next to the firm's office on Wall Street, Allen Dulles provided the excuses to deflect criticism of the firm's support of lending in Europe. In better times, Arthur Dean would raise the good-natured toast "Thank God the sun has set and the statute of limitations run out on another one of my errors." Allen Dulles would have liked to say the same. In fact, he had to admit, the sun had not yet set on the loans the firm had promoted.

He detailed Sullivan & Cromwell's work on ninety-four foreign securities issues from 1924 to 1931, involving $1.15 billion, mostly bond issues but also American shares of foreign companies. The "fact that many [are] in default [is] no reflection on [the] legal work involved. [The firm provided the] finest legal protection. [There is] no safeguard against economic conditions such as during the last few years," he said. "Generally foreign held loans [are the first to be defaulted] since maintenance of internal credit [is] essential to continued national economy."

He did admit that the firm "permitted debt to pile up too fast and too high and took bad moral risk." He came closest to criticizing his brother when he conceded in a lecturing tone, "bonds of foreign borrower[s] are only payable out of excess revenues of debtors after meeting his internal costs of administration and political exigencies; default has moral and not legal consequence[s] as the obligor is without effective remedy."

The mounted antlers and rustic wooden walls of the Down Town Association were an appropriate setting for this demonstration of the hunters' fear of becoming the hunted. "In the foreign bond situation," Allen Dulles conceded, "there was the added risk from currency problems and inability to transfer [payments to bondholders]; in fact, the foreign bond, except in being a promise to pay [a] certain amount of money, has few of the attributes of a bond."

Never had a Sullivan & Cromwell Society dinner sounded so much like a law school class. "In future foreign financing [the] bare pledge of revenues should be eliminated." He reminded the group of the "desirability of agreement among lenders for equal treatment," something Foster Dulles had failed to get from Schacht.

Despite the continuing flow of drink and supply of cigars, the lawyers found the speech sobering. It came as a blow. Something that was reliable about the firm, its judgment, perhaps even its integrity, had been lost. They walked out in the cold night of New York, realizing that the firm had glided through the deepening crisis of its clients and the country without a scratch. It had almost escaped without ever acknowledging its role in the devastating loss of $10 *billion* caused by irresponsible foreign lending.

Allen Dulles gave another, similar speech two years later about $250 million in South American loans. He reiterated that "lawyers cannot set up [in] bond issues proof against economic disaster or political revolutions." He again admitted as the "chief hindsight criticism [an] emphasis on pledges which [are] of little value unless collected by outside agents." This time he had suggestions about getting government support and establishing a fund in prosperous years to guarantee repayment. But he confined his remarks to the lawyers present, unprepared to risk drawing public attention to Sullivan & Cromwell's role in the economic debacle of the 1930s.

If the firm had put its decade-long German lending policy behind it, Foster Dulles's collaboration with the Hitler government was far from over. His actions became only more discreet and secretive.

Sullivan & Cromwell represented I. G. Farben's biggest subsidiary in the Western Hemisphere, the General Aniline & Film Corporation, which had been set up originally as the American I. G. Corporation. With assets by the mid-1940s of $80 million, it was among the largest dyestuffs and film manufacturers in the country.

The company tried to evade confiscation as enemy property during the war by having its stock held by I. G. Chemie of Basel, Switzerland. Investigators in the United States determined that Chemie was in fact controlled by I. G. Farben in Germany, and during World War II President Roosevelt ordered its stock seized by the Alien Property Custodian. "The facts regarding the control of Chemie were, however, cloaked in the greatest of secrecy," a government investigation reported, "and the Swiss have refused to concede that the company was in fact controlled by Farben.'' Throughout the war, ''the fog around the ownership of General Aniline was never dissipated.''

According to Chester T. Lane, the general counsel of the SEC in the 1930s, Sullivan & Cromwell's closest and most brazen dealing with the Nazis occurred in 1938. Lane recalled: ''The German government, acting through its representatives here, its financial counselors and its attorneys, who, as I remember, were Sullivan and Cromwell, filed a registration statement with us looking towards the refunding of many of its securities held in the United States. It was obviously designed as a public relations gesture.'' To deter the Germans, Lane required Hitler's registration statement ''to give us a complete blueprint of his economy, including all its indirect assessments through party dues, its indirect taxes, and its whole financial structure.''

Ultimately the Germans withdrew the effort, barely leaving a trace behind, but Lane concluded: ''If Hitler had succeeded in establishing a new refunding issue and had met its terms, it would have meant that we would have had large numbers of individual investors in this country, as well as large numbers of institutional investors, whose personal interests would have depended, to the extent of their holdings, upon the maintenance of the solvency of Hitler's government and on maintenance of satisfactory relations between the United States and Nazi Germany, which might have had a very profound effect on our attitude after Hitler started in Poland in 1939.''

On the rare occasions when his activities became public, Dulles hid behind clients, acting as if he was just doing them favors. He helped organize the America First campaign to keep the country out of European entanglements for a banking client, Edwin S. Webster, Jr., a partner of Kidder, Peabody. It was merely a courtesy, Dulles claimed, even though on November 5, 1941, a month before Pearl Harbor, Dulles donated $500 to America First and Janet Dulles pledged to match another donor's large gift. Webster effusively thanked Janet Dulles for helping pay the cost of a rally honoring Charles A. Lindbergh, a major America First proponent.

When criticized for contributing to such a cause, Dulles said it was his wife's money, though she had never shown any independence of mind before (or after). Dulles's partner Arthur Dean was more candid about the firm's role in America First. Webster had originally approached Dean to set up the organization in New York. When Dean refused, Webster got Dulles to have a young lawyer in the office draw up the papers to establish the New York chapter of America First. Dean was furious and remembered telling Dulles, "It was from his standpoint a tragic mistake, and I thought from Sullivan & Cromwell's standpoint it was something we ought to get out of the office and get out fast." Ultimately, Dulles agreed and told Dean, "I think I was wrong to have allowed it to be incorporated in the office." Later Dulles denied having had any contact with the organization.

To the degree that America First was isolationist, Dulles legitimately claimed that he did not agree with it. He remained a staunch internationalist, but his extensive dealings in Europe did not improve his judgment, as when he wrote in 1937, "One may disagree, as I do, with many of Hitler's policies and methods, but . . . [Mussolini and Italy] involve more serious threats to the general peace than any act of Hitler's."

In contrast, Allen Dulles bridled at his brother's convoluted defense of Hitler. To his wife, Clover, he referred to "those mad people in control in Germany" and recalled that when he had met Hitler in the spring of 1933, Hitler was already making ominous threats about Poland. Allen Dulles ran unsuccessfully for Congress in 1938 on a platform of trying to get America prepared to face up to the Nazis. While Foster was formulating his thoughts in *War, Peace, and Change* about the "excessive external restraints [that] have created unsound internal conditions" to justify the repression in Germany, Italy and Japan, Allen Dulles collaborated with Hamilton Armstrong, the editor of *Foreign Affairs*, in writing two books defending Britain and France: *Can We Be Neutral?* in 1936 and *Can America Stay Neutral?* in 1939.

Soon after the first collaboration Armstrong discovered that his wife, Helen, was having an affair with columnist Walter Lippmann. Allen Dulles discreetly arranged for the Armstrongs' divorce in Nevada, writing to a Reno attorney that his client Armstrong "was a writer of note and editor of a non-commercial publication so we hope you could keep the fees on an economical basis." The Nevada lawyer charged $200.

The brothers' political disagreements ultimately affected their personal relations. ''They had heated debates, and there were tensions about it,'' Avery Dulles recalled, ''because they were both writing letters to *The New York Times* and were often confused when something Allie said was attributed to Foster, or vice versa.''

Still, as part of his responsibilities at Sullivan & Cromwell, Allen Dulles continued to do business with the Germans. In 1937 he joined the board of directors of J. Henry Schroder Bank, the American subsidiary of the London bank that *Time* magazine in 1939 called ''an economic booster of the Rome-Berlin Axis.'' In 1938 and 1939 he tried to help the Germans buy out American Potash and Chemical Corp., a company that had developed a way to extract potash from bauxite, a plentiful mineral in America. When the effort failed, Hitler lost a monopoly on potash, a crucial component of glass, fertilizer, and photography. The price of the mineral plummeted, and Germany was deprived of a major source of hard currency in the period immediately prior to World War II.

In the summer of 1938, Foster Dulles represented the Bank of Spain in its effort to collect $15 million on behalf of the Franco government from the Federal Reserve Bank. The case revolved around the question of whether the anti-Franco Barcelona bank could sell its holdings of bullion independent of the Spanish central bank. He prepared his case all summer, reading it over and asking for comments from his family, including his teenage children. Though Dulles was fifty years old, it was the first case he had ever argued in court. Sullivan & Cromwell lawyers treated it as a major event, watching Dulles face his friend Henry L. Stimson, the former secretary of state who represented the Federal Reserve.

Even Dulles's children showed up to see their father in action. Avery, a college student, was surprised that his usually meticulously dressed father had his shirttails sticking out of his trousers as he spoke to the judge with his back to the gallery. He also criticized his father's courtroom manner: ''His speaking ability could be improved. It all seemed legalese and his general manner of speaking was not impressive on that occasion.'' A Sullivan & Cromwell associate was more blunt: ''It was a big disappointment. Dulles droned for twenty or thirty minutes, and what he said was incomprehensible.''

Dulles established that the anti-Franco Barcelona government had no right to sell the bullion to the Federal Reserve Bank, but ''the court said we can't go behind the principles of international comity,'' noted Glen McDaniel, a Sullivan & Cromwell associate who acted as Dulles's assistant on the case. ''It was similar to sovereign immunity. So you just lost your money.'' McDaniel admired Dulles because he ''fought and fought and fought. Even when the ship was going down''—the firm appealed unsuccessfully to the Supreme Court—''he never stopped fighting.''

In a three-way dinner debate at the Economics Club in March 1939, Dulles boldly asserted, ''Only hysteria entertains the idea that Germany, Italy or Japan contemplates war upon us.'' Standing between the isolationist, Senator Burton K. Wheeler, and the interventionist, a banker named James Warburg, Dulles ''came down flatly on Wheeler's side,'' Warburg remembered. He ''took a curious kind of metaphysical position that as we were incapable of making a decent peace, we mustn't get involved in a war because we would just make a mess of the peace again.'' Warburg concluded, ''Dulles has been called an elder statesmen, but I think he's elder without being a statesman.''

Wendell Willkie, the Republican presidential candidate in 1940, told Dulles, ''Foster, that is the most persuasive speech on the wrong side of a subject I ever heard.''

When Hitler's *Blitzkrieg* overran Poland on September 1, 1939, to start World War II, Dulles's long defense of Hitler crumbled along with the once beautiful buildings on the fabled Danzig waterfront. Dulles had to abandon the remarkable self-deception that Germany did not threaten world peace and retreat to his fallback argument that the Axis could not help being aggressors after the suffering caused by the Treaty of Versailles following World War I.

This position sounded like blaming the victims for Germany's attacks, as a disillusioned Eustace Seligman told Dulles in a memo in October 1939. Such wishful thinking was finally shattered when the war began and Seligman wrote Dulles, you ''apparently take the view that Germany's position is morally superior to that of the Allies.'' Seligman, who often argued by example, pointed out how ludicrous

Dulles's excuses for Hitler had become. ''A fair analogy is a man who is in a poker game and who finds that he has been cheated of $100 by marked cards. He immediately grabs $100 from the pot and then shoots all the players and also the bystanders.'' (The full text of Seligman's memo appears as Appendix 2.)

Rogers Lamont, who was closely associated with the firm's German policy, having worked in the Berlin office and eased Allied Chemical into the I. G. Farben chemical cartel, resigned his partnership, went to Canada, and volunteered for the British Army. He fought with the British troops retreating toward Dunkirk; on May 27, 1940, while observing enemy artillery fire from an armored car, he was killed at close range by a German tank shell.

He was the first American officer to die in the war and Sullivan & Cromwell's only casualty in two world wars. Lamont's colonel reported that he was ''extremely daring and cool-headed in action.'' The firm established a scholarship at Princeton that is still awarded annually ''to that member of the sophomore or junior class who has maintained good scholastic standing and in addition has exhibited qualities which characterized the life'' of Rogers Lamont.

Why Lamont resigned from the firm to fight the war will never be known. Heinrich Albert, whom the Nazis chose in 1936 to head the Ford Motor Company in Germany after Albert & Westrick was disbanded with the loss of Sullivan & Cromwell business, wrote Dulles in December 1939, ''Is it true that Lamont has gone as volonteer [*sic*] to England in order to fight us? I have not grown old without an understanding for the most unbelievable actions of men but I am sorry because I liked him and I am afraid he would not have done that if he would not hate Germany very much notwithstanding the good friends he has got here [*sic*].''

To Albert and Dulles, who waited six months to announce Lamont's death, it seemed a betrayal of a long and close relationship with the Germans. But Lamont, who had been particularly happy in Berlin because of his love of Wagner and beer-hall revelry, was well aware of the Nazi policies and intentions that had captured Germany. As a member of Sullivan & Cromwell he had known more than most Americans about the Nazi schemes for nearly a decade.

And where Dulles wanted to appease them, Lamont could not stomach them.

To Joe Prendergast, who had known Lamont at Princeton and worked with him in Berlin before sharing a house with him in New York, Lamont's fervor about the war had resulted from disappointment in his partnership, "which was probably not all that it was cracked up to be." It is possible that Lamont wanted to assuage the guilt he felt about the role he and the firm played before the war. If so, his sacrifice was a high price to pay to camouflage John Foster Dulles's Nazi collaboration.

9

THE DULLES WAR MACHINE

I am generally accused of being too sympathetic to Germany.—JOHN FOSTER DULLES

John Foster Dulles knew war was coming to America. In 1940 the Robert Bosch Company of Stuttgart suspended licensing payments from its subsidiaries in "any country of the Western hemisphere with which Germany might in the meantime be at war." Because Dulles represented American Bosch, he knew the Germans were anticipating war with America.

Dulles began to hedge his bets. He had helped Thomas Childs, an associate in the Paris office in 1937 and 1938, get a job as general counsel to the British Purchasing Commission. When the Nazis were marching into Paris, Childs arranged for the British to take over the French contracts to buy American arms and planes. The British purchasing commissioner, Arthur Purvis, got authorization from the permanent head of the British treasury to buy any French equipment or obligations in America. Purvis asked Childs if the telegraphed authorization was sufficient to satisfy American contractors. Childs said yes but offered to check his answer with Dulles, who was asleep at his retreat in Cold Spring Harbor. "The call woke Foster up, but he was alert and agreed to come right over, arriving after midnight," Childs recalled. Dulles concurred, and with signatures in hand Childs spent the next day frantically switching the deals and getting the French to use up their money before the Nazis got it—or Washington confiscated it. Childs gave Dulles credit for getting the telegram accepted, even though they had no legal standing, as both lawyers knew.

When in 1940 the British were forced to sell their American holdings to raise money to pay for armaments, Childs wanted to use Sullivan & Cromwell to represent the British government. Childs mentioned that Dulles had recently been in the newspapers as having met with Hitler's American representative, Gerhard Westrick (former partner in Albert & Westrick). Westrick had come to America in 1940, as Childs put it, "to declare blindly that the war was over—there was nothing more to fight about—let's get back to normal relations."

Westrick, who was run out of the country, brought into disrepute the people willing to meet with him. Childs claimed Westrick "called uninvited on Foster Dulles, the press tailed Westrick and made headlines of the event." In fact, Dulles met willingly with Westrick, as did Dulles's son Avery, then a Harvard undergraduate, who remembered, "I saw him at his suite at the Plaza. He said it would be an absolute disaster if the phony war led into real war and he was hoping to arrive at a peaceful settlement."

The British, Childs reported with regret, "recalled the Westrick ploy then, and thought it serious enough to turn away from Sullivan & Cromwell."

When the Japanese attacked Pearl Harbor, Dulles had to create firm policy about the lawyers who left to fight. Would they be promised places on their return? He spent two days deliberating, writing draft after draft of his memo, trying to mollify the lawyers, though the message was clear. "[We] cannot assure . . . at the termination of their government service [that associates will] resume their relationship with us where they left off.'' The patriotic firms had no problem saluting the boys off to war with a promise of jobs when they got back.

At Sullivan & Cromwell the associates had to ''envy the crippled,'' Glen McDaniel admitted, because they had not lost their jobs. Dulles's decision was deeply resented. Franklin O. Canfield, who worked for Sullivan & Cromwell in Paris, said Dulles ''had the attitude of an American Firster.'' Still, four partners and thirty-five associates—more than half the firm's sixty-six lawyers—enlisted. They served honorably on all fronts, usually as officers and often for some branch of intelligence. Sullivan & Cromwell was, despite Dulles, a badge of honor that earned them places at the heart of the war.

Inzer Wyatt, a young litigation partner, went to Bletchley Park, England, to learn about Ultra, the penetration of the German and Japanese secret codes. He headed the group responsible for keeping the secrets while applying the information to the China-Burma-India theater. He picked Sullivan & Cromwell lawyers for the delicate task, which included lieutenants like Karl Harr briefing brigadier generals.

If the Germans had wanted to identify crucial spots in the American war machinery, they could have done worse than to see where Sullivan & Cromwell lawyers were stationed. William Piel, Jr., prepared daily intelligence reports in the Pentagon for use by the President and Joint Chiefs of Staff. Glen McDaniel worked on aircraft procurement with Undersecretary of the Navy James Forrestal, later the first secretary of defense. In Europe Franklin O. Canfield was the liaison between the Office of Strategic Services (OSS) and the Supreme Headquarters Allied European Forces (SHAEF) FORWARD. Lieutenant Colonel Arthur Roseborough was the chief of Secret Intelligence in Algiers.

It came back to haunt Dulles that he had been so uncharitable to the associates (the partners had their places guaranteed and money paid to their wives throughout the war). When Dulles ran as a Republican for the Senate in 1950, Joseph Broderick, a Sullivan & Cromwell associate, managed the Democrats' downstate campaign, which focused on Dulles's refusal to guarantee the fighting men jobs on their return.

Dulles looked as though he was spending the war years paying public penance for his prewar support of Germany. In fact, he found new collaborators from neutral countries, who emerged extremely wealthy and influential from the war, and continued to use Sullivan & Cromwell long after its German collaboration was forgotten.

At the same time, the war marked a watershed for the firm. It lost the cohesiveness of autocratic rule because Dulles no longer represented his partners. He destroyed his effectiveness within the firm by isolating himself with unsympathetic clients and questionable actions. While they fought from Europe to India, Dulles stayed home and used sanctimonious pronouncements and politics to rehabilitate his image without giving up his secret German ties.

Dulles's most significant wartime activity hindered America's manufacture of diesel-fuel injection motors that the army, navy, and air forces all needed for trucks, submarines, and aircraft. The Economic Warfare Unit of the Justice Department lamented that "there is no known substitute for direct fuel injection equipment in diesel motors," making it a vital product above mere commercial consideration. While the Economic Warfare Unit plotted to bomb diesel plants in Germany, the Germans prevented America from manufacturing more efficient fuel injected diesel motors with the legal maneuvers of Sullivan & Cromwell.

Dulles had this power through a convoluted scheme he had hatched for the Germans after their experience in World War I when enemy property was seized by the Alien Property Custodian. Dulles handled the legal end of the arrangement, and George Murnane the operational end. In 1934 the Robert Bosch Company sold its international subsidiaries to Mendelssohn & Company of Amsterdam with a right to repurchase them; it was a way around Nazi leader Hermann Göring's demand that German companies borrow money to secure hard currency for prosecuting the war. The company was afraid that an inability to repay loans in the future would mean foreign confiscation of its assets. The "sale" had the advantage of satisfying Göring without ultimately losing the company, in return for which Bosch paid Mendelssohn a $100,000 "bonus or commisssion for acquiring the shares." Mendelssohn accumulated dividends for the German company to offset management fees and interest Bosch owed Mendelssohn.

In 1935 Murnane joined the board of directors of the American Bosch Company, the exclusive licensee of the Robert Bosch Company, the owner of one of Germany's most valuable patents—for fuel injection in diesel motors. The head of Mendelssohn, Fritz Mannheimer, admitted he was an agent of the Germans. But Murnane told Mannheimer "he was going to see to it that he never made any inquiry as to how the Bosch shares came into the hands of Mendelssohn & Co. because he always wanted to be in a position to say honestly that so far as he knew the shares were the property of Mendelssohn & Co.," according to the Amsterdam banker.

In 1937 Murnane became the chairman of American Bosch and, as anti-German feeling spread in September 1938, ordered that all new employees of American Bosch be Americans. After assuming office, Murnane urged Dr. Otto Fischer, the Robert Bosch executive in charge of the company's worldwide subsidiaries, to deal with him instead of the president of American Bosch. Murnane wrote, "In these delicate times on matters having to do with the whole Bosch structure it would be well to initiate matters through me. I am sure our understanding on that point is adequate and no more need be said about it."

In this period, American Bosch tried to get the German company to reduce the 5 percent royalty it paid on the German patents because "the high United States prices of pumps and nozzles, due to the royalties, were retarding the use of diesel engines in this country. . . . In many cases the diesel engine is three or four times the cost of similar gasoline engines."

Cutting the royalty had to be approved by the German government. To induce the Germans to agree, American Bosch volunteered information about costs, selling prices, and other competitive data that revealed a great deal about American engine manufacturing. American Bosch went so far as to send Albert Zimmerman, the company's director of inventory and production planning, to Stuttgart. He proudly reported, "Mr. Fellmeth, who has an excellent head indeed, cross examined me for about two hours about the whole diesel business in the U.S.A., and as I was able to answer all of his questions very thoroughly and apparently to his entire satisfaction, he turned me over to Mr. Durst, whom I know very well, for further investigations, particularly in regard to our production times for pumps, nozzles and nozzle holders."

The German government, which was delighted with the industrial intelligence, refused to give the company permission to lower the royalty rate. One of the only German companies operating in America, Bosch gave the Nazis a stranglehold on American engine production comparable with the better-known, highly resented agreement in which I. G. Farben manipulated Standard Oil of New Jersey over Buna rubber patents and almost created a crippling shortage of rubber in the United States. The Germans were happy with American Bosch just the way it was.

Then in August 1939, Fritz Mannheimer of Mendelssohn & Company committed suicide, precipitating the collapse of the Dutch bank. The Germans had to find a new owner for American Bosch that would remain subservient to the German parent company. When General Motors and Chrysler both expressed a strong interest in buying Mendelssohn's shares, Murnane had to dissuade them, telling them that "the attitude of Stuttgart toward any potential American buyer will be absolutely decisive as to whether or not the latter obtained anything of real substance in the purchase." He claimed that Bosch had the right to approve the transfer of the German patents and would disqualify American bidders that might "be destructive of the world's structure for Bosch products."

It was a delicate predicament for Murnane and the Germans. American buyers were disqualified because of their unwillingness to abide by Bosch's international cartel, but potential European buyers were either Nazi allies or enemies, the former unsuited as a cloak for the Germans and the latter unwilling to be their cloak. One possible buyer was an English company with blocked assets in Germany that Bosch could take in return for the company, but its future friendliness was by no means guaranteed.

So important was the future of American Bosch to Germany that Hjalmar Schacht, the German economics minister and Reichsbank president, sent a German banker to Sweden to ask the Stockholms Enskilda Bank to help dispose of the American company. The Enskilda Bank was owned by Sweden's richest family, the Wallenbergs, whom both Murnane and Dulles knew from the Kreuger & Toll bankruptcy. The Wallenbergs bought the major Kreuger assets out of bankruptcy, including Swedish Match and the L. M. Ericsson Company, a phone company that was the only major international competitor of American Telephone and Telegraph and International Telephone and Telegraph.

The German government was already doing business with Marcus Wallenberg, who, between September 1939 and April 1941, bought $2 million of German bonds in New York for only $520,000, acting "with a free hand" from the Reichsbank. Since Sweden was officially neutral, Wallenberg was an appropriate buyer of American Bosch, but the Swedes drove a hard bargain. In contrast with the $100,000 paid to Mendelssohn & Company to buy American Bosch in 1934, Bosch paid Wallenberg more than half a million dollars to take over the company, for which, the Stockholms Enskilda Bank paid $2,297,351 (30 percent less than an American company was willing to pay).

It was a particularly good deal for the Wallenbergs because Murnane recognized that it might be necessary to sell more than half the company to Americans for "qualifying American Bosch with its own government in the United States," as he wrote in the midst of the negotiations. They were in a position to realize an immediate profit by selling half the company in America, so with great confidence, the Wallenbergs bought the company on July 22, 1940.

The contract of sale excluded Robert Bosch's right of first refusal to buy the company back, but a secret agreement of the same date "provided for Wallenberg's definite obligation to sell more than a majority of all outstanding capital stock of American Bosch at a stated price." The secret agreement also included the Germans' right to dividends, to be held by the Wallenbergs until the end of the war.

Dulles stepped in to handle the sale of half the shares to Americans. This was obviously impossible while keeping the Germans in control, but Bosch was desperate to be taken for American. After American Bosch had been confiscated by the Alien Property Custodian during World War I, the company got detailed information about the United States' extensive research into shortwave and high-frequency sound waves. When German Bosch rebought the company after the stock market crash of 1929, that information became the basis of "the lightweight 'walkie talkies' of the German parachute troops, the intertank and ground-air radio communication systems and the short wave sets with which every twelfth German soldier is equipped,'' American intelligence reported during the war.

To get around the sale of Bosch shares but make the company look American, Dulles devised an intricate network of companies that *seemed* American without transferring power out of Germany. He had the Wallenbergs put their shares in a Delaware company, Providentia, Ltd., of which Dulles was the sole voting trustee. Under the terms of the irrevocable trusts, Dulles had full authority to handle or dispose of the shares.

Murnane and Dulles thought they had evaded government control under the pretense of making American Bosch American. They also renegotiated the licensing arrangement with the German parent company, paying a lump sum of $150,000 for all royalty payments ``for a period terminating with the conclusion of peace,'' an eerie anticipation of American entry into the war when it was signed in 1940.

Donald P. Hess, whom Murnane appointed president of American Bosch, noted defensively in the company's annual report that ``in May, 1941, the Corporation arranged complete suspension of the agreements for the full duration of the war.'' But when the Navy Department wrote to American Bosch in July 1941, supporting the Caterpillar Tractor Company's intention to manufacture fuel injection equipment, it responded, ``American Bosch is entirely willing to modify the exclusive nature of its present rights. . . . However, as pointed out, this Corporation's rights are indivisible and it therefore cannot itself confer the desired rights on Caterpillar Tractor Company.''

In May 1942, five months after the United States entered the war, American Bosch was finally confiscated by the Alien Property Custodian. Lacking absolute proof of the German ownership of the company, the investigative unit of the Alien Property Custodian contended there was ``a very strong presumption of an overall German-controlled pattern.'' It cited the Wallenberg takeover of the company's shares despite a higher American bid, Murnane's discouragement to potential American bidders and ``the fact that in the postwar period (in the absence of contrary action by the Custodian) the various agreements with RBAG [the German parent] will automatically become effective once again. Such agreements, even though suspended, are, therefore, of considerable potential importance.''

The Wallenbergs and Germans had heated discussions about who should bear the loss of the seizure by the Alien Property Custodian. They initially divided the loss one third to Wallenberg and two thirds to Robert Bosch; then the Wallenbergs insisted that the Germans take the total loss, which indicated that actual ownership lay in Stuttgart.

The ownership issue was still not fully resolved. In May 1943 German Bosch lawyers told Wallenberg they had deposited in a Swiss account the amount required to buy back American Bosch. German Bosch wanted to eliminate the high interest it was paying on the shares held by Wallenberg, an open acknowledgment that the shares were never sold to the Swedes. Wallenberg agreed to eliminate the interest but refused to turn over the shares because, he claimed, he could not make use of the funds deposited in Switzerland. The German lawyer said Wallenberg could surely get the money in Switzerland since both countries were neutral and the Wallenbergs had had numerous transactions there.

But taking the money would have been an admission that Wallenberg had previously lied in claiming there was no further German interest in American Bosch when the Swedes took the shares. Wallenberg told the Germans not to worry because he "had confidence that he could hold on to the ABC shares. Murnane would have written if there were a new proceeding against ABC shares."

Under American control, American Bosch increased its production so that it paid dividends for the first time in twenty years and tripled profits in 1943 to $1.3 million on an almost doubling of sales from $31 million in 1942 to $50 million in 1943. On December 29, 1942, a court order in an antitrust suit against American Bosch forced the company to cancel the agreements with the German parent company and license all Bosch patents "to American manufacturers without royalties for the duration of the war."

A secret government document dated October 11, 1944, noted Dulles's collaboration with the conclusion "Dulles, as attorney for Wallenberg, and with considerable experience in the international field certainly must have known that the American Bosch Company was German owned."

* * *

The Justice Department's antitrust lawyers found that other Sullivan & Cromwell clients were prominent among the causes of bottlenecks in the war effort. But antitrust prosecutions of Allied Chemical and many others had to await the end of the war because, as Secretary of War Henry L. Stimson wrote to the attorney general, ''war production must inevitably suffer if executive or production personnel is required to devote any substantial amount of time to activities other than the conduct of the munitions business of the respective corporations and such comparatively small amount of commercial business as may still be carried on.''

The chemical company defendants signed a consent decree in 1946, paying a minimal $5,000 fine. Other Sullivan & Cromwell clients who faced and lost (or signed consent decrees in) antitrust actions included the American Agricultural Chemical Company, the Merck Company, which was accused of illegally dividing world drug production with the German Merck Company, and Sofina, a European public utility with extensive international holdings.

These activities contrasted sharply with Dulles's public representations during the war. He ostentatiously represented European governments-in-exile in widely reported cases. Dulles brought the Bank of France case on behalf of the exiled Belgian and Polish governments, which had had almost $300 million deposited in France for safekeeping against German invasion. Belgium and Poland instructed the French government to send the money to America. Dulles explained, ''Although the Bank of France shipped most of its own gold to New York, it shipped the Belgian and Polish gold to French West Africa where it was lost to both institutions.'' The Germans repatriated the gold to Berlin after they invaded and occupied France and its possessions.

Dulles asked the federal court to have the Poles and Belgians paid back in French gold held in New York. He won the suit, thanks to having what he never had with the German loans in the previous decade—collectible assets at home.

Cloaking himself in the pious raiment of a good Christian, he did not shrink from the arrogance of speaking for all Protestant churches through his Commission on a Just and Durable Peace, which was sponsored by the Federal Council of Churches. It was a new role for him, supposedly traceable to a conversion in 1937, when he attended a religious convocation in Oxford, England.

Dulles's son Avery, who himself converted to Catholicism and became a priest, attested to his father's enduring pragmatism. Applied to religion, it would allow a calculated use of piety to hide other activities. Dulles's sanctimonious unlegal phrases sounded like cosmic faith healing, not the Bible: "Let them rather draw the world unto them, knowing that as they in truth form part of Christ's church, then they are that Tree of Life whereof the leaves serve the healing of the nations." He collected money from John D. Rockefeller, Jr., to buy radio time and voluminously reprint his statements. He made 700,000 copies of some of them, rivaling the circulation of *The New York Times*.

Dulles had the International Nickel Company conduct an advertising campaign with the slogan of his pronouncements, "A just and durable peace," which appeared in 250 magazines and newspapers in 1943. Inco and Dulles shared the guilty secret of their collaboration, which ended for Inco when the Nazis confiscated its nickel mines in Norway. The Inco effort served its purpose when the Ottawa *Journal*, desperate for advertising during the war, endorsed the campaign with an editorial that was striking for its self-serving piety, not unlike Dulles's own: "The great corporations of this country are meeting their responsibilities with loyal and realistic appreciation of all that is at stake in this war, and such advertising as that sponsored by International Nickel is bound to be of real service to the country."

Allen Dulles's war showed the alternative course for a Sullivan & Cromwell partner closely connected with high-ranking Germans but also loyal to the Allies. He spent a year heading the COI (the Office of the Coordinator of Information) out of headquarters he rented after evicting the existing tenants in Rockefeller Center in New York. He then went to Switzerland, in an outpost of the Office of Strategic Services (OSS), the precursor of the Central Intelligence Agency. In Bern he found a neutral spot close to Germany from which he could eavesdrop safely on the Nazis.

On the day that the Germans took over unoccupied France, Allen Dulles arrived at the French border with Switzerland. The Vichy government had just issued an order to detain all Americans and British trying to cross the border and report them directly to Marshal Pétain, the head of the French government collaborating with the Nazis. Allen "took the gendarme aside and made to him the most impassioned, and I believe, most eloquent speech that I had ever made in French," he reported. "Evoking shades of Lafayette and Pershing, I impressed upon him the importance of letting me pass."

The gendarme did not seem to be listening, and Allen Dulles contemplated escaping across the border. But as soon as the Gestapo agent left his post for lunch, the gendarme put Allen back on the train and within minutes he entered Switzerland, "one of the last Americans to do so until after the liberation of France," he boasted.

Just getting in made Allen Dulles famous. "One of the leading Swiss journals produced the story that I was coming there as a secret and special envoy of President Franklin D. Roosevelt," he reported. "Offhand one might have thought that this unsought advertisement would have hampered my work. Quite the contrary was the case."

Always able to put a good face on things, he explained that "nobody knew who the British intelligence agent was but everyone knew who was there for the United States." He claimed "that was why certain information about what was going on in the enemy countries came to me." When, after the war, he became deputy director and later director of the CIA, young American spies learned the precept Dulles derived from his experience: "Never try to conceal what cannot or need not be concealed."

The lawyers in the Paris office, who escaped two days before Hitler's troops marched down the Champs-Élysées, reopened the office in a Bordeaux hotel. Taking as many files as they could, they stayed three months when they "left France on the last American ship crowded with European refugees," recalled Franklin O. Canfield, an associate who had joined the French office only the year before.

Cromwell had departed Paris in 1937, never to return. But his possessions, which were kept in a room-size vault at the Chase Bank in the Place Vendôme, interested the Nazis. They inventoried the tapestries, paintings, and silverware while Cromwell kept in touch with old friends by sending them woolly pajamas and words of encouragement throughout the war.

Philippe Monod, a French lawyer in Sullivan & Cromwell's Paris office, quit to join the French Army on the day war broke out in 1939. He collected French intelligence in Lyons and in 1943 made his way to Switzerland to confer with Allen Dulles and Max Shoop, another lawyer from the Sullivan & Cromwell office in Paris. Behind the lines, Monod's group collected a surfeit of information but had no way of getting it out. He persuaded Allen Dulles to give him the American code so any transmitter could pick up the messages, making the Sullivan & Cromwell old boy network the link for America to get information about conditions inside German-occupied France.

The war ended in 1945 with Foster Dulles getting his feet wet in politics, as twenty-five of the firm's lawyers who had left to fight in the war, including the four prewar partners, returned. Only one, Rogers Lamont, had been killed in action.

When Dulles had first embarked on his public career as a foreign policy expert, he failed to impress President Roosevelt and the 1940 Republican presidential candidate, Wendell Willkie, who politely returned Dulles's position paper, "Statement of an American Foreign Policy." But Dulles did not give up and was able to ride the coattails of Thomas Dewey, the New York governor and Republican presidential nominee in 1944.

As foreign policy adviser and prospective secretary of state, Dulles was treated to respectful press coverage during the 1944 presidential campaign, including a long *Life* magazine profile which showed him at his desk, pipe stuck in his mouth, over the caption "The world's highest-paid lawyer, Senior Partner Dulles presides over Manhattan's immense law factory, Sullivan & Cromwell, from his penthouse office at 48 Wall St." The article began with the comment "To look at him you might think he had just finished contact with a green persimmon; and to listen to him on the subject of his business (he is top senior partner in the Wall Street firm of Sullivan & Cromwell) you would only begin to guess that he can distil the poetry of action as well as a big income out of such things as reshuffling the corporate structure of the International Nickel Company."

Politics made Dulles's bad judgment public, even when he tried to keep quiet. President Roosevelt, in formulating policy for the prospective world body that became the United Nations, promised American troops would be deployed under U.N. command. Dulles advised Dewey to reject the compromise of sovereignty, which caused a breach with the Allies while the war was still being fought. Dulles drafted the extremist remark Dewey used in the campaign: "Mr. Roosevelt has so weakened and corrupted the so-called Democratic Party that it is readily subject to capture . . . [by] the forces of Communism."

Dulles also wanted to charge the Democrats with unpreparedness because they had not anticipated Pearl Harbor. The claim might have opened a debate over the Japanese secret code, which was still in use on the Asian front. Cooler heads recognized the subject was far too sensitive to debate, and it was dropped.

In the middle of the campaign, Dulles found himself subject to a comic chase scene that generated the mocking headline YOOHOO, MR. DULLES, THERE'S A MAN TO SEE YOU in the New York *Post*. The cause was a suit by a former employee of Harrison Williams's Union Electric Company who claimed that he had been forced to take the rap (and a two-year jail sentence) for the corruption scandal that was actually the fault of the company board, including Dulles. Dulles was so incensed by the gumshoe detective's stakeout in front of his Manhattan town house (which produced a subpoena and the offensive front-page photo in the New York *Post*) that he wanted to sue the liberal paper. No suit was filed and Dulles evaded the substance of the Union Electric suit.

Besides his close ties to Dewey, Dulles inveigled his way into Republican politics by befriending Michigan Senator Arthur Vandenberg. A classic isolationist who became a decisive internationalist under Dulles's tutelage, Vandenberg collaborated with Dulles on the foreign policy portion of the 1944 Republican platform. When President Roosevelt wanted the senator to go to the organizing meeting for the new United Nations, Vandenberg insisted that Dulles accompany him to the San Francisco parley in September 1944.

The President resisted, telling Secretary of State Edward Stettinius, "I won't have Foster Dulles. He will play it his way; he will leak things; he will be a disruptive force. I don't like Foster Dulles. I won't have him there." Vandenberg persisted, and Dulles went. But Roosevelt's reluctance proved well founded when Dulles leaked information about the American delegation, undermining the agreed-upon bipartisan protocol. According to one delegate, "Whenever you had Foster in on bipartisan policy, you had to have a Democrat with a Democratic leak to counterbalance the Republican leak which Foster would already have made; otherwise you would be cheated out of the next day's headlines."

The end of World War II marked the first time in thirty-five years that John Foster Dulles was not among the Americans closest to events and leaders in Germany. This time he was among the investigated as the American Army swarmed over the occupied territory, interrogating the people Dulles knew and had dealt with for all those years. Long armored convoys, protected by airplanes overhead, streamed across Hitler's prized, but now otherwise deserted, autobahns, bringing back looted gold. One investigator, digging behind false walls in a Stuttgart salt mine, found the secret agreements between the Wallenbergs and Robert Bosch, detailing Bosch's right to repurchase American Bosch, which had supposedly been renounced.

The revelation did not alter the Wallenbergs' determination to claim American Bosch, but it made the job harder for Sullivan & Cromwell. Dulles cleverly turned the case over to his brother, Allen, who had emerged from the war with his reputation enhanced. Allen Dulles had negotiated Operation Sunrise, the surrender of the Nazi army under Supreme Waffen SS General Karl Wolff. The surrender prevented northern Italy from suffering a German scorched-earth retreat; but Operation Sunrise is credited with starting the discord between the United States and Soviet Union that resulted in the Cold War as Stalin suspected Allen Dulles of negotiating a separate peace to gain an advantage over the Red Army. Historian Arthur M. Schlesinger, Jr., called Operation Sunrise "the episode which provoked Stalin to charge Roosevelt with seeking a separate peace and provoked Roosevelt to denounce the 'vile misrepresentation' of Stalin's informants."

Operation Sunrise became public knowledge almost immediately from an article in *The Saturday Evening Post* in September 1945, by which time Allen Dulles had taken a leave of absence from Sullivan & Cromwell to recruit former Nazi spies for a new American anti-Soviet spying unit that would be incorporated into the Central Intelligence Agency. In six months he instituted the postwar policy that the Soviet

Union, not Germany, was the enemy before returning to Sullivan & Cromwell in New York.

When he got home Allen Dulles applied to the Wallenbergs his own strategy of claiming that his German contacts helped the Allied war effort, suggesting to Marcus Wallenberg in February 1946, "Talk to your brother and get from him a report with regard to his contacts with Goerdeler and the July 20th group [to assassinate Hitler]. I am moving along fairly rapidly in collecting my material and hope to begin writing something in the near future. . . . What I have in mind is that it would do no harm if it were known that the contacts which your brother had on the other side of the lines were, in instances such as the July 20th affair, put to uses which benefitted the Allied cause."

Allen Dulles wrote in his 1947 book *Germany's Underground,* "The German underground's most valuable contact in Stockholm was with the Wallenberg family, the well-known Swedish bankers." This public vindication of his client contrasted with an American government report in 1945 that had found that the Wallenbergs' "Enskilda Bank has been, in the past, an implement of Axis policy, Japanese as well as German, to an extent which should eliminate it from considerations of trust." The fact that Marcus Wallenberg operated in the West while brother Jacob consorted with the Nazis "is not an expression of neutrality," the report concluded, "as much as an evidence of power with no assurance that between the two members of the family there does not exist a tacit 'playing of both ends.' "

In the midst of the wrangle, Marcus Wallenberg wrote a letter to Foster Dulles's personal secretary, Florence Snell, asking for her "efficient cooperation in getting me the desired measurements as quickly as possible" for him to "arrange with an English gunbuilder to build a gun so it suits Mr. Dulles perfectly. As I know that Mr. Dulles in most arts and sports is a marksman of the highest quality, I am sure that he will also earn that same reputation with a shotgun."

Their murky politics kept the Wallenbergs from attempting to rescue their famous cousin, Raoul Wallenberg, who helped Jews escape from Hungary under the Nazis and was arrested by the Soviet Army. In 1947 Marcus Wallenberg turned down President Harry Truman's offer to help locate Raoul with an offhanded remark: "He is probably dead by now."

In 1948 when the Alien Property Custodian announced its intention to keep the proceeds of its sale of American Bosch as enemy property, Sullivan & Cromwell took the agency to court, arguing that Swedes owned the company, not Germans. The firm failed to stop the auction, which was won by New York investment bank Allen & Company for $6 million, twice the Wallenbergs' investment. The government specified that the company be owned by Americans because its products were essential to American defense.

The Wallenbergs pursued their suit to get the proceeds of the sale, a case that turned, as United States Attorney General Tom C. Clark wrote to Secretary of State George C. Marshall, "for technical legal reasons, [on] the question of whether the Bank acted with good faith and honesty in disclosing its agreement with the Germans." An employee of the bank contended that it had. John Foster Dulles gave a deposition from his town house and Sullivan & Cromwell lawyers went to court to prevent the Wallenbergs from having to testify.

Ultimately Sullivan & Cromwell worked out a settlement for the Wallenbergs to get $2.6 million of the sale price, practically reimbursing them for their original investment, though they also agreed to pay $420,000 in legal fees. The rest of the proceeds of the shares went to the United States War Claims Commission to pay Americans with "unusual hardships" during the war, deserving benefactors who had to share the money with the Wallenbergs. Janet Dulles, who knew the Swedes socially, wrote to her brother-in-law Allen Dulles, "I am glad to have the Wallenbergs straightened out."

10

OUTSIDE MAN/INSIDE MAN

You can spend many of your evenings uptown attending the Foreign Relations Council and having dinners with people and talking about big affairs, but none of that gets into the ledger as revenue for the office.—DAVID R. HAWKINS, SULLIVAN & CROMWELL PARTNER

John Foster Dulles periodically ventured uptown to polish off a bottle of champagne over lunch with William Nelson Cromwell and give the old man a perfunctory account of firm activities. Now well into his nineties, Cromwell still approved new partners, though he usually could not remember who they were even while he was talking to them.

The firm devoted several partners' meetings to discussing funeral arrangements for the founding father, only to see him survive a few more years. But he finally died, aged ninety-four, on July 19, 1948, to the relief of Rockefeller Center, which promptly erected a new thirty-three-story office building on the site of his house. His death marked the beginning of an era for Rockefeller Center but the end of one for Sullivan & Cromwell. More than two dozen honorary pallbearers included the firm's partners and George Sullivan, the eighty-eight-year-old son of Cromwell's original partner, who had joined the firm in 1882. A blanket of red roses covered the casket lying in state in the domed silence of St. Bartholemew's Church on Park Avenue, which was steeped in floral arrangements, among them a replica of the cross of the Legion of Honor in red and gold flowers. More than five hundred people attended the funeral.

Like an old dowager, Cromwell had spent his declining years proposing changes in his will that he ultimately never made. Even after his death, his $18 million legacy occupied lawyers' time in court because he gave money to law societies that needed to prove their eligibility for tax deductions. He also made a $300,000 bequest to Russian War Relief. The executors—John Foster Dulles, Edward Green, and Eustace Seligman—successfully claimed that the beneficiary was no longer functioning. Charles G. Rodman, the associate who worked on the estate, learned the valuable lesson he called "the Rule of Construction—that the intent of the testator is the one perceived by the executor." Green was chairman of the gifts committee for Columbia University where Seligman's father had been a famous economist. They shifted the money from Russian War Relief to the Columbia University law library, which thereafter bore Cromwell's name.

Cromwell's largest individual bequest went to his Paris secretary, Jane Renard, his reputed mistress, who got $35,000. Another beneficiary (of $10,000) was Helen Keller, whom Cromwell knew from the Permanent Blind War Relief Foundation he established during his years in Paris.

John Foster Dulles stayed at the firm for only a year longer, resigning on July 7, 1949, to accept an appointment as United States senator to fill the unexpired term on the death of Robert Wagner. The appointment was a consolation prize from New York Governor Thomas Dewey for Dulles's not becoming secretary of state, as had been expected after the 1948 election.

Dulles had been Dewey's faithful foreign policy adviser through two unsuccessful presidential campaigns, the second of which was thought to be a Dewey shoo-in until the votes were actually counted.

By 1948, much of the previous controversy, like Dulles's support for America First, was forgotten. James Reston wrote in *The Saturday Evening Post:* "Because he stubbornly persists in the old-fashioned habit of thinking before he opens his mouth, [his speech] seems sensible and dependable. During office hours such pronouncements from a senior partner of Sullivan & Cromwell would probably cost about three times what you figured, but Mr. Dewey got them free, and he evidently was impressed."

A full-page photo of Dulles accompanying the article had the caption "The man who may succeed Secretary Marshall has a lawyer's mind, a philosopher's outlook and a diplomat's training." It shows Dulles in a three-piece suit grasping his own lapels, his jowls showing just a faint hint of fat covered in a patina of suntan. Less formal than the average Wall Street lawyer, he looked more formal than the average politician, just the note to strike for his emerging political career. In fact, he scribbled his signature across the bottom of the photo and sent it out as a postcard during his unsuccessful 1950 senatorial campaign.

Both Dulles brothers were pursuing their internationalist interests outside the law firm. The kind of work they had done as lawyers taking the initiative in foreign policy had, since the war, become the concern of politicians and the prerogatives of the government.

While older brother Foster worked on the American presidential campaign, Allen took a leave of absence to work for the CIA to counter Communist propaganda during the Italian national elections. The headline in the Boston *Globe,* DULLES MASTERMINDS NEW 'COLD WAR' PLAN UNDER SECRET AGENTS, described the country's new role in foreign affairs. The CIA gave Allen Dulles $20 million for propaganda and for supporting the Christian Democrats and right-wing parties, which produced a stirring anti-Communist victory in Italy. Historian Paul Johnson called the 1948 Italian vote "one of the most important of the post-war European elections, for it set a pattern of relative stability in Italy for a generation."

While still a partner at Sullivan & Cromwell, Allen Dulles helped formulate postwar intelligence through the Jackson-Dulles-Corea Committee, which made recommendations for the future of the CIA. He was part of the group that founded Radio Free Europe as a private corporation before it was taken over by the government in the 1960s. He was also instrumental in negotiating among the competing intelligence factions in the government to make the director of the CIA the preeminent head of American intelligence. This achievement was ratified by a National Security Council intelligence directive in 1956.

Both brothers were destined to be in Washington, as their foreign policy for clients was overtaken by the government's foreign policy. If they wanted to continue to promote their private agenda, they now had to do it as government policy, not dictated by private interests as it had been before the war.

Few people who knew Foster Dulles doubted that he aspired from an early age to the job held by his uncle and grandfather—United States secretary of state. John F. Thompson, an executive of the International Nickel Company, a principal client of the firm, who had known Dulles for forty years, considered his lawyer "really an internationalist with legal background, who in his youth was introduced into diplomatic life, and liked it. It came naturally to him. He enjoyed doing it. He devoted his life to it, and everything that he did was touched by this internationalism, this connection with diplomatic affairs so that he tended to think of things, I think, the way a diplomat would. . . . And when he became secretary of state, that was exactly what he wanted to be."

Dulles's grandfather knew from his own experience that the best entrée to the State Department was a legal career, not the Foreign Service. Throughout his period heading Sullivan & Cromwell, Dulles took advantage of the State Department's being "a quaint place," according to George F. Kennan, whom Dulles fired when he did become secretary of state. Kennan, whose Foreign Service career subjected him to the whims of political maneuverers like Dulles, thought the department "embodied . . . kindliness and generosity in the approach to all who were weaker and more dependent, which constitutes, it seems to me, our finest contribution to the variety of the human species in the world and comes closest to embodying our national ideal and genius." It was not the Dulles approach to foreign policy.

This foreign policy heritage of Dulles's maternal side made a strong potion when combined with his father's Protestant ministry to create a uniquely self-righteous, self-confident, and self-promoting world view.

At the end of the war, he was ready to latch his vision onto the power and focusing interests of the country itself. He worked in President Truman's administration as a representative of a bipartisan foreign policy meant to bring the country out of the war with a cohesive view of the world. He negotiated the peace treaty with Japan, which excused the former enemy with the same leniency that he advocated for Germany.

He used bipartisanship to gain a foothold in government, but when he became secretary of state, he was ready for a more independent course. The anticommunism of Joseph McCarthy gave Dulles a convenient means to undermine the bipartisanship which had benefited him when he was out of power. Despite his own personal ambivalence toward the Soviets, which he expressed to his brother and other intimates, he used anticommunism to gut and reorganize the State Department to suit his own demands. He was no administrator at Sullivan & Cromwell, and he continued his disregard of details as secretary of state.

But under the cloak of anticommunism, he rebuilt West Germany the way he had tried to rebuild Germany after World War I. He equated the national interest with the interests of private enterprise, using the State Department to thwart Justice Department antitrust investigations, particularly of the oil business (as discussed in Chapter 13). His virulent anticommunism reflected a fear of losing markets for American exports, a shrinking of the realm in which American business could operate. This, too, came from his background at Sullivan & Cromwell. Most biographies of John Foster Dulles practically begin with his secretary of state years, even though the position was the culmination of a lifetime of international work for his law firm and its clients.

That he moved his base of operations to Washington meant changes for the firm as well as for Dulles. Sullivan & Cromwell was no longer divided between foreign and domestic work. Securities registrations, to which Dulles had objected so strongly, were now becoming the backbone of the postwar Sullivan & Cromwell and allowed the firm to transcend the mixed legacy of the Dulles stewardship.

Dulles's successor, Arthur H. Dean, had actually run the firm for most of Dulles's tenure. The hours Arthur Dean put in at the office made him, unlike his predecessor, fully knowledgeable and approachable about all of the firm's business. One lawyer tried to impress Dean by not leaving till he went home. As Dean departed one night, he stuck his head around the door and asked, "What's the matter? Can't you get your work done on time?"

Dean also had a pedagogic streak that became part of firm tradition. Before the war, partners marked up associates' work like schoolmasters, telling them what they had missed and making them redo assignments. "There was no cost-containment rush," according to William Piel, Jr., who became the firm's primary litigator after the war. "Training was a conscious effort and there was time to do it."

During the war, the work remained but the manpower diminished, so Dean "speeded up the process of producing legal product." Dean, who spent the war at the office, relieved by stints in the Coast Guard, supervised the acceleration and maintained it thereafter. Piel sadly noted, "Never again was there the wonderful, relaxed, ample time for everything."

Instead, Dean spent more time with associates outside the office. While Dulles was senior partner, most firm events, like the annual alumni cocktail party, took place en masse at the Dulles town house on East Ninety-third Street in Manhattan, but Dean started taking lawyers out individually to his Oyster Bay, New York, house. They would have long leisurely weekend walks and ruminate about the law to get a philosophical appreciation of what they were doing.

Lawyers who could not get home for Christmas joined his family for the holiday. After a formal Christmas dinner Dean himself got up the next morning to make breakfast, a display of humility that never failed to impress the young associates.

The difference between Dulles and Dean, the former an "outside man" and the latter the firm's ultimate "inside man," was that Dulles's philosophical streak was exposed only to the clients, not the associates. Dulles instructed each new head of a corporation for which he was general counsel that if there were ever a conflict between the executive and the company, Dulles would have to side with the company. He cited the "law of harmony" when he advised clients on something he could not justify on legal grounds. Sullivan & Cromwell lawyers got to see the ruminative side of Dulles only as a faraway forbidding look that made him a cold, calculating, and distant figure for whom Dean was the intermediary.

The transition away from Dulles's tenure was eased considerably by the administrative talents of David Hawkins, who played a role in the firm that in later years would be taken by a computer. In the firm, Hawkins was known as a "super abacus." He compiled statistics with dogged determination and ruthless results.

He got his start in running the back office soon after his arrival at the firm in 1921, when he told Royall Victor that the stenographic pool could be better organized. Victor assigned Hawkins to do it; it was the launching pad for the young lawyer who was to become a partner in the short period of six years and enjoy a stellar career that lasted until 1964. For forty-three years he applied to Sullivan & Cromwell the detailed statistical and financial methods associated, especially in that era, only with public corporations. His administrative talents allowed the firm to grow after World War II beyond the bounds any law firm had ever contemplated.

He knew everything, broken down into detailed records kept relentlessly year after year, year compared with year, hour by hour, on the recorded hours, caseloads, numbers of matters and cases by subject, fees earned, and proportions put in by senior, middle, and junior lawyers. It was clinical and exact, a function of the kind of mind Hawkins had, but the Confidential Statistical Report also had a devastating effect on careers when it was circulated among the management committee.

His work almost automatically put Hawkins on the management committee. His heyday working with clients was the 1930s, when he helped the public utilities resist registration under the Public Utilities Holding Company Act of 1935, but his clients gradually took up less of his time as his administrative responsibilities grew.

Besides keeping partners apprised of their worth to the firm, Hawkins took control of recruitment and the nonlegal staff. Every six months the partners received a confidential office memorandum marked "Do not file." It discussed new recruits and listed all lawyers in the firm by department. Associates had the dates of their entries into the firm next to their names; partners did not. Hawkins had a definite idea of the kind of man he was looking for: ''We've gotten in a state of mind now [the early 1960s]—which seems ridiculous to me—where we call a person of thirty a youth. My idea is a man should be a man by 21, and he should quit being a young man around 18 or 19, and be a probationary man, if you will, between those years and 21 or 22.''

His judgments on individuals were quick and harsh. His semiannual reports on prospective new associates were peppered with instant analyses—''best all around man available for New York''; ''good likeable Irishman of the litigation type''; ''exceptionally good mind but has not over worked''; ''somewhat negative personality.'' Richard M. Nixon applied for a place at Sullivan & Cromwell in 1937, when Hawkins noted his ''shifty-eyed'' manner in comments that were read to an annual Sullivan & Cromwell dinner during the Watergate scandal in the 1970s.

Hawkins had a gruff manner that, along with his statistical tables, made people fear and dislike him. To him a joke was seeing how different he could make his signature on Sullivan & Cromwell paychecks before the banks would bounce them. Even his secretary, Phyllis Macomber, who enjoyed as easy a relationship with Hawkins as anyone in the office, finally got tired of the relentless routine. She decided, ''I had been doing Dave Hawkins' tables for so long that there is another part of life I should see.'' She also did his tax returns. After she quit, she went to work at the public relations firm Hill & Knowlton until Dulles hired her to work for him when he was secretary of state.

A generation later the work Hawkins did would not necessarily have qualified him to be a partner, let alone one of the most senior partners. But he started the field of legal administration and became a consultant throughout the profession. With his close supervision of personnel and finances, he did the work that was usually assigned to chief executives in corporations but that in partnerships was left to volunteers or subordinate employees.

He gave Sullivan & Cromwell the advantage of being open to recruiting throughout the year in contrast to firms like Davis, Polk & Wardwell and Cravath, Swaine & Moore, where recruiting was done only at Christmastime. Until recently law school students went to the firms to get their jobs rather than wait for campus recruiters. Numerous Sullivan & Cromwell associates and partners had their first contact with the firm when they dared look for a job outside the normal Christmas hiring time. Despite rebuffs elsewhere, Sullivan & Cromwell had someone for them to talk to—Dave Hawkins.

He also gave Sullivan & Cromwell the reputation for taking care of its employees. He instituted health insurance and made sure that everyone took a designated four-week vacation because he "figured everyone worked hard so they should get a good vacation." He provided a lunchroom at the firm and made sure the secretaries had a Christmas party, though it was different from the lawyers'.

Hawkins organized the firm so that "the doors never closed at Sullivan & Cromwell," having the phones manned twenty-four hours a day, seven days a week. Secretaries made $37.50 a week just after World War II, when a room at a women's hotel, including two meals a day on weekdays and three a day on weekends, cost $18.95 a week. Stenographers could work their way up to secretary, though some preferred the stenographic pool, where the pay included allowances for dinner, time and a half for overtime, and double time on Sunday and after midnight. Later they were given allowances for taxis home after hours. Dulles had two secretaries in an office adjoining his, but most partners' secretaries shared an office near, though not adjoining, their bosses.

The turnover in associates had something to do with Hawkins's good-guy, bad-guy role. He did not hesitate to tell associates when they would not make partner in order to give them a chance to look elsewhere. He told Ruth Austin Hall, the fourth woman to join the firm, that she could not expect to make headway as a woman in New York and ought to return to her hometown, Kansas City, to realize her ambitions. She did.

To most secretaries Hawkins had a benevolent countenance compared with that of Jesse Sansom, the stern, no-nonsense office manager. She made the secretarial staff wear gloves and hats to the office (hats were eventually abandoned). First names were never used; Mrs. Macomber made Dulles repeat her name when he first called her Phyllis and that was not at Sullivan & Cromwell but at the State Department.

The firm's Spanish and French staff interpreter, Amalya C. Sartorelli, had three associates courting her in 1932. The stunning, dark-haired woman eventually married associate Joseph Prendergast. But they had to keep the marriage secret when they both were still at the firm; she left their Washington Square apartment half an hour before he did to prevent detection by two associates living across the square. Prendergast quit the firm six months later, and she could then appear in the office as a respectably married woman. One former Sullivan & Cromwell associate of the 1950s said, "In my day the lawyers and staff were in different worlds; now all the lawyers are chasing the paralegals."

The strict, proper environment changed abruptly in the 1960s when a more open, flagrant era hit Sullivan & Cromwell. A partner hired a woman associate because of his own personal social designs, and several partners divorced their wives to marry paralegals. But such behavior was not countenanced under Dave Hawkins's strict control of the staff in the long period that straddled the eras of Royall Victor, John Foster Dulles, and Arthur Dean.

It was a time in which Sullivan & Cromwell had no rivals in applying a system that got a maximum amount of work out of associates. One former associate, who ultimately became a lawyer in Washington, said with admiration, "One thing about Sullivan and Cromwell is that they knew how to drive the young lawyers and make money off of [*sic*] them. Not everybody can do that. It's a skill that they have," which Hawkins made sure functioned whoever was head of the firm.

PART III

THE LAWMAKERS

11

THE PROFITS OF BLAME

The expense of preparing the registration statement will add materially to the cost of raising money.—ARTHUR H. DEAN

The modern Sullivan & Cromwell was founded on a hot Saturday afternoon in the early spring of 1933. Arthur Dean, a thirty-five-year-old partner, was sitting in an airless room in a modest Georgetown house with members of President Roosevelt's Brain Trust to draft the Securities Act of 1933. As previously noted, Dean had gone to Washington with John Foster Dulles to argue against the proposed act and its restrictions on business. When Dulles left in a huff, Dean stayed. William Nelson Cromwell had chosen him to accompany Dulles because the younger man had much less invested in the existing securities system. Dulles could not admit that the activities he had supported and promoted in the 1920s should be regulated.

Dean, who had been made partner in 1930, projected the image of a reasonable adversary with advice that could make the act workable. He admitted, "A fair-minded man, cognizant of the revelations in the past few years, [cannot] say the Securities Act is unnecessary." But at the same time the act, he said, presented practical problems, in fact a host of practical problems that were "so complex and difficult to understand that the commonplace transactions of business and the marketplace could not be carried on."

Dean had not come to Washington, like Dulles, as the senior lawyer in the country's major law firm, prepared to lecture and browbeat the opposition. Above all, Dean advocated conciliation. The act should not perpetuate a climate hostile to business, since the country was already suffering from a lack of confidence and investment in the stock markets. He said that the new act, even before its passage by Congress, was "seriously interfering with the flow of capital to industry at a time when it is sorely needed." The act had the chance to restore confidence by matching penalties to offenses, but in its present form it threatened to erode even further the public's and even the bankers' interest in the future of capitalism. He claimed, "Officials of corporations with impending maturities are finding it difficult to get bankers to undertake commitments, and those seeking new capital are baffled by the complexities of the Act."

Dean was the age of the men around him, the "hot dog boys," protégés of Harvard Law Professor Felix Frankfurter who went to Washington to put President Roosevelt's sweeping legislative program into words. James Landis, a Harvard teacher aged thirty-four, went to Washington for a single weekend to write the Securities Act of 1933. The front-desk clerk at the Carleton Hotel gave him a room just under the suite of J. P. Morgan, Jr., who was testifying before the relentless Ferdinand Pecora, counsel to the Senate Banking and Currency Committee, which was investigating bankers' excesses. Landis was amused to note that while he was reforming the securities industry, Morgan was testifying that despite his multimillion-dollar income, he had arranged, quite legally, to evade taxes for the previous three years.

Morgan's testimony lasted weeks, but the securities legislation had to be prepared in one weekend because Landis had a class in Cambridge the following Monday morning. He was convinced the bill could be thrashed out in two days, and it was (though the need to present it to Congress forced him to postpone his return to Harvard by a day).

Landis worked with Benjamin Cohen, thirty-nine, an employee of the Public Works Administration and another Harvard protégé of Frankfurter's. The third member of the group, Thomas Corcoran, was only thirty-three. Later famous for his talents as a Washington lobbyist, he had a quick Irish smile and a nose for backroom political intrigue. He was a key New Deal legislative draftsman, said to run the "fourth branch" of government out of the Georgetown town house he shared with Ben Cohen.

The young men had written the Securities Act by the time Dulles and Dean got to Washington, and though Sam Rayburn strongly resisted showing it to representatives of Wall Street, Roosevelt's close Brain Trust adviser Raymond Moley insisted. Dulles's ill-informed and emotional attack confirmed Rayburn's doubts, but Dean showed an entirely different side of the opposition. He was reasonable, thoughtful, and modest. Short, inelegant, and informal, he had the face of a bulldog and the manner of a country farmer, peppering insightful and detailed analysis with homespun aphorisms. When his adversaries went too far, he nudged them back in line with the comment "It seems hardly necessary to burn down the house to exterminate the vermin."

He admitted that "issuing corporations and their lawyers have attempted to make the registration requirements look ridiculous." But he just wanted the drafters to understand the challenges he as a corporate lawyer faced. "One who has never prepared a registration statement for a large company cannot realize the enormous amount of time, energy and effort that goes into such a statement," he contended. He came with a long list of items that seemed to make the legislation unworkable.

The group broke for lunch and then reconvened at the "little red house," Corcoran and Cohen's Georgetown home that had become an information and networking center frequented by journalists, businessmen, and government officials. Dean spent the day with Cohen, Corcoran, and Landis, endlessly picking at details.

Dean deftly couched specific advice in generalities to describe what was wrong with the highly detailed registration requirements:

- "Undue emphasis on the historical aspect of a situation may serve to distort the present situation."
- "Frequently the information most difficult to obtain is of the least value."
- "Highly pertinent and important facts may be buried in a mass of irrelevant detail."

His listeners responded. They confined their law to a more orderly and regulated environment for issuing stocks and bonds to the public. Dean guided the drafters away from passing on the merits of investments and confined them to the truthfulness of the presentation to the public, as set forth in the preamble to the act: "to provide full and fair disclosure of the character of securities sold in interstate and foreign commerce, and through the mails, and to prevent frauds in the sale thereof."

Buried in the bill, the twenty-ninth of thirty-two scheduled requirements for a registration, was a short clause demanding "a copy of the opinion or opinions of counsel in respect to the legality of the issue." The future of Sullivan & Cromwell and the whole Wall Street legal profession was embodied in this one phrase.

Despite Dean's advice, the Securities Act as passed on May 27, 1933, did not dispel the harsh climate for investment. Washington assumed Wall Street was purposely holding back new issues and refusing to take the responsibility ascribed by the new law. Some blamed the banks; some, including Felix Frankfurter, blamed the lawyers. The truth, however, was that the environment in 1933 for investment was growing worse. So was the economy. Other Sullivan & Cromwell lawyers took part in criticizing the act. Eustace Seligman, a contemporary of Dulles's with a penchant for analogies, was particularly bothered by one provision in the law: the bankers' responsibility for all the registration statement's faults and inaccuracies. He vigorously argued to limit responsibility to what could be proved as their fault. He considered the provision comparable to a man's having his car demolished by a tree and getting the whole car replaced because the dealer claimed the windshield was shatterproof. "It is a material misrepresentation," Seligman noted in an article in *Atlantic Monthly,* which was quoted in *The New York Times,* "and so under the new Truth in Automobiles Act, I can get back the whole amount I paid for the car."

Dean was called to Washington to confer in the drafting of the Securities Exchange Act of 1934, which regulated the stock exchanges and put modifying amendments into the 1933 act. Among the provisions of the new act was a reduction in bankers' responsibility from the whole of an issue to their proportionate share, as Seligman had advocated.

Dean took particular pride in instituting a voluntary self-regulating system for the over-the-counter market to be supervised by the National Association of Securities Dealers. The act also sanctioned combined dealers and brokers, who could bring stocks to the market and trade them as well. This was a major victory for Wall Street, which had been soundly criticized for the high-pressure tactics of the 1920s, when banks promoted new stocks and bonds through extensive sales networks.

Twenty-five years later, Dean claimed that "self-regulation by broker-dealers, carried out through the medium of the National Association of Securities Dealers, has been a conspicuous success." But twenty-five years after *that,* these provisions became the basis of the scandals of the mid-1980s, when arbitrageurs took insider information from their stock-issuing colleagues for insider trading. Prominent among those accused of offenses by the Securities and Exchange Commission in the 1980s were one Sullivan & Cromwell employee and officials of Sullivan & Cromwell clients Goldman, Sachs & Company and Kidder Peabody.

Dean had obviously convinced Washington that punishing Wall Street was hurting the national economy. Besides the amendments limiting the liability of each underwriter to his portion of a new issue, he got the bank's responsibility reduced from that of a "person occupying a fiduciary relationship" to that of a "prudent man in the management of his own property."

Dean helped the banking industry in tough but informal negotiating sessions he conducted over months of commuting to Washington. Author Martin Mayer noted in his thorough study *The Lawyers,* "Probably the greatest compliment a lawyer can receive from his profession (a compliment never publicized) is an assignment to draft a major law"; but Dean managed to get tremendous mileage out of the work through two articles he wrote for *Fortune* about the new law.

Billed as "one of the foremost experts on securities legislation in New York," Dean and Sullivan & Cromwell were prominently noted in the articles' headlines, each of which was given more than a dozen pages in the prestigious business publication.

The first article, in August 1933, was a dense, almost impenetrable analysis of the new legislation. The magazine editors prefaced it with the warning "What here follows is a stern and technical legal analysis. It is not easy reading. Those who are not concerned with the problems presented by the Act are advised to avoid it as they would an explanation of the Mass Energy Equation."

A half-page outline of the article should have made it easier going, but its forty items proved as off-putting as Dean's prose, which started by defining terms like "through the mails" so extensively that the major points got lost. Dean's article was accompanied by one by Felix Frankfurter, whose elegant style, with sweeping historical references and penetrating analysis, made Dean sound pretentious and evasive. Frankfurter infused his prose with pithy statements like "Legislation is not anticipation. It is response." After putting the securities acts into perspective, Frankfurter focused on their logic with the contention "Many practices safely pursued in private lose their justification in public. Thus social standards newly defined gradually establish themselves as new business habits."

Dean's public writing career did not arise by accident. It was encouraged by John Foster Dulles, whose own career had been boosted by articles that he started writing to impress his superiors at Sullivan & Cromwell. When Dulles appointed Norris Darrell as head of the firm's tax department, Darrell recalled, the senior partner told him to "train and develop assistants so that I could find time to write, lecture and do whatever I could to establish the firm's tax reputation." Though such an aggressive effort to get publicity went against the spirit, if not the letter, of American Bar Association canons, it was the modus operandi at Sullivan & Cromwell.

Dean never succeeded again in reaching an audience as large as he did with his first efforts about the securities acts in *Fortune*. Subsequent pieces appeared in law journals. He also wrote a biography of William Nelson Cromwell, which was privately printed and for twenty years given to new associates at the firm.

Dulles always wrote his own articles on long yellow legal notepads that he filled with doodles along the margins. Dean had another method, as explained by Lawrence McQuade, later a senior vice-president of W. R. Grace & Company, who ghostwrote Dean's articles as a Sullivan & Cromwell associate in the 1950s. "He would call me in and say, 'I want to write about Japan and say this, this, and this.' He'd tell me details. I'd write a draft and send it in. He'd mark things to add, and I'd fix up the syntax. The first draft was always the best because you say what you think. Every word after that must be negotiated with Dean." McQuade did not think that meant the articles were his rather than Dean's. "Senior partners are hired for their opinions. The ideas were his and so it was his article." McQuade's role was as the "architect of the piece."

The new securities legislation gave the Sullivan & Cromwell lawyers much to write about. Dulles, who would have nothing to do with the law and its enactment, found a subject in "The Securities Act and Foreign Lending" to write for *Foreign Affairs.* While the article was meant to justify his previous foreign lending policies, its illogic confirmed their folly. He complained about the "complicated registration certificate" and the "difficulty of qualifying the transaction under the Securities Act" while asserting, in his own feeble defense, foreign "defaults are not normally attributable to a debtor's insolvency but rather to a national shortage of foreign exchange."

Dulles's continual self-justification indicates some inkling of guilt, though no improvement in his reasoning, since countries, which print their own money, can always pay debts, except in a foreign currency that provides an international standard of value. Where Dean edited associates' work on his articles, Dulles wrote his own and used his brother and Dean as his editors. Dulles wisely followed Allen's suggestion to remove the third sentence of the piece: "As a people we are inclined to swing from one extreme to another with a volatility which we prefer to ascribe to the southern races." Dean's advice corrected Dulles's imprecise understanding of the act and its impact. Eustace Seligman contributed to the securities act debate with an article that began "Is the fundamental purpose of the Securities Act sound? The answer is clearly 'yes,' " a proposition Dulles never accepted.

Dean was not as shortsighted as Dulles. He was ready to milk the legislation for all it was worth, both in the time and authority it gave lawyers to exact from clients. Even better, it was boring, rote work that could be done by lowly associates at handsome rates of pay.

On behalf of clients Arthur Dean noted, "The work in connection with the issue and sale of securities is increased by the act *fivefold* and the expense *twofold.*" Though it sounded like a bargain that five times the work cost only twice as much, that expense to the corporations went directly into the pockets of lawyers and investment bankers. The registration questionnaire, which was only 6 pages, elicited responses that were often 140 pages, benefiting the largest and best-organized firms that could assign teams of young associates to do the work. Moreover, few clients complained publicly about the lawyers' hours or output, however excessive they were, for fear of appearing less than fully compliant with the requirements of the acts.

After the acts were instituted William Curtis Pierce, the son of partner Henry Hill Pierce and the grandson of William Curtis, Cromwell's first partner after Sullivan's death (in the only three-generation family in the firm), spent nine months in Chicago working on a refinancing issue for client First Boston. Pierce found the securities acts "new and terrifying. The forms to be filled out required vast quantities of even less relevant detail than are now required." "Back in those days," recalled William Ward Foshay, who became the senior partner of Sullivan & Cromwell on Dean's retirement in 1972, "every registration statement was a first time. Every question you ran into had never been answered. The amount of midnight oil was monumental, you never got home for dinner. It's too bad for the young lawyers today; registration statements now are just updating." From then on, the general practice group, which handles this work, has employed half the lawyers in the firm.

The securities acts held authority jointly with the states' own blue-sky laws against misrepresentation in the sale of securities, forcing a Sullivan & Cromwell lawyer to check the laws of all the states as well as the demands of the SEC. New lawyers in the firm from that time onward first worked on blue-sky and securities registrations. Over the years the work became more routine and more lucrative. With the routinization of securities work, what the firm lost in complexity it

Algernon Sydney Sullivan (left) and William Nelson Cromwell in 1879 at the founding of the firm. Its office was on the fourth floor of the Drexel Building, J. P. Morgan's headquarters at Broad and Wall streets.

Cromwell's first partners after Sullivan's death in 1887 were (from left) William J. Curtis, Alfred Jaretzki, Sr., and Royall Victor, all of whom served terms as managing partner.

After World War I, Cromwell made considerable donations in France, including (from left) the memorial to the Lafayette Escadrille, a poster announcing a lace-making prize, and a lace-making school in Bailleul, France, with Cromwell's bust in the overgrown courtyard.

The 1914 Sullivan & Cromwell Society dinner in Cromwell's house. Seated left to right surrounding a portrait of Sullivan are John Foster Dulles, George H. Sullivan, Edward H. Green, William J. Curtis, William Nelson Cromwell, Waddill Catchings, Hjalmar Boyesen, Eustace Seligman, Ralph Royall, Reuben B. Crispell, Alfred Jaretzki, Sr., William F. Corliss, Francis D. Pollak. Standing left to right are Ralph L. Collett, Donald D. Dodge, Royall Victor, Roger Farnham, Robert McC. Marsh, Edward B. Hill, Emery H. Sykes, Clarke M. Rosencrantz, Max Shoop, and Albert S. Ridley.

Cromwell's houses at 10 and 12 West Forty-ninth Street, New York City. He owned the one on the left and rented the one on the right from Columbia University.

Cromwell returns to New York in 1925, after dedicating the Legion of Honor Museum in Paris, France, which he endowed.

$10,000,000

Fried. Krupp, Ltd.

(FRIED. KRUPP AKTIENGESELLSCHAFT)

7% Five-Year Merchandise Secured Gold Dollar Notes

To be dated December 15, 1924 — Interest payable June 15th and December 15th — To mature December 15, 1929

These Notes will be issued under an Indenture which will provide for the transfer to a Trustee, as security for the Notes, of merchandise and raw material in salable form having at all times a value at cost or market, whichever is lower, equal to at least 150% of the amount of the outstanding Notes.

We are advised by our counsel that the Treaty of Versailles and the London Agreement of August 9, 1924 between the German Government and the Reparation Commission providing for carrying into effect the Experts' Plan "Dawes Plan" do not impose any charge or lien for reparation upon property of the character agreed to be provided as security for these Notes, and do not restrict the right of the Company directly to acquire the foreign exchange necessary to meet its external obligations evidenced by these Notes.

Goldman, Sachs & Co., Fiscal Agents for the Loan

[illegible] is given in the [illegible] letter signed by Dr. Gustav Krupp von Bohlen und Halbach, Chairman of the Executive Committee of Fried. Krupp Aktiengesellschaft, which letter has been summarized in part as follows:

Description of Notes

These Notes will be in bearer coupon form in denominations of $1000 and $500. Principal and interest will be payable at the New York office of the Fiscal Agents for the Loan in United States gold coin of the present standard of weight and fineness. The Company covenants that net interest receivable from it by the holders of the Notes shall not fall below 7% per annum, and that net payments by way of principal and sinking fund shall not fall below the specified amounts, by reason of any German taxes, present or future, which the Company may be required or permitted to deduct or withhold. The Notes may be redeemed only as a whole, except for sinking fund as below stated, on any interest date at 102 and accrued interest on three months' prior notice.

The Notes will be issued pursuant to the terms of an agreement with the National Bank of Commerce in New York, defining the obligations of the Company, and an agreement with the Dresdner Bank, Germany, as Trustee of Pledged Assets.

The Company will covenant to retire $750,000 principal amount of Notes on or before December 15th in each of the years 1925 to 1928, inclusive, Notes to be purchased at not to exceed 102 and accrued interest or called for redemption at 102 and accrued interest.

Sullivan & Cromwell approves the first private loan under the Dawes Plan for the Krupp steel works in 1924.

John Foster Dulles (left) walks in Berlin alongside Sullivan & Cromwell associate Francis X. Downey in 1933, with Harry Winter in the background.

PRINCETON UNIVERSITY

History and Business

Fried. Krupp Aktiengesellschaft (Fried. Krupp, Ltd.), organized in 1903 to continue the industrial enterprises theretofore conducted for nearly 100 years under the firm name of Fried. Krupp, operates one of the best known and most important steel works in the world. The activities of the Company cover virtually every important steel and iron product in its various phases of manufacture.

The enterprise is entirely self-contained and thoroughly integrated, running from the production of iron ore and fuel, through pig iron and steel, up to the manufacture and sale of semi-finished and specialized goods. Under the allotment of the "Ruhrkohle" (Federation of Ruhr Coal Mine Owners), the Company's coal production is placed at 9,500,000 tons a year, ranking it among the largest coal-producers in Germany. The steel plants of the Company have an output capacity of 2,200,000 tons per annum. The Company owns facilities for transport as well by river and canal as by rail. At Essen alone it owns about 140 miles of railroad. The sales organization of the Company is highly developed through sales companies and agencies throughout the world. In the half year ending September, 1924, the value of the Company's total sales in foreign countries amounted to $7,800,000; thus a constant supply of foreign exchange may be relied upon.

Although the name of "Krupp" has been widely associated with the production of war material, yet such production before the year 1914 did not represent more than 5% in weight of the entire iron and steel output of the concern. Since 1919, the Company has been exclusively engaged in the production of industrial articles such as, among many other things, rails, locomotives and rolling stock, forging and steel castings, motors and motor trucks, structural steel, agricultural machinery and implements, Diesel engines and cash registers.

The Company's business has been thoroughly adjusted to a peace-time basis. With the return of stable conditions in Germany and improving business conditions throughout the world, the Company looks forward to a renewed period of prosperity.

Relation to "Dawes Plan"

The obligations of the Company with respect to the payment of reparation ("Dawes Plan") will take the form of a requirement that the Company pay annually an amount not exceeding 6% upon a capital sum which has not yet been definitely determined but which in all probability will not exceed 30,000,000 gold marks, or about $7,200,000. No payment whatever is required for the first year ending August 31, 1925. For the second year the rate is 2½%; for the third year, 5%. For the fourth year, it attains 6% whereof 1% is as amortization of principal. As there is no provision for accelerating the maturity of the capital sum, the average annual payment required of the Company for account of reparation during the life of these Notes would thus not exceed $306,000. The liability of the Company for reparation will be secured by a charge in the nature of a first mortgage upon the fixed assets of the Company, but such charge does not extend to assets of the character to be pledged as security for these Notes.

Neither German law nor any international engagements assumed by the German Government involve any restrictions upon the acquisition by the Company of the foreign exchange requisite to permit the Company to meet the external obligations evidenced by these Notes.

Purpose of Issue

The purpose of this issue is to reduce the Company's current indebtedness and to assure adequate working capital for the future.

Assets and Liabilities

Working assets of the Company, before giving effect to this financing, on October 1, 1924 amounted to in excess of $33,000,000, after eliminating inter-company items. Such assets in themselves substantially exceed the entire indebtedness and liabilities of the Company, including its liability for reparation at the capital sum of $7,200,000 but excluding items of inter-company indebtedness, transitory items and reserves. The plant and fixed assets were conservatively valued at approximately $45,000,000. Liberal depreciation and reserves have been taken. The net worth of the Company, exclusive of subsidiaries, is in excess of $40,000,000 after including in liabilities items of inter-company indebtedness, transitory items and reserves aggregating approximately $12,000,000 and reparation at the capital sum of $7,200,000.

Price 99¼ and accrued interest, to yield about 7.18%

This offering is made in all respects when, as and if issued and accepted by us and subject to the approval of Messrs. Sullivan & Cromwell, of New York. We reserve the right to reject any and all subscriptions in whole or in part, to allot less than the amount applied for and to close the subscription books at any time without notice.

It is expected that delivery of temporary notes or interim receipts will be made on or about February 5, 1925 at the office of Goldman, Sachs & Co., New York, N. Y., against payment therefor in New York funds.

J. & W. Seligman & Co.

54 Wall Street, New York

December, 1924.

As the within letter has been transmitted by cable, its contents and statements based thereon are subject to cable errors. We believe the information contained in this circular to be correct, but do not guarantee it. For the purpose of this circular, conversion between dollars and marks has been made on the basis of 1 gold mark equals 24 cents.

SULLIVAN & CROMWELL
JUNE 25, 1934

PRINCETON UNIVERSITY

The 1934 Sullivan & Cromwell Society dinner. From Norris Darrell (with glasses) in the lower left, they are Rogers S. Lamont, Allen W. Dulles, Reuben B. Crispell, Edward H. Green, William Nelson Cromwell, Wilbur L. Cummings, Horace G. Reed, Stoddard M. Stevens, S. Pearce Browning, Jr., David W. Peck, Arthur H. Dean, David R. Hawkins, John C. Higgins, John Foster Dulles, Eustace Seligman, Alfred Jaretzki, Jr., and DeLano Andrews.

Three of the best caricatures drawn at the dinner were of (from left) Eustace Seligman, Allen W. Dulles, and Arthur H. Dean.

PRINCETON UNIVERSITY

PRINCETON UNIVERSITY

William Nelson Cromwell on his ninetieth birthday talks with his executors, Edward H. Green, John Foster Dulles, and Eustace Seligman.

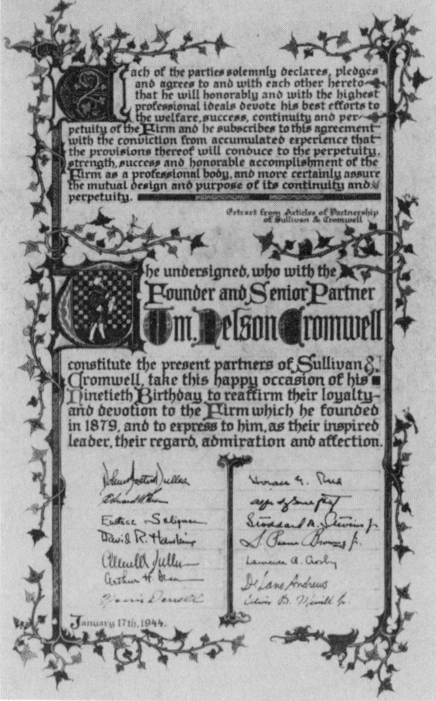

Each of the parties solemnly declares, pledges and agrees to and with each other hereto that he will honorably and with the highest professional ideals devote his best efforts to the welfare, success, continuity and perpetuity of the Firm and he subscribes to this agreement with the conviction from accumulated experience that the provisions thereof will conduce to the perpetuity, strength, success and honorable accomplishment of the Firm as a professional body, and more certainly assure the mutual design and purpose of its continuity and perpetuity.

Extract from Articles of Partnership of Sullivan & Cromwell

The undersigned, who with the Founder and Senior Partner Wm. Nelson Cromwell constitute the present partners of Sullivan & Cromwell, take this happy occasion of his Ninetieth Birthday to reaffirm their loyalty and devotion to the Firm which he founded in 1879, and to express to him, as their inspired leader, their regard, admiration and affection.

Eustace Seligman

David R. Hawkins

Lawrence A. Crosby

DeLane Andrews

January 17th, 1944.

The scroll presented to Cromwell from his partners.

PRINCETON UNIVERSITY

The 1951 dinner at Arthur Dean's Oyster Bay home after the firm's annual Piping Rock Club outing.

Brothers Allen Dulles (left) and John Foster Dulles meet at the airport in 1948.

Ambassador Arthur H. Dean (right) briefs President Eisenhower and Secretary of State John Foster Dulles on his return from Korea in December 1953.

UPI/BETTMANN NEWSPHOTOS

made up for in volume. It developed a securities cottage industry that absorbs most of the time of the young associates today just as it did in the 1930s, when Lauson Stone called it "treadmill, departmentalized work." The revision in 1934 somewhat simplified the reporting procedures, but not the principle of government being the intermediary between business and the public, with lawyers controlling business's access to the government *and* the public.

For Sullivan & Cromwell the new regulatory environment came at a perfect time to deflect attention from John Foster Dulles and refocus it on the firm as a defender of business interests. By midnight, October 1, 1934, every public company had to register with the SEC and the country's twenty-four exchanges. Sullivan & Cromwell was also involved in the first registrations for raising new money, Pacific Gas & Electric's $45 million bond issue and Southern California Edison's $75 million issue of 3¾ percent bonds. The hunger in the market for these securities showed the pent-up demand over the period of resistance to the new laws; the end of the logjam created an enormous amount of business for the firm.

As much as Dulles resisted and ignored the new investing environment, Dean brought Sullivan & Cromwell into the modern world by using the new laws to rebuild and redefine the firm during the thirties. Dulles could continue his private work with the Germans, while Dean led the rest of the lawyers into a new relationship with clients, one based on legal requirements rather than on personal contact and judgment. Dean was by no means devoid of good judgment, but as a thirty-five-year-old junior partner, he did not have the clout of Dulles in advising senior executives.

For Dean's kind of work, judgment was not the primary issue. He had to get the papers prepared that brought companies into conformity with the new laws. Dulles's alienation from the new laws could have destroyed Sullivan & Cromwell. He and his like-minded anti-New Deal executives would have prospered fighting tooth and nail to stick to their old ways, and they would have died happy in their resistance. But the firm would have shriveled into a desiccated relic of the old order.

Dean brought the firm back to the legal mainstream through his Washington experience and the work it brought. He had been Dulles's right-hand man and firm administrator, but his rise in the firm was the result of his participation in the writing of the security laws in 1933 and 1934.

If Dulles was Moses, Dean was Aaron, the new blood for the Promised Land. He reflected what the new era was all about: a rejection of the high-handed slick banking practices of the 1920s, which Dulles participated in and defended. At a time when Frankfurter could complain that the "real culprits" resisting the new legislation "are some of the leading law firms who make such a fat killing out of the abuses which brought the Securities Act into existence," the same firm was making even more money supporting the new laws.

Dean fitted this new role by background as well as temperament. The son of a Cornell law professor, he grew up in Ithaca, New York, where he had to earn his way by clerking in a bank and being a night porter in a local hotel.

A graduate of Cornell and Cornell Law School, he was originally introduced to Dulles by an economics professor who passed on a book review Dean wrote of Keynes's *Economic Consequences of the Peace*. Dean accepted Keynes's argument that reparations demands were greater than Germany's ability to pay, a conclusion that also echoed Dulles's but, Dean later reported, "Mr. Dulles took me to task for expressing an opinion upon such a difficult economic problem when I didn't know any of the background. Only later did I learn he had given the same advice in Paris."

Dean retained a lifelong ability to name plants by their Latin name, an Ithaca legacy he transferred to the more elegant setting of his country homes in Oyster Bay and Nantucket. He remained a country bumpkin on Wall Street. In later years when he joined the Council on Foreign Relations, where most members discussed America's place in the world, Dean imparted the knowledge that the Brooklyn Dodgers had gotten their name because Brooklynites dodged the New York trolleys that turned around there. His shirttails often stuck out of his trousers; he sat at his desk with his hat on, and he wore red and white striped socks that wrinkled around his ankles. He was the archetypal inside man, who helped Sullivan & Cromwell overcome the legacy of its archetypal outside man.

12

TRUST IN ANTITRUST

> Some lawyers get to be fortyish, fiftyish, living in the suburbs, playing golf on weekends—then suddenly the client is faced with some new and very tough problem, and he takes his business somewhere else. In many cases where a law firm loses a client, you'll find the lawyers had too comfortable an experience.—ARTHUR H. DEAN

Arthur Dean was considered the consummate client contact, able to handle seventeen things at once and yet provide full assurance to each executive that he was intimately conversant with any problem brought before the great legal mind. Dean's prescience came from associates, who briefed him fifteen minutes before the client arrived. By the time the visitor was ushered into his large twenty-first floor corner office, Dean could expatiate on the problem with full reference to research and background, while the associate was the only person in the room who actually knew the law under discussion.

Dean would tell the executive, "Oh, well, I remember when we tried to draft that provision in the act and I had a hell of a time with that government lawyer. Those guys don't know what they're talking about, but still I had to make a compromise, and so the language is ambiguous, but I think you could rely on it.''

His approach to the law and clients perfectly suited the investment bankers' antitrust case, *United States of America* v. *Henry S. Morgan, Harold Stanley, et al. doing business as Morgan Stanley & Co., et al.* After all, the securities laws really did come out of meetings Dean had attended in 1933 and 1934, which he could make the most of.

Dean was not a litigator, but he argued the case because he was the only one initially willing to fight the government's suit; the industry and most other lawyers were inclined to settle. Dean, so closely associated with the original securities legislation, knew that the government later regretted not forcing banks to conduct financings by public sealed bidding. He would not easily give in to litigation-inspired revision of the legislation, when he had fought so hard for the leniency of the securities acts.

Postponed by World War II, *U.S.* v. *Morgan,* the granddaddy of modern antitrust cases, was at the top of the firm's agenda when the war came to an end. Dean mobilized his forces, inviting Bill Piel to become a partner specifically to handle the investment bankers' case. For the same reason eighteen new associates were hired in 1946, in addition to the nineteen who returned to the firm after the war.

It required as much—if not more—organizational skill as it did rhetorical brilliance to handle the case. Sullivan & Cromwell represented five of the seventeen defendants. Dean assigned an associate to each defendant, while Piel and Roy Steyer, who became a partner in 1953, acted as chiefs-of-staff for Dean.

The government accused the investment banks of dividing up new securities issues according to tradition in a way that eliminated competition and allowed price fixing. The defendants supposedly reserved the cream of the business for themselves to the exclusion of 200 other investment banks. The government made sixteen different accusations, claiming there was no freedom of choice for companies wanting to issue securities, no alternative means to raise money; that there were also dictation of financial terms by the defendants, hindrance in the growth of small businesses, and domination of investment banking by New York houses.

Dean wanted the bankers to explain the business in their own words while he gathered statistics to prove that no pattern existed in the underwriting history of these investment banks. He wanted to show that bankers usually waited to hear from clients rather than solicit business, and that no conspiracy existed when so many banks took syndicate leadership in a random fashion.

Because the government had interviewed few witnesses, Dean knew that the Justice Department was relying on statistics, which he would counter with his own story in numbers. He put four Harvard Business School researchers in specially rented space above Delmonico's restaurant to compile the charts and tables he needed. They used a rudimentary computer system—cards with holes in designated spots for each category of question—to analyze 10,000 new securities issues and private placements over the previous fifteen years. It took the researchers three years to finish the charts, which showed that banks often moved from first position in the number of syndications they led one year to sixth or seventh position in the following year; cooperation between banks also changed dramatically from year to year.

Dean led the laborious task of taking depositions, with the witnesses being prepped before their appearance and armed with documents for examination and cross-examination. A week's deposition filled five volumes of transcripts, which were then culled into short excerpts for the court. The defense filed 160 interrogatories to make the government be more specific in its accusations. Among other things, it wanted to know when the conspiracy had allegedly started and by whom.

After ten months the government responded, specifying that the conspiracy had begun with a Morgan syndicate on a large Anglo-French loan of 1915, but to keep the trial from lasting an eternity, the judge ruled that evidence would be confined to the period after January 1, 1935.

After three years of preparation, the case finally came to trial on November 28, 1950, in the classic federal courthouse in Foley Square. The granite columns of the courthouse, behind New York's modest colonial-style City Hall, are deceptively imposing, but inside, the building is full of small rooms painted an institutional green. Sullivan & Cromwell used one of the rooms for the spillover of papers and books from the wood-paneled courtroom of Judge Harold Medina, who was famous among generations of New York lawyers for his bar examination course. The lawyers' back room was shared with twenty to twenty-five attorneys from other firms who were involved in the case, including major partners of each firm and the best litigators in the city.

The government submitted statistics to show that the defendants had issued 85 percent of the prime securities marketed between January 1938 and April 1947, representing $14.4 billion in transactions that constituted 68.9 percent of all securities issued in that period. The prosecution alleged that the banks had excluded competitors from these transactions, employed similar practices and identical policies, all meant to thwart competitive bidding for new issues.

Almost on the first anniversary of the trial, on November 19, 1951, the prosecution dropped a number of its charges, including the claim that the defendants had tried to restrict investment banking to New York, neglected small companies, refused to work for clients' competitors, and coerced other investment banks outside their circle to refuse to become agents for new issues. Still, the government, referring to the defendants as "Club 17," considered its main argument intact and pursued its case with thousands of letters, memorandums, syndicate records, and other documents sifted for months on end from the files of the defendants.

The government, presenting a theoretical and statistical case, intended to rely exclusively on documents to show the pattern of conspiracy with little reference to the way a bank actually worked. It showed a pattern of operation in which clients relied on a single bank syndicator, who brought into the transaction those who had included them in other issues. The evidence of this cozy reciprocal arrangement made the judge admit that had the trial ended after the first year, he would have ruled for the prosecution.

But Dean pugnaciously rebutted the charges. In Dean's colorful phrase, government attorneys "compiled their statistics according to the age-old recipe for horse and rabbit stew—fifty horses and fifty rabbits." Dean built his case around figures and charts showing that "the First Boston Corporation, for example, started out in third place during the period 1935–1937, fell to tenth place in the triennial

1941–1943, and climbed to second place by the end of 1949.'' Such vicissitudes proved that the banks had not conspired to divide their business in any set pattern.

Dean used the court as a classroom in the history of securities law. A little deaf, not too articulate, and unpracticed, he had none of the accoutrements of the trial lawyer. Allen Wardwell, a fellow defense lawyer from Davis, Polk & Wardwell, admitted, ''I don't think Arthur Dean is a good trial lawyer, but I think he knows those cases so thoroughly and is so alive to the issues that are involved—it's not a trial case like a murder case with a jury—that I think he is getting it before Judge Medina perfectly well. While I don't think that he knows how to ask a question, he knows his stuff. I don't think anybody would go to Sullivan & Cromwell and ask for Arthur Dean to try a case for larceny or murder.''

But Dean was effective at examining witnesses because he knew the banking business and the people he was interrogating. The government case was built around three malcontents who had reasons of their own to force competitive bidding on the industry. Robert R. Young, chairman of the Alleghany Corporation, was fighting Morgan Stanley for control of his own company; Cyrus Eaton believed his Otis & Company bank in Cleveland was excluded from the New York money circle; and Harold Stuart's Halsey, Stuart & Company, had lost some status as an important New York investment bank when its major utilities client, Samuel Insull, collapsed in the stock market crash.

Once Dean's witnesses pointed out that clients approached banks, not vice versa, and profits had diminished with competition, the prosecution felt compelled to call its own witness. Harold Stuart, seventy-one when the case began and considered the dean of the Wall Street community, was so thoroughly questioned that he commented, ''I felt as though I had run down Wall Street naked.''

On cross-examination, Dean asked Stuart, ''Did you ever suggest to Mr. Insull . . . that he ought to put his securities up at public sealed bidding?''

''No, sir,'' Stuart replied.

''Why not?'' Dean asked.

''Because we had the business,'' Stuart admitted.

The prosecution rested its case in March 1953. Dean spent two months presenting motions to dismiss. The brief supporting the motion relied to a large degree on Stuart's testimony. A lifelong member of the Wall Street fraternity, Stuart remembered the noncompetitive syndication for loans long before the supposed beginning of the conspiracy in 1915.

"Mr. Stuart, the acknowledged champion of 'open price competition,' " the 404-page Sullivan & Cromwell brief noted,

> . . . has also testified that he did not recall a single instance in which he called upon the officers of an issuer, at a time when negotiations were going on with another investment banker, and offered them a better price. This was not because of any arrangement or understanding with other bankers, but, as Mr. Stuart has testified, the reason was that he did not think it would be a good way to get business because "I think it would probably cause great resentment on the part of the seller unless he asked you, and I think you would erect a wall against yourself immediately."

Judge Medina deliberated for six months over the defense motion to dismiss the case. For the defense to present its case would have taken another couple of years. On September 22, 1953, Judge Medina called a procedural conference to announce his verdict: He dismissed the case on grounds of insufficient evidence, echoing Dean's description of "a pattern of no pattern." Judge Medina added to the 57,971 pages of court transcript a record-breaking 424-page opinion. He dismissed the case "on the merits" and "with prejudice," meaning the Justice Department could appeal but not retry the case on the same complaints. The judge's opinion is considered a solid history of the investment banking business, for which he acknowledged Dean's guidance.

On a more personal note, one day the judge inquired about the absence of a lawyer, who, he was told, was awaiting the birth of a baby. When the lawyer appeared the next day, the judge congratulated him and asked him to keep score of the number of babies born to lawyers in the case. At the end of the trial, the lawyer reported there were twenty-one births, ten boys and eleven girls, all of whom got their pictures in *Life* magazine to mark the end of the case.

The investment bankers treated their victory with—above all—relief after five years of government lawyers' sifting through their files compiled under "instructions from Sullivan & Cromwell not to destroy one piece of paper." The case cost the banks $5 million to $7 million in legal fees which did not include the cost of the time the bank partners spent sitting in on the trial and the disruption to their businesses.

The real victory belonged to Sullivan & Cromwell. *It* was the one to benefit most from taking on the government in the first place and seeing the case through to the victory in court. The firm had hired new lawyers just for the case, a decision that was justified by the business its victory brought in subsequent years.

There was also a certain irony in Dean's victory in *United States* v. *Morgan*. He had shown that the investment banks were always competitors, even when they organized syndicates together. But as the lawyer for almost a third of the defendants, he revealed that Sullivan & Cromwell itself exercised considerable influence on Wall Street. Sharing a lawyer "brought the cost down a little bit, thank goodness," claimed Walter Sachs of Goldman, Sachs, which paid $700,000 for its defense. But the case also, if anything, proved only that power on Wall Street is diffused among the banks but concentrated in one law firm, which netted handsome fees for its effort. Sullivan & Cromwell demonstrated that it could make a group of bankers work together to face the law in a way the law would have forbidden their doing in business.

The case marked the second major contribution of Arthur Dean to the firm. It was a natural outgrowth of his work on the Securities Act of 1933 and the Securities Exchange Act of 1934. An expertise in antitrust law was a distinct specialty for a new, burgeoning area of government regulation of business. In 1950 Congress tightened the antitrust provisions of the Clayton Act by stopping mergers of companies that competed "in any line of commerce in any section of the country," a more stringent standard than had previously been applied. Though a number of lawyers had been hired specifically to deal with the investment bankers' antitrust case, they stayed as long as nine years with the succession of cases that helped define the new antitrust boundaries.

The firm could look back in increasing amusement at the memo Dave Hawkins wrote to the top partners in 1948, worrying that "at the end of the year we shall have 80 lawyers in the office. We have desks in rooms for 79. The excess over 79 must sit in the library." Lawyers soon got used to sitting in the library as their number grew from 83 in 1950 to 90 in 1958, and then to 102 in 1960. The library became so stuffed with lawyers that it was easier for them to do research at the New York County Lawyers' Association, which Cromwell had conveniently endowed near the office.

Four lawyers in a bullpen no longer represented the lowest rung on the Sullivan & Cromwell ladder on the way to getting a single room, which was a privilege but no great luxury. A new recruit asked the novelist Louis Auchincloss, when he was an associate with his own room at Sullivan & Cromwell, if he worked much at night. Auchincloss, whose tiny window looked out on a dark airshaft, answered, "I don't know."

The first signs of bureaucratic rigidity came in Dave Hawkins's memo about lawyers in the library. His solution was to "not take on another man unless one of the following partners concludes that he wishes the particular man to join his working group, regardless of the number already in the office." Restricting hiring to the group heads, which the memo suggested, established a structure that would become more pronounced as the firm got bigger.

In the 1950s Arthur Dean was already telling associates that partners were made "for three reasons: intellectual ability, dedication and the need of the firm for a partner, which was the most important. We may lose some good attorneys, but there will be others down the line, too." The quality of the individual had begun to be submerged into the needs of the organization. Eventually partners were chosen on the library-seating principle of filling vacancies. It came to be called the "slot system," which was run by group heads whose jurisdictions expanded from hiring associates to making partners.

Dave Hawkins established the myths of the new bureaucracy to foster loyalty with comments like "One thing we pride ourselves on here is that all of us have grown up in the firm. . . . The result is that it's a homogeneous firm. And it's never called for some bright specialist to come in. . . ." In fact, John Foster Dulles offered partnerships to lots of prominent lawyers. All turned him down, including John W. Davis, who went on to build Davis, Polk & Wardwell as a formidable New York firm; Thomas Dewey, who reentered the profession after his political career and resuscitated what became Dewey, Ballantine, Busby, Palmer & Wood; and John J. McCloy, who turned Dulles down in 1945 to go with what became Milbank, Tweed, Hadley & McCloy.

Dave Hawkins, however, wanted to perpetuate a myth that the firm refused to hire lateral partners. The firm had become self-sustaining; he wanted young lawyers to know the intensity of the commitment expected from them and given to them by the firm. In the 1950s it was still possible for Sullivan & Cromwell lawyers to get a job anywhere else on Wall Street or in corporate America by virtue of their experience at the firm. It was a golden name that conveyed the highest quality of law, rectitude, and influence. It had also grown faster than other firms, which could use Sullivan & Cromwell associates in order to expand.

Sullivan & Cromwell kept lawyers as long as it needed them, since it knew they would find work when they left. This, too, maintained morale and intensified young lawyers' commitment to the firm. More than 100 Sullivan & Cromwell attorneys have gone to work at client companies; at least seven became chief executives. Only a few associates thought the firm exploitative, taking advantage of their Depression mentality that made them grateful to be there and willing to accept a place in the bureaucracy.

There was plenty of work for the firm. In the 1950s the government brought antitrust suits against the Brown Shoe Company to prevent its merger with G. R. Kinney Company, Inc., and against Crown Zellerbach's merger with the St. Helens Paper Company. George C. Kern, Jr., eventually the firm's merger-and-takeover specialist, traced his expertise to his first merger case, *Brown Shoe,* which produced a landmark decision on permissible mergers. He worked in the company's headquarters, compiling data and taking affidavits for that antitrust case. When Arthur Dean relayed the request of Brown Shoe president Clark R. Gamble that Kern be a little tidier, Kern screamed, "He can have a charwoman or meet the injunction," and threw things around the office in a fury.

Dean argued the Brown Shoe Company's defense in the Supreme Court against the solicitor general, Archibald Cox, who would become famous a decade later as special Watergate prosecutor during the Nixon administration. Cox succeeded in convincing the justices in the *Brown Shoe* case that the merger of the third and the eighth largest shoe companies *did* violate antitrust laws because, as Chief Justice Earl Warren wrote in a unanimous opinion, "any decline in competition that might result need not have a uniform effect throughout the entire country. It is sufficient if the record proves that . . . competition will generally be lessened. . . ."

The shoe company had to dispose of its Kinney acquisition after losing the case in the Supreme Court, but the decision had taken seven years from the inception of the case in 1955, during which time Brown Shoe operated Kinney as a subsidiary. Kern had pioneered the argument that rather than postpone or prevent the merger in the first place, it should be allowed and held separately while justice took its course.

This argument proved particularly valuable for Crown Zellerbach, which had taken over St. Helens to provide a quick boost in papermaking capacity while it expanded its own facilities. Marvin Schwartz, later a partner of Kern's in takeover cases, was a young associate who spent four months on the West Coast deposing witnesses in the Crown Zellerbach antitrust suit. The case took four years, and though the firm lost in its defense, based on the failing companies' argument which allowed takeovers to prevent bankruptcy, Crown Zellerbach got what it wanted: the right to operate St. Helens while it increased its own papermaking capacity.

Antitrust work was the most lucrative, time-consuming legal specialty. It required hordes of lawyers, experts, detailed supervision, and dogged persistence. Sullivan & Cromwell was well qualified to do the work as a result of the habits long ingrained in the firm by Cromwell. But beyond the firm's discipline, it developed complex litigation management as a separate practice skill for antitrust and other remunerative work, while establishing a reputation for understaffing its cases.

It was astounding how few could do so much. Two lawyers put together the purchase of the Matador Land Company, one of the most complicated land deals ever devised. It took three days to close because it ultimately required 2,200 signatures on 600 documents. One of the lawyers, Bob McDonald, later joked that only two lawyers did it because "to explain the transaction would take more time than to do the work." But that was how the firm operated. It was expected, yet it was extraordinary, and it made a difference to the fate of the client. George Ames, a senior partner at Lazard Frères, for whom McDonald and partner John Raben did the Matador Land deal, considered it "an important milestone in the development" of the investment bank.

Ames watched—and helped—McDonald and Raben work night and day for eight months as the deal got progressively more complicated. Lazard had offered $18.9 million for the 800,000-acre Matador property, the second largest spread in Texas. Because it was owned by a Scottish company (whose shares had previously sold on the London stock market for one third of the American offer), the transaction involved British and American taxes, a division of the mineral rights to cut the Scots in on any oil discoveries, and special permission from the British government to let the sellers reinvest their money in the United States. Raben collapsed from exhaustion a month before the end of the deal, and McDonald had to finish alone. His stamina won him a Sullivan & Cromwell partnership in 1952.

The firm's reputation in the 1950s was enhanced by a detailed, prodigious, and sometimes unbelievable output that could save or earn clients millions of dollars on seemingly inconsequential points of law. Such projects responded to increasingly complicated and specialized laws in which the stakes could be as large as the issues seemed narrow and picayune. The firm perfectly suited the elitism of the Republican fifties. Anything was possible as long as the clients could afford it. Sullivan & Cromwell gave the best, cost the most, and never complained (just charged).

Litigation partner John Dooling got his client the American Metal Company extra deductions on foreign tax credits *(American Metal Co.*

Ltd. v. *Commissioner),* and in corporate litigation successfully argued that Ford had infringed an International Nickel Company patent on an intricate piece of modular iron machinery (*International Nickel Company Inc.* v. *Ford Motor Co. and Caswell Motor Co.*).

He also saved Smith-Corona from a takeover by Meshulam Riklis, later famous for marrying and supporting the career of singer-actress Pia Zadora, in an immensely convoluted and compact six-week case, tried before a Special Master in a conference room on the thirteenth floor of the Sullivan & Cromwell offices. Dooling's pioneering cases in the 1950s reflected the country's expansive, innovative activities, reaching into new areas of commercial enterprise, in which Sullivan & Cromwell participated as the foremost business-law firm.

Dooling saved longtime firm client Babcock & Wilcox, a major industrial construction company, from having to pay the full wartime excess profits tax by reinterpreting the interest due on those profits (*Babcock & Wilcox Co.* v. *Pedrick*). George Kern mastered the basics of nuclear physics to be able to represent Babcock & Wilcox before the Atomic Energy Commission in a long and persistent effort to get the regulators to see the point of view of those who are regulated. A boilermaker in conventional power plants, Babcock & Wilcox was an early participant in nuclear reactors. Kern helped formulate the Price Anderson Act, which limited the liability from nuclear disasters, and sought consistent approval of licenses for the design and building of plants so that companies would not face having a completed plant rejected after the original design was accepted.

Kern was on Babcock & Wilcox's board of directors, succeeding firm partners John Foster Dulles and Stoddard Stevens. In 1978 he defended the company in an all-out takeover defense against United Technologies. Seven litigations were going on at once, including an antitrust battle in Ohio, when the company was ultimately taken over by the white knight J. Ray McDermott Company.

Harry Gray, United Technology's combative chairman, blamed Kern for not getting Babcock & Wilcox, the first prey that he had failed to devour. After the leak at the plant at Three Mile Island, Pennsylvania, which Babcock & Wilcox had built, Gray thanked Kern for fending him off. Since that disaster occurred soon after the merger, Kern was no longer involved with the company, but the contracts he wrote limited Babcock & Wilcox's liability exposure in the ensuing legal nightmare.

The general practice of Sullivan & Cromwell dealt with the complexities of increasingly large public stock offerings. In 1955 William Ward Foshay, whose office was next to Arthur Dean's for thirty years, was called to organize the biggest public offering up to that time for Ford Motor Company.

Foshay was the partner in charge of securities work, but this was a significant step up for him because the lead underwriter, Blyth & Company, picked Foshay rather than the firm, establishing his reputation as one of the best securities lawyers in Wall Street, if not *the* best.

Foshay supervised teams of lawyers, who had to become familiar with all the loans and agreements the company had undertaken and to meet all states' regulations in the blue-sky provisions, many of which were more stringent than the SEC's. He confirmed the firm's ability to work not only as a cohesive group, but also as the leader of various law firms and investment banks brought together for a major underwriting. Only a year before in 1954, Sullivan & Cromwell handled the largest initial public offering to date—Campbell Soup's $51 million sale of shares. The Ford Motor Company's initial public offering in January 1956 was more than twelve times larger—$643 million.

The Ford deal required an unusually large contingent of Sullivan & Cromwell lawyers, who represented four underwriters as well as Blyth & Company. The five-car private train taking the financial team to Detroit included fifteen Sullivan & Cromwell associates among a concentration of the top business minds of the era. Charles Blyth, Sidney Weinberg of Goldman, Sachs (the Ford family banker), and senior Lehman Brothers bankers secretly boarded the train in New York for a trip on which the liquor flowed freely, the talk lasted late into the night, and "everybody was very, very up about it," a young Sullivan & Cromwell participant recalled.

For all the teamwork, these men were highly motivated, high-strung professionals who were trained to treat work as the reward for their positions. Not to work was punishment or an affront. As John Foster

Dulles once told Dave Hawkins (who took it as a compliment), "You know, Dave, I think there are only two people in this office that [*sic*] are willing for other people to do the work. And that's you and me."

Tensions surfaced publicly only once. In the late 1950s, a memo was circulated in the office that litigation partner Inzer Wyatt had resigned. Associates remembered that "Inzer and Dean got into a showdown. Dean sent around the memo, but in fact Wyatt had not resigned. The resignation memo was followed by a second one reversing the first."

It was a shocking admission of rumblings in the hierarchy, though no one talked about such things then. Associates interpreted the trouble to mean that "Inzer was not considered the royal road to advancement at the firm." The resignation memo remained a sensitive issue a quarter of a century later, when Wyatt, asked to elaborate on the two memos, said testily, "I did not resign. I never resigned before I resigned to go on to the bench." In 1962, President John F. Kennedy appointed Wyatt to the federal district court in the southern district of New York.

The Wyatt-Dean conflict was unusual for Sullivan & Cromwell. The firm remained remarkably free of the fiefdoms that powerful partners in some firms cultivate. The reconciliation between Wyatt and Dean was attributed to clients' telling Inzer they wouldn't stay with either him *or* the firm, a confirmation that clients tended to be Sullivan & Cromwell clients, not those of individual lawyers.

But Wyatt did have a little coterie in the litigation group in which he handled corporate as well as litigation clients. They were firm clients, to be sure, but Wyatt seemed intent on matching the senior partner's breadth of interests. Wyatt succeeded the Dulleses as the lawyer for the Wallenberg brothers, bringing them in as investors in the world's largest iron-ore deposit in Liberia. Wyatt represented Johnson Avery, a Canadian prospector, who had spent twenty years looking for minerals in Africa, only to come across the iron-ore lode on Christmas Day, 1955.

Avery's company, the Liberia-American Mining Company (Lamco), started with little more than a "hunting license" from the Liberian government. Wyatt sent associate Ken Scott to Liberia, where he spent months straightening out Lamco's contract with the Liberian government. The contract was originally "not too precise or clear. So there was room for definition and greater precision. As the concession agreement was turned into a more finely crafted legal document, the Liberian government's share went up," Scott admitted.

Living six degrees above the Equator, Scott was subjected to two seasons, both hot: one dry as dust, the other drenched with rain. He lived and worked out of Monrovia's best hotel, which elsewhere would be called a boarding house. Scott had to defend Lamco's share not only against the Liberians but also against other companies with capital and expertise that Wyatt had brought in, such as the Wallenbergs' Swedish mining company. Scott performed chores like delivering a commencement address at the University of Monrovia, standing in for Johnson Avery (including the use of his tuxedo), and attending state dinners, where he knew his rank from the Johnny Walker Black Label scotch on the table, compared with the Red Label tables of the lesser guests.

Wyatt specialized in marathon litigation, like the complicated, decades-long dispute over the Bata shoe empire. Thomas Bata, the man who built the international company based in Prague, Czechoslovakia, later handed over the company to his brother, Jan, with the understanding he was to pass it on to Thomas Bata, Jr., a seventeen-year-old at the time of the transaction in 1931. Thomas Bata died a year later.

In 1939 the son was dismissed by his uncle, Jan, who was determined to keep Bata on good terms with the Nazis, while Thomas, Jr., and his mother were Allied partisans. In the midst of the war 826 previously unknown shares of the Bata holding company were found in a safe-deposit box that both Jan and Thomas, Jr., claimed. The company's dispersal and radical changes in Czech law after World War II made it an exceedingly complicated case, especially since the disputed shares constituted a controlling interest in the company.

Wyatt, representing Thomas, Jr., and his mother, conducted litigation almost continuously from 1942 to 1961, "using corresponding law firms in places throughout Europe. I would be there as a consultant," Wyatt said, "because I was not familiar with the customs and practices there. Even if I was permitted to appear in court, it would have been unwise to do so." The case kept getting reversed on successive appeals, depending on how the judges interpreted the senior

Thomas Bata's intentions. It was clear that he would have given the shares to his brother, Jan, had they not been hidden in the safe-deposit box, but that he hid them and wanted his son to take over the company persuaded some courts to reestablish the original intent of the bequest.

After a partial victory in the Delaware Supreme Court, Wyatt negotiated a favorable comprehensive settlement for the widow and Thomas Bata, Jr. But after Wyatt's appointment to the federal bench, the opposition, headed by frequent presidential candidate Harold E. Stassen, renounced the settlement. Further litigation ensued in Philadelphia, England, and Holland, postponing a final settlement for a decade, after which Sullivan & Cromwell partner Robert MacCrate earned a place as a senior adviser to the conclave of the Bata Shoe Organization.

Antitrust work continued with little letup. Bill Piel represented the Flinkote Company in *U.S.* v. *Masonite,* a case the government brought to stop Masonite from fixing prices on its patented hardwood boards, which were made by exploding wood chips into a white, cottony substance that was then compacted under heat into grainless boards. Every hardwood board supplier wanted the product and had spent two to three times the amount of Masonite's license to find a competitive product, but the government deemed the licenses anticompetitive.

The government appealed to the Supreme Court after losing in the lower court. Piel faced a deathly silence when he entered a strategy meeting for the Supreme Court argument. The other defendants wanted another firm to represent Flinkote, having calculated that Harlan Fiske Stone held the crucial vote in what would otherwise be a 4–4 decision. They did not want him to sit out the case.

Dean told Piel to say that Sullivan & Cromwell would not drop out of the case, but the Supreme Court brief could delete its name. In the end Stone was just one vote in a unanimous verdict against the defendants. "So much for projections," Piel chuckled. It was a time when the government lost few antitrust cases.

Still, Arthur Dean gave the firm a solid legacy of substantial, remunerative work, as he remained the senior partner, but followed the Dulles brothers to Washington.

13

THE GOVERNMENT AS CLIENT

> I wonder a good deal about the desirability of bringing to Washington at this initial juncture a second partner of Sullivan & Cromwell, having in mind that with me as Secretary of State, with Allen as Deputy CIA and with [Norris] Darrell as Under-Secretary of the Treasury, a rather frightening picture could be drawn by unfriendly persons.—JOHN FOSTER DULLES

In April 1952 Eustace Seligman walked excitedly into the office that John Foster Dulles kept at Sullivan & Cromwell. He said that General Lucius Clay had just called him to discuss the possibility of Dulles's going to Paris to meet Dwight David "Ike" Eisenhower after Henry Cabot Lodge, an elder statesman of the Republican party, had convinced Ike to run for President. Ike had Clay call Seligman, a fellow board member at Marine Midland Bank, a longtime Sullivan & Cromwell client.

Dulles could hardly contain his excitement. He realized he had not lost his final chance to be secretary of state when Dewey failed to beat Truman in the 1948 election.

Dulles, who retained an office on the eighteenth floor though he was officially retired from the firm, called in Dean to help figure out what he should say to Ike. Seligman advised that the general was more likely to have a military policy than a foreign policy, and Dean added that his popularity was based on well-publicized efforts to minimize the number of American casualties in the war. Someone at the Council on Foreign Relations attributed Ike's genius to knowing as early as 1940 that the American public would not support an unpopular war that produced senseless American deaths.

Seligman said that "massive retaliation" was the modern strategy, using nuclear warheads to frighten enemies into peace and keep American boys from having to fight. Dulles went to Paris the following week, where Ike was delighted with Dulles's up-to-date and sensible policy of massive retaliation. They did not bother to discuss foreign policy.

Every lawyer in Sullivan & Cromwell followed the 1952 presidential election with a deep personal interest. When vice-presidential candidate Richard Nixon gave his Checkers speech explaining a secret political slush fund, the partners hovered over a radio on the eighteenth floor near Dulles's office, while the associates gathered in a room downstairs off the library to hear it.

Not all the lawyers were conservative Republicans. The Hiss case had already shown how divided the partners could be, with Seligman giving the money to reconstruct the "Woodstock typewriter" in Alger Hiss's defense against accusations of his spying for the Communists. When a third Hiss trial was planned in 1952, Seligman asked Dulles to review his previous testimony about hiring Hiss as president of the Carnegie Endowment for International Peace, of which Dulles was chairman. Hiss claimed that Dulles asked him to be president. In the first trial, Dulles admitted this, but in the second changed his testimony to say he was not at the meeting at which Hiss was hired.

A seemingly minor point, it was important as one of only half a dozen contradictions pinned on Hiss. In reading the transcripts of the two trials, Seligman noticed the inconsistency in Dulles's testimony, but Dulles refused to jeopardize his political career by standing up for Hiss despite Seligman's urging.

Such divisiveness did not dampen the impression in the early 1950s that the firm and the business interests it represented were on the threshold of power and influence they had not enjoyed for three decades. "There was a hum of expectancy along Wall Street and at Sullivan & Cromwell," recalled associate James Thacher, a Democrat stopping at the firm on his way back to his family law practice in San Francisco. "One had the feeling that the men who guided the firm and their clients in the worlds of finance and business were, or shortly were to be, in or near the saddle of events and, more importantly, that events themselves could be ordered by the considered application of sound thinking by men of prudence, character, and intelligence."

Even Democrats in the firm had reason to celebrate Ike's victory over Adlai Stevenson. Marvin Schwartz, though a second-year associate and a liberal Democrat, had during the campaign researched for Dulles legal questions about the effect on American law of the United Nations charter, especially as it related to human rights.

Janet Dulles wore to the inauguration an emerald necklace that had been given to her by William Nelson Cromwell. Only when it was appraised after she died nearly two decades later did her children learn that the necklace was a fake. Each generation had its own reasons for remembering Cromwell.

So wide did Dulles seem to be opening the door of government to his former clients that at his polite confirmation hearing for secretary of state, Michigan Senator Homer Ferguson pointedly asked, "Could you tell us whether or not there are any fees that may come in the future in which you would in any way be interested?"

Dulles, who two days before had received a final $45,000 settlement from the firm, responded, "There is not one single cent that I am entitled to receive or expect to receive from S&C or any clients or any fees from now on." The lump-sum payment was far less than his $200,000 income in the 1940s, but it was about five times what the firm had been paying him. Since his resignation in 1949, Sullivan & Cromwell had picked up the tab for Dulles's rented house in Washington, with servants, food, and utilities which cost about $900 a month. The settlement was also double the yearly $22,500 he would earn as secretary of state.

But the benefit to Sullivan & Cromwell in Dulles's new position was not lost on the firm's new clients, starting with Standard Oil of New Jersey, which hired Dean for its impending criminal antitrust case. This was a legacy of Dean's own reputation in antitrust, but the political overtones of the case made Sullivan & Cromwell's connections at the top of the new administration an essential part of the defense's strategy. Accusations that oil companies fixed prices went back to wartime investigations, but the Justice Department postponed prosecution on security grounds for the duration of the war. The oil-cartel issue came up again in 1948, when the European Cooperation Administration, which organized the Marshall Plan in Europe, discovered that the oil companies were overcharging them.

The Federal Trade Commission produced a 400-page secret report in 1951—published a year later by the Senate Select Committee on Small Businesses—which detailed the history of collusion in the oil markets and exposed their intricate sharing arrangements around the world. But only in the summer of 1952 did the Justice Department produce an internal memo noting the "existence of a series of agreements among the seven largest oil companies in the world to divide markets, to distribute on a quota basis, to fix prices and to control the production of oil throughout the world. These agreements are in violation of the antitrust laws of the United States." The delay in bringing the case against the oil companies worked very much in favor of the defendants and their new lawyer, Arthur Dean.

On January 11, 1953, the same week as Dulles's confirmation hearing, the Justice Department offered to drop criminal charges and bring only a civil suit against the oil-cartel defendants if they would produce the documents requested in the criminal case. *The New York Times* speculated that the change "could easily end in a compromise and consent arrangement whereby the companies might agree to end the practices complained of."

The offer was a last-minute effort by the outgoing Truman administration to salvage the case in the strongest terms it could before the Republicans took power. But Dean was in no mood to compromise. He called the offer "outrageous blackmail." After meeting with the attorney general, who conveyed the President's proposal, Dean spoke for the thirty-five lawyers representing the oil companies, fuming, "He gave us until 11:00 A.M. tomorrow to go along with this. His statement was the most insulting I have ever heard during twenty years at the bar.''

Dean told reporters that the attorney general ''glared at us and told us peremptorily to sit down. He said he would not make any further explanation of the offer.'' Mixing vitriolic metaphors as he warmed to the subject, he continued, ''When I asked if he wasn't holding a gun to our heads and demanding that we swallow his offer hook, line and sinker or not at all, he said we could take it or leave it—that if one company rejected the offer that was sufficient to nullify the proposition. It seemed to us that this was cold blackmail by a high Government official, and we said so.''

Dean added, ''That kind of thing happens behind the Iron Curtain, but I didn't think it would happen here.'' Reminded that the attorney general spoke for the President, Dean replied, ''That's right. And speaking for the Standard Oil Company of New Jersey, I said I wanted no part of his proposition and rejected it in its entirety.''

Asked why he would not cooperate, Dean revealed his basic defense, which would hold good for the following eight years: ''If it were not for the question of national security, we would be perfectly willing to face either a criminal or a civil suit. But this is the kind of information [on European oil delivery contracts] that the Kremlin would love to get its hands on. Once it is produced in compliance with the subpoena, it is public property.''

A national security defense had nothing to do with the merits of the case, but it did get two of the most powerful members of the administration involved in the client's cause.

Following his brother into government service, Allen Dulles became the director of the Central Intelligence Agency in the first week of the Eisenhower administration. Norris Darrell, who originally was going to be made undersecretary of the treasury, remained in New York because, Dulles wrote to Leonard Hall, the head of Eisenhower's transition team, ''I wonder a good deal about the desirability of bringing to Washington at this initial juncture a second partner of Sullivan & Cromwell, having in mind that with me as Secretary of State, with Allen as Deputy CIA and with Darrell as Under-Secretary of the Treasury a rather frightening picture could be drawn by unfriendly persons.'' But even from New York, the administration used Darrell to devise the Internal Revenue Code of 1954, which was the basis of American taxation for more than thirty years.

Dean asked the judge presiding over the oil antitrust grand jury to postpone the defendants' answers to subpoenas to "give the new Administration time to consider if it wants to act or not." Two months later, the new administration abandoned the criminal investigation of the oil cartel without asking concessions from the companies. The civil case continued, but the companies were not under the same obligation to produce documents.

The Dulles brothers undertook a persistent and effective policy to obstruct the case on national security grounds. In exasperation the Justice Department cataloged Foster Dulles's actions, particularly in the National Security Council, where the "Secretary of State believed that the suit would prejudice our foreign relations unless conducted with due regard to all matters affecting foreign relations as well as national security." Dulles got the National Security Council to set up a special committee to "screen evidence and segregate from public disclosure evidence with national security implications."

The national security implications of the United States' oil business were raised during preliminary discussions of the case in the Truman administration, but by the secretary of the interior, not the secretary of state. Dulles's actions had the effect of making the case pass through his office, a clear conflict of interest, considering his close ties to the defendants'counsel.

Other aspects of the relationship with Sullivan & Cromwell were less concealed. Dulles asked Dean to negotiate the prisoner exchange at the end of the Korean War, though he recognized, he told Republican National Committee Chairman Leonard Hall, "there might be criticism about his taking someone from his old firm but it was a terrific problem to get anyone as capable." While anxious to take the Korean assignment, Dean would not let it interfere with the oil litigation because, he told Dulles, he had "interviewed the 60 oil operating head[s] abroad and [have] been working on the case for 18 months, no one else is prepared." A week later the judge who was supposed to hear the argument withdrew for health reasons, and all proceedings in the case were indefinitely postponed. Dean was then free to take the Korea job.

Hall thought Dulles should pick someone else, but Vice-President Nixon told Dulles to "go ahead with it" even if "there would, of course, be the inevitable criticism." The President agreed that "we should [not] be prevented from getting the services of able people merely because of this type of criticism."

Henry Ess, a Sullivan & Cromwell partner, told Dean there was a disturbing ambiguity in the law about conflict of interest. It could be interpreted to mean that a lawyer could not work for the government if his firm was involved in any case against the government. Dulles "didn't think this was sound law. Evasion was one thing, and the possibility of evasion another." Dean said he "did not want any criticism and would do whatever was necessary to avoid it." After numerous leaks had forced the issue, the State Department just ignored the objections. On September 15, 1953, Dean was appointed "Deputy to the Secretary of State in preparation for the prospective Korean Political Conference and to serve at that Conference as Deputy Chairman of the Secretary of State on the United States Delegation" with the rank of ambassador.

Dean had made his choice and now had to lie in a hard soldier's bed in the knee-deep mud of an American army base in South Korea instead of his luxurious New York apartment near the mayor's mansion in Gracie Square. Compared with the services provided by Dean's butlers and maids in New York, his army camp existence was indeed "a great sacrifice," as Dulles had originally claimed to Leonard Hall. Dean started every day with a helicopter flight to face hours of verbal abuse from the other side before returning to the primitive conditions near the Korean border separating north and south.

Arthur Dean, trudging through the mud of Korea, epitomized Sullivan & Cromwell at the crux of world events, negotiating for seven weeks with the Communist Chinese and North Koreans. Dean was known for his disarming sense of humor, which usually enlivened tough negotiations or diverted the opposition.This negotiating table, across which no hands were shaken, no politeness exchanged, had a line down the middle exactly on the thirty-eighth parallel between

North and South Korea. Across it Dean was called a "capitalist crook, rapist, thief, robber of widows, stealer of pennies from the eyes of the dead . . . a murderer lying in the gutter with filthy garbage, wallowing in the filth of a ram." This seemingly harmless, good-natured little lawyer with the rumpled clothes and sagging socks legitimately represented something that, to the Communists, symbolized the enemy. What he represented could be taken to be the firm, the law, his country, and even the United Nations, whose troops were fighting the North Koreans and Chinese.

The routine was draining. Dean finally got fed up with the harangues, shouted back, and suddenly walked out of the negotiations. Dulles, annoyed, led a policy debate that spilled into public criticism, especially when Dean got back to New York just in time for his son's wedding. W. Averell Harriman, an experienced negotiator, thought "what Arthur Dean did in Panmunjom was absolutely wrong. He tried to outshout the Koreans. . . . He descended to the Korean level." The government was deluged with letters, like the one the President got, complaining, "Mr. Dean [is] returning to this country for the Christmas holiday and for his son's wedding when the peace in Korea and the world hangs in the balance."

Back home, Dean got into further trouble when he contradicted government policy and advocated recognizing Red China "with a view toward splitting Communist China from the Soviet Union without military action," as the Cleveland *Plain Dealer* reported. He also said "the U.S. would not drop an atomic bomb in Korea," which as Dulles told him, "was contradictory to the general line taken." Dean had Sullivan & Cromwell associate Lawrence McQuade prepare an article on recognizing the two Chinas for *Foreign Affairs,* which caused a sensation when it was printed. *The New York Times* considered the article worthy of a front-page story.

To most people who knew Dulles and Dean, it was hard to believe that Dean would write an article on China without consulting the secretary of state. McQuade, who actually wrote the article, did not know but assumed Dulles was aware of what he was writing. But the secretary of state told his brother, "Arthur Dean has been talking too much," and would have dropped him from the resumed negotiations except he was afraid that "it will look like a Communist victory which they might take advantage of."

Dean's sudden interest in foreign policy was an ironic twist to his career in the law, in which the Dulles brothers had kept Sullivan & Cromwell's international dealings mostly to themselves. Dean had negotiated Japanese bonds in 1928 and occasionally gone to Europe for the firm, but the Dulleses always led the way and formulated policy. Not being in the firm, Foster Dulles could no longer control Dean the way he once had. While the fate of Dean's ambassadorship was being debated in Washington, he found a way to keep up his foreign policy work at home. As mayor of Upper Brookville, Long Island, he conducted the sale of the Soviet Union's thirty-eight-room mansion for nonpayment of local taxes. Because he was hard of hearing, Dean had his wife, Polly, wield the auctioneer's mallet in their living room on a Duncan Phyfe mahogany drop-leaf table.

Unlike at Panmunjom, this encounter with communism occurred as the participants sipped coffee in front of a blazing hearth, surrounded by the Deans' collections of antique pewter, china, and glass. The high bid was $544.88 for the fifteen-acre estate, which was valued at more than $100,000. But the Soviets had two years to match the bid to redeem it themselves or get a tax exemption on the property, as they ultimately did.

As for Korea, *The New York Times* story about the auction called Dean the "former special envoy to the Korean peace negotiations." Sullivan & Cromwell, as the Dulleses had shown for thirty years, did better behind the scenes.

Being a hard-boiled and aggressive anti-Communist became Dulles's public image once he got involved in politics. But privately he was more ambiguous. When Dewey lost the presidential election in 1948, Dulles wrote to his brother that he would have liked "to shape things up so as perhaps to break the tension with the Soviet Union. It calls, I think, for a kind of coordinated effort and over-all planning that I do not think possible under Truman." His legal career was also a long exercise in compromise and internationalism, which may have had no direct bearing on relations with the Soviet Union but did show a pragmatic side of the man that seemed to disappear when he took office.

His dogmatic reputation was not unearned. As secretary of state, Dulles became a red-baiter who stripped the State Department of some of its most devoted civil servants. He forced the resignation of George F. Kennan, the career diplomat credited with conceptualizing containment in a *Foreign Affairs* article. Arthur Dean echoed the sentiments of the secretary of state when he said, ''he was glad to know that Kennan was out'' because ''he was an introvert who didn't understand Russia at all.''

Dulles attacked containment as a policy of being ''satisfied as long as the Communists didn't actually get into our front yard.'' He wanted to roll back communism in contrast with the Truman administration's policy that, he said ''destroyed the hopes of these [East European] people, and they more readily became the victims of Soviet aggression than if we had given them more vigorous support.'' He also shocked civil libertarians for his acquiescence to the spirit of McCarthyism by having ''instructed the FBI to make a thorough investigation of all aspects of my past. They have done so and reported'' to Eisenhower. ''I did that as an example which I thought should be followed generally.''

Three reasons account for Dulles's seeming change from a pragmatist to a dogmatic anti-Communist. His previous support of Alger Hiss to become president of the Carnegie Foundation had made him vulnerable to attack; anticommunism helped deflect criticism from himself. Second, in the Truman administration, Dulles had supported a bipartisan foreign policy. Aggressive anticommunism was a way to dominate the State Department and avoid sharing power with the Democrats. Third, anticommunism was the easiest way to rehabilitate Germany, as a bulwark against the enemy in Eastern Europe. All three of these issues concerned Dulles. The handwritten notes for his confirmation hearing in January 1953 contained references to ''Hiss,'' ''bipartisan foreign policies,'' and ''Cromwell estate,'' the last dealing with aid to the Soviets. The senators did not ask questions on these subjects, but Dulles was obviously worried that they would.

Dulles turned to Sullivan & Cromwell to carry out his support for Germany; the firm in turn could expect Dulles to safeguard the interests of its clients. He publicly endorsed a bill proposed by the raspy-voiced Republican Senate leader, Everett Dirksen, to return all the property held by the Alien Property Custodian to its previous owners. The accumulated value of Nazi-owned property that the United States confiscated during the war was put at between $15 million and $200 million, depending on the valuation of Sullivan & Cromwell client General Aniline & Film.

Dulles justified the return of the property for a number of reasons: There were "humanitarian and policy considerations"; "it seemed like ruthless confiscation"; and "historically we have been for private ownership of property." One reason he did not mention was the benefit to Sullivan & Cromwell clients.

Attorney General Brownell, who opposed the bill, claimed that even Konrad Adenauer, the German chancellor, "said when he was here that he would not raise the point. The property," he added, "was taken instead of reparations."

Dulles defended the Dirksen bill before a Senate Judiciary subcommittee despite the loud objections of the horrified Allies and Nazi victims. Holland, for instance, had already confiscated $100 million, a small fraction of the damage done by the Nazi invasion. The Justice Department used the international reaction as an excuse to kill the bill, despite the lobbying of the secretary of state, who should have been among the most responsive federal officials to foreign governments.

Dulles tried to get the attorney general to cancel or at least to postpone the Alien Property Custodian's sale of the Hugo Stinnes Corporation, which held the assets of the "coal king" of the Ruhr Valley. Legally, anyone could bid on the company, but Dulles called Arthur Dean to get help in making sure Germans bought the shares. Dean spoke with André Meyer of Lazard Frères, who, Dean reported to Dulles, "might be able to handle it on an able and confidential basis."

Just before the bidding closed, *The New York Times* carried a long story with four photographs on the extensive assets and revived fortunes of the company under its postwar president, Milton Rosenthal, operating for the Alien Property Custodian. The *Times* noted that a number of companies might be interested in the shares, but when the bids were opened, majority ownership went for less than the prevailing stock market price to the sole bidder, the Deutsche Bank of Frankfurt.

Dean's role in the sale remains submerged in classified documents, including a series of conversations among Dean, Meyer, and Dulles that were not released publicly, even under Freedom of Information requests made in 1985, nearly thirty years after the event. Whether Dean discouraged other bids (through Meyer or on his own), the truth is locked in files tantalizingly identified only as "Stinnes matter."

The oil companies' antitrust case gave the firm a role in the Middle East foreign policy crises in the Eisenhower years. Through Allen Dulles, the firm represented the Anglo-Iranian Oil Company, which suffered a major loss when the pajama-clad hysterical populist prime minister of Iran, Dr. Mohammad Mossadeq, nationalized the company's oil fields and confiscated its property. Allen Dulles engineered a CIA plot to overthrow Mossedeq and bring back the shah, a longtime acquaintance. Anglo-Iranian's concession was renegotiated, with Sullivan & Cromwell smoothing the way for a redivision that cut the major American oil companies in on the British concession. The company felt compelled to change its name to British Petroleum in recognition of the loss of its exclusive title in Iran, but over the succeeding years, Sullivan & Cromwell helped it develop the exceedingly profitable oil fields on the North Slope of Alaska, take over Standard Oil of Ohio, and build an Alaskan pipeline. Sullivan & Cromwell also got BP removed as a defendant in the oil antitrust case because of the sovereign immunity of the British government, which owned the company.

In the 1956 Suez crisis, Arthur Dean acted as intermediary among the secretary of state, the oil companies, and the State of Israel. Promising Dulles to "go back and get hold of execs of Standard Oil of NJ and see what they can do" about "the oil companies moving M[iddle] E[ast] oil through the Canal," Dean was in a position to keep the oil companies abreast of the crisis.

On October 3, 1956, Dean had a breakfast conference with the Israeli ambassador to the United States, Abba Eban, to discuss the "denial by Egypt of her [Israel's] rights to send ships through the Canal," as Dean reported to the secretary of state. Two months later Golda Meir and Eban breakfasted with Dean and pulled out a topographical map of the canal to show "where the Arabs used to fire on the Israeli boats coming up through there [and] they have some soldiers there now. . . . [I]n an effort to keep the Gulf open they have advised [UN Secretary-General Dag] Hammarskjöld that they want to keep those people there until there has been some overall UN policy with respect to the relations between Egypt and Israel."

Throughout Dean emphasized to both foreign diplomats and Americans that, as he affirmed in a letter to Dulles, "you didn't . . . ever authorize me to have any role in the matter. I tried to make it very clear . . . that my function was only to listen and to analyze some of the problems and to pass on to you some of the thoughts which might be helpful, as I had absolutely no authority from you in the matter."

Dean offered to withdraw: "I don't want to cross any wires or give anyone any false impressions and if you think it preferable that I should simply decline to discuss this extremely difficult subject, I would be very glad to get your views." Dulles replied, "Let me say first that I am very glad that many of our mutual friends are in communication with you about this situation. . . . If it [Dean's offer to withdraw] meant that you have no official status in the matter, of course, that is correct."

With the firm's role in the Middle East compromising the Justice Department's case against the oil companies, government lawyers took another tack to get Sullivan & Cromwell disqualified. A young partner, Garfield Horn, who had been to college with Dulles's son Avery and eventually bought Dulles's Cold Spring Harbor home, had been with the Economic Cooperation Administration, which discovered the oil companies' discriminatory oil pricing. Horn supposedly gained "special knowledge" of the case through that work. The firm hired the eminent litigator Bruce Bromley of Cravath, Swaine & Moore, to fight the Justice Department's accusation. Though Horn may have theoretically been in a supervisory position in the investigation of the oil companies' abuses, he had had no personal role in it. On that basis, the government lost its case to disqualify Sullivan & Cromwell.

In the main antitrust case the Justice Department forced the oil companies to produce thousands of pages of documents about their international operations and dealings with each other. Dean had a constant flow of correspondence resisting demands, particularly over foreign operations where other governments were unaware of the oil companies' agreements and procedures. Serious negotiations began in the second term of the Eisenhower administration. They were not concluded by the time Foster Dulles died in May 1959. Finally, the companies agreed to end collusive activities within months of the end of the Eisenhower administration, settling the case that had started as the President took office eight years before.

The firm's role in foreign policy switched from a private international operation on behalf of clients in the heyday of the Dulles brothers to a subordinate role designated by the Dulles brothers once they were in government. The new position suited the firm, which had lost its independent foreign policy creators anyway and could now call the government its client. In 1958 Dulles gave Dean a new job, negotiating the Law of the Seas treaty, which was later taken over by John R. Stevenson, a successor to Dean as senior partner of Sullivan & Cromwell. The foreign policy traditions of the firm were thus both perpetuated and tamed when the Dulleses joined the government and gave Sullivan & Cromwell an official part in the country's international relations.

14

COUNTER COUNTERCULTURE

Hello, "Company Man."—JUDGE DAVID W. PECK TO A NEWLY APPOINTED SULLIVAN & CROMWELL PARTNER.

Despite Sullivan & Cromwell's close association with the Eisenhower administration, John F. Kennedy's Democratic victory in the 1960 presidential election did not immediately sever the firm's Washington connections. The firm would of course have been better off with the election of Richard M. Nixon, who had admitted to John Foster Dulles, "If you had given me a job, I'm sure I would be there today, a corporate lawyer instead of Vice-President."

But Foster Dulles died in May 1959, having resigned the month before, gaunt and ravaged by cancer. In one of the first decisions of the new administration, Kennedy announced the reappointment of Allen Dulles as director of the Central Intelligence Agency. Arthur Dean was considered for a number of posts. McGeorge Bundy wrote in exasperation, "Arthur Dean's name gets considered for almost every important appointment." He was finally chosen negotiator of the nuclear test-ban treaty in 1961 and 1962, with the rank of ambassador.

Allen Dulles diminished the firm's influence in Washington after the Bay of Pigs fiasco when Cuban exiles under CIA control mounted an abortive invasion against the Fidel Castro regime.

The planning for the invasion had started in the Eisenhower administration, when the Dulles brothers had access to information about Castro through Laurence A. Crosby. Crosby was a Sullivan & Cromwell partner who had resigned from the firm in 1946 to live in Cuba, where he held a number of executive positions in sugar companies and was the chairman of the U.S. Cuban Sugar Council from 1954 to 1960.

To the Dulleses, intervention in Cuba was nothing new. Foster had gotten President Woodrow Wilson to protect the interests of firm clients by sending 1,600 troops to Cuba in 1917. By the time of the Bay of Pigs, Allen Dulles was carrying the banner alone, somewhat isolated from the center of power in the Kennedy administration. But he got the blame for a misguided policy that Kennedy came to feel "was one of those rare things in history, a perfect failure," according to historian Arthur M. Schlesinger, Jr., who added, "It led to Kennedy's having great skepticism about the experts he had inherited from the previous administration. He never trusted them again."

Dean invited Allen Dulles back to the firm as a $50,000-a-year Of Counsel elder statesman, serving on the boards of mutual-fund clients and writing books on intelligence and on his wartime service in Switzerland. Refusing to relinquish his lifelong romance with intrigue and covert action, he wrote Dean, "Espionage in the field of business seems to be assuming new proportions which does not particularly surprise me as I have often wondered why there was not more of it. Undoubtedly you are considering, with our old clients, some of the problems involved in the whole problem of industrial intelligence. We might have a word about this when we next get together," he wrote tantalizingly with no further elaboration.

Allen Dulles was called back to Washington in 1963 to be a member of the Warren Commission on the Assassination of President Kennedy, after which he returned to Sullivan & Cromwell with a reduced annual stipend of $16,000.

The firm's continuing links to Washington eventually became a liability, since the Vietnam War proved unpopular and Dean was advising President Lyndon Johnson as one of the "wise men" chosen to rally the country around presidential policy. Dean ingratiated himself by sending the President obsequious telegrams on his election in 1964 and his State of the Union message in 1965.

But he could not manage to have the President meet with a client, Frank Coolbaugh, president of Amax. Coolbaugh wanted to justify a price increase for molybdenum, a steel alloy used in weapons, which increase the government rescinded. Dean was forced to take his client to see presidential adviser Joseph Califano; still, when the company raised the price six months later, the government did not interfere.

Dean continued to support the President and his foreign policy. He proposed starting a new organization to rally support for the war called the Committee for an Effective and Durable Peace in Asia. With a name echoing Foster Dulles's platitude about a durable peace after World War II, the group placed a large advertisement in *The New York Times* soliciting funds to be sent to Sullivan & Cromwell at 48 Wall Street.

The ad was little more than a public relations effort for the war, but it misleadingly claimed a higher purpose: "to enlist economic aid for the entire area and to assure the people of South Vietnam their right to choose a government of their own, free from assassination, threats of violence or other forms of intimidation." John J. McCloy, also a presidential adviser and a Wall Street lawyer, criticized Dean's disingenuous high-mindedness, writing, "I do not feel disposed to put my name on a manifesto which calls for contributions and which by implication at least suggests that this committee is going to follow this whole Viet Nam situation and if at any point the committee feels the Government is not going along the right direction we will speak out and try to put them on the right track."

But McCloy ultimately did sign the manifesto along with four dozen other business leaders, including Sullivan & Cromwell clients, Frederick W. Colclough of Inco (and a former firm associate), André Meyer of Lazard Frères, Robert D. Murphy of the Campbell Soup Company, and Harold Zellerbach of Crown Zellerbach. Dean's foray into politics isolated him from the growing revulsion and protest against the war, even though, as the chairman of the board of trustees of Cornell University, he was exposed to some of the earliest manifestations of campus unrest, with draft card burnings and pitched battles among students of the left and right.

The firm suffered from Dean's absence, starting in 1963 when the President instituted an interest-equalization tax to eliminate the advantage foreigners had in the American financial markets. Instead of immediately setting up the same service in London, where Sullivan & Cromwell could have operated beyond the jurisdiction of the new American law, the firm let its foreign securities work lapse, causing a sharp curtailment of an important part of its business.

Dean, a fervent internationalist who worked in the Dulleses' shadow but who also had long experience handling the firm's foreign bond issues, might have acted on the threatened loss of international business. William Ward Foshay, Dean's right-hand man, cared less about the international business.

John R. Stevenson, who succeeded Foshay as firm chairman, admitted, "The large volume of international financings was sharply reduced in the 1960s when the interest equalization tax and other restrictions on U.S. foreign investments were introduced."

Stevenson, who arranged World Bank bond issues and financings for the governments of Norway, Finland, Denmark, Sweden, Oslo, Copenhagen, and Helsinki, personally took advantage of the lost business since "it enabled me to spend four years away from the firm in Washington, from 1969 to January 1973, while the U.S. capital market was in effect closed to the foreign governments and companies with which I had worked so much at Sullivan & Cromwell."

The firm continued to respond slowly to the antiestablishment, egalitarian spirit of the country. Its once-fabled noblesse oblige, both in its hiring practices and its generosity as an employer, turned into an institutional rigidity, typified by its policy on hiring women. Foster Dulles brought four women lawyers into the firm in 1930. Though they never expected to become partners, it was a highly unusual move, attributable to his respect for his sister, Eleanor, who pursued a career in the State Department.

In 1956 when Barbara Schlei graduated top in her class and law review at Yale, she interviewed at the three most prestigious New York firms: Davis, Polk & Wardwell; Cravath, Swaine & Moore; and Sullivan & Cromwell. Davis, Polk took her out to lunch and told her they were not hiring women. After she went through Cravath's daylong interview process, the interviewers told her they were not quite prepared to take on a woman, but did hire one the following year.

Sullivan & Cromwell, Schlei felt, "was refreshingly liberal and open-minded." The firm already had two women in the trusts and estates group, but litigation had been a male sanctuary. She believed "it was a very traditional and conservative but at the same time open-minded place." It hired her, and, as far as she was concerned, "the road to partnership was open. It sounds remarkable to say so but I thought so." She found the firm had no reticence to introduce her to clients. "The standards were so high that they had the security that if they presented me to a client, I would be accepted. Sullivan and Cromwell was very secure as a law firm and felt confident in taking risks."

Schlei left three years later, not because of any disgruntlement with the firm—in fact, she felt they conveyed and imbued in her the highest standards—but to take a job in the Kennedy administration in 1961. She believes that she has "done a huge variety of things and my ability to do them is attributable to the skills learned at Sullivan and Cromwell." Eventually Schlei became a Los Angeles labor lawyer and a member of the city's police commission but she continued to meet firm partners years after leaving Sullivan & Cromwell. "There was a real sense of family in the firm and quite a remarkable caringness, yet they were still tough-minded and maintained high standards."

Schlei's confidence that she would have been considered for a partnership was never tested. But throughout the 1950s and 1960s, the firm limited the prospect of any woman becoming partner by hiring, at most, one a year. Only in 1971 did it match John Foster Dulles's hiring of four women associates in 1930.

And in 1971 the firm was acting under duress, with the filing of a law suit brought by Diane Serafin Blank, a New York University Law

School graduate who claimed, according to the suit, that "she had been discriminated against on account of her sex when the Firm failed and refused to offer to employ her as an associate. . . ." Statistics compiled for the case showed that Sullivan & Cromwell had two women associates, only 2 percent of all associates hired from 1961 to 1970.

The case, which was handled by labor partner John Cannon, dragged on for three years. Sullivan & Cromwell tried to have Federal District Court Judge Constance Baker Motley disqualified because she was a woman and had been a civil rights attorney. That effort failed. Eventually the firm agreed "not to ask any routine questions of women with regard to marital status, family plans, child care arrangements or spouse's occupation that are not also asked of men. . . ." The firm would "not . . . indulge any arbitrary or general assumptions that solely by reason of sex a person is either more or less qualified for professional work which requires travel, dealings with clients, long hours, appearances before particular tribunals, or labor or other negotiations."

The agreement stipulated that for three years Sullivan & Cromwell would submit recruitment records to the New York City Commission on Human Rights to monitor the firm's offers to women. The number of women associates gradually increased, with three hired in 1972, five in 1973, four in 1974, three in 1975, until a breakthrough occurred with ten women in 1976.

The focus shifted to the issue of a woman partner. But by then the firm's reputation was such that women were discouraged and did not want to put up with the likelihood that even if they became associates, they could not expect to make partner. With so many women in law school, Sullivan & Cromwell's obvious reluctance to promote a woman to partnership was hurting recruitment, with only five women joining the firm in 1980.

Sullivan & Cromwell had no women partners in 1980, at a time when other old-line Wall Street firms had begun to change. Davis, Polk & Wardwell; Shearman & Sterling; Cravath, Swaine & Moore; Simpson, Thatcher & Bartlett, and Milbank, Tweed, Hadley & McCloy all had woman partners by then. White & Case had two;

Cleary, Gottlieb, Steen & Hamilton had three, and Philadelphia-based Pepper, Hamilton & Scheetz had five.

The women who were in the firm complained that they could not expect the same treatment as men. They lacked mentors to foster their careers. Critics, citing the aggressive spirit of Sullivan & Cromwell, recalled litigation partner William Piel, Jr.'s comment defending associate Lynne Dallas against charges that she had harassed jurors in the *Berkey* v. *Eastman Kodak* antitrust case. Piel said that Dallas had "about the build and ferocity of a song sparrow." Another woman associate pointedly asked, "Would you pick a sparrow to be a partner at Sullivan & Cromwell? The answer is no—they want only eagles." Asked why she quit the firm, Marcia Paul, an associate from 1972 to 1977, said, "I didn't want to become one of the boys."

The firm resisted giving in to pressure. Stevenson argued that the lack of a woman partner was only "a coincidence—a matter of luck and numbers and time—and that the situation is sure to change soon. We have every expectation that we will have women partners."

Finally, in 1982 the firm chose its first woman partner. But she and her successors raised more questions than they answered. Margaret Pfeiffer, the first female partner, worked in the Washington office, making it seem as if the whole issue had been sidestepped. The Washington office, after all, had been considered a failure. It never acquired a major clientele of its own, and it did not attract important partners from New York. Apart from Pfeiffer, associates sent to Washington did not make partner, giving the impression that Washington was a convenient place to placate criticism over the discrimination issue.

Yvonne Quinn also made partner under unusual circumstances, which set her apart from other associates and showed the lack of senior mentoring most women face at the firm. Quinn came to the attention of a member of the management committee, William E. Willis, when her original firm, Cravath, Swaine & Moore, asked her to leave because she had married one of its partners, Ronald Rolfe. Recommended to Willis by Cravath's powerful partner Thomas Barr, Quinn had a number of offers and went to Sullivan & Cromwell with a "certain amount of fanfare." She worked almost immediately with

Willis fighting a Federal Communications Commission order to take away three of client RKO's television stations. A skillful litigator, she proved herself once she had the chance, but it is a chance that most associates, particularly women, feel they never get.

Sullivan & Cromwell resisted equal treatment of women at a time when men showed decreasing interest in a career at the firm. This was particularly obvious in the 1960s, when the firm needed lawyers. Partner Stanley Farrar, who opened the Los Angeles office, recalled, "In August 1968 most of my colleagues were at Ralph Nader or the SEC. Wall Street was not fashionable at that time. So Sullivan and Cromwell saw me as a warm body. Most are hired in the fall, and I went in in late summer. It would be much harder to get a job today." The firm needed twenty-four associates in 1968, a sharp rise from only six ten years earlier and nine in 1964. A disproportionately large number of these "warm bodies" from the 1964 group went on to make partner.

The firm's ethos ran counter to the era of sit-ins, be-ins, and love-ins. The style of old and new clashed in the elevator, where associates could expect to be chastised for not wearing hats. The contrast could be striking, the old-timers reflecting a bygone era in their dress and manner that seemed to be its own form of ostentation. The firm prided itself on the conversation in the elevator that was all about work, compared with the conversation at Davis, Polk, which, according to Sullivan & Cromwell, was about lunch. But when partners were in the elevator, there was no conversation at all.

Sullivan & Cromwell represented much of what the young generation was protesting against; it affected the partners' personal lives when Arthur Dean's son became an art photographer, and when head litigator William Piel's children chose professions like teaching yoga and working for the Ringling Brothers and Barnum & Bailey Circus World.

The values of the firm remained rooted in the ambitious, hardworking 1950s when family took a backseat to professional advancement, and the office provided companionship as part of one's career. David Peck, a highly respected, well-loved mentor to the litigation group, took three or four lawyers at a time by limousine to the opera, gave them fine bottles of wine for Christmas, and provided them with the intoxicating sense of life at the top.

He was tough on his son and sent him to a psychiatric hospital when he could not adjust to boarding school. M. Scott Peck turned out to be the most famous child of a firm partner when he authored one of the best sellers of the 1980s, *The Road Less Traveled.* In the book Peck credits the choice of hospitalization over returning to Exeter as a turning point in his life because it made him grow up and choose his own path. The book is dedicated to his parents with the measured appreciation "To my parents, Elizabeth and David, whose discipline and love gave me the eyes to see grace."

The firm came closest to the spirit of the 1960s when partners ditched their first wives and families to marry office associates, secretaries, or paralegals. Though this seemed to adapt the love-in to a Wall Street legal practice, it also reflected a work ethic that had undermined their personal lives and presented the incestuous alternative of seeking the comforts of home at work.

Home life was more than alien to the practice of law at Sullivan & Cromwell; it even seemed threatening to the insulated hothouse atmosphere, sweaty with the odor of success. William Ward Foshay, firm chairman in the mid-1970s, kept associates hard at work by bragging that he had missed his wedding anniversary and the birth of a child. He had not even been able to take them home from the hospital, calling his wife at the last minute to tell her to grab a cab.

One former associate attributed his escape from Sullivan & Cromwell to the influence of his wife. Far from being henpecked into failure or obscurity, as would be assumed at Sullivan & Cromwell, Ronald Dworkin rose to eminence as professor of jurisprudence at Oxford University. Looking back, he recognized the insidious mixture of exclusively male, exclusively work-oriented attitudes that pervaded the firm. Judging from his experience, the exclusion of women is more than just an oversight.

"The religion of work I think is rather special—the combination or the idea that it is a kind of macho to work very very hard at a desk. There was the kind of pride that people would say, 'I haven't been home before midnight for three weeks; I haven't taken Sundays off in two years.' There was the idea of male bonding—'We are a legion against the world.' It would be wrong to exaggerate that because the work was there and had to be done, but it was the special gift of masculine achievement and virtue just in the fact one was working that hard.

"My wife used to come down for dinner. . . . She was the only wife who ever did. Early on I was sort of brought to my senses by her, about the self-deception of this misconception of work. . . ."

The spirit of the firm was instilled at the dinner "training table" conducted by litigation partner John Dooling. Famous for his prodigious memory, drinking three martinis, and uttering instructive aphorisms, Dooling ate every night at Massoletti's, an undistinguished restaurant in the basement of the Cities Service Building. Though crowded at lunch with Wall Street workers, at dinner its cavernous space was practically left to Dooling and his crew, who pulled up tables as more arrived.

In 1933 Dooling was the first Sullivan & Cromwell summer intern. He greatly impressed the partners, who sent him to Harvard Law School to complete his education and then return to the firm. With his thick glasses, wide smile, and hairline defining the dome of his head, Dooling was the genuine insider at Sullivan & Cromwell.

To those who participated in these gatherings they were a re-creation of a meeting with Socrates in ancient Greece, mixed with the fun of trying to find a subject Dooling was not expert in. In the midst of a rambling conversation, he slipped in legal precepts, like "Never let a stubborn adversary goad you into behavior damaging to your client"; "It is sometimes best to fight fire with a down pillow"; and "The three components of a good trial lawyer are preparation, insight, and nerve."

Through his training table, he perpetuated the values and the sense of shared interest that he had acquired as the firm's one charity case. When an associate asked him why he stayed so long at the office and ate every night at Massoletti's instead of going home, Dooling told him, "Because all I'd be doing there would be playing bridge with 'the girls.' "

After Dooling was appointed a federal court judge in 1962, the firm opened an office cafeteria, which had neither the feeling nor the wine cellar of Massoletti's. (Massoletti's cellar was a legacy of the 1939 World's Fair, the proprietor having bought the wine from the pavilions that had to abandon it when war broke out as the fair was disbanding.) Having turned a valued tradition into an institutional convenience, the firm was embarrassed to find the cafeteria had been cited in 1984, along with Dante's Pizza and the Oasis Lounge, for violations by the New York Health Department. Partner H. Rodgin Cohen quipped, "I'm OK. I use paper plates."

The firm had to settle for "warm bodies" because it was busy. It was tied to the tail of a business community that was living the exhilarating but scary vicissitudes of boom and bust, both of which provided work for lawyers.

As the stock market soared, any company with the suffix "onics" shot up in share price. George Kern recalled a company that proposed to go public to manufacture artificial sweat. Companies were being bought and sold at fantastic multiples of their assets, profits, or profit potential. Kern advised Goldman, Sachs in what, two decades later, would be called "risk arbitrage." At the time, the practice had no title and little competition, so the rewards were much greater for buying the stock of takeover candidates.

But the antitrust laws were also more stringently enforced. Gus Levy, the head of Goldman, Sachs, had Kern advise him on whether the government would ultimately prevent a merger. "He had a lot of money riding on the answer," Kern recalled, and Levy repeatedly warned Kern, "You'd damn well better be right."

Sullivan & Cromwell was intimately involved in the first forays of Japanese companies into the American stock market, where they wanted to have their shares traded in conjunction with selling Japanese goods abroad. Akio Morita, the founder of Sony Corp., pioneered the strategy of "becom[ing] a citizen of the world," as he quaintly put the internationalization of his business. He turned to Jack Stevenson at Sullivan & Cromwell, who considered the Sony public offering his "most interesting international experience." Stevenson had to reassure "many investment bankers [who] had said it would be impossible even to offer Japanese securities in the United States because of Japanese traditional opposition to disclosing corporate information."

Stevenson gives credit for overcoming the barriers to Morita, "who has always been quite different from the traditional Japanese businessman. . . . He was always most innovative in finding ways to do things consistent with Japanese tradition yet in a manner that was feasible and responsible to the needs of United States investors and the regulations of the Securities and Exchange Commission."

But it was Sullivan & Cromwell associates who did the work, which entailed overcoming the resistance of the Japanese government as well as businessmen. Associate Frederick Seibold spent ten weeks in Tokyo organizing the SEC registration for Sony at a time when Sony's annual sales were $80 million, primarily in transistor radios, tape recorders, and little black-and-white televisions. Seibold recognized the "excellent design" of their products, but didn't buy any stock. "It was too bad because the shares went up about a hundred times what they were then," he added with a shrug. (Only with the publication of an office manual in 1970 did the firm forbid lawyers' investing in firm-related companies.) Seibold met Mr. Honda in his garage when he was still making pedicycles, which required no driver's license, and predicting, with precious little evidence, that he would one day be a major automobile manufacturer.

In 1962 Seibold went to Japan to arrange a convertible debenture for the flagship unit of the Mitsubishi industrial empire, Shin Mitsubishi. It was the first convertible debenture—a bond secured by the general credit of the corporation convertible into stock—ever done there. "I worked with the Ministry of Finance and the SEC, which decided additional legislation was not required for a convertible debenture. I had worked out how to do it," Seibold said.

Much of the Japanese securities law was part of the legacy left by General Douglas MacArthur's occupation after World War II. So when Sullivan & Cromwell lawyers assured the ministries of finance and justice that no new legislation was required, it was eventually accepted, but only after days of repeating the same argument to different bureaucrats and finally distributing 200 copies of their opinion throughout the two ministries.

Seibold learned that Japanese and American securities laws were by no means identical, and the sticking points might be details, but they were crucial. "Japanese corporate law had a provision that a company could not issue new stock until the day *after* it was paid for. The SEC wouldn't go for that." After four days of deadlock, the Japanese agreed to make payment a minute before midnight, which would allow the shares to be traded, according to American law, the same morning at ten o'clock in New York. The first closing was done by telex and had an electrical effect on the Japanese stock market, which jumped a hundred points in one day.

Ten weeks was not a long time to spend on one Japanese deal, and even after such arrangements became routine, they took six weeks. Sullivan & Cromwell had five lawyers at a time working in Japan until the interest-equalization tax law was unexpectedly announced by President Kennedy in 1963.

Marvin Schwartz and George Kern had ringside seats in one major market bust when they were phoned in the middle of the night by a Chicago commodities trader. Kern spent hours on the phone with the trader, who explained how the commodities market worked and why he wanted to stop all commodities trading the next day.

The trader was holding $10 million in forged warehouse receipts. He was just one of the more than fifty creditors of Tino De Angelis, who had perpetrated one of the largest swindles of all time. This scandal unraveled on the same weekend that President Kennedy was shot, and the markets closed the following Monday as the repercussions spread from commodities to the stock markets. One small but respectable stockbroker, Ira Haupt & Company, became insolvent. It had the same problem as Schwartz and Kern's client. It held receipts for carloads of salad oil that did not exist.

Schwartz became lead counsel for the more than fifty plaintiffs because he recommended subpoenaing mounds of documents from the American Express Company, whose warehouse receipts Tino De Angelis had forged in an effort to prop up his faltering salad-oil business and reckless commodities trading. Using the rarely invoked Section 21 of the Bankruptcy Code to rifle through confidential American Express documents, Schwartz produced a book of documents to show that American Express was responsible for its subsidiary's carelessness, because officials of the parent company made decisions as though the two companies were the same. Schwartz even went to the telephone directory, a favorite source used by litigators to show deceptive practices, to note that American Express did not differentiate itself from the subsidiary—until trouble started.

Dean said proudly at a partners' lunch, "Schwartz must be doing a helluva job because Howard Clark"—the American Express chairman—"called me twice last week to call him off." After years of wrangling, American Express used the specter of its own bankruptcy to arrange a settlement for $60 million, which Schwartz agreed to only if his client, the Chicago commodities broker who had awakened him in the middle of the night, got paid in full on his $10 million claim. He did.

The firm developed an entirely new area of work in the 1960s, based on the return of David Peck from being chief judge of the New York State Appellate Court. Peck combined a taste for limousines, the opera, expensive wines, and exclusive schools for his sons with connections at the top of New York society.

His high-society contacts started when he became a member of the Young Republicans in the 1920s. A country boy from Crawfordsville, Indiana, Peck went to rustic Wabash College and joined Sullivan & Cromwell only after a stint in the U.S. attorney's office and on the legal staff of the International Telephone and Telegraph Company. He joined the firm in 1930, when the litigation group consisted of one partner, John Higgins, and three associates. It was less than a stimulating environment under Higgins, who had been hired away from his private practice on the West Coast. Higgins was a workaholic with no ability to make the work interesting for his associates. When he was finished with firm business for the day, he started making calls to the West Coast business associates he had retained. Most of the firm's lawyers considered litigation a dead end, but Peck liked courtroom work and stuck with it.

In 1938, when Higgins succumbed to an ulcer from overwork, Foster Dulles tried but failed to recruit Thomas Dewey to head the litigation group by offering a guaranteed $150,000 a year. Dewey accepted the offer, but before he started work, was drafted to run for district attorney and won. Peck, at the age of thirty-six, became chief litigator and was just beginning to make real money when Governor Dewey offered him a position on the appellate court in 1944. Peck said he would take the job for five years or so. When he was appointed chief judge in 1947, he decided to serve out his term and ultimately stayed until 1958.

Peck returned to the firm having had a rewarding and full career. Despite Sullivan & Cromwell's pride in its anonymity, Peck and his social prominence provided a new specialty in glamour litigation.

Brooke Astor, who had been married to Vincent Astor for only five years before his death in 1959, asked Peck to fight off a claim by her husband's half brother, John Jacob Astor III, for half the $120 million estate. It had the makings of a sensational case, but it ended anticlimactically when he settled for $250,000. Two Sullivan & Cromwell partners and a former Sullivan & Cromwell associate remain on the board of the Astor Foundation.

The case of the four adopted children of Muriel McCormick Hubbard was a knock-down-and-drag-out court battle involving five law firms. An heiress from both sides of her family, Hubbard died with a $4 million estate, derived largely from stock in the International Harvester Company, supplemented by a much larger $9 million Rockefeller Foundation trust, all of which she wanted her children to share.

Because the children were adopted, John D. Rockefeller III, Mrs. Hubbard's cousin, claimed the Rockefeller trust was forfeited to charity. The guardian of the children, who were all less than seven years old, hired Sullivan & Cromwell for the trial, which was fought on the pages of the daily papers. But Sullivan & Cromwell lost, so most of the trust money went to Rockefeller's favorite charity at the time—Lincoln Center, of which he was chairman. The money helped build the Juilliard School of Music, which was just having its foundation laid as part of the Lincoln Center complex in 1959 when the litigation started.

Sullivan & Cromwell brought Hollywood director Otto Preminger's case against Columbia Pictures over his film *Anatomy of a Murder*. Preminger had the right of final cut, which he claimed allowed him to prevent interruptions for commercials during a network television screening. Sullivan & Cromwell associate Thomas E. Patton spent three months poring over documents in Preminger's Fifth Avenue office, while stars like Laurence Olivier and Carol Lynley prepared their roles for Preminger's *Bunny Lake Is Missing*. Preminger lost, despite testimony by director Elia Kazan and a dramatic defense that disrupting the screening was tantamount to shredding a Picasso painting.

Peck defended free speech against Jacqueline Onassis when he represented *Look* magazine in its effort to excerpt William Manchester's *The Death of a President*. It was a prime example of Peck's legal diplomacy, working with Mrs. Onassis's lawyer, Simon Rifkind of Paul, Weiss, Rifkind, Wharton & Garrison, who pored over every word. Rifkind would say, "This is offensive," and Peck would reply, "Oh, come on, that's not so bad." Peck "would offer to take out this word but not that one" and, according to a Sullivan & Cromwell associate who watched them one Saturday afternoon in the firm's office, "They essentially rewrote the damned article to settle and compromise in a very statesmanlike fashion."

Peck was a shrewd attorney, capable of elevating clients to his level of prestige and rectitude. Or so Frank Lloyd thought in 1974 when he asked Peck to handle an embarrassing case against the Marlborough Gallery. The heirs of the abstract painter Mark Rothko, who had committed suicide in 1970, claimed the gallery did not get full value for the works, especially the ones it bought itself. Judge Peck lost the case amid a glare of publicity that had come to characterize his career.

Peck entertained numerous offers from rival law firms when he retired from the bench, but he returned to Sullivan & Cromwell in part because so many of the lawyers he had known in the 1930s and 1940s were still practicing there.

Edward Green, who joined the firm in 1908, was still wearing spats and being driven by a liveried chauffeur in a green Cadillac. Green's uncompromising opinions were not confined to his expertise in company law, as for example when he told an associate who had just arrived from Yale Law School, "Yale was a nice country law school until that fool Sterling gave them all that money." He wrote curt, impolite notes if he had any criticisms of an associate. "He was not a man to suffer fools easily and was not in the business of protecting personalities," one former associate recalled. Another said, "Edward Green did not get close to anyone because, one, he didn't want you to, and two, because no one wanted to."

Eustace Seligman, who started at the firm in 1914, continued wearing a high celluloid collar long after the fashion died. He impressed associates because of the Dürer print he kept on his wall, but he would have preferred to impress them about the moral standards of the firm, for which he took personal responsibility. He used the death of a former client as a lesson for the firm. "Our relations to the client were excellent," he wrote when the president of the Flinkote Company died, "until Mr. Harvey called me up and told me that his son was graduating from law school and he would like us to give him a job. The boy unfortunately did not measure up to our standards and we refused, and he went with White & Case instead. Not too long thereafter—as we had feared—Mr. Harvey told us quite frankly that in order to help his son he was transferring from S&C to White & Case.

"This is of course only one of a number of instances over a period of years where we have refused to lower our standards of admission notwithstanding the request of a client."

Seligman's brother-in-law, Alfred Jaretzki, Jr., was another old-timer. He started at the firm in 1916 and continued to represent mutual funds, on whose behalf he had contributed to the formulation of the Investment Company Act of 1940. Quiet, with a wry sense of humor, Jaretzki had an outstanding collection of modern art and, as a reminder of the comparative wealth of Sullivan & Cromwell partners in earlier times, lived like his brother-in-law in a New York town house.

By the time Green died in 1963, the three relatives had been at the firm for a total of 151 years; Jaretzki continued until 1969, Seligman until 1971.

And they were not the only ones.

Stoddard Stevens, an expert on utility rates, joined the firm in 1917, became a partner in 1929, and stayed until 1975. He gained prominence in the 1950s when his client Chester Dale, a partner in an investment bank specializing in utility financings, gave his remarkable Impressionist collection to the National Gallery of Art in Washington, D.C. Stevens became the lawyer for the National Gallery, and through it, brought to the firm the business of the Gulf Oil heir Paul Mellon and his various trusts. Special counsel to the National Gallery became a Sullivan & Cromwell position taken after Stevens by Jack Stevenson who eventually became the museum's president, while Sullivan & Cromwell associates continued to work on the Mellon trusts.

Oliver Merrill, who started in 1929 and retired in 1974, epitomized the group of unassuming, exceedingly modest lawyers (often working in utilities) who provided the backbone of the firm by acting as intermediaries between its well-known stars and its hardworking associates. Merrill, known as "June," had been a college athlete who developed an ulcer and drank milk at his desk. "His opinions were accepted because of his intellect rather than his force of personality," said a former associate.

The slot system ordained that when a partner retired, his shares would be allocated among new partners. Lawyers of such vintage left large shares, which could be divided among several new partners. In the 1960s and 1970s, when the firm suffered from recruitment ills, it had room for increasing its number of partners. In 1968, at the height of the protest era, the firm made six partners, double or triple the number in the average year.

Sullivan & Cromwell was finally suffering from the arrogance of Arthur Dean's claim that there were always good lawyers in the next batch. The firm was filling its ranks, not with the outstanding men it had had previously, but with a new type of middle manager, who could organize a litigation, not argue it. These were "chiefs-of-staff" who took on increasing prominence as heads of client groups that were filled with large numbers of associates but reported to the same few prominent partners.

The chiefs-of-staff became the new partners, though not with the highest client contact, a prerogative that remained with the senior partners. The firm developed procedures, detailed in the office manual of more than sixty pages issued in 1970, that revealed how distanced the major partners could be from a client.

"Each younger lawyer is always expected to take the initiative in maintaining contact with the seniors on the team," the manual asserts, "so that the seniors will be fully informed as to all matters on which the younger lawyer may be working. In the case of unusual occurrences, the seniors should be informed immediately so that they will have the knowledge necessary to discuss the matter intelligently if the client should call them."

In some ways, partners are associates' clients. For partners who are directors of companies, "it is extremely important that any partner who regularly attends board of director meetings of a client, either as a director or as counsel, be kept fully informed on a current basis of all developments in the affairs of such client. Any such partner should be sent copies of opinions and other important documents relating to such client and must be advised in advance of each meeting of the board concerning developments in affairs of the client with which others are familiar and particularly concerning the details of all matters which other lawyers know are to come up at the meeting."

It was, perhaps, no different from Arthur Dean's being briefed before a client came in. But there were new pitfalls. As clients developed their own in-house legal departments, a Sullivan & Cromwell lawyer was more likely to be dealing with another lawyer (even a former Sullivan & Cromwell associate). He had to be more knowledgeable, and the subject was likely to be more precise or arcane if the in-house department was not handling it.

The firm had long practiced in client groups, which divided responsibility among the members, as opposed to firms where associates were personal assistants to partners (like judges' clerks) or part of only one client team. Sullivan & Cromwell has an atomistic structure that young associates find exhilarating because it gives them responsibility almost immediately, and as members of several teams they can see how different partners function.

The system relies on getting top graduates who are quick to learn and anxious to work. Bill Piel told successive generations of associates what he had been told as an associate: ''You must learn to say no, to save your health and sanity; but if it is your habit generally not to use that word, you will find that somehow there is time for everything.''

But by the end of the 1960s, the firm had to question just how good its system was if it could not always get the recruits it wanted. The question would recur, to the firm's chagrin, in future years.

15

THE POWER OF TRADITION

There was the extraordinary, most extraordinary, situation at Sullivan & Cromwell that, at least officially, the partners did not know how much each other made. That to me is mind-boggling from my point of view as a partner at another firm.—FRANCIS CARLING, SULLIVAN & CROMWELL ASSOCIATE, 1974–80

While struggling with its own growing pains, Sullivan & Cromwell was overtaken by rivals it had paid little attention to before. Others found it easier to expand because they were not hampered by traditions and established practices. Sullivan & Cromwell would not hire partners from other firms or merge with another firm.

The idea of building from within was so ingrained that even when the firm did decide to open offices in other cities, it looked for former associates who had originally been turned down for a partnership to come back to Sullivan & Cromwell. But following tradition required a selective memory. No one was still around who remembered that in the 1930s the firm had considered merging with Cotton & Franklin, the predecessor firm of Cahill, Gordon & Reindel. The deal fell through because the Cotton & Franklin partners were earning more than Sullivan & Cromwell's.

The firm's memory went back only to the early postwar period when Malcolm MacIntyre, a Sullivan & Cromwell associate in the 1930s offered the firm American Airlines as a client if MacIntyre and another of American's lawyers were taken on as partners. The airline was moving its headquarters from Washington, D.C., to New York and only part of its outside law firm was going with it.

Sullivan & Cromwell partners entertained the proposition until Edward Green declared, "Making partners just to get clients is the beginning of the end." Debevoise & Plimpton accepted the arrangement and got the American Airlines account.

There were Sullivan & Cromwell partners who felt they had made a mistake, especially with the postwar boom in air travel, airline conglomerates, and massive liability cases. But firm policy had been set, and that was that.

MacIntyre had learned more from Sullivan & Cromwell than the firm did from him. As president of Eastern Air Lines, he started the New York–Washington shuttle, the most successful route in aviation history, because he remembered the overnight train he was forever having to take to get to the SEC by the time the stock market opened the next day.

Sullivan & Cromwell lawyers regularly used the shuttle, but came only late and halfheartedly to the idea of a Washington office. Less reluctantly, the firm reopened its Paris office in 1962 and its London one in 1972. But these were obviously outposts for American lawyers in other countries. Their services were circumscribed by the amount of American law, dealmaking, and bond issuing that was needed, all taking their direction from New York.

Washington was different, presenting a dilemma that forced the firm to face up to an identity crisis that had been brewing since the rapid expansion in the 1960s. Other white shoe firms were tied to dominant clients, like Shearman & Sterling to Citicorp and Cravath, Swaine & Moore to IBM, which was particularly demanding because of a government antitrust case against the computer giant that lasted most of the 1970s.

The firms that were growing so spectacularly tended to be located outside New York or new ones. Sullivan & Cromwell was unique in that it had a more wide-ranging practice than most old firms and more traditions than new ones. It was not prepared to shake loose from the hold of the New York office.

It hesitated about expanding until Jack Stevenson forced the issue in 1977. He had been in Washington from 1969 to 1973 as legal adviser to the State Department in the first Nixon administration. (Unlike Dean and others, Stevenson had had to resign to take this appointment, emphasizing the loss of the firm's close links to the government.)

It was clear to Stevenson that Washington firms had greater access to government than did Sullivan & Cromwell. For far too long the firm mistakenly assumed that Washington lawyers could never intrude on its relationships with its clients. But the growth of in-house legal departments weakened the ties to companies' outside firms, while clients found that "all I had to do was pick up the phone, ask my question and have the lawyer in Washington deal with his former colleagues in government to get the answer. At Sullivan & Cromwell they would have spent hours researching the question in law books and only come back with a hypothetical answer," according to Lawrence McQuade, a former Sullivan & Cromwell associate who became senior vice-president of W. R. Grace & Company.

When the firm opened its Washington office in 1977, it sent lawyers down from New York. Stevenson had gone back to New York, but he promised associates assigned to Washington that he would be there often, a condition they felt important for their own careers. They realized that being away from the mainstream at the firm could harm their futures at Sullivan & Cromwell as much as refusing to take the Washington assignment.

At the same time, the Washington office was expected to generate its own clientele, even though it was competing with other firms headed by well-known Washington figures hired out of government or politics. Sullivan & Cromwell had opted for the worst of both worlds, raising expectations that would be hard to fulfill. It wanted the office to act like a new operation without offering the benefits that competing firms had.

Even Stevenson failed to support the office, showing up infrequently and leaving the associates who had gone there feeling abandoned. As a last-year associate, Frank Zaffere was told to go back to New York to improve his chances of becoming a partner; but he had already uprooted his family once to go to Washington and did not want to do it again, with the prospect, if he did not make partner, of having to move in another year. He stayed in Washington and did not make partner.

Washington was just one example of ill-considered or badly handled policies. The firm failed to take advantage of important opportunities that did not fall into the pattern of its normal work. The only substantial client the Washington office attracted was Turner & Newall, a British defendant in the large and lucrative litigation over asbestos liability.

Sullivan & Cromwell failed to make a partner of Charles E. Dorkey III, the associate who handled the British company. The client gave part of its business to Dorkey when he left, and eventually he got it all. Dorkey estimated that Sullivan & Cromwell could have expected yearly revenue between $10 million and $20 million from product liability work. If Turner & Newall did not interest the firm as part of the biggest litigation in American history, it should have recognized that the area of product liability, of which asbestos was but one example, was blossoming into a major concern of its corporate clients.

The firm also failed to take advantage of investment banking clients' development of mortgage-backed financing and collateralized mortgage obligations in 1977. It did not assign a full-time person to handle it, even though client First Boston was the second-largest underwriter in the field. Phillip Pollock left Sullivan & Cromwell to join a firm known as Brown, Wood, Ivey, Mitchell & Petty to work in that area, only to be hired away by Skadden, Arps, Slate, Meagher, & Flom, which started a satellite San Francisco office to accommodate him and what blossomed into his specialty in structured finance.

These failings reflected a management crisis based on unresolved attitudes toward growth and new offices. On the one hand, senior partners were judged by the growth of the firm in their tenure. The firm biography of Arthur H. Dean notes, "By January 1972, the firm had grown to 154 lawyers from 85 lawyers in 1949, and there were more than 85 lawyers in the General Practice Group alone.'' His successor, William Ward Foshay, got credit for opening the Washington office, while the instigator of the new office, Jack Stevenson, became *his* successor. The next firm chairman, John E. Merow, had proposed the new offices started under Stevenson.

And yet lawyers in those offices were, at least at the beginning, practically outcasts, in part because they were so far away from New York and in part because the offices were not deemed successes. The firm seemed intent on growing, but directionless.

A key link between the older generation and the young lawyers was John Raben, considered heir apparent as firm chairman, whom most younger lawyers admired and emulated. Called affectionately ''Tiger'' Raben, he had natural leadership abilities ''and fabulously good judgment,'' according to Paul Sheeline, chief executive officer of Intercontinental Hotels, who worked with Raben as an associate at Sullivan & Cromwell.

Peter T. Jones, an associate who went to work at Levi Strauss, remembered ''going to a meeting of investment bankers with John where they decided to make a public offering in six months. After the meeting, John said, 'We'll have to go back and get into it and work over the weekend.' ''But John, it's six months away,'' the associate had to remind him.

Professor Ken Scott of Stanford University Law School puts the same qualities in another perspective: ''Raben was a classic driven, upward strung, early mortality individual if there ever was one. He was endlessly striving. He was not typical of the firm. Typical of the firm was hardworking but externally in control. Maybe they have ulcers but the tension doesn't show. Raben had his tension externalized. It showed.''

On at least two occasions, Raben overworked himself to the point of not completing an assignment—one a complicated pipeline deal where Paul Sheeline had to spell him at the printer's and the other the Matador Land deal that Bob McDonald finished alone.

A pain Raben developed after being in a taxi accident turned out to be an advanced case of cancer, from which he died, aged fifty-eight, in 1975. The leadership of the firm fell to Jack Stevenson, once a protégé of John Foster Dulles, who was known for an extraordinary skill in getting people to agree with him without seeming to push his ideas onto them. He could also disagree with someone on the phone by merely repeating his initial comment as an answer to anything the other person said. Like Dean, he was hard of hearing. He treated associates as he was treated by his mentor Foster Dulles, making sure they stayed far in the background while he dealt with the client. He was a surprising choice as firm chairman, especially since he had left for the State Department for four years in 1969. Stevenson returned from Washington more as an elder statesman than active lawyer or firm manager.

For a firm that prided itself on its training of associates, growing numbers complained of being "cannon fodder" for big cases, office slang for having to work full time on one large, dull, profitable case. For such cases, even the pretense of training associates, as opposed to using them, was missing; and Stevenson did not see his job as placating associates, even though associates—and first-year associates in particular—became an increasing percentage of firm personnel.

An unnamed Sullivan & Cromwell partner told *American Lawyer* the firm's theory of why no lawyer should work full time on a case—"We like to stay slightly understaffed—you know, real trim. We don't like to have dozens of partners and associates in there tripping all over each other . . . [so that] no one ever gets trapped working on just one case,"—a good intention that did not always work out in practice. He was discussing *Berkey* v. *Kodak,* in which Sullivan & Cromwell took the case on appeal, after Berkey won a $113 million judgment and a lawyer on Kodak's original defense team from Donovan, Leisure admitted to retaining a document he claimed was destroyed. Sullivan & Cromwell associates went through the whole transcript and documents in the original case to prepare an appeal of Berkey's claim that Kodak monopolized the camera, film, and developing business.

Jerrold J. Ganzfried, a fourth-year Sullivan & Cromwell associate, remembers spending night and day in a conference room to turn 20,000 pages of court transcript into an appeal within a month. Robert MacCrate, the partner in charge who got the assignment because he had worked with Kodak's general counsel on another antitrust case, felt, "To pick up a large assignment is always tremendously time consuming. But I don't think the time frame was anything that stressed us to the limits.''

To associate Ganzfried, who did the work, however, ''We had to go through that testimony, pick out the best arguments, marshal them. There was so much work to do in such a limited time. Three of us climbed into a conference room for a month and emerged thirty days later with the two briefs.''

The judge threw out most of the previous jury verdict and Kodak settled for $6.8 million. But the work was not over. Ganzfried was assigned to negotiate the fee for Berkey's counsel. He had to argue with the number-two litigating partner at Parker, Chapin, Flattau, & Klimpl. They ''had guidelines from the judge but the range was substantial. It started mid- to late afternoon and lasted until one A.M.'' The negotiation had to be finished and a statement readied for the judge by the next morning.

It was a testimonial to the work and achievements of a Sullivan & Cromwell associate, though Ganzfried got little of the credit. Bill Piel, who argued the appeal in court, was generous to John Warden, the young partner on the case, who, he said, was the ''real creator of an appellate victory. He was in charge of the brief; I criticized it and counseled him, but seventy-five to eighty-five percent of the credit belongs to him and Philip Howard who worked on the brief.''

The Kodak case required only a month's concentrated effort. Alan Reinke spent virtually the whole of his Sullivan & Cromwell career working on one case: the defense of Goldman, Sachs in the celebrated Penn Central Commercial Paper Case, which resulted from the largest bankruptcy in American history. Three dozen savvy investors including Walter Annenberg, the American ambassador to Great Britain, and Getty Oil Company sued Goldman, Sachs for selling them bonds months before the railroad collapsed but after, they claimed, the bank knew it was in trouble.

The investors produced internal Goldman, Sachs documents that showed the bank reducing its own inventory of Penn Central commercial paper after recognizing its financial problems five months before the collapse.

The case required a lot of hard work because, Reinke said, ''the basic strategy was one of delay. There were technical defenses but jury sympathy would be with the investors who clearly lost their money. So the strategy was to delay the inevitable. Huge amounts were already being spent on legal fees, so this was not a deterrent. Cubic yards of money got thrown at this case.''

It was a strategy that the client favored. ''Goldman, Sachs was a general partnership and every partner would have been individually liable for the eighty-two million dollars and interest and attorney's fees,'' Reinke said. ''They probably had that much but not more. The longer it was before they had to pay the money, the more their reserves grew to pay off any liability.''

To carry out the strategy, Sullivan & Cromwell ''made full use of pretrial procedures that are allowed in civil law. Many cases can be advanced at a snail's pace until one chooses to go to trial. Nothing was done solely as a delaying tactic. Lawyers didn't make frivolous motions just for delay. The judge would have been wrathful if he had seen us doing that.''

Finally Bill Piel argued the lead trial involving three Goldman, Sachs customers. He tried to show that although Goldman, Sachs had adverse information about Penn Central, ''it felt the Penn Central would be able to pay off the IOUs when they came due.''

The firm lost, and Goldman, Sachs had to pay the full face value of the bonds plus interest; but litigation on the other cases continued, depending to a large extent on when the investors bought their commercial paper. ''There was a famous memorandum that came to light at Goldman, Sachs.

''Two days before they sold their shares, someone wrote, 'First quarter earnings will be disastrous.' The smoking gun was that they were selling their own inventory of securities while continuing to market those shares to other people to hold. That was the time that mattered.''

Reinke quit Sullivan & Cromwell after three years. ''If I had stayed, I would have had no choice but to continue on these cases and I didn't want to. My bonus was four times greater than any other associate's. Had I known how much they appreciated me, I probably would not have left.'' He added, ''But it would have been a mistake to stay.'' The reason: ''This case was so thinly staffed. One wonders, if the purpose is to delay, delay, delay, then why not have more attorneys?''

He answered his own question: ''The point is to maximize partners' profits. It causes associate burnout. But they have five to ten applicants for every spot, so who cares?''

The discontent was not confined to the litigation group. Boyd Blackburn, a tax lawyer, felt, ''My experience was so specialized, I could only use it at another New York City law firm.'' He needed to retrain himself to practice in San Francisco.

Growth made the firm more impersonal. It started producing an annually updated ring binder, one lawyer per page, with a photo and details about each person's background and family life. Known as the pig book, it was proof that all the lawyers no longer knew each other.

In this, as with so much at the firm, Arthur Dean led the way. Until his retirement at the end of 1971, he met annually with associates to give them their bonuses and salary increases. He pretended to know who they were, but his deafness made the pretense comic, since a secretary had to shout each person's name in his ear.

The growing impersonality affected the firm practice as well as personal relations. Frank Carling saw, from the time he was a summer associate in 1969, associates' gradual loss of latitude as partners ''do not allow people under them to make the same sorts of intuitive expansive kinds of judgments that they were able to make.''

Less involved with senior partners, the associates dealt with young partners who themselves suffered from and imposed ''constant pressure for political conformity. Bureaucracy always takes the safe route. The kind of people who succeed at Sullivan and Cromwell today are safe people,'' according to Carling. '' 'Safe people' is defined as preferably a very bright workaholic drone, someone who can be relied upon to consistently produce.''

In contrast to the dwindling enthusiasm at Sullivan & Cromwell, associates saw other firms being more attentive to their young lawyers. Competition from other firms forced Sullivan & Cromwell to raise salaries—money was never a problem—but not to make the system more humane or considerate of the associates. It continued to operate as though any Sullivan & Cromwell alumnus would have no trouble getting a job at a client company or another law firm. But the other firms were building from within and the companies were filling up their legal departments.

Professional recruiters pressured Sullivan & Cromwell associates to consider other jobs sooner with statements like "By the end of your third year out of law school you'll be totally unmarketable and you'd better make up your mind now." To counter the pressure of recruiters, the firm cynically continued to encourage associates to think they would become partner, even though only about one in ten would.

"You're on the track" was the standard blandishment, which meant only "You are one of that vast horde who has not been eliminated definitely but whose odds of making it are slim, at best," according to an associate of the 1970s. The firm purposely suspended the decision on partners as long as possible to let associates nourish their own hopes.

"By and large," an embittered former associate commented, "they have discovered that you can keep people's hopes alive . . . by the merest signal, the smallest plum. Associates are so hungry for approval that they will take almost anything you say in the most positive way possible. You don't really have to lie to make associates think that they are making it when they are not. You just have to not be very negative and their own fantasies will do the job for them."

Such behavior looked increasingly archaic compared to other firms. Wald, Harkrader & Ross in Washington started giving associates detailed evaluations every six months and after three years ranked them on a scale of one to four on their chances of making partner. Hogan & Hartson in Washington adopted a policy of telling associates within four years whether they would be made partner, as did King & Spaulding in Atlanta.

Sullivan & Cromwell's policy hid a deep-seated hypocrisy toward associates, which bred a group in the 1970s who remained hostile to the firm long after they left. To the outside world, Sullivan & Cromwell wanted the firm's lawyers to be treated equally, but within the firm, the partners knew all and the associates knew nothing. Compare this to the policies of Morrison & Foerster, an old-line San Francisco firm, which started inviting associates to the firm's annual retreat, where the partners discussed hourly rates, partners' share and client relations. When it was pointed out that this differed from Sullivan & Cromwell's secrecy, one Morrison & Foerster partner replied "We trust them with client confidences, don't we?"

The only consolation to Sullivan & Cromwell associates was that partners got similar treatment. The Partnership Agreement resolutely resisted the democratic wind blowing through other legal practices. The firm made the pretense of sharing power—without actually reducing the role of the all-powerful seven-man Committee in a redraft of the Partnership Agreement that chairman William Ward Forshay recommended just before his retirement in 1979. The amendments as drafted by Jack Stevenson, his successor, merely hid the Committee with a deft sleight of hand. In an accompanying memo, Stevenson admitted his version "deletes (except in those few instances where it is desirable to provide expressly for a determination or action by the Committee) the specific references to the Committee in reliance on a broadening of the general powers of the Committee. . . ." [This version of the partnership agreement is reprinted in Appendix 1.]

The Committee appeared to stop making the decisions it continued to make. For instance, where the old agreement said "no payments shall be made . . . except with the written approval of the Committee," the new provision said "except with written approval on behalf of the Partnership" without designating who gives the approval. (The subject was giving former partners permission to work for other firms without losing their pensions.)

The description of the division of profits deleted the phrase "the Committee" three times. But it was replaced with nothing. So the first sentence of the section used to read, "The Net Profits of the Partnership for any fiscal year shall be determined *by the Committee* as follows: a calculation shall be made of the gross income . . . less all expenses and losses paid during, and other charges determined *by the Committee*. . . ." Those determinations were then just made, period.

More interesting were the places where the Committee was *not* deleted. The allocation of the reserve percentage—the discretionary payments beyond the fixed amounts—"will be made among the Partners, or some of them, by the Committee. . . ." Later, in the discussion of the capital that remains unallocated, the agreement noted, "It is intended that at all times the aggregate capital of the Partnership shall not be less than the amount that the Committee considers appropriate. . . ."

In a slight concession to the growing number of young partners, on several decisions "majority in number" replaced "majority in interest." This was important in a large firm with more than seventy partners, where half were under the age of forty-six; with the continuous addition of new partners, the average age kept falling, with eighteen partners under the age of forty and thirty-seven under the age of forty-four.

The majority in number could reduce other partners' shares without their consent, admit new partners, and dissolve the partnership altogether. The majority in number could also amend the Partnership Agreement.

These rights sounded truly democratic, even revolutionary, except that "The term 'majority in number' of the Partners," the deft counter revolution stated, "whenever used in connection with taking any action under this Agreement, shall mean a majority in number of the Partners acting on a proposal of the Committee."

The Committee had not lost power after all, just camouflaged itself.

A new retirement policy in the revised Partnership Agreement forced Sullivan & Cromwell lawyers to give up their lucrative practices at the age of seventy and take less money in the three years preceding retirement. William Nelson Cromwell's longevity and fat partnership share that spanned a good part of two centuries made his successors jealous of their rights to get *their* money on an ascending scale throughout their lives. Though an improvement on the previous system that gave doddering old partners a stranglehold on younger lawyers' earnings, it still promoted the idea of the rich getting richer, since a retired important partner could still make more than an active young partner.

Under the new provisions, three years before a partner retired, he got 80 percent of his average percentage (the average of his five highest-paying years), then 60 percent, and finally, the last year before retirement, 40 percent. In retirement, a former partner got 20 percent of his average percentage as long as it fell within a specified boundary of the "minimum amount" and the "maximum amount." In the late 1970s, the minimum rose from $50,000 to $65,000 and the maximum rose from $125,000 to $165,000. While the set minimum and maximum amounts changed every year, the agreement also stipulated that the minimum would never fall below $50,000 a year and the maximum below $125,000 a year.

As the firm grew, so did the number of associates and rejected associates. With newsletters and annual parties, the firm continued to cultivate the Sullivan & Cromwell connection. These annual events trace their history to William Nelson Cromwell's first Sullivan & Cromwell Society dinner in 1908, which evolved into New Year's parties at John Foster Dulles's and Eustace Seligman's. Arthur Dean invited the firm to his house for dinner after a sporting day at the Piping Rock Country Club in Locust Valley, Long Island. After Dean's retirement the day continued without the dinner at his place.

Firm alumni were invited to an annual eggnog party at the Colony Club on Park Avenue. Mike Maney, a smooth-looking litigation partner with slicked-back hair and wide-set piercing eyes, confided to an alumnus, "The Christmas eggnog party for alumni shows what a special place the firm is. People usually return to alumni functions at places where they left under happy circumstances. At Sullivan and Cromwell the alumni are all people who didn't make it." Such is the power of the firm's tradition.

16

THE TRADITION OF POWER

It's a little more difficult for me, but who can be light on their feet should be.—GEORGE C. KERN, JR.

On April 2, 1979, 558 lawyers, wives, and friends of the firm were invited to celebrate its centennial at a dinner at the United States Customs House. As appropriate as the venue was to the firm's long history in international commerce, most partners were more anxious to point out the firm's new offices down the street at the foot of Broad Street overlooking the harbor. The sixty-six page history of Sullivan & Cromwell given to the guests featured photos of the firm's founders, who knew the Customs House as a place to trace clients' goods, not eat them.

It was one way to measure the firm's progress, from "players" to "gentlemen," for having gradually risen above the fray and hurly-burly of common law to the pinnacle of the profession. The problems of the 1970s reflected the dilemma of wanting to keep doing things the old way, with the quiet superiority of the Dulles generation that had provided a patina of respectability to the obstinate aggression of the Cromwell years.

On such an occasion, guests overlooked the skeletons in the firm's closet; instead, they greeted old friends during the assorted hors d'oeuvres and reminisced through the mousse of salmon, stuffed breast of veal, spinach gnocchi, raspberry ice with cassis sauce, and cordials. They laughed over "Centenary," a thirty-stanza firm ballad, written by Howard D. Burnett, a second-year associate aware of both the players and the gentlemen, but couching their excesses in light verse that only emphasized the tradition imbued in even the youngest lawyers.

So youngst'r Cromwell, thirtee-three,
Thus founde himselfe command'n–
And litigation (Sulliv'n's strengthe)
Was mightee neare abandon'd.

....

(A footnote here–Cromwell's advyce
For long, productive lyves:
Champagne eache lunche, and at fyrme feastes,
Kisse all your partn'rs' wyves.)

'Twas Dean in charge by '49,
And borne was "Ye Committee"
(Whose memb'rs dare ye not revile,
For purse strings show no pittee).

....

But as th' century nexte unfoldes,
Heede welle this sounde advyce:
At S&C, th' highest only–
Charact'r, qualitee, pryce.

Head litigation partner Bill Piel had a chance to indulge his original aspiration to be a writer by organizing *Lamplighters*, a compilation of biographies of every lawyer who had ever been at the firm. The book substituted for the failed efforts to get a book-length firm history. Arthur Dean never fulfilled his intention to write one to accompany his biography of Cromwell, which was written with eventual partner

Mitchell Brock in the late 1950s and privately printed for distribution to new associates. The firm hired a professional writer to do a history, but, according to Piel, "the points of view couldn't come together and the firm can't write about itself because of client confidences."

Lamplighters was meant to be ready for the centennial, with living lawyers asked to contribute autobiographical segments, and biographies of the deceased lawyers pieced together by a paralegal drawing on the Sullivan & Cromwell files. The title came from the couplet by James Russell Lowell: "As one lamp lights another, nor grows less/ So nobleness enkindles nobleness." It aroused opposition for its pretentiousness, but since it appeared on a bust of Algernon Sydney Sullivan, which still stands in Van Cortlandt Park in New York, the firm chairman approved it.

In his own reminiscences, Piel described his career in "S&C's litigating three-ring circus. Most of my years have been spent . . . scrubbing and feeding the antitrust elephants," he wrote, in a metaphor he got to know better than most when his son became ringmaster in Ringling Brothers and Barnum & Bailey Circus World. An heir of the Piel's beer family and stalwart of the firm, who would be played in the movies by James Whitmore, Piel noted that his arrival at the firm "coincided with the lumbering into the tent of that massive pachyderm, the *Investment Bankers* antitrust case, for which mahout Dean was in need of a trainer-feeder handy with broom and bucket."

The 739 lawyers who spanned the century from April 2, 1879, to April 2, 1979, measured the distance the firm had traveled. Its accelerating growth was obvious in the fact that the midway point in number of lawyers came in 1958, crowding half the group into two decades.

Piel catalogued the careers of the lawyers, those who became partners in 142 other firms and those who joined 136 business and financial companies, "clients in many cases, of the firm," he noted. One alumnus, Harlan Fiske Stone, became chief justice of the United States; others joined federal and state benches across the country. There were law professors and deans, ambassadors, senators, a secretary of state, an attorney general, and a director of the Central Intelligence Agency. It was a group for whom, for the most part, Sullivan & Cromwell provided the launching pad of successful, if not stellar, careers; among the group, the elite remained those who became Sullivan & Cromwell partners, even if it was their only accomplishment.

Though the centennial was an excuse to look back at the glory of its history, 1979 was also the year the firm started to look forward, or at least take the first steps to continued growth with more purpose and direction.

The change was sparked by the defense of an old-line client fighting a hostile takeover, one of many it had contested over the years. After all, the firm's old-line industrial companies were the constant victims of young aggressive managements of new companies able to use their market capitalizations to challenge older, staider companies much larger than themselves. Sullivan & Cromwell's defenses went back to the 1950s in SCM's repulsing the advances of Meshulam Riklis and continued in celebrated cases like McGraw-Hill's fending off American Express, and Babcock & Wilcox's fighting off United Technologies.

Such work was handled by the lawyers on the client teams, like any other matter. Sullivan & Cromwell even advised the acquirer in a hostile takeover in the mid-1970s, before unfriendly acquisitions had earned the respectability provided by increasing volume and fees. That case, Inco's acquisition of Electric Share & Battery, proved to be a costly and unsuccessful investment, but Sullivan & Cromwell showed its willingness to help clients on either side of the deal.

The year 1979 was significant because it marked the second battle over Kennecott Copper, a client that had been fighting off Curtiss-Wright for two years. The first defense ended in a standstill agreement arranged by Marvin Schwartz, in which Curtiss-Wright, which held 10 percent of Kennecott, agreed not to mount a proxy battle for two years in return for getting four seats on Kennecott's board of directors.

When the standstill agreement was expiring, George Kern advised Kennecott's new combative chairman, Thomas Barrow, to shake off Curtiss-Wright by buying *it* instead.

Kern had already defended a hostile takeover attempt when United Technologies went after Babcock & Wilcox in early 1979. A white knight, J. Ray McDermott, eventually took over Babcock & Wilcox in what Kern considered a blueprint for takeover defense because it was so elaborate. That case had all the elements—litigation, the search for a white knight and demand for regulatory review played out over six months.

Though by later standards it would seem to have been done in slow motion, Kern got invaluable practice in the various defense mechanisms, and he saw that hostile efforts were no longer an exception but increasingly the rule. For Kennecott, he speeded up the process, which gradually blurred the distinction between aggressor and defender as the two companies tried to arrange the takeover, reverse takeover, and eventual truce when they bought back their own stock.

After the end of the Kennecott–Curtiss-Wright fight, and before going on holiday to his favorite retreat, Greece, Kern suggested to chairman William Ward Foshay that the firm set up a separate mergers and takeover group. When he got back, Foshay told him to start the group. Kern was glad to get the assignment, even though he considered the group just a public-relations gesture, formally recognizing work the law firm was already busy with.

The formation of the mergers and acquisitions group signified that Sullivan & Cromwell would advise on hostile takeovers and take transactional business from previous nonclients. Kern felt that the Inco-Electric Storage Battery case had clarified the firm's position on hostile deals, but some clients, including Lazard Frères and First Boston, had already hired other firms, thinking Sullivan & Cromwell would not play the aggressor.

The role perfectly suited Kern, whose constant kinetic energy and booming voice made him a fish out of water with staid old-line clients. He looked particularly incongruous when he moved into the firm's Park Avenue office, which was founded in 1971 for the uptown dowager and executive clientele of the trusts and estates group. As he himself remarked, in a voice that could reverberate through the body of a frail person, "My God, we wouldn't put me on some old lady's estate, some widow in Palm Beach." But he was there, a thirty-block walk from his Park Avenue apartment and close to corporate and banking clients.

Part litigator, part corporate lawyer, Kern looks like a disheveled teddy bear who, aged sixty-one in 1987, has the curiosity of a child and a genuine warmheartedness behind a frenetic exterior that is constantly chopping the air with sharp gestures and fidgeting in his chair.

His generalist skills followed the career of Arthur Dean, whom Kern assisted in the unsuccessful defense of Brown Shoe's takeover of Kinney in 1956. Kern took his own cases to court, including his longest antitrust trial, a criminal defense of Tenneco, which implicated the heads of Equitable Life Assurance, American Natural Gas, and Northern Natural Gas, "three of the most eminent people ever indicted under the Sherman Act," he claimed with the hyperbole of enthusiasm. He argued up to the Supreme Court that individuals could not be indicted under the Sherman Act and, when he lost, argued that the collusion of these people in building a pipeline to the Midwest was so overt, they could not be guilty. After five years, they were let off: "They were wrong," Kern admitted, "but it was an honest mistake."

He handled cases before the Federal Trade Commission over the labeling of furs and pricing in the brick industry. Following his quick education in physics to handle regulatory matters for Babcock & Wilcox's nuclear reactors, in the 1970s he became the firm's expert on wage and price guidelines. He stopped appearing in court when his takeover practice got too time-consuming to commit to a complete trial.

But Kern believes in the importance of litigation experience for corporate lawyers and deal-making experience for litigators. His mergers and acquisitions group, which grew from eight to thirty people in less than a decade, gives lawyers lots of experience in both. The group is purposely small, in the firm's tradition of understaffing; he calls it a "flying squad geared for instant response."

His cross-practice skills were not the traditional way to get on in Sullivan & Cromwell, but with mergers and acquisitions, all of Kern's talents were finally focused. It gave him not only a *raison d'être* within the firm, but also its most profitable group, bringing in as much as a third of the more than $100 million in annual billings. In 1986, Kern's group was involved in more than $50 billion worth of transactions.

Kern delights in thinking up new wrinkles to throw into a situation. He assured client American Standard Inc.'s friendly $511.3 million takeover of the Trane Company in 1983 by getting an option to buy 60 percent of Trane. Trane agreed, even though this violated stock-market rules limiting options to 18.5 percent. "A lot of people thought it was a misprint when they saw it," admitted Sullivan & Cromwell partner David Kies. "It violated the rule, but the rule isn't a law." Kern disingenuously claimed it never broke the rule because the option was not exercised. "It was a way to protect the deal against uninvited guests. And there haven't been any."

He takes credit for pioneering several strategies that became part of the standard mergers and acquisitions game plan. He first used the "breakup fee," paid to a white knight to induce a bid, in the takeover of Ogden Corporation, the validity of which was confirmed in court. "It has to pass the smell test," Kern said, meaning that the breakup fee is within reason, and in eliciting higher bids, serves the shareholders. The fact that it is payable whether the white knight succeeds or not also increases the price to the hostile offerer.

He stunned T. Boone Pickens several times. In Unocal Oil's defense against Pickens, for example, Kern proposed to buy back stock at a higher price than Pickens's offer—from all shareholders but Pickens. Pickens fought the action in the Delaware courts and lost. This first major loss by the corporate raider forever changed aggressors' strategies, since they could suddenly lose out even on another's successful bid. Thereafter, raiders felt compelled to offer cash to all shareholders to prevent a partial response from management.

Kern originally thought up that strategy to defend Gulf Oil from a Pickens raid, but "Jimmy Lee [Gulf's chairman] wanted to know what it would do to the stock. When I told him it would go down, he rejected it because he was ready to sell the company to the highest bidder." To keep Pickens from "piecemealing" the company by getting seats on the board of directors and disrupting Gulf's normal functioning, Kern quickly registered the company in Delaware, shades of the quick-footedness of William Nelson Cromwell fighting the original antitrust legislation of the nineteenth century. The Delaware registration allowed Kern to eliminate accumulated voting with which Pickens could have voted all of his shares for one board member and gotten himself elected.

After the price of Gulf got too steep for Pickens, Kern orchestrated a three-way battle among Arco, Chevron, and Kohlberg Kravis Roberts & Co. "It was a period of relaxed antitrust enforcement," he said. "A few years before, you would have been sent to an institution for even thinking such deals were possible. I had to get Chevron to agree in a contract that regardless of what they had to do to get the merger through, they'd do it. I had to be able to tell the Gulf board there would be no antitrust problem with the offer." Chevron agreed, and "since then," according to Kern, "people keep trying to get the same sort of 'Gulf-type' contract."

In the days of more stringent antitrust enforcement, Kern was the first to horse-trade with the SEC, arranging British Petroleum's investment in Sohio in return for the divestiture of some of the gas stations it had acquired in the purchase of Sinclair Oil.

Kern's strategy is aimed at one goal: to get the highest price for the company he is defending. He admits that in the decade since hostile transactions set the tenor of takeovers, "you have to be a metaphysician to tell the difference between a hostile and a friendly transaction." For clients who want to take over another company, he suggests waiting until a third party makes the initial offer so that his client will look like a white knight.

He does not believe in poison pills or other artificial defensive mechanisms. "Look what happened to Crown Zellerbach," he said, gesticulating with a karate chop to a mahogany conference table. "The poison pill backfired, so Goldsmith did not have to take it over to gain control. It was the worst of all worlds—losing the company without getting your price."

He resists clients' requests for poison pills. "To them it's a macho thing. They hear one of the companies they're on the board of has one so they want one. The best defense is a well-run company," he adds.

Many of the deals in which Kern's group is involved are for the investment bank Goldman, Sachs, a long-term firm client. In a takeover, representing the bank allows Kern to act without embarrassment to existing relationships between a company and its lawyers.

He has not sought, but neither has he avoided, the publicity his competitors used to establish their names in takeovers. He does not write journal articles, as Martin Lipton does, and did not appear in *Fortune* magazine, as Lipton and Joseph Flom did on the subject of takeovers, but neither did he shun *American Lawyer*'s offer to put his picture on the cover of the magazine's first Corporate Scorecard supplement, subtitled, "The Biggest Dealmakers of 1983." The issue made public the degree of Sullivan & Cromwell involvement in mergers and acquisitions, in which it came in third place behind Skadden, Arps, and Wachtell, Lipton, two firms dominated by their takeover practices.

Sullivan & Cromwell was the only firm to place in the top three of all three lists the magazine compiles for its annual survey that includes, besides mergers and acquisitions, stocks and bonds and initial public offerings. In subsequent years, *American Lawyer* capitalized on the popularity of the lists to compile an overall winner, which is often Sullivan & Cromwell, emphasizing Kern's pride in the breadth of the firm's practice.

Kern is unabashedly a businessman, who is unembarrassed to admit that he sells his services to clients. "It's not just a question of getting invited in the first place. That comes up in all kinds of ways: Someone recommends us or you meet someone on the board of a company you're dealing with. But it's a matter of following up over time, keeping in touch, informing them of current developments on evolutionary things, like restructuring."

Kern's business skills have moved the firm back toward being "players" again; others would not admit to soliciting business, being too much the "gentlemen," but who can argue with the man who uses a tenth of the staff to produce as much as a third of the firm's income? Thanks to his "paternal interest," other specialist groups now exist for real estate, banking, commodities, mortgage-backed securities, and other investment banking specialties. "In an age when financial markets are moving so fast, you must keep very much on the alert to deal with changing tides," according to the wisdom of George Kern.

He is particularly glad to have real estate develop because of its affinities to his own work as bankers evaluate real estate and use it for backing securities. The banking group under H. Rodgin Cohen works closely with Kern because the entry of foreign banks to America in the late 1970s and 1980s was accompanied by numerous takeovers. Cohen's group also deals with regulatory issues at the SEC and negotiations of mergers and acquisitions.

Kern thinks of the specialties as marketing ploys that announce to the world Sullivan & Cromwell is doing what it always did anyway. He treats it as a new label on old wine, but acknowledges its success, which addresses the needs of clients who have lost their traditional loyalties to law firms.

A good example is First Boston, which started its own in-house legal department only in 1977, with former Sullivan & Cromwell associate David Sexton. It was Sexton, as a member of the First Boston client team at the firm, who suggested the idea to the investment bank. He boosted the personnel to six lawyers and now distributes work among a lot of law firms, including Sullivan & Cromwell, which gets more work than ever before from the bank, but not all the work, as it once did.

Kern is used to dealing with chief executives, as he has always done. But for the other lawyers in the firm, the label of their specialty establishes an expertise that in-house counsel is seeking.

Kern's help in refocusing the firm on client-attracting specialties came at a time of clarifying the role and relationship of the satellite offices in other cities. Under Jack Stevenson, the firm opened offices in Melbourne in 1982 and Los Angeles in 1984. John Merow, who initiated the new offices and the strategy to focus on the expanding Pacific basin, clearly saw the new offices as outposts of the New York office with no pressure to bring in their own business.

Melbourne happened because Merow, who represented important Australian clients like Broken Hill and Kaiser Aluminum and Chemical Corp., wanted to rehire a former associate, Jeffrey Browne. When Merow asked Browne to return to New York, Browne suggested instead they open an office in Melbourne, where he was living.

The Los Angeles office opened in 1984 after Merow had his secretary keep track of the number of lawyers traveling to the West Coast. "On any given day," he found, "we had ten lawyers out there. It made sense to open an office." He polled clients, who approved of the idea, as did Stevenson.

To find someone to head the office, the firm called Stanley Farrar, a Sullivan & Cromwell associate from ten years before, who thought the offer came from "out of the blue." His contacts with the firm since leaving in 1973 were intermittent. He had attended the centennial dinner and been in negotiations either allied or opposed to Sullivan & Cromwell lawyers. For Farrar, the decision to rejoin the firm was "like moving from regional opera to the Met," a reflection of his modesty and his wife's being an opera singer, if not the shape of his practice at that time. His assignment, according to Merow, was "not to build an independent law firm in L.A. We want it to be an extension of the New York City practice.''

In the summer of 1987, the firm opened a Tokyo office headed by Mitchell Brock, a partner in the securities field who had worked for the SEC. He found support staff within the firm: a Japanese paralegal from the Washington office to go as office manager and a Japanese-speaking Hawaiian associate who had graduated from Yale Law School to go as an associate.

Merow, who became the firm chairman in July 1987, pushed the Pacific basin strategy because ''they've got all the money in the world.'' Kern approved because ''the Japanese will take seriously someone making the commitment to be there.''

The firm already has a number of major Japanese clients, including Nippon Steel and Daiwa Bank. Kern fought the Japanese company, Dainippon, in its hostile takeover attempt against Reichhold Chemicals. He did not think by temperament the Japanese would be aggressive takeoverers. ''They also take a longer view, which would favor building a new plant on a green acre site rather than buying out another company.''

But the fall in the value of the dollar might attract Japanese to the takeover market because American companies had become just too cheap to overlook.

The firm showed further adaptability in improving its treatment of associates. In the Reagan years, there were fewer complaints anyway, with young professionals prepared for the duress of the business world. The major disgruntlement was the comparison with investment bankers, where young MBAs were getting bonuses in excess of their salaries. As a result, a number of lawyers went to work for investment banks, including Sullivan & Cromwell alumni. Sullivan & Cromwell also paid associates more, raising starting salaries to $71,000 and senior associates' to $177,000.

To those who stayed, the firm gave notice more quickly about their prospects for making partner. By the mid-1980s, the only associates still at the firm by the last year of their associate period were those who were assured of or had a good chance to make partner. Bill Willis, a member of the Committee and the firm's administrative head, conceded, "It *is* more fair, isn't it?"

The firm also began to hire lawyers as permanent associates, a practice that originated with William Nelson Cromwell himself and which Dulles maintained before it fell into disuse under Dean. In the 1980s, permanent associates are not associates who did not make partner, but lawyers hired after practicing elsewhere in the specialty they are hired for. Of the sixteen permanent associates at Sullivan & Cromwell in 1987, nine or ten worked in the area of clearing securities registrations, and others in oil and gas taxes, wills, and litigation.

Since permanent associates earn less than the other associates, they make business sense for the firm in routine matters that can be handled more cheaply. As Willis noted, "At an investment bank, they don't ask whether you are a partner or a vice-president. We should be able to do the same thing without a stigma attaching to the lawyers who are employees rather than partners."

But it is a sign of the gentlemen reverting to players, being more conscious of their financial position than of appearances, in contrast to the long period when permanent associateships went into eclipse. It may also be a sign of growing financial pressure on the firm. Under the "slot system," new partners were made when old ones retired. Now six are made at a time, when only one partner may go senior.

The continuing growth of the firm provides another financial strain—real estate. Sullivan & Cromwell's original five floors at 125 Broad Street were leased in 1979, during a real estate recession that saw prices at a fifth of what they became five years later. When American Express moved out of the building in 1987, the firm took two more floors, but at market rents of the later period.

The higher salaries for associates are only part of the greater expense they represent: The space they occupy may double their cost to the firm. The only consolation of the Tokyo office is that its cost makes American real estate look cheap. (Merow commented, "We were happy when Japan had a rule it wouldn't have foreign lawyers there; once the rule changed, though, we had to be there.") But if higher expenses helped make the firm wake up to the competitiveness of the 1980s, with the need for specialties and a better focus on its growth, the price was cheap for recognizing the necessity of adapting to the times.

17

THE TRIALS OF SULLIVAN & CROMWELL

In a generation we'll look back and laugh on our efforts to do things the way we used to.–WILLIAM E. WILLIS

In the past, the highlight of the firm's annual outing at the Piping Rock Country Club in fashionable Locust Valley was dinner at Arthur Dean's house nearby. After his retirement in 1971, the firm had to find other entertainment. In 1987, the highlight was *Sullivan & Cromwell—The Movie,* associate John Hardiman's effort to give the firm a good laugh at its own expense. The half-hour-long *Saturday Night Live*–style skits projected the subliminal message of pillar of the establishment, the archetypal old-line aristocratic law firm uncorrupted by the sharper practices and lower standards that were creeping into the profession.

In a takeoff on the Bartles & Jaymes wine-cooler commercials, slow-talking "Ed" Cromwell explains that he and "Frank" Sullivan were opening "a second office on Wall Street. We prefer morning appointments and tall ones for lunch." "Sullivan & Cromwell," the end credit read, "the premium law firm."

The new Tokyo office came in for a ribbing when Hardiman opened a closet door to reveal what was supposed to be the new office—cramped, as expected, with standard Sullivan & Cromwell office decor: a nineteenth-century Currier & Ives print of a New York scene of horse traders that, as much as anything, symbolizes old-fashioned, stuffy Sullivan & Cromwell. No modern art for this firm.

The film showed off the different-sized offices allotted to junior and senior partners and "the broom closet for the sixty-fifth summer associate." Newly appointed partner Ted Rogers claimed his promotion would not change his relationship to the associates, while the camera panned down to show a younger lawyer shining Rogers's shoes.

One sequence noted how fast the firm had grown. "It has expanded by a third in the past ten years. In the past two years there have been thirteen new partners, which means thirteen new summer houses, thirteen new mortgages." It caused confusion, with four Andersons, including a John D. and a John E., three McKeons and two Baumgardners; as a result, the front desk, which calls the limousines to take late-working lawyers home, did a routine resembling the famous Abbott and Costello dialogue "Who's on First?"

The final scene alluded to the risk in assailing the firm's carefully nurtured and prized self-image, with Hardiman telling the new firm chairman, John Merow, "Well, sir, the film is finished," to which his superior rejoined, "So are you."

Through the middle of 1987, Sullivan & Cromwell seemed to be coasting comfortably in the spirit of the Piping Rock movie: It could make fun of its own pretensions, which had been adjusted to the times with no ostensible change in its fundamental image or self-confidence. It was invigorated by the sheer dimensions of its success in mergers and acquisitions and the other specialties, as well as in keeping the confidence of its major clients, most of whom were prospering in the twilight of the Reagan years.

Sullivan & Cromwell was growing; it was making money; and it had changed remarkably little. The firm culture had held intact with little more than a few adjustments.

Then the century-old facade suddenly crumbled.

Within a week of the expansive Piping Rock outing, the firm was making headlines, with lawyers accused of unethical or illegal behavior. Not once or twice, but three times. In early August, a front-page article in *The Wall Street Journal* headlined LEGAL NIGHTMARE projected all of those cases across the country and added another one. To an outsider, the firm had fallen apart; inside, partners were meeting with each other, calling clients, and reeling from the unwanted publicity. Associates said they were trying to work normally, but rumors circulated about the firm's having to face up to an unprecedented crisis.

"It is a matter of great concern to us," John Merow admitted on taking over the chairmanship July 1, 1987. "I really didn't expect these particular matters," he said, like a man watching the stock market destroy his net worth in one day. Much of the whispering alluded to the decline and fall of a great legal institution.

The firm had been in the news before, but not because of lawyers' troubles. In 1983, Alan Ihne, a thirty-six-year-old manager in office services, including messengers and the Xerox machine, was arrested for insider trading on information obtained about George Kern's takeover work. Though the firm had to conduct a yearlong investigation with FBI agents swarming over the office and administering lie-detector tests, Marvin Schwartz was confident no lawyer was involved. He knew that of the ten stocks traded from firm information, the insider lost money on two purchases where he bought shares of the acquirer, not the defender. "A lawyer would not have done that," said Schwartz, who headed the firm's investigation.

Ihne had obtained his information from photocopies of documents, forcing a tightening of procedures. Kern was advised to speak more softly and the list of possible deals, which runs into the hundreds of companies, had to be kept in a locked file on a computer diskette accessible only to one person, whom everyone had to ask before trading in stocks.

The firm might have preferred it if the new allegations *had* been about insider trading. An inside trader would have been dismissed as a rotten apple and thrown out. (Ihne also got a three-year sentence of which he served eleven months.) Instead, the firm faced accusations about the way lawyers handle cases and clients, a far more serious matter. The publicized cases involved some of the most prominent lawyers in the firm and two important, highly visible areas of practice, the takeover group and estates litigation.

A judicial investigative committee was considering whether to bring charges against the managing partner of the litigation group, Robert Osgood. The charges, coming from the celebrated *Johnson* v. *Johnson* will contest, accused Osgood of improperly attempting to influence witnesses on behalf of the firm's client, the widow, Mrs. Basia Johnson.

The charges were a reminder of the trial, something the lawyers might have preferred to forget. Even to get its fee, the firm had to apply to the court, exposing the client's disgruntlement and the firm's failure to get its full $10 million.

It was a black eye for the previously successful glamour-litigation group. As Peck moved toward retirement in 1972, the firm chose Donald Christ, a suave litigator with a dry sense of humor and an understated, serious courtroom manner, to move from litigation to the trusts and estates group. Where Peck discreetly handled litigation for celebrities, Christ (whose name rhymes with "mist") specialized in defending widows against the children of their husband's previous marriages.

One earlier case in particular brought Mrs. Johnson to the firm. After fifteen months of marriage, Jaquine Lachman inherited half of the $30 million fortune earned by her husband, Charles, from the Revlon cosmetic company. Lachman's fourth wife, Jaquine was forty years younger than he. The will required that the couple not be "divorced or separated by decree or written instrument or by the voluntary act or fault" of the wife.

Jaquine was traveling in Europe when her husband died. Nurses conducted the lonely vigil in his palatial Fifth Avenue apartment and sided with Lachman's daughter Charlene when she brought a suit claiming that the couple were separated. In fact, house staff and nurses testified, Lachman was ready to start divorce proceedings but died before his previous lawyer, whom Sullivan & Cromwell replaced in the last months of his life, got back from vacation.

Though successfully handled, the case proved embarrassing for Sullivan & Cromwell for several reasons. First, the firm had represented both husband and wife, a potential conflict of interest the firm tried to get around by assigning two different lawyers to handle the couple's interests. But Donald Christ, Jaquine's lawyer, admitted to seeing early drafts of Charles Lachman's will prepared by his partner Frederick Terry, the head of the trusts and estates group. Second, the will stipulated that Sullivan & Cromwell be counsel for the estate, a provision that was worth $600,000 to the firm. Third, the will also disinherited anyone who contested it, a clear advantage for Jaquine, Sullivan & Cromwell's original client.

Christ called the accusations against Jaquine "a stew of kitchen gossip, moonshine and wishful thinking [by] the nurse, the maid, the secretary . . . [and] the old flame." A three-month case in surrogate's court brought the ruling that it was a "somewhat unhappy marriage" but not enough to overturn the will.

The *Johnson* v. *Johnson* litigation started as a typical Sullivan & Cromwell glamour case. A man died and left all his money to his third wife, forty years younger than he; the children got nothing and sued.

So tailor-made was the case for Sullivan & Cromwell that Shearman and Sterling, one of Wall Street's most distinguished firms, called Christ to represent its own associate, Nina Zagat, who wrote the will, and its client, the widow Johnson. She was willed a half-billion-dollar estate, after entering Johnson's life as an attractive but barely English-speaking maid to his previous wife.

Though Sullivan & Cromwell normally shunned the press, it exposed the lurid details of the children's lives that provided the case with the makings of a major spectacle, as the largest will contest in New York history featuring characters for whom the challenge of money was how to spend it. Sullivan & Cromwell conducted depositions, later handed out to the press, to establish that the Johnson children did not deserve to inherit anything from their father's estate.

The documents strongly supported Christ's case. The six children, having already been given trust funds in the 1940s, which would have grown to $100 million each if left intact, had not been included in their father's will since 1966, two years before he even met Basia. Some had squandered their fortunes; others had shamed the family with public scandal. The oldest, son Seward junior, had tried to commit suicide. A daughter, Jennifer, had given money in a divorce settlement to a former husband, who committed suicide and left the money to his new wife. One family member contended that a grandchild had injected his dog with heroin and watched the animal's frenzy, while another planned to blow up a local police station.

Mrs. Johnson was so confident of winning that she vowed never to settle with the children, adding insult to the injury inflicted by their father. He had shown little love for his children, forcing them to live, according to one account, in a rat-infested chicken coop after his first divorce. Yet he lavished favors on Basia, buying her before their marriage a Sutton Place apartment which he filled with expensive art. Once married, they built a $30 million mansion near Princeton, New Jersey, that rivaled the royal palaces of her native Poland.

While Basia Johnson was the mistress of her palace, *Jasna Polona,* the ornate, turn-of-the-century surrogate's court was clearly the domain of Judge Marie Lambert, who gave herself a colorful but dominating role on the judicial stage. Though considerate and attentive to the jury, to the lawyers she was tough and demanding, quick to tell them to move on to new points or to accuse them of letting their witnesses give opinions rather than facts.

Sullivan & Cromwell, in particular, she portrayed as plodding and unprofessional. She frequently interrupted Christ's slow and hesitant examination of witnesses. He read questions mechanically from a loose-leaf notebook with no clear objective.

The opposing counsel, Edward Reilly of another distinguished Wall Street firm, Milbank, Tweed, Hadley & McCloy, seemed sharper and better prepared. He battered Christ's witnesses on cross-examination. One Sullivan & Cromwell medical witness gave laboriously detailed testimony about a series of X rays of Seward Johnson senior's skull. On cross-examination, Reilly got the doctor to admit these were two separate series of X rays, not, as he had originally asserted, one continuous one. Sullivan & Cromwell started calling its adversary "Mad Dog Reilly" but he *was* more familiar with the medical evidence than Sullivan & Cromwell's own witness.

Reilly's first witness was a Polish maid who had made a tape recording of Basia Johnson berating her before the poor girl got fired. Over more than one hundred objections from Osgood, the tape was played in court to show Basia's terrible temper. Sullivan & Cromwell never pressed the girl on why she was tape-recording the confrontation, but Osgood asked to take the jury down to Basia's mansion to play the tape in the bathroom where the conversation took place.

After a long argument the judge finally agreed, when Sullivan & Cromwell withdrew the request. It never realized the damaging impact on the jury of the sumptuous, intimidating mansion where its client browbeat a defenseless maid, but Mrs. Johnson did not want camera crews there. After this fiasco, Osgood never returned to the courtroom and refused repeated requests to explain his disappearance.

The tape incident highlighted the arrogance and bullying of a Sullivan & Cromwell trial. It had been slow to produce documents, even omitting important items that Reilly explicitly asked for. Both sides requested thousands of items and made more than ten times the normal number of pretrial motions.

During the trial, Reilly submitted a memo to the judge accusing Osgood of paying potential witnesses. Those accusations later became the basis of the judicial inquiry.

According to the memo, the facts of which Osgood did not deny, he paid $27,000 to John Peach, a Johnson employee at the Florida estate where Seward Johnson died. Peach, a potential witness, was hired by Sullivan & Cromwell as a litigation assistant to help the firm locate and prepare witnesses. For this and his caretaking duties Mrs. Johnson paid him $135,000. Judy Smith, one of the nurses who served Johnson in his last months, had a serious car accident for which Mrs. Johnson paid the $23,000 medical bills, though the nurse had long since stopped working in the Johnson household. At the trial, Smith changed her testimony from Mr. Johnson's being "confused," as she had originally said, to just "exhausted."

Marvin Schwartz was called in to keep Osgood from having to testify on his handling of witnesses. After all, he reasoned, there was no evidence of witnesses "having [their] legs broken or . . . noses broken." Schwartz appealed to Judge Lambert in her chambers, silently buttressed by fellow partner and American Bar Association president-elect Robert MacCrate. Ironically, considering the firm's objections to the inquiry when it happened, Schwartz told the judge that the appropriate forum for such accusations was an investigation after the trial. The judge, while not sealing the memo, restrained the lawyers from attacking each other and directed them to focus on the litigants.

The kind of case the firm had handled so easily before was unraveling, and as it did, more Sullivan & Cromwell partners came to participate. Compared to its proudly understaffed way of handling most clients, this trial brought lawyers out of the woodwork. With eight attorneys actively involved in the courtroom, more than seventy worked on the case back at the office. On the other side, Reilly presented his case with only one junior partner.

Christ said he would make his key points in his summation, as though the aimless boredom in his handling of witnesses would suddenly be forgotten. The number of Sullivan & Cromwell lawyers who appeared in court confused the jury and exasperated the judge. The idea of building rapport with the jury—let alone sustaining an argument—was ignored, an obvious failing for which the firm blamed the judge's intrusions. But Christ, who admitted he was not used to dealing with juries, floundered. He did not know how to recover as his case fell apart.

The two sides became increasingly embittered and alienated during the course of the trial. The children gloated; Basia kept a brave, impassive face. As the four-month courtroom debacle came to a close, the two sides reached a settlement just before the summations, but not before Basia Johnson hired one more attorney, former Judge Frederick Lacey, from LeBoeuf, Lamb, Leiby & MacRae, to replace the advice of her trial lawyers.

The trial could not have been a more wasteful and futile exercise. But the confident widow and her overconfident lawyers had to go through the humbling process of nearly failing before they would settle. The children persued their case through the Harbor Branch Foundation, which Seward Johnson had formed and the children controlled after his death. The settlement gave Harbor Branch $20 million, and the children got $6.2 million each after taxes, with an additional $8 million for Seward junior, who was named an executor and trustee in the will.

Basia Johnson claimed victory because the judge collapsed her marital trusts so that instead of getting only the income from a $500 million estate, she got $350 million outright. But it was a humiliating victory that made Basia Johnson refuse to pay the remainder of her bill, which was ultimately settled for a total fee to Sullivan & Cromwell of $7 million.

The firm tried to get Ed Reilly to withdraw his memo on bribing witnesses as part of the settlement. Reilly, a member of the character committee of the American Bar Association, refused. John Merow called Milbank, Tweed, Hadley & McCloy "outrageous" for pursuing a vendetta against Osgood. Though the disciplinary committee had supposedly initiated the investigation itself, the group had two Milbank partners on it, leading Sullivan & Cromwell to assume that Reilly had put them up to it.

Osgood's lawyer is John Dickey, one of the few eccentric Sullivan & Cromwell partners, who lives in Greenwich Village and whose office looks like an antiquarian bookstore. Had he been available, he could have played in the Bartles & Jaymes routine in the Sullivan & Cromwell movie, with his affable, bearlike presence.

Dickey recognized that much of his job was a public-relations effort to combat as best he could the publicized allegations against Osgood.

Sullivan & Cromwell felt victimized, in part by the investigation but also by the publicity given it, when such proceedings are supposed to be confidential. The firm would not admit that it had been hoisted by its own petard, having itself launched the pretrial campaign against the Johnson children, which brought the case so much notoriety in the first place.

To important partners in the firm, the most shocking thing was the disloyalty of the profession. Sullivan & Cromwell had been outmaneuvered. It had reluctantly joined a battle of character assassination that affected the clients on both sides, only to see the accusations extend to its own lawyers, much to its embarrassment.

The second problem of Sullivan & Cromwell's summer, which could have the greatest consequence for the way the firm functions, also comes out of the glamour litigation area. The New York state appellate court threw Garrard R. Beeney, a sixth-year associate, off a case because he issued a subpoena without informing the other side. Merow "wishes he had not made the error," but feels the punishment was worse than the crime.

The court called the firm's justification of Beeney's action "preposterous" and "far-fetched," its offenses "blatant abuse" in a "deliberate and thoroughly unprincipled effort to obtain a litigational advantage by whatever means seemed useful, including deceit." The court said Beeney had violated attorney-client privilege and tricked another lawyer into giving up documents Sullivan & Cromwell had no right to ask for.

Beeney's error has grave implications for a firm that prides itself on the autonomy and capabilities of its associates. The firm likes to think it still gets the best law-school graduates and, in a tradition going back to Cromwell, immediately puts them to work on clients' matters. On-the-job training is a Sullivan & Cromwell hallmark prized by the law firm; now clients may question its benefit to them.

Beeney, a well-liked Sullivan & Cromwell litigation associate who wears a Zapata moustache and has eyes permanently ringed in tired-looking circles, thought his information would win the case. He represented Martin Wynyard in a drawn-out effort against his sister to get his share of the family trust set up by their father. Beeney's break in the case came when he obtained the family's legal files from another firm to prepare questions for Wynyard's sister, Rotraut Beiny, who controls the family trusts.

Mrs. Beiny claimed, as far as she knew, her father had died with few assets; her mother gave her the bulk of her $20 million trove of antique porcelains, gold, and jewelry, though their father Hans Weinberg was the major antiques dealer in London and New York.

Beeney went to depose Rotraut Beiny in London, armed with documents that would surely embarrass her and might even force an advantageous settlement for Dr. Wynyard. Beeney led his witness carefully and painfully through the incriminating letters. He quoted her advice to her father, "In this way you would make up a statement of wealth of goods which belonged to you and the rest of the goods in the safe could be Horst's [Martin's] and mine."

"Do you recall writing that to your father?" Beeney asked.

"No, I don't," she answered.

He asked triumphantly, "If you believe your father owned no assets as you've testified, can you tell me why in this handwritten note you suggested that he defraud the Inland Revenue by hiding certain assets?" She had no answer.

After giving her deposition in London, Mrs. Beiny found out from the newspapers that her lawyers, Shearman & Sterling, were being represented by Sullivan & Cromwell in the Johnson will case. She angrily fired the firm and hired Patterson, Belknap, Webb & Tyler, whose lawyers accused Beeney of obtaining his information improperly from the family's law firm, violating client-lawyer privilege, and neglecting to notify Mrs. Beiny of the subpoena to get the documents. The appellate court agreed and removed Sullivan & Cromwell from the case.

As a result of the firm's motion to have the decision reconsidered or be allowed to appeal it, the court looked askance at "an appeal that is before us solely because of the misconduct of lawyers in pursuit of a fee." Besides denying the motion, the court "refer[red] this proceeding to the Departmental Disciplinary Committee for investigation . . ." over "intentional misconduct" and "Sullivan & Cromwell's inexcusable and sustained efforts to squeeze from the improperly obtained documents every bit of advantage they might bestow upon their holder."

Pointing out that Beeny was "as he now claims, hopelessly confused" in his excuse for not following proper procedures, the opinion also criticizes Donald Christ, the partner in charge of the case, who "must have known at the very least of the way Beeny had acquired the privileged papers[;] still nothing was done to right what must have seemed to Mr. Christ to have been wrong." According to John Merow, the firm welcomes an investigation as an "opportunity to obtain the hearing before the committee or its staff which we feel has not been afforded to us by the court."

The case is proving costly to Sullivan & Cromwell; it had agreed not to accept a fee until a settlement was reached. Merow argued that technically it was not a contingency fee, something that the most reputable firms supposedly do not accept. But having spent $200,000 in expenses and $2 million in time, the firm faces a complete write-off and even a lawsuit from Mrs. Beiny for having jeopardized her business through strong-armed judicial tactics such as having a receiver appointed for the disputed trust.

After the Beeney disqualification, Merow went so far as to say he was willing to review the firm's procedures for training associates, but later concluded no changes had to be made. He does "not discount the concern and the problems of quality" that occur when the firm takes in fifty associates a year, as it does now, compared to six when he joined twenty-nine years ago.

Sullivan & Cromwell's third problem involves George Kern, the tireless takeover expert who beat T. Boone Pickens at his own game. Kern was accused by the SEC of not publicizing a relevant development in the hot battle over Allied Stores Corp., the parent of a host of familiar names in retailing like Brooks Brothers, Ann Taylor, Bonwit Teller, and Plymouth Stores.

Kern felt he could not announce Allied's possible sale of some of its shopping centers to Edward J. DeBartolo Corp. because they were subject to DeBartolo's obtaining financing, which it ultimately failed to do. A sale would have signaled to the investing community the intention to restructure Allied. It would have meant that the pieces were in place to outbid the hostile offer from Campeau, with the shopping-center sale as a centerpiece of the rescue.

Kern thinks the SEC is so gung-ho about full disclosure that it loses sight of the harm it can do. "If someone can trigger the need for disclosure by making a telephone call, then speculators would have a field day with the SEC's blessing. If you put out stuff that doesn't happen, you compound market uncertainty. It is no place to swing the black ax of government." He distinguishes between "the people on this island," meaning the professional securities industry, and "the lady in Omaha," who would interpret the same press release differently. Kern could not give a misleading signal to a market "where credibility is everything."

Fighting the SEC on principle, not practicalities, he mentions only in passing that he actually had a press release ready to announce a deal to save Allied Stores (on whose board of directors he sat). But when the financing fell through, he withdrew it.

Kern assumes he will lose in his first appearance, in front of an SEC administrative judge, where, he said, "they are judge and prosecutor." But he expects to win on appeal to the federal court, with the backing of colleagues around the country who called to offer their support against every lawyer's fear of unwarranted government interference in legal judgment and advice.

When companies face the same charges as Kern, lawyers, including Kern, recommend they settle because the only penalty is the admonition not to do it again. For himself, Kern is fighting for "the court to tell the SEC it's wrong."

Fearing to lose his credibility with savvy investors got Kern in trouble with the SEC, which wanted disclosure of the facts regardless of their interpretation. The authorities spoke for another audience than the cognoscenti Kern wanted to address, a situation reminiscent of the making of the securities laws in which Arthur Dean helped cut the public at large in on the deals of the insiders in the 1920s.

All of Sullivan & Cromwell's problems stem to some degree from dealing ineptly with the public. The fourth problem to hit Sullivan & Cromwell was brought by a group of ninety investors who accepted $2.7 million from defendant Prudential-Bache Securities after charging that they were not adequately warned about the risk of an investment. When the plaintiffs later learned that Pru-Bache had been under investigation by the New York Stock Exchange for its investment advice, the plaintiffs felt they had settled for too little and sued both Sullivan & Cromwell and Pru-Bache for failing to reveal the investigation. The suit threatens to cost the firm and the securities company an additional $2 million.

Marvin Schwartz, the Sullivan & Cromwell lawyer who negotiated the first settlement, contended, "I had absolutely no obligation to reveal the investigation, because the letter [about the investigation] did not come into existence until many months after we had responded to the plaintiffs' document demands."

Sullivan & Cromwell sought to have the case against it and Pru-Bache dismissed if the plaintiffs would not disgorge the previous settlement while pursuing more money. In federal court, the disgorgement would have been permissible, but not in New York. "It was debatable whether we could get it," Schwartz claimed.

To outside observers, the request for the refund looked like bullying;

it seemed as though the firm was raising the stakes to discourage the other side from pursuing its case.

The events of 1987 and the press they attracted returned the firm to the reputation it had acquired under William Nelson Cromwell for aggressive client representation with no regard for wider issues of public concern and the national interest. On taking over as chairman, John Merow's first reaction to the news stories about the firm was "Clients may even think it is a great thing to have a law firm that's aggressive."

Cromwell capped his career with the extraordinary achievement of getting America to build in Panama a canal it did not want so his French client would get a $40 million payment. The Alabama Bar Association passed the first code of legal ethics and Cromwell retreated to France, eventually turning the firm over to the more circumspect John Foster Dulles.

For the next half a century, Sullivan & Cromwell was synonymous with high-level legal service to business, but the public rarely knew what it was doing. In 1935, Allen Dulles admitted in a speech at the firm's annual dinner that they made fundamental mistakes in drawing up the prospectuses on more than $1 billion in foreign bonds that ultimately went into default.

Dulles's admission remained a secret within the firm. The banks the firm represented were brought under government regulations, which Dean helped draft. Foster Dulles was a public figure, to be sure, but clients' interests became the abstract issues of *Foreign Affairs* articles, while the actual dealings were secret, and sometimes discreditable.

In 1987, Sullivan & Cromwell faced a world that no longer tolerated the secret pursuit of clients' interests. The same public right to know that inspired investigative journalism in the 1970s and left even the President of the United States more accountable than ever before had finally come to the legal profession.

And Sullivan & Cromwell was found wanting. To the Johnson jury, the firm seemed out of touch; to the Pru-Bache litigants, it seemed arrogant; to the appellate division, it seemed "outrageous"; and to the SEC, it seemed unresponsive. While Sullivan & Cromwell continued to call Ed Reilly of Milbank "Mad Dog Reilly" a year after the *Johnson* case, it failed to acknowledge the commitment he had made to *his* client rather than to professional colleagues.

John Merow saw no excuse for Reilly's behavior; when Patterson, Belknap succeeded in getting Garry Beeney thrown off his case, Merow acknowledged that it gave the opposition a tactical advantage against Sullivan & Cromwell. Asked whether the firm would do the same if it benefited the client, Merow answered, "I don't know."

But other lawyers do know and increasingly take the part of their client to extremes that seem ungentlemanly but win court cases. The explosion in malpractice suits in so many professions comes down to the issue of practitioners siding with the victims rather than fellow professionals. There are excesses—excesses, by the way, perpetrated by lawyers—but the thrust of holding professionals accountable has made them more responsible.

It is not surprising that the legal profession has finally been subjected to the same scrutiny. After all, lawyers have handled the prosecution of all the other professions. Their turn had to come. Now it has. Sullivan & Cromwell's actions have had a consistency over a century. They have been "advocates," as their profession designates they should be.

But such a one-sided role also deserves the wider scrutiny of society. As Sullivan & Cromwell itself has argued in the Beeney case, "attorney-client privilege" is a specific protection that does not cover all communications between lawyers and clients. Lawyers have hidden behind it long enough. Recent events have shown that when the firm wants to talk about itself and its clients, it does.

Lawyers are not just transparent protection for their clients. Their abilities determine the success of clients; they have their own agendas for which they draw client participation; and they act as a network among clients. Not surprisingly, the growth of the legal profession has kept pace with the growth of government, for lawyers protect people and companies from the government. By keeping a closer eye on America's lawyers and law firms, people will have a better idea of when they need protection from their protectors.

EPILOGUE

LEGAL ADVICE

18

HOW TO MAKE PARTNER—OR WHAT THEY DON'T TEACH YOU AT HARVARD LAW SCHOOL

There are four ways to make partner at Sullivan & Cromwell:

1. Make yourself indispensable to George Kern, Jr., the mergers and acquisitions leader. Responsible for as much as a third of the firm's billings, he is the key man in Sullivan & Cromwell today. Get close to him, put in the hours he demands, tolerate his exuberance and think up a few clever gimmicks when takeover clients are in trouble. This is the royal road to riches at the firm.
2. Invent a new securities instrument (and we mean a securities instrument—other creativity may go unrecognized). Securities instruments replace banks with bonds. The field got started in 1983,

when the Federal Home Loan Mortgage Board found the price of borrowing could be substantially reduced by issuing bonds instead of mortgages.

This does not, as it may seem, require an economics or business degree. Lawyers play an essential role in structuring deals involving securities law, tax, bank regulations, and bankruptcy law. Though complicated and structured under tremendous pressure in a short time, it is a specialty that gains immediate recognition. Litigators in the firm may do the same amount of work and be considered just routine grunts, while Joseph Shenker, a star in security invention, put together major real estate financings with public securities and became a Sullivan & Cromwell partner at the age of thirty.

3. Pick your practice group on the basis of a careful assessment of which will be expanding or replacing partners when you are a seventh-year associate. It is practically a blind guess eight years in advance, especially because the competition, your fellow associates, are likely not to be at the firm by then. But it is the crucial calculation: Partnerships today are doled out on the "slot system" that relies on the places available more than on the quality of the candidate.
4. George Kern says, "Now more than ever you have to find the people with a spark, whether it's legal brilliance or client-getting ability or writing an appeal brief. And then you make sure that he's been exposed to enough people."

But most partners in the firm are drones, the chiefs of staff who can manage assignments and associates to get the most done in the shortest time. It is a talent, to be sure, but it makes you indistinguishable from most of the other lawyers in the office, whether partners or associates. You need not be a great trial lawyer, just be able to prepare briefs, supervise the preparation of briefs, organize evidence and generally keep the operation working behind the great lawyers and litigators who were made partner in previous generations. It is the talent of fitting in, being a "company man," as an older partner might call you when you meet in the hall and he cannot remember your name.

But even though most partners do come from this pool of capable lawyers, it is, contradictorily, the hardest way to make partner. The reason is that it merely gives you a sweepstakes ticket, and while everybody has an equal chance in a sweepstakes, the chance is small. Very small.

The greatest number of associates become Sullivan & Cromwell partners by fitting into the structure, but it harms their chances to become rich at the firm. So how *do* you become rich at Sullivan & Cromwell? It is a common mistake to assume that all partners get rich or even that they get incomes anywhere near each other. That may be true at Cravath, Swaine & Moore, which gives all partners of equal duration equal pay. Not so at Sullivan & Cromwell, not by a long shot.

Sullivan & Cromwell is an increasingly less manageable bureaucracy of 345 lawyers and 92 partners as of January 1988. It does not compare in size to clients like Exxon or Nippon Steel, but it is unwieldy because lawyers operating in partnerships ostensibly have a measure of equality. Every law firm treats this supposed equality differently, either as real equality, as at Cravath, or as a Byzantine structure with endless gradations of unequal pay, as at Sullivan & Cromwell.

The best way to get rich at Sullivan & Cromwell is to become a partner working in the lucrative mergers and acquisitions area or by inventing your own specialty. In other words, to make a lot of money *at* the firm, make a lot of money *for* the firm.

The next partner to get as rich as Kern will replace him as the main Sullivan & Cromwell mergers and acquisitions partner. Anyone entering the firm now has to look down the road to the year 1996 to see who will head the lucrative group when Kern retires.

The other way to get rich at Sullivan & Cromwell is to be on the management committee. This is not the rather large group of ten partners who make policy, but the smaller Committee of seven that distributes more than half the firm's annual profits on merit.

Neither of these routes obviously offers much hope of riches for large numbers of lawyers, even though Sullivan & Cromwell is an exceedingly wealthy firm. It does not rank among the highest in gross revenue, as calculated by *American Lawyer*. Its $115 million in 1986 ranks twelfth compared to $228 million for top-ranked Skadden, Arps. But unlike so many other firms, it does not divide its income democratically, allowing a smaller number of partners to become a lot richer (with the concomitant problem that a large number of partners make a lot less).

Even the run-of-the-mill partners make incomes that would be the envy of law-school classmates who went to practice in other cities. It may not mean, however, that the Sullivan & Cromwell partner has the same life-style he would have elsewhere because million-dollar apartments on Park Avenue and country houses on Long Island remain the prerogative of the older partners, not the new ones.

There are traps to avoid on the way to a Sullivan & Cromwell partnership. For instance, it is easy to get caught as cannon fodder in some worthy and perhaps important litigation that consumes all your time but makes no contacts to help you into a partnership. You may also get fed up before you get near partnership consideration. Alan Reinke, an associate in the mid-1970s, left the firm after three years, having almost single-handedly conducted the work on a major case for investment banking client Goldman, Sachs. He worked eighteen-hour days six days a week and ten hours on Sunday because the case was so thinly staffed. He felt he was on his own and stuck with the one case for as long as he remained at Sullivan & Cromwell.

It does your chances no good to have the firm lose a client on whose team you work. This is a matter of chance, not negligence, because the firm can lose clients when they are taken over by other companies. The mergers and acquisitions group may get the client the most money possible for the loss of its independence, but that usually ends the relationship—and some poor associates' chances for a partnership. Though associates serve on several client teams, the risks are high because Sullivan & Cromwell represents so many traditional old-line companies that get taken over. Such major clients as General Foods, American Motors, Allied Stores, Kidder Peabody, and Babcock & Wilcox have lost their independence in recent years.

An associate has to be careful to cultivate important senior associates and partners rather than be sidetracked by those who cannot do him any good. Some associates refer to their sponsors as "rabbis" who shepherd them through the years toward general recognition and a partnership. For the past two decades, as a consequence of the slot system of making partners, the young lawyer need not come to the attention of the head of the firm, just of his group and other key partners. Partners are allotted among the group so the managing partner of the group makes the decision that was once the preserve of William Nelson Cromwell, the long-lived senior partner, and then his successors as chairman.

While the aspiring associate has to please the important partners in his group, he also has to be wary of displeasing junior partners. Sullivan & Cromwell's secret pay scales and strict hierarchy resist the democratic trends in Wall Street. John Merow, who became firm chairman in 1987, thinks the pressure for democracy waned in the Reagan years. But among the very few concessions to younger members of the firm is the right to veto new partners. To the senior partners, it is a minor sop to democracy. There is no danger of upsetting the hierarchy, and like the coercive methods in police states, it encourages underlings to prey on those below them. This gives them a sense of importance and reconciles them to their own inferiority because they are at least superior to *someone*.

This power does not overtly threaten associates, since it is rarely used; but when it is, the policy of placating junior partners does not always seem like such a good idea. Overriding more senior partners is usually done for reasons other than quality of work, since the senior partners are the best judge of that. The young partners can take out competitive anxiety on the associates they reject.

In a job-satisfaction survey Lynn Gracin conducted among a small sample of associates for a course in industrial organizational psychology, the most generally accepted conclusion, agreed to by 91 percent of the respondents, was that it was easy to make enemies at Sullivan & Cromwell.

All associates get asked what club they want to join midway through their lives in the firm. The one with the greatest prestige and social cachet is the Down Town Association, a hunters' clubhouse in the middle of Wall Street. One associate from a poor background who had the temerity to want to join it—and did—was one of the rare prospective partners turned down by the junior partners, to the dismay of the head of his group. Despite the strong support he had within his group, his joining the Down Town Association and a particular run-in with a young partner over a matter of professional conduct worked against him. He was promptly offered a partnership in another major Wall Street firm, a rare occurrence in the present competitive mood of the legal profession.

One of the things *not* needed to make partner at Sullivan & Cromwell is a knowledge of the history of the firm. Senior lawyers are surprisingly unaware of the firm's background. With Arthur Dean's retirement in 1972, a repository of firm lore and history was gone. His successors seemed more intent on covering than recovering the past. It is not a backward-looking place. There is not even a portrait of John Foster Dulles, the senior partner for twenty years, on the walls of the office.

Partners do not want to seem dependent on the past or acknowledge that much of the firm's power today derives directly from its inherited relationships. Still George Kern's mergers and acquisitions specialty arose because the firm represented so many major industrial companies in their dotages. What William Nelson Cromwell built, George Kern sold, a direct link that included hundreds of lawyers, all working under the name of Sullivan & Cromwell for more than a hundred years.

19

WHAT A SULLIVAN & CROMWELL CLIENT GETS

It is only somewhat easier to become a Sullivan & Cromwell client than a partner. Partners have to follow an elaborate procedure for introducing new clients to the firm. Even lawyers' relatives have to be approved by the new client committee, which meets every Thursday.

In order to get approval, the partner has to write a two-page single-spaced letter justifying the new client to the firm. The criteria include, according to the firm's office manual, "(i) reputation of the prospective client and its principals; (ii) background of the firm . . . and, if the prospective client has or had other lawyers, the reason it is not or is no longer using them."

There are a total of nine subjects the partner has to explain about a potential new client for the firm. It is much less complicated to turn down prospective clients, but here too the firm has rules that make the matter pass through the client committee before final rejection.

Of course, the main criterion for becoming a Sullivan & Cromwell client is wealth. The firm will represent the rich in almost any way, shape, or form. A favorite way of representing rich individuals is on foundation boards of directors. Two partners sit on the board of the Vincent Astor Foundation. Sullivan & Cromwell lawyers past and present work for Paul Mellon in his various trusts and foundations, which endowed the National Gallery of Art and continue their benevolence toward numerous arts and science beneficiaries. The trusts and estates department will also look after an individual's investment portfolio, as partner Donald Osborn did for CBS Chairman William S. Paley, thereby winning a seat on CBS's board of directors.

Such positions contributed to Sullivan & Cromwell's reputation for dispensing largess to cultural and charitable institutions in the grand tradition of the American aristocracy. If not lucrative, these assignments are prestigious and spread across the whole firm the patina of distinction that actually applies to a very few old partners. Distinguished young lawyers, such as Robert Hayes of the Coalition for the Homeless and Philip Howard, who represents the Municipal Arts Society, are *ex*-Sullivan & Cromwell associates.

Do not expect Sullivan & Cromwell lawyers to sit on a corporate board of directors. The firm has long been weaning partners from positions that detract from billable time and can cause conflicts of interest. George Kern's being on the board of Allied Stores Corp. helped persuade the SEC to bring a suit.

Still Chairman John Merow sits on the boards of several Kaiser entities in California and claims the experience has helped his understanding of how business works. He quotes firm policy not to encourage board memberships, but adds that "it cannot be ruled out completely. It is part of a total client service and could be useful for foreign companies with subsidiaries here."

Only the closest Sullivan & Cromwell clients have partners as board members, like Bank of New York, USLIFE Corp., and Daiwa Bank & Trust Co. Most clients deal with the firm on a transactional basis during some major event in the organization's history—being bought, sold, merged, or bankrupted. Corporations tend to come to Sullivan & Cromwell for individual one-off transactions that cannot be handled in-house, specializing in securities registrations performed for companies that need to get SEC approval to issue stocks and bonds. Tedious, formulaic work for which the firm uses permanent and freshman associates, it is an extremely lucrative training ground for young lawyers.

Because of Sullivan & Cromwell's close relationships with Goldman, Sachs and other investment banks, the firm's lawyers may prepare a registration statement as the bank's lawyer rather than the company's. This role has gained the firm a reputation for dogmatic and callous disregard of business concerns in favor of a self-serving, cautious pursuit of self-protection for itself and its own client. The attitude reflects priorities as well as the inexperience or low status of the lawyers assigned to the work, which can make an important difference to a corporation's future.

At its best, as performed for instance by lawyers working under Jack Stevenson, registrations need not be the routine, demeaning experience that many clients find it. In the 1960s a number of partners and associates went to Tokyo to arrange the first postwar securities registrations for Japanese companies in the United States. They spent weeks arguing with the Japanese Ministry of Finance over minor matters like changing the wording from "fruits of the investment" to "dividends" and reconciling the Japanese law that stock must be paid for a day before it is issued with the American demand to get the stock when paid for.

For the first convertible debenture in Japan, Sullivan & Cromwell had to convince the Ministry of Justice that additional legislation was not required, a process that entailed daylong explanations with charts and graphs, followed the next morning by a call from the ministry asking again, "But why do you think it is legal under Japanese law?" Then lawyers had to explain it again, but ultimately the point was made and Sullivan & Cromwell could boast that it wrote the memo to tell the Japanese why their law was applicable.

The more desperate a company's predicament, the better suited the firm is to handle it. The First Boston Corporation, a leading investment bank, had its existence threatened in the complicated *Piper* v. *Chris-Craft* case where Chris-Craft sued Bangor Punta and First Boston after Bangor Punta as a white knight took over Piper Aircraft for it to escape Chris-Craft. Losing would have ruined First Boston, but John Arning of Sullivan & Cromwell successfully argued in the Supreme Court that a company already taken over had no standing to sue.

In the 1960s heavy electrical equipment manufacturers lost a landmark antitrust case when the government proved a long and detailed conspiracy to fix prices by a variety of means, including the assignment of supposedly competitively bid contracts by the phases of the moon (rotating every two weeks). The defendants lost an estimated $500 million in penalties, costs, and refunds, but M. Bernard Aidinoff, head of the tax group at Sullivan & Cromwell, got the Internal Revenue Service to let General Electric deduct the antitrust damages from its taxes. The other defendants, including Westinghouse Electric Corporation and Allis-Chalmers Corporation, then got the same deduction before Congress changed the law to eliminate such a seemingly unfair escape from punishment.

Desperate clients suit Sullivan & Cromwell because partners will be closely involved. Routine work is handled by associates, often led by a senior associate. The firm attracts top law-school graduates because it gives them responsibility, client contact, and major matters to handle on their own. But even as top graduates, the associates are still only beginners. A large majority of them will not make partner, part of the firm's arcane politics that should give clients pause to consider the value of the Sullivan & Cromwell label on their work.

Any client has to worry about the firm's financial interest in having work handled by the most junior lawyer.This is true in any firm, but Sullivan & Cromwell has a very large number of juniors, especially first-year associates, who comprise 15 percent of the whole firm, a much greater proportion than in the past. The firm wants the world to treat all its lawyers as equal representatives of its high standards and efficient work. This assumption works for long-standing clients, the ones that merit client teams at Sullivan & Cromwell.

These dozen to fifteen major banks and corporations include the Bank of New York, Marine Midland Bank, British Petroleum, and

Exxon, where the firm has long known how to match its staff with the clients' needs. Midlevel lawyers within the firm deal with counterparts in the companies. They carry on their work in the context of senior people on both sides overseeing major policy matters and assignments. The Sullivan & Cromwell partner is fully available to his executive client, while the team is more or less a coherent group that brings to the client continuity and confidence.

Not everyone can expect to be so lucky, and different clients can be treated very differently, as shown in the handling of billing. The firm prides itself, as the *American Lawyer Guide to Law Firms* notes, on being the "only firm in the Guide that does not use an hourly billing rate. The partner in charge of each matter determines the amount to be billed." Sullivan & Cromwell charges substantially more than many other Wall Street firms, often adding a premium for work done successfully and under time pressure.

Even major clients, like Allied Stores, admit that their bills arrived with only a total on it, which the client is expected to pay, no questions asked. Another major client, Lazard Frères, gets detailed bills, which sometimes cause it to ask the firm to justify the amount billed. Why the discrepancy? The firm's office manual blatantly concedes, "The amount of detail to be included in the bill will depend upon the customary practice in billing the particular client involved."

Sullivan & Cromwell does make a concerted effort to help clients anticipate the size of their bills. Once a partner gets a monthly readout of an outstanding balance due, he is supposed to discuss it with the client. Showing how reliant the partner is on associates' work, the office manual reminds the partner, "For the purpose of determining the amount to be suggested and discussing it informatively with the client, it is most important that the partner in charge know the details of the substance and status of the matter." Associates supply those details.

The bills themselves go back and forth to the billing department three times. First, the partner sends the billing department a draft of each bill; to this the billing department adds disbursements and returns the total to the partner, who passes it to the junior partner or associate who prepared the bill to look it over again. The billing department gets it back and a final check is made by a bill-reviewing partner.

As for collecting its bills, notes a partner in another Wall Street firm,

"Sullivan and Cromwell is very good about getting paid. Sullivan and Cromwell is able to take a very aggressive stand with clients. All clients complain about bills, particularly in this era of much greater competition than there was even ten or fifteen years ago."

Clients complain about bills but Sullivan & Cromwell takes the position, "We are very expensive, and we are very good, and if you think it is too expensive, by all means get another law firm." The firm is well placed for getting paid because Sullivan & Cromwell turns away so much work. Thus it can insist on being paid its rates for doing the work it chooses.

To a client that refuses to pay, the firm might say, "If you don't think this is fair, pay whatever you think is fair, but then please get another firm to handle the rest of the matter for you. Don't ask us to do anything more for you." The client usually pays.

Like any brand name, Sullivan & Cromwell represents a certain standard, but because the law is a highly individualistic practice, the actual service can vary enormously.

In hiring Sullivan & Cromwell, the client is employing the firm, which picks the lawyers to work on the matter. In the 1930s associate Joseph Prendergast brought in a client that wanted him to handle its work. The firm would not let the client dictate its lawyer, so Prendergast took himself and the client to another firm. Today the firm will try to accommodate clients but an autocratic philosophy permeates the firm's modus operandi. Its letterhead mentions no individual lawyers, a long-standing practice that emphasizes the group over the individual.

At the same time, the strict and inviolate hierarchy of lawyers creates a fundamental contradiction that Sullivan & Cromwell clearly does not trust associates with firm confidences. A hiring partner at the firm admitted that anyone being interviewed at a law school who asked about partners' pay would not be invited to work at Sullivan & Cromwell. In a period like the 1980s, when the country was overrun with law school graduates, hard work usually submerged questions of employee rights and consideration. The high pay on Wall Street also put other issues in the background, with starting salaries as high as $71,000 in 1987. But the growth of regional firms and the increasing difficulty rejected associates have in getting comparable new jobs reduce the firm's appeal.

At one time an entrepreneurial law school graduate would find Sullivan & Cromwell excellent grounding for any kind of legal or business career. Today the greater specialization of its work makes the firm less appealing for enterprising lawyers. They are just the ones who may not even be considered for a partnership at Sullivan & Cromwell, since they are less conformist and less fixated on playing safe to get the ultimate reward of a firm partnership.

There are other, subtler reasons that the firm may not be getting the best lawyers. Its bureaucratic growth encourages a mentality and promotes a lawyer different from those that made the firm great. The great litigators choose as partners their seconds-in-command, the chiefs of staff behind them. They are not the equal of their seniors.

Like any bureaucracy, the firm has a long, eighty-nine-page office manual that no one reads. Lawyers cannot even take their copies home. But the manual exists to show that there is a policy when something goes wrong.

The firm puts its own politics ahead of client needs in its refusal to hire lawyers with government or business experience. It prides itself on internal promotion to encourage loyalty, but loyalty alone does not a great lawyer make. One former Sullivan & Cromwell associate realized the weakness of his old firm when, as a business executive, he found a Washington firm much better placed to answer questions on relations with the government.

The firm tenaciously pursues its own policies, like using former associates to open new offices in other cities, but a client has to wonder how he benefits from his lawyers' quirky habits and traditions.

Potential clients have many alternatives to Sullivan & Cromwell among attorneys who were trained in the Sullivan & Cromwell system. The profession is filled with former Sullivan & Cromwell lawyers working in other firms and on their own, many of whom handled some of the firm's most important cases, the kind that attract clients. They have advantages their former firm lacks: A client can expect to get more partner attention and be assured that a young associate is not doing all the work on the case. The cost will be less, or if it is the same, it will reflect more partners' hours devoted to the case.

Sullivan & Cromwell has never had to pay a price for its practice of filling its office with associates who will not make partner. But greater publicity being given to lawyers and their operations is gradually exposing the real features behind monolithic brand-name law like Sullivan & Cromwell. Clients can find out who the lawyers they really need are and go to them directly after they have left the firm.

Lawyers can make a tremendous difference, as William Nelson Cromwell did to the clients he helped, who in turn were instrumental in the growth of Sullivan & Cromwell. Lawyers can also look better than they perform, as was true of Cromwell's handpicked successor, John Foster Dulles, who used clients to pursue his own foreign policy and cozy relationship with Germany after World War I. The near-anonymous lawyers at Sullivan & Cromwell have only recently relinquished their secrecy under pressure of adverse publicity, which more than ever raises the question, Is the premium the firm charges worth it? Beyond that, how will the firm perform in an era of greater public awareness of legal actions and results.

Sullivan & Cromwell has kept the biggest, most successful clients satisfied over a long period. It has maintained a century-long tradition with remarkable tenacity, despite vast changes in the law and American society. A hundred years ago most lawyers earned their livings in court, convincing judges and juries of the innocence of their clients. Today, the biggest law firms consider litigation a specialty, compared with the overwhelming prevalence of corporate law. In the transition from the courtroom to the office, Sullivan & Cromwell dominated the practice of law.

But the firm's salvation—its venerable name and established clientele—has become its nemesis. Tradition has prevented Sullivan & Cromwell from adapting easily to the overt competition of contemporary practice. The firm has trouble accepting a world that claims a right to know and wants even lawyers to be accountable publicly for their actions. It objects to legal advertising because it benefited for so long from unique name recognition. Having to share the limelight—and seeing it expose more than the firm can control—guarantees Sullivan & Cromwell a future different from its illustrious past.

NOTES

CHAPTER 1: SULLIVAN VERSUS CROMWELL, *pages 15–23*

Page	
	The primary sources for Chapter 1 are:
	Anne Middleton Holmes, *Algernon Sydney Sullivan* (New York: Southern Society, 1929).
	William Piel, Jr., and Martha Moore, compilers, *Lamplighters: The Sullivan & Cromwell Lawyers 1879–1979,* 1981.
	Sullivan & Cromwell 1879–1979: A Century at Law 1979.
18	"As a lawyer he was not given . . . case.": William J. Curtis, *Memoirs* (Portland, Maine: Mosher Press, 1928), p. 46.
18	"other things being equal . . . case.": Curtis, *Memoirs,* p. 44.

CHAPTER 2: NOTHING BUT A PAID ATTORNEY, *pages 25–38*

Epigraph: William Nelson Cromwell to Henry Villard, Feb. 28, 1886, Henry Villard Papers, Baker Library, Harvard University.

27 His fee was $50,000: Matthew Josephson, *The Robber Barons* (New York: Harcourt, Brace & Co., 1934), p. 382.

28 "an illegal and invalid . . . incorporated.": Arthur H. Dean, *William Nelson Cromwell* (Privately Printed, 1957), p. 99.

28 they threatened to throw Cromwell in jail: Curtis, *Memoirs,* p. 81.

30 "Frankly . . . do for me.": William Nelson Cromwell to Henry Villard, Feb. 28, 1886, Henry Villard Papers, Baker Library, Harvard University.

33 party line: Dean, *Cromwell,* p. 28.

33 "Accidents don't happen . . . misadventure.": Dean, *Cromwell,* p. 117.

33 "I did not recover . . . for some years.": Curtis, *Memoirs,* pp. 128–129.

33 "annual Reports . . . securities": Dean, *Cromwell,* p. 114.

34 "you will notice . . . methods.": Dean, *Cromwell,* p. 114.

34 Ivy Lee, averred: *World's Work,* June 1904.

34 Carnegie confided: Frederick Lewis Allen, *The Great Pierpont Morgan* (New York: Harper & Bros., 1949), p. 176.

34–35 National Tube consolidation: Josephson, *Robber Barons,* p. 422.

35 "malefactor of great wealth" and an "enemy of the Republic": Walter Isaacson & Evan Thomas, *The Wise Men* (New York: Simon & Schuster, 1986), p. 41.

36 proxy battles: *New York Times,* "Harriman Railroads," Nov. 12, 1906.

36 Cromwell forged an alliance: *New York Tribune,* "Mr. Fish Quits Mutual," Feb. 24, 1906, p. 1.

36 "board . . . Illinois Central.": *New York Tribune,* "Harriman Has Board," Nov. 6, 1906, p. 1.

37 "All that is wanted . . . complications.": *New York Times,* "Harriman Ousts Fish from Illinois Central," Nov. 8, 1906, p. 1.

37 *New York Times* editorial: *New York Times,* "The Ousting of Mr. Fish," Nov. 8, 1906, p. 8.

37 Richmond *Times-Despatch* quoted in *New York Times,* Nov. 10, 1906, p. 8.

37 Cromwell sent . . . associate through New England: *New York*

Times, "Harriman's Blind Pool in Wells, Fargo & Co.," July 17, 1906.

38 Cromwell . . . saying of Harriman: *New York Times,* "Harriman Smothers Wells, Fargo Minority," Aug. 10, 1906, p. 1.

CHAPTER 3: CROMWELL THE REVOLUTIONARY, *pages 39–52*

40–41 Curtis and Cromwell in Washington. Curtis, *Memoirs.*

42 "Advise the . . . case": Dwight Carroll Miner, *The Fight for the Panama Route* (New York: Columbia University Press, 1940), pp. 101–102.

42 340 documents: David McCullough, *The Path Between the Seas* (New York: Simon & Schuster, 1977), p. 275.

43 Morgan's infuriated speech: Report from the Senate Commission on Interoceanic Canals, May 16, 1900 (Washington: U.S. Government Printing Office, 1906).

43 "control, own and manage.": U.S. Congress, House, Hearings on the Rainey Resolution before the Committee on Foreign Affairs (Washington: U.S. Government Printing Office, 1913), p. 236. (Hereafter cited as "Rainey.")

43 Commission valuation: Hearings before the Senate Committee on Interoceanic Canals on H.R. 3100 (Sen. Doc. 253, 57th Congress, 1st Session) (Washington: U.S. Government Printing Office, 1906), pp. 2147–2148. (Hereafter cited as "Investigation on Panama Canal Matters.")

44 Bunau-Varilla telegram: Charles D. Ameringer, *American Historical Review,* "The Panama Canal Lobby of Bunau-Varilla and William Nelson Cromwell," January 1963; Bunau-Varilla cable to brother Maurice, Jan. 26, 1902, p. 350, in Bunau-Varilla Papers, Library of Congress.

45 Spooner Amendment: *American Historical Review,* January 1963; Cromwell to Spooner, Jan. 21, 1902.

45 "bulldoze like damnation . . .": Spooner to William J. Curtis, Sept. 20, 1894, Henry Villard Papers, Baker Library, Harvard University.

45 The Nicaragua band of red dots: McCullough, *Path,* p. 319.

46 "Hannama canal.": Herbert Croly, *Marcus Alonzo Hanna* (New York: Macmillan Co., 1912), p. 384.

46 Morgan traces "this man Cromwell": Miner, *Fight,* p. 151.

46 Morgan: "crowd of French jailbirds . . .": Miner, *Fight,* p. 198.

47 Roosevelt called them "foolish and homicidal . . .": Elting E. Morison, ed., *The Letters of Theodore Roosevelt* (Cam-

bridge, Mass.: Harvard University Press, 1952), Vol. 3, p. 599.

47 The New York *World* "special report": Rainey, p. 344.

47 The organizers of the revolution: Miner, *Fight,* p. 288.

47 Cromwell promised to "go the limit": Rainey, p. 349.

47 The secretary of state's promise: Rainey, p. 360, and Miner, *Fight,* p. 348.

48 Cromwell bombarded the secretary of state: A.L.P. Dennis, *Adventures in American Diplomacy* (New York: E. P. Dutton, 1927), p. 321.

48 Bunau-Varilla underwrote, provided and demanded: Miner, *Fight,* pp. 356–357.

49 Cromwell was incensed and cabled: Rainey, p. 34.

49 Cromwell fed the New York *World* a news story: Rainey, p. 730.

49 Waldorf-Astoria celebration: Rainey, p. 479.

49 Morgan transfer: Rainey, p. 731.

50 The liquidator's distribution: William J. Curtis, Address, Alabama Bar Association, 1909.

50 Roosevelt's arbitration: *New York Tribune,* "Panama Company's Bill," May 21, 1904, p. 3.

50 Curtis' visit to Poincaré: Curtis, *Memoirs,* pp. 108–109.

50 The firm got . . . $200,000: Gerstle Mack, *The Land Divided* (New York: Alfred A. Knopf, 1944), p. 482.

50 Cromwell became Panamanian general counsel: Rainey, p. 477.

51 Cromwell collected stock: Taft to Cromwell, January 16, 1905, William Howard Taft Presidential Papers, Butler Library, Columbia University.

51 *New York Times* report on Farnham: April 18, 1905.

51 Cromwell's grandiloquence: Cromwell to Taft, Dec. 12, 1904, Taft Presidential Papers.

51–52 "There is nothing theatrical . . . an acrobat.": New York *World,* Oct. 3, 1908.

52 "We possibly . . . strangers.": Curtis, *Memoirs,* pp. 109–110.

CHAPTER 4: CHANGING OF THE GUARD, *pages 53–68*

Epigraph: Cromwell in *Lamplighters.*

53 Interoceanic subcommittee hearings. Investigation on Panama Canal Matters, p. 1094.

54 *Headline* CROMWELL DODGES, MORGAN LEARNS LITTLE.: *New York Tribune,* Feb. 28, 1906.

54 STILL AT MR. CROMWELL . . . LOCKJAW.: *New York Tribune,* March 1, 1906.

54 "The assets . . . no conditions.": McCullough, *Path,* p. 262.
54 Editorial, "farm dog . . . hole.": *New York Times,* June 21, 1906, p. 8.
54 "the patience . . . lightning.": *New York Times,* June 21, 1906.
54 Roosevelt warned Taft: Morison, *Roosevelt Letters,* Vol. 5, Roosevelt to Taft, July 3, 1905, pp. 1260, 1262.
55 Taft admission and urging: Taft to Cromwell, Aug. 6, 1908, Taft Presidential Papers.
55 Cromwell refusal: Cromwell to Sheldon, July 29, 1908, Taft Presidential Papers.
55 Cromwell sues blackmailers: Curtis, *Memoirs,* p. 98.
56 Cromwell's denial: New York *World,* Oct. 3, 1908.
56 Roosevelt forwarded papers: *New York Times,* "Where Panama Payments Went," Dec. 15, 1908, p. 1; Morison, *Roosevelt Letters,* Vol. 6, p. 1416.
59 "all relatives.": Louis Auchincloss interview, March 1, 1985.
59 "violently anti-Semitic": Hazel Goldmark interview, Feb. 27, 1985.
59 Edison's next batch of inventions: Dietrich G. Buss, *Henry Villard: A Study of Transatlantic Investments and Interests, 1870–1895* (New York: Arno Press, 1978), p. 210.
60 "Never had the architects . . . mystification": Arthur M. Schlesinger, Jr., *The Crisis of the Old Order* (Boston: Houghton Mifflin Co., 1957), p. 118.
61–62 Grandfather's reminder: John Watson Foster to John Foster Dulles, Aug. 20, 1911, John Foster Dulles Archive. (Hereafter cited as "JFD Archive.")
63 "there was no nepotism involved": Leonard Mosley, *Dulles,* (New York: Dial Press, 1978), p. 43.
63 "It did not seem . . . its clients.": Dulles to Lansing, Jan. 13, 1913, JFD Archive.
63 "he was appointed . . . desirable.": State Department, 819.51/53, April 10, 1915, National Archives.
64 "I trust . . . a passport.": Dulles to Lansing, April 2, 1915, JFD Archive.
64 "telling them right.": Dulles to Janet A. Dulles, May 7, 1915, JFD Archive.
65 Dulles on Tinoco in Costa Rica: Ronald W. Pruessen, *John Foster Dulles: The Road to Power* (New York: Free Press, 1982), p. 23.
66 "the best means . . . considered.": Lansing to JFD, July 29, 1916, JFD Archive.

66 37 Dutch ships scheme: Philip Crowe, Dulles Oral History Project, JFD Archive (Hereafter cited as "DOHP").

67 "unusual and diversified means . . . immediately.": State Department, 337.11/241, March 1, 1917, National Archives.

67 "the strong moral . . .": quoted in Russell Fitzgibbon, *Cuba and the United States, 1900–1935* (Menasha, Wis.: George Banta Publishing Co., 1935), p. 161; Dean, *Cromwell,* p. 62.

67 protection for . . . until 1922: Memo of Activities Relating to Cuban Affairs, Feb. 13–Feb. 20, 1917, JFD Archive.

68 "the Government . . . capacity.": State Department, 311.54/31, Sept. 4, 1918, National Archives.

68 "New York . . . character.": State Department, 611.519/50, March 13, 1915, National Archives.

CHAPTER 5: PARTNERS FOR PEACE, *pages 69–75*

Epigraph: Cromwell in *Lamplighters.*

72 "to accept . . . terms of peace.": Memo of confab at Wilson hotel, April 1, 1919, JFD Archive.

73 Colonel House concluded, "I thought . . . lunacy.": Pruessen, *Dulles,* pp. 33–34.

73 the Brazilians were impressed: Memo, April 22, 1919, JFD Archive.

73 "McCormick, Baruch . . . disappointment.": JFD to Janet A. Dulles, June 27, 1919, JFD Archive.

74 "our Government has consented to . . . new oppressions, subjections and dismemberments—a new century of war.": quoted in Schlesinger, *Crisis of the Old Order,* p. 14.

74 President Wilson wrote, "I hope . . . handling.": Wilson to JFD, June 27, 1917, JFD Archive.

75 Dulles to New York *World,* "Without . . . affected.": New York *World,* "Our Last Economic Expert Quits Paris Peace Comm," Aug. 14, 1919.

CHAPTER 6: DULLES'S PRIVATE FOREIGN POLICY, *pages 77–95*

Epigraph: JFD to Bernard Baruch, March 19, 1945, JFD Archive.

78 "In truth . . . energy.": Cromwell to Dulles, March 13, 1923, JFD Archive.

79 "Because . . . honor.": Legion of Honor archive, Paris, France.

80 "Above all . . . conduct.": Memo, Jan. 20, 1922, JFD Archive.

80 Dulles preferred gin: Charles I. Avery to Dulles, Oct. 1, 1921, JFD Archive.

81 He was embarrassed to visit Paris: Dulles to John W. Davis, Jan. 13, 1920, JFD Archive.

81 Dulles's foreign languages: Blanche Wiesen Cook, *The Declassified Eisenhower* (New York: Penguin Books, 1984), p. 151.

83 Dulles and Schacht: "The Young Plan in Relation to World Economy," Foreign Policy Association, October 20, 1930, p. 12, JFD Archive.

84 $15 million cotton deal: JFD to JAD, March 28, 1920, JFD Archive.

84 "Today we . . . in abeyance.": JFD to AWD, March 28, 1920, JFD Archive.

86 The *Times* letter: *The Times* (London), "The Indemnity Terms," February 14, 1920.

86 Bernard Baruch, *The Making of the Reparation and Economic Sections of the Treaty* (New York: Harper & Bros., 1920).

86–87 "The reparation . . . all time.": JFD to Bernard Baruch, March 19, 1945, JFD Archive.

87 New York Life Insurance policies outstanding: Mira Wilkins, *The Emergence of Multinational Enterprise: American Business Abroad from the Colonial Era to 1914* (Cambridge, Mass.: Harvard University Press, 1970), pp. 104–106.

87 Court case: Edward S. Greenbaum, Columbia Oral History Project, p. 154. (Hereafter cited as "COHP.")

87 Amount and number of policies: *New York Times,* "Plot of Soviet Seen in $40,000,000 Suits," Dec. 24, 1925.

88 "It was . . . on it.": Frederick Seibold interview, July 17, 1985.

88 Dulles to American Bankers Association: Dulles to Drum, Nov. 12, 1920, JFD archive.

88 German inflation: Gordon Thomas & Max Morgan-Witts, *The Day the Bubble Burst* (New York: Penguin, 1980), p. 36.

89 Dulles to the German chancellor: Memo of Conference with Mr. Cuno, July 2, 1923, JFD Archive.

89 The Hamburg-American line represented by Sullivan & Cromwell: Arthur H. Dean quote in Eleanor Lansing Dulles, COHP, Part 2, p. 57.

89 Cuno pleaded with Dulles: Cuno memo, July 2, 1923, p. 76, JFD Archive.

89 Louis Loucheur to Dulles: Memo of conference with Louis Loucheur, July 7, 1923, p. 83, JFD Archive; memo of conference with Mr. Theunis, July 10, 1923, p. 88, JFD Archive.

90 Dulles's pro-German solution: Proposed German Memorandum in form of July 16, 1923, and as then approved by Mr. Cuno and

by Messrs. Maltzar, Ritter, and Gans of the Foreign Office, p. 4, JFD Archive.

91 State Department rebuke: State Department, F. W. 862.51/1859, Dec. 27, 1924, National Archives.

91 Krupp prospectus: "$10 Million Krupp Dollar Notes Out," newspaper clipping, not dated, JFD Archive.

92 Dulles in *Foreign Affairs,* October 1926, p. 33.

92 The German government warned against loans: Robert R. Kuczynski, *Bankers' Profits from German Loans* (Washington: Brookings Institution, 1932), p. 15.

92 Prussian state loan prospectus: Robert R. Kuczynski, *American Loans to Germany* (New York: Macmillan Co., 1927), p. 123.

92 Dulles called it "a pretty poor effort . . . working.": Dulles to H. Reed, Oct. 21, 1925, JFD Archive.

93 Robert E. Olds recruited: "American Ministers of Foreign Finance," *New York Times,* June 17, 1928.

93 Dulles praised himself; "financial . . . nation.": *The Power of International Finance,* Foreign Policy Association pamphlet No. 51, Series 1927–28, May 1928; and *Constructive Forces of International Finance,* March 24, 1928, p. 202, JFD Archive.

93 Dulles admitted to a partner, "In . . . matters.": Dulles to Curtis, Sept. 26, 1926, JFD Archive.

93 Bavarian bond deception: Kuczynski, *American Loans,* p. 79.

93 Competition for a city of Budapest loan: Cleona Lewis, *America's Stake in International Investments* (Washington: Brookings Institution, 1938), p. 377.

93–94 Dulles chased the Dresdner Bank: A. Hubbe to Dulles, July 31, 1925, JFD Archive.

95 Saxon State Mortgage Institution clause: quoted in Kuczynski, *American Loans,* p. 15.

95 Loans handled from 1924 to 1931: Office dinner notes, Oct. 30, 1935 and Nov. 18, 1937, Allen W. Dulles Archive (Hereafter cited as "AWD Archive").

95 Albert and Westrick started to serve Sullivan & Cromwell: U.S. Counsel for the Prosecution of Axis Criminality, Records of Dr. Gerhard A. Westrick, Oct. 9, 1945, Nuremberg Interrogation, p. 3, Military Archives Division, National Archives.

95 Albert a German spy during World War I: James Stewart Martin, *All Honorable Men* (Boston: Little Brown, 1950), pp. 52–53.

95 "to create . . . the Government.": *Boston Transcript,* "Germany's Plot and Plotters," Aug. 17, 1915.

95 "impudent activities.": *New York Times,* "Showing Up the Propagandists," Aug. 17, 1915.

95 Dulles claimed, "It is . . . responsible.": *Foreign Affairs,* "Our Foreign Loan Policy," October 1926, pp. 44, 46.

CHAPTER 7: THE RISE AND RISE OF JOHN FOSTER DULLES, *pages 99–118*

Epigraph: Michael E. Parrish, *Securities Regulation and the New Deal* (New Haven, Conn.: Yale University Press, 1970, pp. 190–191.

100 Sullivan & Cromwell offer to Stone: Alpheus Thomas Mason, *Harlan Fiske Stone: Pillar of Law* (New York: Viking, 1956), p. 143.

101 Interview at Sullivan & Cromwell: William O. Douglas, *Go East, Young Man* (New York: Vintage Books, 1974), pp. 149–150.

101 Sharp on Dulles: George Sharp, DOHP, pp. 18–19, JFD Archive.

102 "Having convinced . . . return address": Arthur H. Dean, DOHP, JFD Archive.

103 Polly Dean: Arthur H. Dean, DOPH, JFD Archive.

104 Goldman Sachs Trading Company: Catchings to JFD, Nov. 28, 1928; JFD replies, Dec. 3, 1928, JFD Archive.

105 Reaction to market crash: Pruessen, *Dulles,* p. 136.

105 Suits against Goldman, Sachs: Walter Sachs, COHP, p. 50.

108 Cromwell and Mellon: *Congressional Record,* 71st Congress, 3rd Session, Dec. 16, 1930, p. 873.

109–110 Firm restructuring: Dulles to Cromwell, Nov. 5, 1934, JFD Archive.

110 Janet A. Dulles's monthly allowances: JFD personal records, JFD Archive.

111 Lawyers and pauper's oath: Jerold S. Auerbach, *Unequal Justice: Lawyers and Social Change in Northern America* (New York: Oxford University Press, 1976), p. 16.

111 Sullivan & Cromwell and First Boston: Robert Goldsby interview, July 20, 1985.

111–112 Cromwell and Dulles invest in clients: Dulles to Cromwell, Oct. 16, 1934, JFD Archive.

112 Murnane on Kreuger: *New York Times,* "I.T. & T. Challenged Kreuger's Honesty," May 14, 1932.

113 Hoover's joke: Schlesinger, *Crisis of the Old Order,* p. 242.

113 "full publicity": quoted in James Landis, "The Legislative History of the Securities Act," *George Washington University Law Review,* 1933, p. 30.

113 "hopeless . . . Anglo-Saxon law.": Parrish, *Securities,* pp. 54, 55*n.*

114 Dulles on Rayburn: Parrish, *Securities,* p. 40.

114 Dulles advice to utilities: William O. Douglas, *Go East,* p. 277.

115 Stone's refusal: Martin Mayer, *The Lawyers* (New York: Harper and Row, 1967), p. 339.

116 Stone on North American Co.: Mason, *Stone,* p. 703.

116 Eaton on Dulles: Douglas, *Go East,* p. 278.

117 Cummings "pulled . . .": Chester Travis Lane, COHP, p. 533.

117 "slush fund": Chester Travis Lane, COHP, p. 534.

117 Missouri legislature: Chester Travis Lane, COHP, p. 539.

117–118 Chester Travis Lane, COHP, pp. 537–538.

CHAPTER 8: NAZI CLIENTS, *pages 119–142*

Epigraph: Dulles to James S. Patty, April 28, 1950, JFD Archive.

120 "We don't want headlines . . .": Joseph Prendergast interview, July 21, 1985.

120 "the most constructive loan . . .": George Murnane, Jr., interview, April 10, 1985.

120 Schacht horrified: Hjalmar Horace Greeley Schacht, *Confessions of "The Old Wizard"* (Boston: Houghton Mifflin Co., 1956), p. 251.

120–121 Dulles-Schacht debate: "The Young Plan in Relation to World Economy," Foreign Policy Association pamphlet, October 20, 1930.

122 "You'll get your money back, Murnane . . .": Schacht, *Confessions,* pp. 251–252.

122 Shares for Credit Anstalt: Sullivan & Cromwell to State Department, 863.51 c86/–, Sept. 27, 1927, National Archives.

123 Sullivan & Cromwell complained to State Department: 862.51 interest/4, Dec. 22, 1931, National Archives.

123 Debt holders' conference: Dulles to Cordell Hull, June 6, 1933, p. 5, JFD Archive.

124 "precipitate and . . . treatment of the Jews.": Notes on lunch conference with Schacht, June 8, 1933, JFD Archive.

124 Murnane bonds did well: George Murnane, DOHP, pp. 6–7, JFD Archive.

124 Allied's nitrogen factory: *Business Week,* June 7, 1933.

124 Weber justifies secrecy: Weber to Allied Chemical stockholders, June 14, 1933, Scudder Archives, Columbia University.

124 "Much as I deplore . . .": *New York Times,* "Gerard Begins Fight," June 10, 1933, p. 19.

125 Schacht on Jews: Schacht, *Confessions,* p. 296.

125–126 Inco supplied I. G. Farben: *U.S.* v. *Inco,* Civil Complaint, 36-31, May 16, 1946, p. 18.

126 Inco helped Germany process nickel: *U.S.* v. *Inco,* p. 21.

126 Dulles supports arms exports: "Our Foreign Loan Policy," *Foreign Affairs,* October 1926.

126 "it would be impossible . . .": Jamie Swift, *The Big Nickel: Inco at Home and Abroad* (Kitchener, Ontario: Between the Lines Publication, 1977), p. 28.

126 Inco's argument on indirect exports: O. W. Main, *The Canadian Nickel Industry: A Study in Market Control and Public Policy* (Toronto: University of Toronto Press, 1955), p. 119.

127 Dulles to Lord McGowan, Sept. 15, 1943, JFD Archive.

127 "plan for . . . Reichsbank.": Dulles to Schacht, Oct. 12, 1933, JFD Archive.

128 Dulles on Possehl Works: State Department, 360c.1133OV2/5, Jan. 17, 1924, National Archives.

128 "the consortium now owning the shares . . .": State Department, 360c.1153OV2/8, April 2, 1924, National Archives.

128 Dulles reluctant with information: Pruessen, *Dulles,* pp. 62–63.

129 Dulles's ties to Flick: Preussen, *Dulles,* p. 131.

130 AWD charges a client: Mary Bancroft interview, March 8, 1985.

130 AWD entertains Cromwell: AWD to Clover Dulles, May 20, 1932, AWD Archive.

130 "Cromwell hasn't touched a drop . . .": AWD to Dulles, April 22, 1932, AWD Archive.

130 "I dined . . . 'Gregoire.' ": AWD to Clover Dulles, April 18, 1932, AWD Archive.

130 Polish golf: *New Yorker,* 1927.

131 Cobb tries to collect: Candler Cobb, COHP, p. 151.

132 "Heil Hitler.": Lauson Stone interview, June 29, 1985.

132 "the changes which . . . avenues of change.": *Atlantic Monthly,* October 1935.

133 Cromwell on Dulles's argument: Cromwell to Dulles, October 1, 1935, JFD Archive.

133 AWD sees Albert, Westrick: AWD to Clover Dulles, June 3, 1935, AWD Archive.

133 Dulles's deathbed promise: Mary Bancroft, *Autobiography of a Spy* (New York: William Morrow, 1983), p. 139.

134 Foster used the loss of profits argument: Swift, *Big Nickel,* p. 28.

134 AWD argument: Mosley, *Dulles,* p. 92.

134 Dean added . . . : Eleanor Lansing Dulles, COHP, Part 2, p. 59.

134 "in tears.": Swift, *Big Nickel,* p. 28; Townsend Hoopes, *The*

Devil and John Foster Dulles (Boston: Little Brown & Co., 1973), p. 47.

134 "no argument": Eleanor Lansing Dulles, COHP, Part 2, p. 57.

134 Cobb's successes: Candler Cobb to Dulles, April 7, 1936, JFD Archive.

135 "Thank God . . . errors.": *Lamplighters,* James Thacher entry, p. 397.

135 The "fact that many . . . attributes of a bond.": Office dinner notes, Oct. 30, 1935, AWD Archive.

136 "lawyers cannot . . . outside agents.": Office dinner notes, Nov. 18, 1937, AWD Archive.

136 General Aniline & Film background: Martin, *All Honorable,* p. 67.

136 GAF assets: United States Group Control Council, June 10, 1945, National Archives.

137 "the fog": Martin, *All Honorable,* p. 68.

137 Hitler's stock offer: Chester Travis Lane, COHP, pp. 435–438.

137 Dulles organizes America First: Dulles to Edwin S. Webster, Feb. 7, 1941, JFD Archive.

137 Janet Dulles's contribution: New York *Evening Post,* Nov. 1, 1944.

138 America First: Arthur H. Dean, DOHP, JFD Archive.

138 "One may . . . Hitler's.": Dulles to Henry Leech, Sept. 30, 1937, JFD Archive.

138 "those mad . . .": AWD to Clover Dulles, May 3, 1933, AWD Archive.

139 "heated debates . . .": Avery Dulles interview, July 19, 1985.

139 AWD helps the potash monopoly: AWD client list, 1938, 1939, AWD Archive; *Time,* "Potash Politics," July 10, 1939.

140 "fought and fought . . .": Glen McDaniel interview, Jan. 30, 1985.

140 Debate with James P. Warburg: Warburg, COHP, pp. 760–761.

140 Willkie to Dulles: Quoted in *New Yorker,* Sept. 2, 1944.

140–141 Seligman memo: Seligman to Dulles, Oct. 25, 1939, JFD Archive.

141 Lamont's death: *New York Herald Tribune,* "Rogers Lamont Reported Killed at Dunkerque," Sept. 24, 1940.

141 Albert & Westrick disbanded: Charles Higham, *Trading with the Enemy* (New York: Delacorte Press, 1983), p. 154.

141 "Is it true that Lamont . . . here.": Heinrich Albert to Dulles, Dec. 2, 1939, JFD Archive.

142 Lamont's partnership disappointment: Joseph Prendergast interview, July 21, 1985.

CHAPTER 9: THE DULLES WAR MACHINE, *pages 143–159*

Epigraph: Dulles to Dr. H. Borchers, German Consul General, Feb. 14, 1940, JFD Archive.

143 "any country . . . at war.": Draft letter from American Bosch Corp. to Navy Department, Bureau of Ships, July 1941.

144 British purchases: *Lamplighters,* Thomas Childs entry, pp. 163–168.

144 Childs gave Dulles credit: Thomas Childs interview, March 11, 1987.

144 "to declare . . . relations.": *Lamplighters,* Thomas Childs entry, p. 167.

144 "I saw . . . settlement.": Avery Dulles interview, July 19, 1985.

144–145 Dulles memo: December 9, 1941, JFD Archive.

145 "America Firster.": Franklin O. Canfield interview, Nov. 7, 1985.

145 Inzer Wyatt's war: Ronald Lewin, *Ultra Goes to War* (New York: Pocket Books, 1978), pp. 299–302.

146 "there is no known substitute . . .": Memorandum for the Files Feb. 23, 1943, Justice Department, Economic Warfare Unit, National Archives.

146 Mendelssohn's commission: Safehaven Name Files, Robert Bosch, 1945, Record Group 84, Box 12, p. 3, National Archives.

147 "high U.S. prices . . ." Robert Bosch GMBH #6, Justice Department, Economic Warfare Unit, pp. 6, 7.

147 "American Bosch volunteered information . . .": Confidential Report, June 16, 1943, Justice Department, Economic Warfare Unit.

147 "Mr. Fellmeth . . . holders." February 4, 1944, Justice Department, Economic Warfare Unit, p. 4.

148 "the attitude . . . purchase.": Memorandum to Executive Committee of the Alien Property Custodian from Division of Investigation and Research, May 15, 1942, p. 4.

148 "be destructive . . . products." Confidential Report No. 187, June 16, 1943, Justice Department, Economic Warfare Unit.

148–150 Wallenberg involvement: Memo, Aug. 30, 1945, Safehaven Name Files, Robert Bosch, 1945, Record Group 84, Box 12.

149 Bosch between the wars: Confidential Report No. 187, June 16, 1943, Justice Department, Economic Warfare Unit.

150 "complete suspension of agreements . . .": American Bosch, Annual Report, 1943.

150 "American Bosch . . . Company.": Robert Bosch #22, Record Group 60, Justice Department, Economic Warfare Unit.

150 "a very strong . . . importance.": Memo on Capital Stock of American Bosch Corp., May 15, 1942, p. 8.

151 "had confidence . . . shares.": Safehaven Name Files, Robert Bosch, 1945, Record Group 84, Box 12.

151 "to American . . . war.": Martin, *All Honorable,* pp. 250–251.

151 "Dulles . . . German owned.": Memo on William L. Batt's Role, Oct. 11, 1944, Charles Higham Papers at University of Southern California Library.

152 "war production . . . on.": War Department to Attorney General, May 25, 1942, Justice Department, National Archives.

152 "Although the . . . institutions.": JFD Memo in 1944 file, JFD Archive.

153 Dulles quote, "Let them . . .": Pruessen, *Dulles,* pp. 196, 199.

153 Dulles's copies: Pruessen, *Dulles,* p. 205.

153 Nazi confiscation in Norway: Thomas Childs interview, March 11, 1987.

153 "The great corporations . . .": J. Thompson and Norman Beasley, *For the Years to Come: A Story of International Nickel of Canada* (New York: G. P. Putnam's Sons, 1960), p. 244.

153–154 AWD arrives in Switzerland: Allen W. Dulles, *The Secret Surrender* (New York: Harper & Row, 1966), pp. 14–15.

154 Famous for getting in: Allen W. Dulles, *The Craft of Intelligence* (Westport, Conn.: Greenwood Press, 1963), p. 7.

154 AWD: "nobody . . . me.": *New York Times,* "New Era in Intelligence," Sept. 28, 1961.

155 Monod and Dulles: Philippe Monod interview, April 16, 1985.

155 Willkie returns Dulles's position paper: Pruessen, *Dulles,* p. 222.

155 1944 profile: *Life* magazine, Aug. 21, 1944, pp. 85, 96.

156 Dulles drafted remark, "Mr. Roosevelt . . .": Pruessen, *Dulles,* p. 232.

156 YOOHOO, MR. DULLES . . . : *New York Post,* Aug. 22, 1944.

156–157 FDR against Dulles—and justified: Alger Hiss, COHP, p. 244.

157 "Wherever you had . . . headlines": Alger Hiss, COHP.

157 Secrets in the Stuttgart wall: *Washington Star,* "Hearings Set on Move to Call Swedish Bank Officers in Bosch Case," Oct. 5, 1948.

157 AWD and surrender: *Saturday Evening Post,* Sept. 22, 1945, p. 9ff.

157 "the episode . . . informants.": Arthur M. Schlesinger, Jr., *Cycles of American History* (Boston: Houghton Mifflin, 1986), p. 185.

157 AWD recruits Nazi spies: John Loftus, *The Belarus Secret* (New York: Alfred A. Knopf, 1982), p. 54.

158 AWD rehabilitates Wallenberg: AWD to Marcus Wallenberg, Feb. 5, 1946, AWD Archive.

158 ''The German underground's . . . bankers.'': Allen Welsh Dulles, *Germany's Underground* (New York: Macmillan Co., 1947), p. 142.

158 ''Enskilda Bank . . . both ends.'': Memo to Dr. Otto F. Fleischer from Hazel H. Hallinan, ''Undesirable transactions of Stockholm's Enskilda Bank,'' Jan. 27, 1945, Charles Higham Papers at University of Southern California.

158 Gun for Dulles: Wallenberg to JFD, July 19, 1946, JFD Archive.

158 ''He is . . . by now.'': Kati Marton, *Wallenberg* (New York: Random House, 1982), p. 12.

159 Attorney General to Secretary of State: Tom Clark to George C. Marshall, Department of Justice, Nov. 4, 1948.

159 Bosch settlement: *New York Times,* ''U.S. Settles Suit Over Bosch Stock,'' Sept. 22, 1950.

159 ''I am glad to have . . .'': 1947 file on Germany's Underground, AWD Archive.

CHAPTER 10: OUTSIDE MAN/INSIDE MAN, *pages 161–170*

Epigraph: David R. Hawkins, DOHP, p. 8, JFD Archive.

163 ''Because he stubbornly persists . . .'': *Saturday Evening Post,* Oct. 4, 1948, p. 132.

163 AWD in Italy: *Boston Globe,* April 8, 1948.

163 ''one of . . . generation.'': Paul Johnson, *Modern Times* (New York: Harper & Row, 1983), p. 579.

163–164 Allen Dulles intelligence activities: Lawrence Houston interview, Feb. 7, 1984.

164 John F. Thompson on Dulles: DOHP, pp. 39–40, JFD Archive.

164 Kennan quote: George F. Kennan, *American Diplomacy 1900–1950* (Chicago: University of Chicago Press, 1951), pp. 91–92.

168 ''We've gotten . . . 22.'': David R. Hawkins, DOHP, p. 4, JFD Archive.

168 ''I had been . . . should see.'': Phyllis Macomber interview, March 8, 1985.

169 ''figured everyone . . . Cromwell'': Phyllis Macomber interview, March 8, 1985.

170 ''One thing . . . they have'': Max Stolper interview, August 27, 1985.

CHAPTER 11: THE PROFITS OF BLAME, *pages 173–182*

Epigraph: *Fortune,* "The Federal Securities Act: I," August 1933, p. 99.

174 Dean: "A fair-minded . . . on.": *Fortune,* "As Amended: The Federal Securities Act," September 1934, p. 80.

174 Dean: "Officials . . . Act.": quoted in Vincent Carosso, *Investment Banking in America: A History* (Cambridge, Mass.: Harvard University Press, 1970), p. 361.

175 "It seems . . . vermin.": Joel Seligman, *The Transformation of Wall Street* (Boston: Houghton Mifflin Co., 1982) p. 77.

175 Dean: "issuing . . . statement": *Fortune,* "As Amended: The Federal Securities Act," September 1934, pp. 82, 127.

176 "undue emphasis . . . detail.": *Fortune,* "As Amended: The Federal Securities Act," September 1934, p. 127.

176–177 Seligman on truth in autos: *New York Times,* "Proposes Changes in Securities Acts," Feb. 18, 1934.

177 Dean on "self-regulation . . .": Arthur H. Dean, "25 Years of Federal Securities Regulation by the SEC," *Columbia Law Review,* May 1959, Vol. 59, p. 700, n.17.

177–178 "Probably the greatest . . . law": Mayer, *The Lawyers,* p. 51.

178 "What here follows . . .": *Fortune,* "The Federal Securities Act: I," August 1933, p. 50.

178 Dulles to Darrell: *Lamplighters,* Norris Darrell, Sr., entry, p. 110.

179 "He would call me in and say . . .": Lawrence McQuade interview, June 27, 1985.

179 Dulles on foreign lending: *Foreign Affairs,* "The Securities Act and Foreign Lending," October 1933.

179 "Is the fundamental purpose . . .": *Atlantic Monthly,* "Amend the Securities Act," March 1934, p. 370.

180 "The work . . . *twofold.*": *Fortune,* "As Amended: The Federal Securities Act," September 1934, p. 81.

180 "new and terrifying . . . required.": *Lamplighters,* William Curtis Pierce entry, p. 159.

180 Foshay on registrations: Quoted in Mayer, *The Lawyers,* p. 317.

181 "treadmill . . . work.": Quoted in Mason, *Stone,* p. 542.

182 "real culprits . . . existence": Parrish, *Securities,* p. 190.

182 Dean's shirttails: Max Stolper interview, August 27, 1985.

182 Socks: Frederick Seibold interview, July 17, 1985.

182 "Mr. Dulles took . . . in Paris": Arthur H. Dean, DOHP, JFD Archive.

CHAPTER 12: TRUST IN ANTITRUST, *pages 183–198*

Epigraph: *Fortune,* February 1958.

183–184 Dean with clients: Lawrence McQuade interview, June 27, 1985.

184 The law firms and their clients in the investment bankers' antitrust case were: Cahill, Gordon, Zachry & Reindel, representing Dillon, Read & Company and Stone & Webster; Cleary, Gottlieb, Friendly & Cox, representing the Investment Bankers Association of America; Covington, Burling, Rublee, O'Brian & Shorb, representing Smith, Barney & Company; Cravath, Swaine & Moore, representing Kuhn, Loeb & Company and Union Securities; Davis Polk Wardwell Sunderland & Kiendl, representing Morgan Stanley and Harriman Ripley; Donovan Leisure Newton Lumbard & Irvine, representing Harris, Hall & Company; Shearman & Sterling & Wright representing White, Weld & Company; and Choate, Hall & Stewart co-representing First Boston Corp. with Sullivan & Cromwell. The other Sullivan & Cromwell clients were Blyth & Company Inc., Glore Forgan & Company, Goldman, Sachs & Company, and Lehman Brothers.

186 Dean's rebuttal, horse and rabbit: quoted in Carosso, *Investment,* pp. 478–479.

187 Allen Wardwell on Dean: Wardwell, COHP, p. 58.

188 Sullivan & Cromwell's brief: "*U.S.* v. *H.S. Morgan, Harold Stanley, et al.* Brief on General Points in Support of Motions to Dismiss of Defendants Blyth & Co. Inc., First Boston Corporation, Glore, Forgan & Co., Goldman, Sachs & Co., and Lehman Brothers," pp. 176–177.

188 "a pattern . . .": Carosso, *Investment,* p. 478.

188 Dismissal: Carosso, *Investment,* pp. 493–494.

189 "instructions . . .": Walter Sachs, COHP p. 96.

190 Hawkins memo: Nov. 26, 1948, AWD Archive.

190 Auchincloss, "I don't know.": *Lamplighters,* p. 273.

190 "not take on . . . the office.": Hawkins memo, Nov. 26, 1948, AWD Archive.

190 "for three reasons . . . too.": Background interview, June 21, 1985.

193 "to explain the transaction . . . the work.": *Lamplighters,* Robert McDonald entry, p. 224.

193 Matador Land details: George Ames interview, Sept. 3, 1985.

193 London stock exchange price of Matador: Cary Reich, *Financier* (New York: William Morrow, 1983), p. 57.

193–194 Dooling litigation: *Lamplighters,* pp. 178–179.

196 Dulles to Hawkins: ''You . . . me.'': Hawkins, DOHP, p. 14.

196 Wyatt resigns and rescinds: Marvin Schwartz interview, Sept. 1, 1987.

196 ''Inzer . . . firm.'': Kenneth Scott interview, May 27, 1985.

196–197 Lamco: Kenneth Scott interview, May 27, 1985.

197 ''using corresponding . . . so.'': Inzer Wyatt interview, April 4, 1985.

CHAPTER 13: THE GOVERNMENT AS CLIENT, *pages 199–212*

Epigraph: Dulles to Herbert Brownell, Nov. 24, 1952, JFD Archive.

200 Dulles talks to Ike: Eustace Seligman, DOHP, p. 22.

200 Seligman role in Woodstock typewriter: James Thacher interview, May 23, 1985.

201 ''There was a . . . intelligence.'': *Lamplighters,* James Thacher entry, p. 305.

201 ''There is not a . . . from now on.'': Nomination of John Foster Dulles, Secretary of State-Designate, Hearing before the Senate Committee on Foreign Relations, 83rd Congress, 1st Session, Jan. 15, 1953 (Washington: U.S. Government Printing Office, 1953), p. 27.

201 Sullivan & Cromwell paid for Dulles's Washington, D.C., house: JFD and JAD checkbooks, JFD Archive.

202 ''the existence of a series of agreements . . .'': Memo for the Attorney General, June 24, 1952, Department of Justice.

202 change ''could easily end . . .'': *New York Times,* ''U.S. Drops Its Plan to Indict 'Big Five' for Oil Monopoly,'' Jan. 12, 1953.

204 Dean asks for postponement: Quoted in *New York Times,* ''Civil Cartel Suit Will Be Filed Against Major Oil Concerns,'' April 10, 1953.

204 Justice Department complaint, the ''Secretary . . . implications.'': Memo for Attorney General, Nov. 21, 1957, Department of Justice.

204 ''interviewed the 60 oil . . .'': Sept. 4, 1953, JFD files, Eisenhower Library.

205 ''proceedings indefinitely postponed . . .'': Sept. 12, 1953, JFD files, Eisenhower Library.

205 Hall against Dean: Telephone conversation, JFD files, Eisenhower Library.

205 Nixon for Dean and ''didn't think . . . avoid it.'': Aug. 13, 1953, JFD files, Eisenhower Library.

205 Ike for Dean: Sept. 8, 1953, JFD files, Eisenhower Library.
205–206 Dean in Korea: *New York Times Magazine,* "What It's Like to Negotiate with the Chinese," Oct. 30, 1966, p. 54.
206 Criticism of Dean: Ellis Briggs, COHP, p. 61.
206 Harriman's opinion: W. Averell Harriman, COHP, pp. 85–86.
206 Letter to the President about Dean: Dec. 28, 1953, Eisenhower Library.
206 Dean on Red China: Jan. 3, 1954, JFD files, Eisenhower Library.
206 "Arthur Dean . . . much": Jan. 8, 1954, JFD and AWD conversation, JFD files, Eisenhower Library.
207 "it will . . . of.": Jan. 12, 1954, telephone conversation with Sen. Knowland, JFD files, Eisenhower Library.
207 Bid on Soviet estate: *New York Times,* "Communists Suffer 'Capital' Setback," March 10, 1954.
208 Kennan resignation: George F. Kennan, DOHP, JFD Archive.
208 Dean "was glad to know . . .": Arthur H. Dean to Dulles, March 14, 1953, JFD files, Eisenhower Library.
208 Dulles: "satisfied . . . yard.": Hearing before the Senate Committee on Foreign Relations, Jan. 15, 1953, p. 23.
208 Dulles: "instructed . . . generally." Senate Hearing, p. 27.
209 Dulles support for Dirksen bill: Brownell and Dulles conversation, March 24, 1954, JFD files, Eisenhower Library.
209 "humanitarian and policy . . . of property." and "said when he . . . reparations.": Brownell and Dulles conversation, March 24, 1954, JFD files, Eisenhower Library.
209 Dean: "might be able . . . basis.": Arthur Dean to Dulles, April 29, 1957, JFD files, Eisenhower Library.
209 Stinnes sale: *New York Times,* "German Bid Wins Seized Holdings," June 26, 1957.
209–210 Stinnes matter: FOIA Request NLE-258, Eisenhower Library documents 3, 4, 8, NLE MR No. 82–266.
210 Dean talks to executives: Dean to Dulles, Aug. 7, 1956, telephone conversation, JFD files, Eisenhower Library.
210 Dean breakfast conference: Memo, Dean to Dulles, Oct. 3, 1956, JFD files, Eisenhower Library.
211 Dean: "where the Arabs . . . Israel.": Dean letter to Dulles, Dec. 28, 1956, JFD files, Eisenhower Library.
211 Dean: "you didn't . . . matter.": Dean to Dulles, March 22, 1956, JFD files, Eisenhower Library.
211 Dean and Dulles: "I don't . . . correct.": Dean to Dulles, March 27, 1956, Re Middle East, JFD files, Eisenhower Library.
211 Case against Horn: *New York Times,* "U.S. Seeks to Bar Dulles' Old Firm," Aug. 5, 1955.

CHAPTER 14: COUNTER COUNTERCULTURE, *pages 213–232*

213 "If you had given me a job . . .": Earl Mazo, *Nixon: A Political Portrait* (New York: Harper & Bros., 1959), p. 26.

214 "Arthur Dean's . . . appointment.": Name file, Box 637, JFK Library.

214 Schlesinger on Bay of Pigs: *New Yorker,* n.d., p. 36.

215 John J. McCloy to Dean: Aug. 10, 1965, LBJ Library.

216 Interest equalization tax: Frederick Seibold interview, July 17, 1985.

216 "The large volume . . . Cromwell.": *Lamplighters,* John R. Stevenson entry, p. 297.

219 "about . . . eagles.": *National Law Journal,* August 4, 1980, p. 58.

221–222 "The religion of work . . . misconception of work.": Ronald Dworkin interview, June 14, 1984.

223 "becom[ing] . . . world": Akio Morita with Edwin M. Reingold and Miksuko Shimomura, *Made in Japan* (New York: Dutton, 1986), p. 92.

224 "most interesting . . . Commission.": *Lamplighters,* John R. Stevenson entry, p. 297.

224 "I worked with . . . how to do it.": Frederick Seibold interview, July 17, 1985.

231 "it is extremely . . . meeting.": Sullivan & Cromwell Office Manual, p. 23.

232 "You must learn . . . everything.": *Lamplighters,* William Piel entry, p. 186.

CHAPTER 15: THE POWER OF TRADITION, *pages 233–245.*

234 Eastern shuttle: Malcolm MacIntyre interview, July 22, 1985.

235 "all I do . . . answer": Lawrence McQuade interview, June 27, 1985.

236 Mortgage-backed financings: Phillip Pollock interview, May 23, 1985.

236–237 "By January . . . alone.": *Lamplighters,* Arthur H. Dean entry, p. 98.

237 "going to a meeting . . .": Peter T. Jones interview, May 25, 1985.

238 "We like to stay slightly understaffed . . .": *American Lawyer,* August 1979, p. 6.

CHAPTER 16: THE TRADITION OF POWER, *pages 247–258*

249 ''S&C's litigating . . . elephants'': *Lamplighters,* William Piel entry, p. 185.

250–251 Kennecott–Curtiss-Wright fight: James Stewart, *The Partners* (New York: Simon & Schuster, 1983).

251 Kern: ''My God . . . Beach.'': Stewart, *Partners,* p. 251.

CHAPTER 17: THE TRIALS OF SULLIVAN & CROMWELL, *pages 259–273*

The information in this chapter is based on interviews with the people involved and on court papers.

Other references: Barbara Goldsmith, *Johnson v. Johnson* (New York: Alfred Knopf, 1987); *American Lawyer* articles by Ellen Joan Pollock; and Patricia Bellew Gray, ''Legal Nightmare,'' *Wall Street Journal,* August 3, 1987, p. 1.

269 ''an appeal . . . of a fee.'': *National Law Journal,* Dec. 11, 1987.

CHAPTER 18: HOW TO MAKE PARTNER—OR WHAT THEY DON'T TEACH YOU AT HARVARD LAW SCHOOL, *pages 277–282*

281 ''In a job-satisfaction . . . Sullivan & Cromwell.'': Lynn Gracin interview, Jan. 4, 1988.

CHAPTER 19: WHAT A SULLIVAN & CROMWELL CLIENT GETS, *pages 283–290*

284 ''it cannot . . . here.'': John Merow interview, July 15, 1987.

285 Japanese securities work: Frederick Seibold interview, July 17, 1985.

286 Heavy electrical equipment manufacturers antitrust case: The Historical Society of the United States–District Court for the Eastern District of Pennsylvania, Seminar on ''The Electrical Equipment Antitrust Cases,'' October 15, 1987, Philadelphia, Pennsylvania.

287 ''only firm . . . billed.'': *American Lawyer Guide to Law Firms* (New York: Am Law Publishing Corp., 1982–83), p. 1441.

288 ''Sullivan & Cromwell is very good . . . years ago.'': Francis Carling interview, May 21, 1985.

APPENDICES

1. Sullivan & Cromwell Partnership Agreement, with proposed changes in 1979*
2. Eustace Seligman memo to John Foster Dulles, October 25, 1939

APPENDIX 1

AGREEMENT made as of the 1st day of October, 1979, among the persons who execute this Agreement at the foot hereof as parties hereto,

WITNESSETH:

WHEREAS, the parties hereto desire to continue in the practice of the law, under the following partnership agreement, the Partnership of SULLIVAN & CROMWELL (hereinafter referred to as the "Partnership") founded by Algernon Sydney Sullivan and William Nelson Cromwell on April 2, 1879,

NOW, THEREFORE, the parties hereto agree as follows:

ARTICLE I

CONTINUANCE AND DEFINITIONS

SECTION 1. The Partnership shall continue in the practice of the law under the firm name of Sullivan & Cromwell with the parties hereto as Partners thereof.

SECTION 2. This Agreement shall take effect as of October 1, 1979, but shall not apply to fees received on or after such date in respect of services rendered prior to such date except as provided in or pursuant to Articles II, V and XII hereof, and their allocation shall be governed by the pre-existing agreements between the parties.

* Lines scored through text indicate deletions; italics indicate additions for the 1979 revision.

SECTION 3. The Partnership shall continue until dissolved pursuant to Section 6 of Article IV hereof ~~by decision of the Committee hereinafter mentioned with the approval of a majority in interest of the Partners~~.
Neither the termination of status of any Partner, nor the admission of any new Partner, shall dissolve or terminate the Partnership.

SECTION 4. Whenever the following terms are used in this Agreement, they shall have the meanings set forth below unless the context otherwise requires:

(a) The term "Average Percentage" shall have the meaning set forth in Section 3 of Article XII hereof.

(b) The term "Base Percentage" shall have the meaning set forth in Section 1 of Article II hereof.

(c) The term "Committee" shall mean the Committee established by and pursuant to Section 1 of Article IV hereof; *and the terms "Chairman" and "Vice Chairman" shall mean respectively the Chairman and any Vice Chairman of the Committee*

(d) The term "Date of Termination" shall have the meaning set forth in clause (e) of Section 2 of Article V hereof.

(e) The term "Distributable Net Income" of the Partnership for any fiscal year or other period shall mean the net income for such period, as reported on by the Partnership's independent public accountants, before the deduction (i) of any annuities paid for such period pursuant to Sections 6 and 7 of Article XII hereof and (ii) of any contribution for such period by the Partnership on account of Partners to the Retirement Plan.

(f) The term "Early Retirement Date" of a Partner shall have the meaning set forth in Sections 4 and 5 of Article XII hereof.

(g) The term "Estate" of a person shall include, but not be limited to, his legal representatives and each trustee and beneficiary, if any, specified in his Will to receive all or any part of the payments, if any, due after his death under Section 2 of Article V hereof.

(h) The term "fees" shall include all revenues for services rendered, and all executors', trustees' and other fiduciary commissions, received by the Partnership.

(i) The term "fiscal year", except as otherwise expressly provided herein, shall mean: (1) the calendar year with respect to the year ended December 31, 1972 and years prior thereto; (2) the 9-month period ended September 30, 1973; (3) the 9-month period ended September 30, 1974; and (4) each 12-month period ending September 30 commencing with the period ended September 30, 1975.

(j) The term "Former Partner" shall mean a person who was a Partner at any time before or after the date of this Agreement and whose status as a Partner was or is terminated other than by retirement.

(k) The term ''majority in interest'' of the Partners shall mean as of any time Partners having a majority of the Base Percentages at such time.

(l) ~~The term ''majority in number'' of the Partners shall mean as of any time a majority of the persons who are then the Partners of the Partnership~~. *The term ''majority in number'' of the Partners, whenever used in connection with taking any action under this Agreement, shall mean a majority in number of the Partners acting on a proposal of the Committee.*

(m) The term ''Net Profits'' of the Partnership shall have the meaning set forth in Section 5 of Article II hereof.

(n) The term ''Normal Retirement Date'' of a Partner shall have the meaning set forth in Section 1 of Article XII hereof.

(o) The term ''Participation Schedule'' or ''Participation Schedules'' shall mean the schedule or schedules referred to in Section 1 of Article II hereof.

(p) The term ''Partner'' shall mean at any time a person who is at such time a member of the Partnership.

(q) The term ''Partnership'' shall have the meaning set forth in the recital to this Agreement.

(r) The term ''Percentage'' of a Partner shall mean for any fiscal year or other period the sum of his Base Percentage for such period plus the amount, if any, of the Reserved Percentage allocated to him for such period.

(s) The term ''Pre-retirement Period'' of a Partner shall have the meaning set forth in Section 2 of Article XII hereof.

(t) The term ''Reserved Percentage'' shall have the meaning set forth in Section 1 of Article II hereof.

(u) The terms ''retire'', ''retired'', ''retirement'' and ''time of retirement'' shall have the meaning set forth in Section 1 of Article XII hereof.

(v) The term ''Retired Partner'' shall mean (i) a person who on September 30, 1978 was a Retired Partner under the Partnership Agreement of the Partnership as in force and effect on that date, and (ii) a person who was a Partner any time on or after the date of this Agreement and whose status as a Partner is terminated by retirement pursuant to Article XII hereof.

(w) The term ''Retirement Plan'' shall mean the Retirement Plan of Sullivan & Cromwell, adopted by the Partnership, effective January 1, 1968, for the benefit of certain of its legal staff, as in effect from time to time.

(x) The term ''Special Quarter'' shall mean the 3-month period ending December 31, 1973.

(y) The term ''Surviving Spouse'' shall mean a spouse who is married to and living with a Partner as the spouse of such Partner at the time of the retirement of such Partner and continuously thereafter until the death of such Partner.

(z) The term "Terminal Period" shall have the meaning set forth in Section 4 of Article II hereof.

(aa) The term "termination of status" as a Partner (and variants thereof such as "a Partner whose status as a Partner has terminated") shall mean ceasing to be a Partner for any reason whatever, including: death while a Partner; resignation pursuant to Section 1 of Article V hereof; termination of membership in the Partnership pursuant to clause (c) of Section 6 of Article IV hereof or Section 2 of Article IX hereof; and retirement pursuant to Article XII hereof.

(bb) The term "year of termination" shall have the meaning set forth in Section 2 of Article V hereof.

(cc) Words of masculine gender shall include the feminine gender as appropriate.

ARTICLE II

Participation Schedule, Etc.

Section 1. A Schedule designated "Participation Schedule No. 36—Effective October 1, 1979", in which are set forth, as of October 1, 1979, the names of the several Partners, the Base Percentage in the Net Profits of each Partner, and the Reserved Percentage, constituting the unallocated percentage in the Net Profits, signed by a majority of the Committee, is on file at the office of the Partnership in New York City and shall be deemed a part of this Agreement. The profits to which such Schedule shall be applicable shall be the Net Profits of the Partnership for the fiscal year ended September 30, 1980, and unless superseded as provided in the next paragraph, for fiscal years thereafter.

Whenever, as hereinafter provided, any new Partner shall be admitted or any change shall be made in the Base Percentage in the Net Profits of any Partner, a revised Participation Schedule shall be prepared to give effect thereto, and each succeeding Participation Schedule shall be designated by a successive number and by the date as of which it becomes effective. Each revised Participation Schedule shall be signed by a majority of the Committee and filed with the counterpart of this Agreement on file at the office of the Partnership in New York City and, when so designated, signed and filed, shall become a part of this Agreement and shall supersede all prior Participation Schedules with respect to the Net Profits of the Partnership after the commencement of the fiscal year in which the effective date of such revised Participation Schedule falls. The Base Percentage in Participation Schedules applicable to periods ended prior to the commencement of such fiscal year shall continue in effect with respect to fees received after such commencement in respect of services rendered prior thereto subject to the provisions of Sections 4 and 7 of this Article II, clause (*b*) of Section 2 of Article V hereof and Section 6 of Article XII hereof.

The Base Percentage set forth in any Participation Schedule for any Partner who is in his Pre-retirement Period shall be the Percentage determined pursuant to Section 3 of Article XII hereof.

If any new Partner shall be admitted, or any change shall be made in the Base Percentage in the Net Profits of an existing Partner, other than as of the first day of any fiscal year, then, except as otherwise determined by the Committee at the time of such admission or change, (a) the Base Percentage of such new Partner in the Net Profits for the fiscal year of admission, and his Percentage of fees received after the end of such year with respect to services rendered during such year, shall be the product obtained by multiplying his Base Percentage set forth in such revised Participation Schedule by a fraction of which the numerator is the number of months from the date of his admission to the end of such year and the denominator is 12, and (b) the Base Percentage of such existing Partner in the Net Profits for the fiscal year in which such change is made, and his Percentage of fees received after the end of such year with respect to services rendered during such year, shall be the quotient obtained by dividing by 12 the sum of (i) his Base Percentage set forth in the Participation Schedule in effect prior to the effective date of such revised Participation Schedule multiplied by the number of months in such year prior to such effective date, and (ii) his Base Percentage set forth in such revised Participation Schedule multiplied by the remaining number of months in such year.

Section 2. Prior to the close of each fiscal year an allocation of the Reserved Percentage for such year will be made among the Partners, or some of them, by the Committee and similarly signed and filed. There may be included among the Partners to whom such allocation is made any Former Partner whose status as a Partner has terminated in such period. There shall not, however, be included any Partner who is or was in his Pre-retirement Period in such period except with the consent of a majority in number of the Partners. The allocation so made by the Committee of the Reserved Percentage for such period will (like the Base Percentage for such period) be effective with respect to (*a*) the Net Profits of the Partnership for such period, and (*b*) fees received after the end of such period with respect to services rendered during such period, in each case subject to the provisions of Sections 4 and 7 of this Article II, clause (*b*) of Section 2 of Article V hereof and Section 6 of Article XII hereof.

In the case of the termination of status of a Partner prior to September 1 of any fiscal year there will be added to the Reserved Percentage a fraction of his Percentage in the Net Profits of the Partnership for the year of termination of which the numerator is the number of months remaining in such year after the month in which his status as a Partner terminated and the denominator is 12. In the case of a reduction of the Base Percentage of a Partner prior to

September 1 of any fiscal year, a corresponding addition shall be made to the Reserved Percentage. If such termination of status or reduction of Base Percentage occurs after the allocation of the Reserved Percentage for the fiscal year has been made, a further allocation shall be made of any resulting addition to the Reserved Percentage in the same manner as above set forth in this Section 2.

SECTION 3. It is intended that at all times the aggregate capital of the Partnership shall be not less than the amount that the Committee considers appropriate for the then current and prospective working capital and other requirements of the Partnership and that (subject to variation deemed necessary by the Committee in particular circumstances) the amount in the Capital Account of each Partner shall be not less than the level established from time to time by the Committee for him and other Partners with comparable position in the Partnership. Toward this intended result, (a) the Committee shall determine for each fiscal year whether, and, if so, to what extent, there shall be credited to the Capital Account of any Partner a percentage of or an amount out of his distributive share (resulting from his Percentage) of the Net Profits for such period and his Percentages of the fees received in such period for services rendered prior thereto, and (b) from each distribution of Net Profits and fees of the Partnership there shall be withheld and credited to the Capital Account of each Partner the amount so determined, if any, of his share of such distribution (for this purpose, a drawing account for any such period shall not be deemed to be a distribution of Net Profits or fees until the end of that period); provided that the moneys so withheld and credited from any distribution shall not exceed the amount by which the level applicable to him exceeds the amount in his Capital Account at the time of such distribution.

SECTION 4. Neither a Former Partner nor his Estate shall be entitled to share in any fees received after the Terminal Period of such Former Partner. The amount of the fees received in any period after the Terminal Period of any Former Partner which, except for the provisions of this Section 4, such Former Partner or his Estate would have received shall be credited to the profit and loss account of the Partnership for such period. As used in this Agreement, "Terminal Period" shall mean (*a*) for any Former Partner whose status as a Partner is terminated by death, the period ending 36 months after the September 30 which is, or next succeeds, his date of death, and (*b*) for any Former Partner whose status as a Partner is terminated for any reason other than death, the period ending 60 months after the September 30 which is, or next succeeds, the date of such termination of status or, if shorter, the period ending 36 months after the September 30 which is, or next succeeds, his date of death.

The amount of the fees received in any period which, except for the provisions of Section 4 of Article V hereof or the provisions of clause (*b*) of

Section 2 of Article V hereof, a Former Partner or his Estate would have received shall be credited to the profit and loss account of the Partnership for such period.

Section 5. The Net Profits of the Partnership for any fiscal year shall be determined ~~by the Committee~~ as follows: a calculation shall be made of the gross income received by the Partnership during such period, exclusive of fees received in respect of services rendered prior to such period except as provided in or pursuant to Sections 4 and ~~7~~ *6* of this Article II, clause (*b*) of Section 2 of Article V hereof and Section 6 of Article XII hereof, less all expenses and losses paid during, and other charges determined ~~by the Committee~~ to be properly allocable to, such period (including guaranteed payments made pursuant to Section 3 of Article XII hereof, annuities paid pursuant to Sections 6 and 7 of Article XII hereof, and the aggregate contribution by the Partnership for the account of Partners to the Retirement Plan, for such period); provided, however, that (i) effect shall be given to any debits or credits determined ~~by the Committee~~ for such period, pursuant to Section ~~7~~ *6* of this Article II, in connection with fixed amount payments, and (ii) expenses paid which are allocable to more than one period, and depreciation on depreciable assets in which the capital of the Partnership is invested, shall be charged as an expense in the amount claimed in the income tax return of the Partnership which covers such period.

The amount thus calculated shall be adjusted by deducting (a) the income from, and gains, if any, on sales of securities in the proprietary pension fund of the Partnership received or realized during such period and (b) the contributions made in such period by the Partnership to such fund, and by adding (c) the losses, if any, realized during such period on sales of securities in such fund, (d) the expenses of such fund during such period, and (e) the amount of pension payments made during such period out of such fund.

The figure resulting from the above computation shall be the Net Profits of the Partnership for such period for all purposes of this Agreement. In the income tax returns of the Partnership the distributive shares of the Partners shall be computed without giving effect to any deductions or additions made pursuant to the preceding paragraph.

In effecting the change of fiscal year of the Partnership from a calendar year to a fiscal year ending September 30, the Partnership was required to include in its taxable income for the fiscal year ended September 30, 1973, an amount (hereinafter called the "Special Adjustment") equal to the ordinary income of the Partnership for the Special Quarter as computed for Federal income tax purposes. In computing the Partnership's ordinary income for Federal income tax purposes, one-tenth of such Special Adjustment is deductible in each of the ten taxable years of the Partnership beginning with the fiscal year ended September 30, 1973. For Federal income tax purposes, each Partner's share of the Special Adjustment shall be the same as his share of the Partnership's ordinary income for the Special Quarter. The deductions available to the Partnership in respect of the Special Adjustment shall be allocated among the Partners ~~by the Committee~~ over the ten taxable years in which such deductions are allowable so that the aggregate amount of deductions allowable to each Partner or his Estate shall be equal to such Partner's share of the Special Adjustment. ~~The Committee shall endeavor to allocate~~ Such deductions *should be allocated to the extent practicable* so that each Partner will recover the aggregate amount of deductions allowable to him or his Estate over a period of time not longer than that during which he or his Estate will receive distributions of income from the Partnership.

If in any fiscal year the Net Profits of the Partnership calculated as provided above shall result in a net loss, then such net loss shall be charged to the Partners in accordance with their respective Percentages in the Net Profits for such period, except that if such net loss is the result of one or more extraordinary events relating to prior periods it shall be charged, in such proportions as ~~the Committee~~ shall *be* determine*d* ~~in its discretion~~ *to be appropriate*, to the Partners and Former Partners, provided that no Former Partner shall be charged in any period after his year of termination with any amount greater than the payment, if any, which would otherwise be made to him or to his Estate in such period pursuant to clause (*b*) of Section 2 of Article V hereof.

The Net Profits for each fiscal year of any office of the Partnership located outside the United States shall ~~also~~ be *separately* determined ~~by the Committee~~.

~~SECTION 6. Although recognizing the practice that all the Partners send bills to clients and that it is normally the individual decision of the billing Partner (who is in charge of the matter and who is most familiar with the professional work done and the other considerations listed in the Code of Professional Responsibility, as well as with the clients' views) whether or not he will consult with any other Partner in determining the fee for the matter, nevertheless, for all purposes of this Agreement, the Committee in its sole discretion shall have the right to review and determine the amount of any fee to be charged by the Partnership for services, and any waiver or reduction of any fee; to allocate fees to services rendered in such period or periods as the Committee may deem appropriate; and to determine the time or times for billing any fee. The Committee shall also have the right in its sole discretion to determine the amount of and make contributions to the proprietary pension fund, the trusteed employees pension plan of the Partnership and the Retirement Plan, and to make pension payments out of the proprietary pension fund; to determine the amount of any charitable or other contribution of the Partnership; and to make the determinations referred to in Section 9 of Article XII hereof.~~

SECTION ~~7~~ *6*. If a fixed amount payment shall be made to a Former Partner pursuant to clause (*d*) of Section 2 of Article V hereof, as ~~determined by the Committee in its sole discretion,~~ *determined on behalf of the Partnership*, the amount of such payment in excess of the sum of the amounts specified in subclauses (i) and (iv) of clause (*a*) of Section 2 of Article V hereof shall be debited, in whole or in part, to the profit and loss account for the year of termination and any one or more fiscal years in the Terminal Period of such Former Partner, and the share of the Net Profits and fees which, pursuant to subclauses (ii) and (iii) of clause (*a*) of Section 2 of Article V hereof and clause (*b*) of said Section 2, such Former Partner or his Estate would have received had such fixed amount payment not been made, shall be credited, in whole or in part, to the profit and loss account for the year of termination and any one or more fiscal years in such Terminal Period.

ARTICLE III

CAPITAL

SECTION 1. The capital of the Partnership on October 1, 1979 shall be the total of the Capital Accounts of the Partners as shown upon the books of the Partnership as of that date. It shall be increased from time to time by credits made to the Capital Accounts of the Partners pursuant to Section 3 of Article II hereof, and may be increased from time to time by contributions made by the Partners to their Capital Accounts.

SECTION 2. No Partner shall have the right to make any withdrawal from his Capital Account except (a) as many be consented to by the Committee or (b) upon the termination of his status as a Partner as provided in Section 2 of Article V hereof.

SECTION 3. The capital of the Partnership shall be held in cash, or invested in securities and in assets used in the business of the Partnership, including assets which are subject to depreciation, such as alterations and improvements to the office premises, furnishings and equipment, and reading and reference materials. ~~as the Committee shall from time to time determine.~~ In respect of assets which are not charged on the books of the Partnership as an expense of the Partnership at the time of acquisition, an amount equal to the depreciation charged in any period as an expense in calculating the Net Profits of the Partnership for such period pursuant to Section 5 of Article II hereof shall be credited on the books of the Partnership to accumulated depreciation.

SECTION 4. The assets in the proprietary pension fund shall not be included for any purpose in calculating the capital of the Partnership unless and until it shall be dissolved and no successor partnership organized which shall have the right to use the firm name pursuant to Section 1 of Article VIII hereof. The proprietary pension fund shall be invested in cash and/or securities, and shall be credited with all income received from, and gains realized on sales of, such securities, as well as all contributions made by the Partnership to such fund. The proprietary pension fund shall be debited with all losses on sales of securities in the fund, all expenses of such fund, and all pension payments made out of such fund.

ARTICLE IV

~~The Committee~~

Management of the Partnership

Section 1. There shall be a Committee *of the Partnership* which shall consist of at least three members. The Committee as of October 1, 197~~8~~*9* consists of Wm. Ward Foshay, William Piel, Jr., David S. Henkel, Robert J. McDonald, Richard G. Powell, Robert MacCrate, John R. Stevenson and William E. Willis. As and when changes occur in the membership of the Committee, a schedule of the revised Committee membership, stating the effective date, shall be signed by a majority of the then members of the Committee and filed at the office of the Partnership in New York City, and such schedule so signed and filed shall become part of this Agreement from its effective date. A member may resign at any time.

The Committee shall act by a majority of its then members at a meeting or in writing.

The Committee shall have the power from time to time to determine ~~the number of~~ its members, ~~to fill vacancies~~ and to select a Chairman who shall be the chief executive Partner *and one or more Vice Chairmen who will act for the Chairman in his absence.*

~~Section 2. In the event that any Partner's status as a Partner shall terminate, he or his Estate shall be entitled (subject to the provisions of Section 2 of Article IX hereof) to the following payments (which shall be in final settlement) at the following times:~~

~~(*a*) Within 90 days after the close of the fiscal year (such year being herein called the "year of termination") in which such termination of status occurs, an amount equal to~~

~~(*i*) the amount to the credit of his Capital Account on the books of the Partnership on the Date of Termination; plus~~

~~(*ii*) the amount of his Percentage in the Net Profits of the Partnership for the year of termination calculated up to the Date of Termination, and not theretofore paid or credited to him; plus~~

~~(*iii*) the amount of his Percentages of fees received in the year of termination in respect of services rendered prior to such period and not theretofore paid or credited to him; plus~~

~~(*iv*) any other credit balances with the Partnership to his account on the Date of Termination not included in the foregoing~~.

SECTION 2. *Subject only to (a) the power of a majority in number of the Partners to act as provided in specific provisions of this Agreement (which power shall be deemed to be exclusive in respect of such actions) and (b) the limitation on the power of the Committee to act without the consent of a particular Partner as provided in Section 5 of this Article IV, the Committee shall have power to manage the Partnership and to act for and on behalf of the Partnership in all matters relating to the conduct of its affairs and finances and the carrying on of its practice, including, without limitation, the power, in its sole discretion, to make the various determinations and agreements and to take the various actions to be made or taken under this Agreement. In exercising this function, the Committee may establish such committees of Partners with such delegated authority, and shall consult with such other Partners, as it deems appropriate, having regard to the particular area or matter involved and the proper distribution of responsibility for day-to-day action and the general morale of the Partnership. The general powers given to the Committee by this Section 2 of this Article IV shall not be limited to or by the specific powers elsewhere given to the Committee.*

In order to broaden the sharing of over-all responsibility and to assure obtaining the benefit of the counsel of Partners whose experience especially qualifies them to contribute to the formulation of sound firm policies, there may be a Policy Group consisting of the members of the Committee, the managing partners of the various practice groups and such other Partners as the Committee shall invite from time to time to meet together to consider matters of partnership policy at meetings of convenient size.

SECTION 3. ~~Without limiting the general powers given to the Committee by Section 2 of this Article IV or the specific powers elsewhere given to the Committee~~, The Committee is ~~specifically~~ authorized (a) to exercise on behalf of the Partnership any power the Partnership now has or which may hereafter be given to the Partnership to designate an original or successor executor, trustee, or other fiduciary, agent or representative, whether such designee be a Partner or otherwise; *and* (b) to act in behalf of the Partnership in the event the Partnership is designated or appointed to act in a fiduciary or representative capacity. ~~and (c) to act for the Partnership for all purposes of the trusted employees pension plan and the Retirement Plan~~.

SECTION 4. The Committee shall have authority to delegate to one or more Partners or to any investment adviser or other specialist power to invest and reinvest the assets constituting the capital of the Partnership and the assets of the proprietary pension fund in any type of security such Partner or Partners or investment adviser or other specialist shall select. Such Partner or Partners may retain investment advisers or other specialists and may make any such investment or reinvestment with or without recommendations from or assistance of any person so retained.

Section 5. The Committee shall have the power to increase the Base Percentage in the Net Profits of any Partner or with his consent to reduce the Base Percentage in the Net Profits of any Partner and the power to determine the time and amount of the distribution of Net Profits or fees; provided, however, that the Percentage of a Partner who has entered his Pre-retirement Period shall only be increased~~ with the consent of~~ *by* a majority in number of the Partners, as provided in Section 12 of Article XII hereof.

Section 6. ~~The Committee shall have the power, with the approval of~~ A majority in ~~interest~~ *number* of the Partners shall have the power (*a*) *to reduce the Base Percentage in the Net Profits of any Partner* WITHOUT HIS CONSENT; (*b*) to admit a new Partner and to determine the effective date of his admission; (*c*) *to terminate at any time the membership in the Partnership of any Partner;* (*d*) to dissolve the Partnership; provided, however, that in respect of any Partner who had become entitled to retire on an Early Retirement Date, the amount receivable under Article XII hereof shall not be reduced without such Partner's consent, and any action pursuant to clause (*c*) above shall be deemed to constitute the retirement of such Partner pursuant to Section 5 of Article XII hereof; (*e*) *to act for the Partnership, or to appoint a committee of the Partners authorized so to act, in determining the amount of and making contributions to the proprietary pension fund of the Partnership, the trusteed employees pension plan of the Partnership and the Retirement Plan, in making payments out of the proprietary pension fund, and for all other purposes of the trusteed employees pension plan and the Retirement Plan; and* (*f*) *to determine, or authorize the Chairman or a committee of Partners to determine, the amount of any charitable or other contribution of the Partnership.*

Section 7. When any new Partner is admitted, the Committee shall determine his Base Percentage in the Net Profits. In the case of any such new Partner or any Partner serving the Partnership in an office located outside the United States, the Committee shall also determine whether there is to be a guaranteed payment without regard to the amount of such Partner's Percentage and, if so, the period and amount thereof; provided that, in any event, any Partner serving in such an office is hereby guaranteed payment in each fiscal year at the rate of $25,000 per annum and that any such guaranteed payment shall be considered a distribution in respect of such Partner's Percentage in the Net Profits for such period and of fees received in such period for services rendered prior thereto.

For all purposes of this Agreement the readmission of a Former Partner shall be deemed to be the admission of a new Partner.

~~SECTION 8. In order to broaden the sharing of over all responsibility and to assure obtaining the benefit of the counsel of Partners whose experience especially qualifies them to contribute to the formulation of sound firm policies, there may be a Policy Group consisting of the members of the Committee and such other Partners as the Committee shall invite from time to time to meet together to consider matters of Partnership policy at meetings of convenient size~~.

ARTICLE V

RESIGNATION AND PAYMENTS ON TERMINATION OF STATUS

SECTION 1. Any Partner may resign from the Partnership at any time; provided, however, that the resignation by a Partner during the period from the date he became entitled to retire on an Early Retirement Date to his Normal Retirement Date shall be deemed to be a retirement pursuant to Section 5 of Article XII hereof.

SECTION 2. In the event that any Partner's status as a Partner shall terminate, he or his Estate shall be entitled (subject to the provisions of Section 2 of Article IX hereof) to the following payments (which shall be in final settlement) at the following times:

(*a*) Within 90 days after the close of the fiscal year (such year being herein called the "year of termination") in which such termination of status occurs, an amount equal to

(*i*) The amount to the credit of his Capital Account on the books of the Partnership on the Date of Termination; plus

(*ii*) the amount of his Percentage in the Net Profits of the Partnership for the year of termination calculated up to the Date of Termination, and not theretofore paid or credited to him; plus

(*iii*) the amount of his Percentages of fees received in the year of termination in respect of services rendered prior to such period and not theretofore paid or credited to him; plus

(*iv*) any other credit balances with the Partnership to his account on the Date of Termination not included in the foregoing.

However:

(*v*) if the amounts theretofore paid or credited to him in respect of Net Profits for, or fees received in, the year of termination shall prove to be in excess of the amount to which he was entitled under the preceding subclauses (*ii*) or (*iii*), the excess shall be debited to his account; and

(*vi*) any debits to his account, whether resulting from the operation of the preceding subclause (*v*), or otherwise, shall be deducted from the amount to be paid by the Partnership pursuant to clauses (*a*) and (*b*) of this Section 2, or from the annuities to be paid pursuant to Section 6 or

7 of Article XII hereof, as the Committee at its option may elect, and shall, except in case of dissolution of the Partnership and as provided in Section 5 of Article II hereof, be satisfied in full thereby.

(*b*) Subject to the provisions of Section 5 of Article II hereof, Section 2 of Article IX hereof, Section 4 of this Article V and the further provisions of this clause (*b*), there shall continue to be paid to a Former Partner, or his Estate, his Percentages of fees received after the end of the year of termination and prior to the close of his Terminal Period in respect of services rendered prior to the Date of Termination; provided, however, that the total amount payable under this clause (*b*) shall be reduced by the lump sum cash value (other than amounts attributable to voluntary contributions) of the interest of the Former Partner under the Retirement Plan on the Date of Termination, whether or not the Former Partner elects to receive a lump sum payment under the Retirement Plan. The amount of the reduction shall be determined by the Administrative Committee under the Retirement Plan and shall be applied against the first payments due under this clause (*b*) in order of time.

(*c*) No payments shall be made pursuant to clause (*b*) of this Section 2 to any Retired Partner, and each Retired Partner, his Estate and any Surviving Spouse shall be entitled solely to the respective payments and annuities provided for in clause (*a*) of this Section 2 and Sections 6 and 7 of Article XII hereof.

(*d*) In lieu of the payments to be made to a Former Partner or his Estate pursuant to clauses (*a*) and (*b*) of this Section 2, ~~the Committee on behalf of~~ *agreement may be made on behalf of* the Partnership with such Former Partner or his Estate upon a fixed amount to be paid by the Partnership in final settlement, either in a lump sum or in instalments.

(*e*) For the purposes of this Section 2, the ''Date of Termination'' shall be deemed to be the last day of the month in which occurs the termination of status as a Partner.

If the Date of Termination is on or prior to August 31 of any fiscal year, in order to obviate the closing of the books on other than a year-end basis, the Net Profits of the Partnership for the year of termination through the Date of Termination for the purposes of clause (*a*) above shall be determined by multiplying the Net Profits for the year of termination by a fraction of which the numerator is the number of months in such period through the Date of Termination, and the denominator is 12; and for the purpose of clause (*b*) above, the fees received in any fiscal year after the end of the year of termination in respect of services rendered from the first day of the year of termination through the Date of Termination shall be determined by multiplying all the fees received in such fiscal year in respect of services rendered during the year of termination, by the same fraction.

Section 3. Neither a Partner nor his Estate shall have any interest that survives such Partner's termination of status as a Partner in the good will, if any, of the Partnership or its records and files or in the proprietary pension fund or in any reserve upon the books of the Partnership, nor shall he have any right to the use of the firm name.

Section 4. If in any fiscal year during his Terminal Period a Former Partner who has resigned pursuant to Section 1 of this Article V, or if in any fiscal year a Retired Partner, shall engage in the private practice of law in New York City (alone or in partnership or association with others) except with ~~the~~ written approval *on behalf* of the ~~Committee~~ *Partnership*, no payments shall be made in such fiscal year or in any subsequent fiscal year pursuant to the provisions of clause (*b*) of Section 2 of this Article V to such Former Partner or his Estate or pursuant to the provisions of Section 6 or 7 of Article XII hereof to such Retired Partner or to his Surviving Spouse; provided, however, that this Section 4 shall not apply to any Former Partner who on January 1, 1972 was 67 years of age or older.

ARTICLE VI

New Partners

Section 1. Each new Partner shall sign a counterpart of this Agreement on file at the office of the Partnership in New York City and upon his signing the same he shall be a party to this Agreement as of the effective date of his admission to the Partnership with the same force and effect as if he had been one of the original parties to this Agreement.

ARTICLE VII

Depositories, Etc.

Section 1. The Partnership shall keep its bank accounts in such banks as the Committee may from time to time designate, and checks against such accounts shall be signed only by such Partner or Partners or employee or employees of the Partnership as the Committee, or a Partner thereunto authorized by the Committee, shall from time to time designate.

Section 2. The Partnership may rent such safe deposit boxes as the Committee may from time to time deem necessary, and access to such safe deposit boxes shall be granted only to such Partner or Partners or employee or employees as the Committee, or any Partner thereunto authorized by the Committee, shall designate.

Section 3. No indebtedness, outlay, contract or other obligation of any kind shall be created or incurred by any Partner in the name of or in behalf of the

Partnership without the consent or approval of the Committee or of a Partner thereunto authorized by the Committee.

The Partnership will continue to reimburse a Partner for ordinary and necessary expenses incurred by him, in accordance with the usages and practices of the Partnership. However, under such usages and practices each Partner is expected to incur certain of such expenses and bear the cost thereof without reimbursement.

ARTICLE VIII

Firm Name and Dissolution

Section 1. In the event of the dissolution of the Partnership, any successor partnership which includes among its members a majority in interest of the Partners, including among their number a majority of the then members of the Committee, shall have the sole right to the use of the firm name and to its good will, if any, and its records and files, and if there shall not be any successor partnership so constituted, no one shall have the right to use the firm name or to succeed to its good will and the records and files shall be disposed of as shall be determined by the liquidating Partners.

Section 2. In the event of the dissolution of the Partnership, the Committee shall be the liquidating Partners.

ARTICLE IX

Miscellaneous

Section 1. All compensation for professional or other services, including executors', trustees' and other fiduciary commissions, received by any Partner or any Retired Partner or any Former Partner, or his Estate, shall belong and be paid to the Partnership, except for directors' fees and compensation for writings or speeches, which shall be considered as personal emoluments; provided, however, that in the case of any Retired Partner or Former Partner, or his Estate, there shall not belong or be paid to the Partnership: (*a*) any fiduciary commissions that are received for services rendered by him after his termination of status as a Partner in respect of matters which the Committee shall determine are essentially family rather than Partnership matters or are received under or as a result of any instrument executed after such termination of status, unless, in the case of a Retired Partner, such instrument is a modification of, amendment to, or a replacement of, an instrument which was in force *or* effect prior to such termination of status and was prepared by the Partnership; or (*b*) any compensation for professional or other services rendered after his termination of status as a Partner, except as a fiduciary as aforesaid.

The foregoing provisions of this Section 1 shall have no application to any Former Partner who on January 1, 1972 was 67 years of age or older; provided, however, that any such Former Partner shall be subject to the provisions of Section 1 of Article IX of the Partnership Agreement of the Partnership as in force and effect on December 31, 1971.

SECTION 2. It is expressly and mutually agreed that the interest hereunder of each Partner, Former Partner and Retired Partner is personal to him, and is not and shall not be assignable or transferable to any party whatsoever, except the right to receive any payments due after his death under Section 2 of Article V hereof which right may be freely disposed of by his Will, in which case payment will be made in accordance with his Will anything in Section 2 of Article V hereof to the contrary notwithstanding, and except as aforesaid each Partner, Former Partner and Retired Partner agrees not to assign or transfer or attempt to assign or transfer any part of the same; nor shall any such interest be subject to judgment, execution, levy, claims, receiverships or judicial sequestration or other legal proceedings as against the Partnership or any Partners thereof or its property, affairs, good will, if any, or other assets; and each Partner, Former Partner and Retired Partner agrees not to do or suffer or permit to be done any act or thing as respects him which will effect such result, pledging himself at all times so to order his personal affairs as to avoid the risk of any financial embarrassment either to himself or the Partnership.

Each Partner agrees to refrain from stock speculation or other speculative or business operations of a nature or character which the Committee may consider might, in fact or in the estimation of clients, operate to impair his professional judgment and service to the Partnership, or distract his attention from professional matters or otherwise impair or affect his professional standing and reputation in the community. ~~Each Partner hereby further agrees that if the Committee shall determine that he has failed to observe or perform any of his agreements in this Section 2, the Committee, itself and without need for approval by a majority in interest or a majority in number of the Partners, may forthwith terminate his membership in the Partnership. In the event of such a termination of status as a Partner, all amounts, if any, which may at the time be, or which may thereafter become, payable under this Agreement to him or his Estate or to his Surviving Spouse may be withheld by the Partnership so long as the Committee may consider it advisable so to do in the interest of the Partnership to protect it against any present or prospective claim or any losss, damage, or liability, actual or contingent, and such Partner, for his own, his Estate's and his Surviving Spouse's account, hereby irrevocably empowers the Partnership to pay off, purchase, satisfy or otherwise settle or terminate any such judgment, execution, levy, claim receivership, judicial sequestration or other legal proceeding which in the Committee's opinion may be advisable. In the case of a Partner who has~~

~~become entitled to retire on an Early Retirement Date, termination of his membership in the Partnership pursuant to this Section 2 shall be deemed to constitute the retirement of such Partner pursuant to Section 5 of Article XII hereof and, for the purposes of Section 12 of Article XII hereof, shall not constitute a modification of the application of the provisions of Article XII hereof to such Partner.~~

Section 3. Proper books of account and records of the accounts and affairs of the Partnership shall be kept. ~~in such manner as may be approved by the Committee.~~ Such books shall be maintained on the basis of a fiscal year ending on September 30. Each Partner, Former Partner and Retired Partner, for himself, his Estate and his Surviving Spouse, accepts as conclusive and final for all purposes of this Agreement and of his relationship to the Partnership, the books and records of the Partnership and the results thereof and all determinations ~~of the Committee~~ under or pursuant to this Agreement, including, but without limitation, each determination pursuant to or referred to in Section 5 or Section 6 of Article II hereof, waiving and renouncing any right to an accounting, and agrees that under no circumstances shall the Partnership be required to close its books otherwise than at the close of a fiscal year. Upon any termination of a Partner's status as a Partner in the Partnership, the Partnership shall from time to time furnish to him, his Estate or his Surviving Spouse a statement of the amounts due him, his Estate or his Surviving Spouse and any such statements so furnished shall be final, binding and conclusive upon him, his Estate and his Surviving Spouse and upon the other Partners.

ARTICLE X

Interpretation

Section 1. The construction, interpretation or application of this Agreement or any of the provisions thereof by the Committee shall be finally and conclusively binding upon the parties hereto and their respective Estates and Surviving Spouses, even though the members of the Committee should be personally interested in or affected by such construction, interpretation or application.

ARTICLE XI

Amendment

Section 1. This Agreement may be amended by a written instrument executed in one or more counterparts by a majority in ~~interest~~ *number* of the Partners; provided, however, that any amendment to Article XII hereof shall be made as provided in Section 12 of Article XII hereof. Any such amendment shall be set forth in an amendatory or supplemental agreement which shall be filed at the office of the Partnership in New York City.

ARTICLE XII

Retirement and Retirement Annuities

Section 1. A Partner shall retire on his Normal Retirement Date which shall be the September 30 which is, or next follows, his seventieth birthday. A Partner may retire on an Early Retirement Date as provided in Sections 4 and 5 of this Article XII.

As used in this Agreement, the terms ''retire'', ''retired'', ''retirement'' and ''time of retirement'' shall refer to a termination of status as a Partner pursuant to this Article XII, whether on Normal Retirement Date or on an Early Retirement Date.

Section 2. During the three fiscal years prior to the Normal Retirement Date of a Partner (the ''Pre-retirement Period''), the services of such Partner are expected to decrease with respect to his own individual work for the Partnership and he is expected to facilitate the transfer of his functions and activities to other Partners.

Section 3. During his Pre-retirement Period, (a) the Percentage of a Partner in the Net Profits of the Partnership shall be (i) for the first fiscal year of his Pre-retirement Period, 80 percent of his Average Percentage; (ii) for the second fiscal year of his Pre-retirement Period, 60 percent of his Average Percentage; and (iii) for the third fiscal year of his Pre-retirement Period, 40 percent of his Average Percentage; and (b) he shall also receive his applicable Percentages (as provided in Sections 1 and 2 of Article II hereof) of fees received in each such fiscal year with respect to services rendered prior to such fiscal year;~~provided, however, that the Percentage determined pursuant to subclause (i), (ii), or (iii) above shall not exceed his Percentage in the Net Profits of the Partnership for the fiscal year immediately prior to the beginning of his Pre-retirement Period~~; and provided, ~~further,~~ that for each fiscal year of his Pre-retirement Period such Partner is hereby guaranteed payment of the Minimum Amount determined under Section 8 of this Article except that if his status as a Partner shall terminate for any reason during any such fiscal year, the amount of such guaranty for such fiscal year shall be the product obtained by multiplying such Minimum Amount by a fraction of which the denominator is 12 and the numerator is the number of months from the beginning of such fiscal year to the end of the month in which such termination of status occurs.

The ''Average Percentage'' of a Partner for the purposes of this Article XII shall be the average of his highest Percentages in the Net Profits of the Partnership for any five fiscal years (whether or not consecutive) ended prior to the beginning of his Pre-retirement Period or, in the case of early retirement without any Pre-retirement Period, ended on or prior to the Early Retirement Date of such Partner.

Each Percentage of a Partner calculated pursuant to the first paragraph of this Section 3 and the retirement annuity percentage calculated pursuant to the second paragraph of Section 6 of this Article XII shall be rounded to the nearest one one-hundredth of one percent.

SECTION 4. Any Partner may retire voluntarily on an Early Retirement Date which may be the September 30 which is, or which follows, his 65th birthday or any date thereafter.

SECTION 5. If after he is entitled to retire on an Early Retirement Date but before he has completed his Pre-retirement Period, a Partner's status as a Partner shall terminate for any reason, such Partner shall be deemed to have retired voluntarily pursuant to this Article XII and the date of such termination of status shall be deemed to be his time of retirement and to be his Early Retirement Date.

SECTION 6. Following his time of retirement, a Retired Partner (or in the event of death, the Retired Partner's Estate) shall be paid the amounts provided for in clause (a) of Section 2 of Article V hereof at the respective times specified therein. In the event that a Partner shall have an Early Retirement Date which is on or prior to August 31 of any fiscal year, then the amount payable to him or his Estate under subclause (iii) of clause (a) of Section 2 of Article V shall be determined by multiplying the amount of his Percentages of fees received in the year of termination in respect of services rendered prior to such year by a fraction of which the numerator is the number of months in the year to the Date of Termination and the denominator is 12.

Subject to the provisions of Section 4 of Article V hereof, ~~Section 2 of Article IX hereof~~ and Section 10 of this Article XII, following the time of retirement of a Partner pursuant to this Article XII (other than retirement resulting from death), such Retired Partner shall be entitled to receive a retirement annuity for life. Subject to the provisions of Section 9 of this Article XII, the amount of such annuity for each fiscal year shall be equal to the product obtained by multiplying the Distributable Net Income of the Partnership for such fiscal year by 20% of his Average Percentage but shall not exceed the Maximum Amount nor be less than the Minimum Amount determined under Section 8 of this Article XII; provided, however, that if the right to receive an annuity pursuant to this Section 6 shall begin or end during a fiscal year, such annuity shall be payable only for the applicable portion of such fiscal year and shall be determined by the Committee as provided in Section 9 of this Article XII.

Except as provided in this Section 6 (but subject to the provisions of Section 11 of this Article XII), neither a Partner who retires pursuant to this Article

XII nor his Estate shall be entitled to receive any payments whatever from the Partnership, whether on account of fees received by the Partnership or otherwise. The amount of fees received in any fiscal year after the time of retirement of a Partner which, except for such retirement, would have been payable to such retired Partner or his Estate shall be credited to the profit and loss account of the Partnership for such fiscal year.

SECTION 7. If a Retired Partner dies and has a Surviving Spouse, then, subject to the provisions of Section 9 of this Article XII, ~~and to Section 2 of Article IX hereof with respect to acts of such Retired Partner prior to his retirement~~, one-half of the amount of the retirement annuity to which such deceased Retired Partner would have been entitled had he lived shall be paid to such Surviving Spouse but only during the lifetime of such Surviving Spouse and until the expiration of the later of (a) 240 months after the time of retirement of such Retired Partner or (b) 60 months after his death; provided, however, that this Section 7 shall be applicable to the Surviving Spouse of a Partner whose retirement results from his death during the period from the date he became entitled to retire on an Early Retirement Date to his Normal Retirement Date and that, for such purpose, such Partner shall be deemed to have been entitled to a retirement annuity in an amount equal to that which he would have received under Section 6 of this Article XII had his retirement resulted from resignation rather than death and he shall be deemed to be a deceased Retired Partner; and provided, further, that if the right to receive an annuity pursuant to this Section 7 shall begin or end during a fiscal year, such annuity shall be payable only for the applicable portion of such period and shall be determined by the Committee as provided in Section 9 of this Article XII.

SECTION 8. For fiscal years of the Firm ending on or before September 30, 1978, the guaranteed payment and the minimum amount specified in Sections 3 and 6 of this Article XII (the "Minimum Amount") shall be $35,000 per annum, and the maximum amount specified in Section 6 of this Article XII (the "Maximum Amount") shall be $100,000 per annum. For the fiscal year of the Firm ending September 30, 1979, the Minimum Amount shall be $50,000 per annum and the Maximum Amount shall be $125,000 per annum. For each fiscal year of the Firm thereafter, the Minimum Amount and the Maximum Amount shall be adjusted at the beginning of such year (and rounded to the nearest one hundred dollars) for changes in the cost of living in substantially the same manner and to the same extent as the maximum permissible annual benefit is adjusted under Section 415(d) (1)(A) of the Internal Revenue Code for the calendar year in which such fiscal year begins or by use of such other standard or index as may be determined by the Committee to be appropriate; provided, however, that without the authorization of ~~the Committee and the approval~~ of a majority in number of the

Partners, the Minimum Amount shall not exceed $65,000 per annum and the Maximum Amount shall not exceed $165,000 per annum; and provided, further, that the Minimum Amount and the Maximum Amount shall not be reduced below $50,000 per annum and $125,000 per annum, respectively.

SECTION 9. The amount of the retirement annuity payable for each fiscal year to a Retired Partner or his Surviving Spouse pursuant to Sections 6 and 7 of this Article XII shall be reduced each year by the amount of the primary retirement benefit under the Retirement Plan of such Retired Partner (or of his Surviving Spouse, as the case may be), whether or not the Retired Partner has elected to receive such primary retirement benefit (''Primary Retirement Benefit''). The amount of the Primary Retirement Benefit shall be determined (without taking into account any amounts attributable to the voluntary contributions of such Retired Partner) by the Administrative Committee under the Retirement Plan and shall be either (a) if the Retired Partner has a Surviving Spouse, the amount receivable in respect of each such fiscal year by the Retired Partner or by his Surviving Spouse, as the case may be, if the Retired Partner has elected under the Retirement Plan to receive a joint and survivor annuity, with the amount of the annuity payable to his Surviving Spouse being equal to 50% of the amount paid to the Retired Partner or, if no such election has been made, the amount the Retired Partner or his Surviving Spouse, as the case may be, would have received in respect of each such fiscal year had such election been made, or (b) if the Retired Partner has no Surviving Spouse, the amount receivable in respect of each such fiscal year by the Retired Partner if the Retired Partner has elected to receive a straight life annuity under the Retirement Plan, or, if no such election has been made, the amount the Retired Partner would have received in respect of each such fiscal year had such election been made.

The total amount of all annuities paid by the Partnership pursuant to this Article XII for any fiscal year to all Retired Partners and Surviving Spouses of deceased Retired Partners shall not exceed 15% of the Distributable Net Income of the Partnership for such period. In the event such 15% limitation becomes applicable for any period, all annuities payable by the Partnership pursuant to this Article XII for such period to Retired Partners and Surviving Spouses of deceased Retired Partners but for such 15% limitation shall be proportionately reduced, in the proportion that the amount which each such Retired Partner and Surviving Spouse would receive during such period under this Article XII bears to the total amount which all such Retired Partners and Surviving Spouses would receive during such period under this Article XII, in each case such amount to be determined for the purpose of this sentence without the reduction set forth above in respect of the Retirement Plan.

The Committee in its sole discretion may, at any time or from time to time, determine (a) the amount of any annuity payable for a portion of a fiscal year and (b) when and how annuities payable for any fiscal year or portion of a fiscal year are to be paid including, but without limitation, the amounts, and times for payment, of instalments or estimated instalments thereof.

SECTION 10. As a condition to the receipt by him or his Surviving Spouse of payments pursuant to this Article XII, following the time of his retirement pursuant to this Article XII a Retired Partner shall not engage in the private practice of law in New York City (alone or in partnership or association with others) except with ~~the~~ written approval *on behalf* of the ~~Committee~~ *Partnership*.

SECTION 11. A Retired Partner shall not be expected, and shall have no obligation, to render any services to the Partnership. The Partnership may, however, retain the services of a Retired Partner for a particular matter or for any particular period of time, on such terms and conditions as the Committee in its sole discretion shall determine, and the provisions of Section 9 of this Article XII shall not be applicable to payments for such services.

SECTION 12. Anything in this Agreement to the contrary notwithstanding, the provisions of this Article XII may be terminated or amended in whole or in part in any respect, and the application of the provisions of this Article XII to any particular Partner may be modified, if so determined by ~~the Committee with the approval of~~ a majority in number of the Partners; provided, however, that without the consent of the person affected, no such termination, amendment or modification shall result in a reduction in the amounts receivable in accordance with the provisions of this Article XII by any Retired Partner, the Surviving Spouse of any deceased Retired Partner or any Partner who has become entitled to retire on an Early Retirement Date; and provided, further, that a consent by a Partner or Retired Partner during his lifetime shall be binding upon his Surviving Spouse.

This Agreement shall be binding upon and enure to the benefit of the parties hereto and their respective Estates and Surviving Spouses and may be executed in one or more counterparts, each of which shall be deemed to be an original.

IN WITNESS WHEREOF, each of the parties hereto has hereunto set his hand as of the day and year first above written.

____

____

____

____

____

NEW PARTNERS

Name

Effective Date of Admission

APPENDIX 2

October 25, 1939

MEMORANDUM
to Mr. John Foster Dulles
from Mr. Seligman

I regret very much to find myself for the first time in our long years of association, in fundamental disagreement with you.

The point is the one which we discussed so heatedly at a Monday lunch four or five weeks ago. Your position now is that the Allies' position is in no respect morally superior to Germany's, and in fact you even go further by implication and apparently take the view that Germany's position is morally superior to that of the Allies.

This goes far beyond the position which you took in your book. You will remember then that your position was summarized by a sentence which you had at one time intended to use in your preface, namely, that you were analyzing the causes which explained why a person became a criminal but that an understanding of those causes in no way lessened your disapproval of his criminal acts.

Your present position seems to me to be based upon a fallacious argument. Injustice accorded to Germany justifies Germany in remedying such injustice even by violence, but it does not justify Germany going beyond remedying these injustices and creating new and worse injustices. While as a scientist one can understand the reasons which have caused Germany to pursue this path of action, one still must condemn this action as immoral and endeavor to stop further action along the same line.

A fair analogy is a man who is in a poker game and who finds that he has been cheated of $100 by marked cards. He immediately grabs $100 from the pot and then shoots all the players and also the bystanders.

As a scientist one can readily explain the entire chain of events and the approximate cause is undoubtedly the act of one of the poker players. However, the shooting was nevertheless morally unjustified and should be condemned and punished.

My own view has been, as you know, that notwithstanding the anti-Semitic excesses in Germany, Hitler was justified in remedying the injustices of the Versailles Treaty, and I therefore thought he was justified in trying to get back the Sudetenland. His action on March 15, however, was wholly unjustified and, instead of remedying past injustices, it was creating new injustices. Not only were the victims of the new injustices in Slovakia and Moravia justified in calling the action immoral, but so also were the British who thereupon started their policy of defensive alliances to stop further unjustified aggression by Germany.

Accordingly, while as you know I agree entirely with your fundamental position in regard to peaceful change, I can see nothing in it which furnishes any logical basis for the position you have now come to.

I think it unfortunate from your own point of view that you are taking this position publicly, and I am wondering what P.B.* thinks about it.

E. S.

* Pemberton Berman, a Jewish friend of Dulles's.

ACKNOWLEDGMENTS

We interviewed Sullivan & Cromwell partners, former Sullivan & Cromwell partners, associates, and employees, Sullivan & Cromwell clients, and family members of Sullivan & Cromwell lawyers in Los Angeles, San Francisco, Chicago, Washington, D.C., Philadelphia, New York City, London, and Paris. In addition to our hosts Judy Lansing, Peter Kovler, Sami Shad, and Leon Baumgarten, we would like to thank the following people for sharing their time and insights with us during often very long interviews.

Charles E. Allen, Jr., George Ames, Louis S. Auchincloss, Mary Bancroft, William Bardusch, Jr., Robert E. Barnett, Kenneth M.

Bialo, Boyd A. Blackburn, Jr., Norbert Bogdan, Eugene L. Bondy, Jr., Ronald E. Bornstein, Joseph L. Broderick, Spencer B. Burke, Frank V. Calaba, Franklin O. Canfield, Lista M. Cannon, Francis Carling, Diane de Castellane, Mme. Georges de Castellane, Roger D. Chesley, Thomas W. Childs, Donald C. Christ, Paul P. Colborn, Harvey Corn, John W. Dickey, David M. Donohue, Charles E. Dorkey III, Father Avery Dulles, Eleanor Lansing Dulles, Ronald A. Dworkin, Mrs. P. M. Eckstrom, Eleanor Elliott, Stanley F. Farrar, Judge Macklin Fleming, George S. Franklin, Jr., Victor Futter, Jerrold Ganzfried, Jackson B. Gilbert, Hazel Seligman Goldmark, Robert E. Goldsby, Donald A. Goldsmith, John H. Hanes, Jr., Michele Beiny Harkins, Karl G. Harr, Jr., Charles Higham, Lilias Hinshaw, Lawrence R. Houston, Al Ihne, Clover Dulles Jebsen, Harry Leroy Jones, Peter T. Jones, George C. Kern, Jr., Robert T. Kimberlin, Allan Kramer, Rita Lachman, Judge Marie M. Lambert, Walter C. Lundgren, Robert MacCrate, Glen McDaniel, Malcolm A. MacIntyre, Phyllis Bernau Macomber, Lawrence C. McQuade, Margaret D. Merli, John E. Merow, Phillippe Monod, George Murnane, Jr., Robert M. Osgood, Mme. Gaston Palewski, Thomas E. Patton, Judge David W. Peck, William Piel, Jr., Henry Pollard, Phillip R. Pollock, Joseph Prendergast, Madeleine Regnier, Edward J. Reilly, Alan M. Reinke, John Richardson, Jr., Davis R. Robinson, Odile Mallet Rosetti, David A. Rosinus, Barbara L. Schlei, Edwin G. Schuck, Jr., Jeffrey Schwab, Marvin Schwartz, Kenneth E. Scott, Kenneth M. Seggerman, Jr., Frederick C. Seibold, David F. Sexton, Paul C. Sheeline, Marvin S. Sloman, Max A. Stolper, Lauson H. Stone, James F. Thacher, Raymond S. Troubh, Martin Victor, William E. Willis, Inzer Wyatt, Ida C. Wurczinger, Elizabeth K. Yadlosky, William S. Youngman, Frank D. Zaffere III, Nina S. Zagat, Jeffrey I. Zuckerman.

There are others who asked not to be named to whom we are also most grateful.

A great deal of the material that went into the book came from the John Foster Dulles Archive and the Allen Welsh Dulles Archive at Princeton University. Nancy Bressler has meticulously curated the papers in the John Foster Dulles collection. Also we thank Jean Holliday for her cheerfulness and Carl Esche for his patience doing thousands of pages of photocopies.

Thanks to John E. Taylor for guiding us through the Military Archives Division, to Cindy Fox in the Department of Justice records and to Patrice Brown at Suitland, Maryland, all of whom made the maze of the National Archives and Record Service manageable and useful. Leo Neshkes, the Department of Justice Freedom of Information Act officer, diligently pursued our queries over an extended period. The Federal Archives and Record Center at Bayonne, New Jersey, also provided some important material.

Other libraries important to our study were the New-York Historical Society; the New York Public Library; the Butler and Cromwell Libraries at Columbia University; the Columbia Oral History Project; and the Scudder Business Archives. The Library of Congress Manuscript Division held many important items for the research. In addition, the Dwight D. Eisenhower Library, the Lyndon Baines Johnson Library, the John Fitzgerald Kennedy Library, and the Franklin Delano Roosevelt Library provided invaluable materials.

We appreciated gaining access to the Association of the Bar of the City of New York; the American Foundation for the Blind; the Thomas A. Edison National Historic Site in West Orange, New Jersey; the Baker Library at Harvard University for its collection of Henry Villard Papers; and the YIVO Institute in New York City.

We consulted the Public Records Office in London and interviewed people who actually worked with William Nelson Cromwell in Paris in the 1920s and 1930s. Others who did not remember him personally still appreciated his largess to their institutions and cities, opening to us the evidence of his presence and beneficence. We want to thank Mme. Isabelle de Pasquier, the conservateur of the Museum of the Legion of Honor in Paris for patient and generous help; the mayor and the city of Bailleul, France, for their kindness and interest in the project; and M. Guy Oberdorff, sous-préfet of Valenciennes and his secretary, Geneviève Van Helder, for their warm hospitality.

Benjamin T. Pierce generously shared with us the privately published *Memoirs* of his grandfather, William J. Curtis. Charles Higham was generous with his time and papers housed in the University of Southern California Library. Dr. Robert Morison was kind enough to let us rummage around his attic looking at original documents about the building of the Panama Canal. Florence Patterson whetted our interest in early business history with a greatly appreciated starter library and Dorothy Tomassini labored through many transcriptions of taped interviews.

Thanks to Julius Lucius Echeles for his personal and legal advice. Clyde E. Walton and Clarke Taylor made invaluable contributions to the style and content of the book with their detailed reading of and insightful comments on the manuscript.

Finally, thanks to those in the extended and extensive Sullivan & Cromwell family who loaned us books, some of which we kept for more than four years, and others whose introductions and leads put life into the research process. We especially wish to thank our families and friends for their unflagging interest and support.

INDEX